Sailing to the
Far Horizon

T0312224

Sailing to the
Far Horizon

∿

The Restless Journey and Tragic Sinking of a Tall Ship

PAMELA SISMAN BITTERMAN

THE UNIVERSITY OF WISCONSIN PRESS / TERRACE BOOKS

Terrace Books
A trade imprint of the University of Wisconsin Press
1930 Monroe Street, 3rd Floor
Madison, Wisconsin 53711-2059
uwpress.wisc.edu

3 Henrietta Street
London WC2E 8LU, England
eurospanbookstore.com

Printed in the United States of America

Library of Congress Cataloging-in-Publication Data

Bitterman, Pamela Sisman.
    Sailing to the far horizon: the restless journey and tragic sinking
of a tall ship / Pamela Sisman Bitterman.
        p. cm.
    ISBN 0-299-20190-2 (cloth: alk. paper)
    1. Sofia (Schooner) 2. Bitterman, Pamela Sisman—Travel. 3. Shipwrecks—
South Pacific Ocean. I. Title.
    G530.S724B58 2004
    910.4 1—dc22

                        2004005376

ISBN 978-0-299-20194-4 (pbk.: alk. paper)
ISBN 978-0-299-20193-7 (e-book)

This book is dedicated to my father,
who has somehow always trusted that I'd be all right

It is in memory of my mother,
who is holding my hand

And my brother,
a real hero

And the sea will grant each
man new hope
as the sleep brings dreams
of home.

—CHRISTOPHER COLUMBUS

Make voyages. Attempt them. There's nothing else.

—TENNESSEE WILLIAMS

Contents

Illustrations

Acknowledgments

The events in this book occurred nearly twenty-five years ago. That I am able to recount them in such vivid detail is due entirely to the faith that my parents had that I would someday commit the adventure to print. They preserved my letters, journals, photographs, and newspaper and magazine articles. My mother even transcribed the most worn and weather-beaten pages, word for word, in her own graceful script. If I had retained possession of my records of the journey, they would have gone down with the ship and been lost forever. My mom simply believed that my telling this story was *bashert*, Yiddish for "meant to be."

I gratefully acknowledge the following people for their support and inspiration; without them this manuscript might never have completed the long journey to publication:

Sheila McMahon, the editor who saw the book in my story
MaryLee Dungan and Susan Milne, my computer gurus
Steven Milne, for creating the map of the voyage
Tom Barnett, for chapter 5
Tobi Sisman, for watching over the home front
Denise LeVine, my first reader
Rigel and Hallie, the reason
Joey, for the next great adventure

Chronology

20 AUGUST 1978   The author joins the schooner *Sofia* in Boston, where the ship is preparing for her second circumnavigation.

25 OCTOBER 1978   The author sets out of Boston aboard the *Sofia* bound for Martinique in the West Indies.

NOVEMBER 1978   *Sofia* makes Hamilton Harbor, Bermuda, after running from Hurricane Kendra.

NOVEMBER 1978–JUNE 1979   *Sofia* traverses the Caribbean, making port in Martinique, Dominica, Ille de Saints, St. Vincent, Bequia, and Barbados (where she hauls out) in the Windward Island Group of the West Indies before continuing on to the Isla de Margarita in the Lesser Antilles, Puerto La Cruz on the north coast of Venezuela in South America, Curaçao, in the Netherland Antilles and on through the San Blas Islands in the Archipiélago de las Mulatas.

JULY 1979   *Sofia* enters Panama in Central America at Cristóbal on the Atlantic side of the Canal Zone. The author jumps ship to spend the next several weeks back in the United States.

SEPTEMBER 1979   The author travels overland from Bakersfield, California, through Mexico and Central America, to meet the *Sofia* in Golfito, Costa Rica.

NOVEMBER 1979   *Sofia* sails up the coast of Costa Rica from Golfito to Puntarenas.

DECEMBER 1979–JANUARY 1980   *Sofia* departs Puntarenas and enters the Canal Zone at Taboga, via the Bay of Panama.

JANUARY 1980   The Panamanian government charges *Sofia* and her crew with unauthorized entry and international trespassing. Later that month, *Sofia* hauls out in Vacamonté, Panama.

FEBRUARY 1980–DECEMBER 1980   *Sofia* crosses the South Pacific calling into the Archipiélago de Colón (the Galapagos Islands), the Marquesan Islands, the Tuamotu Archipelago, the Societies Islands of French Polynesia, the Cooks, the Samoas (where she hauls out), and the Kingdom of Tonga.

DECEMBER 1980   The author jumps ship in the port of Russell in the Bay of Islands, New Zealand, and again returns to the United States.

JANUARY 1981   The author rejoins the *Sofia* in Nelson, New Zealand.

JANUARY 1981–JANUARY 1982   *Sofia* rests in Nelson, New Zealand, where she undergoes two haul-outs, the construction of a false keel, a failed mutiny attempt, and a significant crew turnover.

FEBRUARY 1982   *Sofia* departs Nelson, sailing "North About," laying over in New Plymouth en route to Auckland, New Zealand.

21 FEBRUARY 1982   *Sofia* departs New Plymouth, New Zealand.

23 FEBRUARY 1982   The schooner *Sofia* sinks off the North Cape of New Zealand.

28 FEBRUARY 1982   The survivors of the *Sofia* are rescued by the *Vasili Perov.*

AUGUST 1983   The U.S. Coast Guard Department of Transportation officially informs Evan of the charges being brought against him.

Sailing to the

Far Horizon

Introduction

This tale is not ancient. It is just twenty-five years old, in fact. However, as part of the tradition of sailors whom it hopes to honor, its years number in the hundreds. And the legacy of the human spirit of which it strives to be worthy is timeless. Nonetheless, in the end, *this* is just my story.

I have written as complete an account as possible of a time long ago. There are many problems inherent in undertaking such an endeavor, and they give rise to questions that warrant answers.

I've constructed the book primarily around the journal entries I made during a nearly four-year voyage aboard the schooner *Sofia.* This journal comprised the bulk of my communication with my family. My mailings often consisted of great hunks of paper ripped from my notebook and sent in a bundle from some remote harbor; a single package could contain several pages detailing the events covering weeks or months, a succession of ports and hundreds of nautical miles. Other letters home were hurried notes scribbled on such random swatches of paper as antiquated charts and the backs of produce box labels. Many were not dated. Some records were lost or destroyed. Consequently, it was at times a challenge to establish specific dates and locations. I've made every effort, however, to ensure that the chronology is generally accurate, if not absolutely precise. And any errors are mine, results of the limitations of human memory.

I have not recreated the journal verbatim; instead I have gone back into the entries and reworked them for the sake of the narrative. And although I haven't falsified any event, some episodes have gone the way of sea stories, told and retold until they became what I remember. I've selectively expanded and carefully crafted other bits to ensure their significance. I have simplified the nautical terminology to avoid sinking the story in a sea of technical detail. And, in reflection, I embellish upon vignettes merely alluded to in letters.

This narrative emerges as a memoir of intimate perception and sentimental retrospection; I do not apologize for this, nor do I consider it anyone's truth but my own. The writing was as much an act of catharsis at the time of the voyage as it became again a quarter century later, when I transformed the adventure into a book. My hope is that the reader will empathize with the teller and gain personal insight from the tale. To sail an old tall ship across vast oceans and beyond is fundamentally an irrational act in which idealism conquers sensibility. Can such a journey be portrayed honestly in any other light? Should it be?

Why did I choose to write the book? In twenty-five years no one else has taken on the task. I must assume no one else will; so the responsibility fell to me by default. To never transmit the events of the final days of the schooner *Sofia* would be a betrayal of all she has meant to so many. And why now? In dealing openly with this last question, I come close to exposing a part of myself that I'd prefer to keep private. I did not choose the moment when the book would be written; the moment chose me. When personal tragedy struck, I discovered I was able to overcome a desperate sense of powerlessness by recalling my *Sofia* days. I could feel the strength of that fearless explorer again—the girl with the bright spirit and the indomitable life force. She resurfaced as I wrote and this book spilled out of me like a dance of redemption. It has been said that through writing we discover what we believe, and so I ride the *Sofia*'s wake one last time.

Sofia

1. Jib boom
2. Bobstay
3. Bowsprit
4. Bow
5. Samson post
6. Bow net
7. Fisherman anchor
8. Stem
9. Waterline
10. Flying jib
11. Outer jib
12. Inner jib
13. Fore staysail
14. Forestay
15. Foremast
16. Fore topmast
17. Course squaresail
18. Course square topsail yard
19. Lower square topsail
20. Lower square topsail yard
21. Raffee
22. Fore gaff topsail
23. Fore gaffsail
24. Main gaff topsail
25. Main topmast
26. Main gaffsail
27. Mainmast
28. Topsides
29. Cap rail
30. Ratlines
31. Baggywrinkles
32. Mizzen gaff topsail
33. Mizzen topmast
34. Mizzen gaffsail
35. Mizzenmast
36. Mizzen gaff
37. Mizzen boom
38. Stern
39. Taffrail
40. Davits

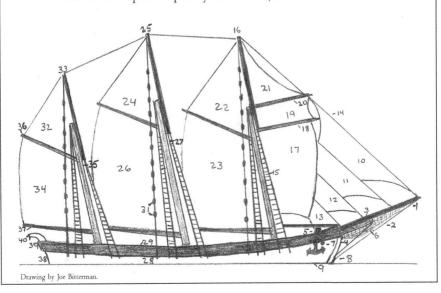

Drawing by Joe Bitterman.

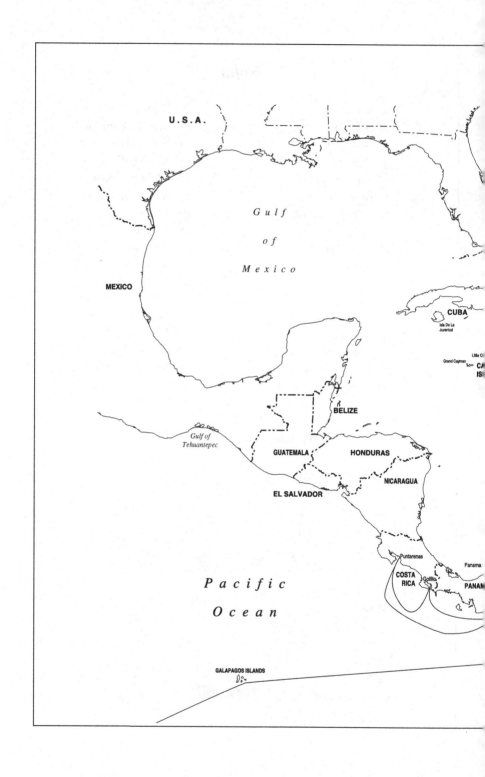

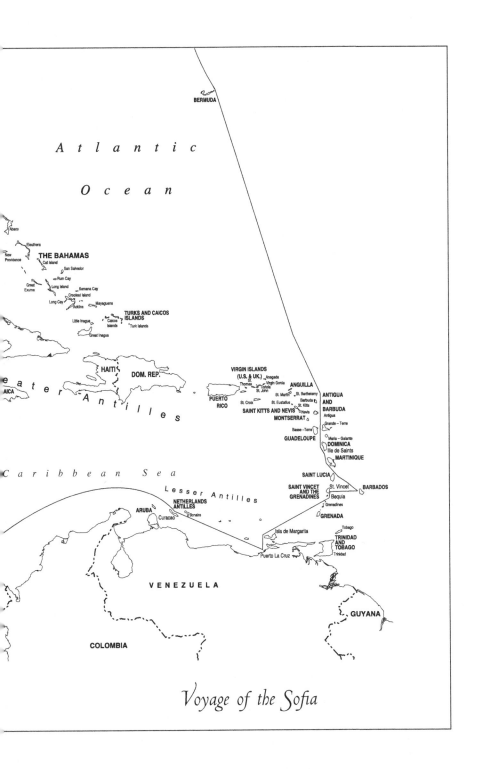

Atlantic

Ocean

Abaco

Eleuthera

New
Providence

THE BAHAMAS
Cat Island

San Salvador

Rum Cay

Great
Exuma

Long Island

Samana Cay

Long Cay

Crooked Island

Acklins

Mayaguana

TURKS AND CAICOS
ISLANDS

Little Inagua

Caicos
Islands

Turk Islands

Great Inagua

eater

AICA

HAITI

DOM. REP.

A   n   t   i   l   l   e   s

VIRGIN ISLANDS
(U.S. & UK.)

Anegada

St.
Thomas

Virgin Gorda

Tortola

St. Martin

ANGUILLA

St. John

St. Barthelemy

PUERTO
RICO

St. Croix

St. Eustatius

Barbuda

ANTIGUA
AND
BARBUDA

St. Kitts

SAINT KITTS AND NEVIS

Nevis

Antigua

MONTSERRAT

Grande – Terre

Basse –Terre

GUADELOUPE

Marie – Galante

DOMINICA

Ilie de Saints

MARTINIQUE

C a r i b b e a n   S e a

SAINT LUCIA

SAINT VINCENT
AND THE
GRENADINES

St. Vincet

BARBADOS

L e s s e r   A n t i l l e s

Bequia

NETHERLANDS
ANTILLES

Grenadines

ARUBA

Bonaire

GRENADA

Curacao

Tobago

Isla de Margarita

TRINIDAD
AND
TOBAGO

Puerto La Cruz

Trinidad

VENEZUELA

GUYANA

COLOMBIA

BERMUDA

Voyage of the Sofia

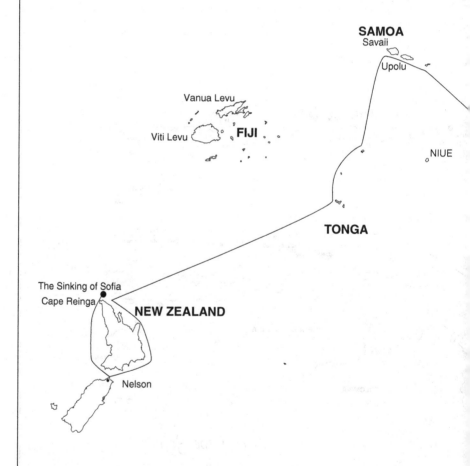

PACIFIC

OCEAN

SAMOA
Savaii
Upolu

Vanua Levu

Viti Levu   FIJI

NIUE

TONGA

The Sinking of Sofia
Cape Reinga

NEW ZEALAND

Nelson

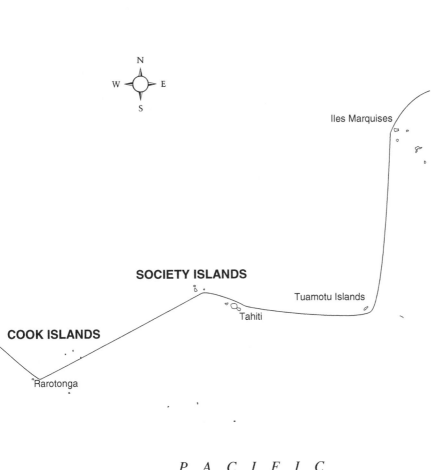

N

W ◆ E

S

Iles Marquises

SOCIETY ISLANDS

COOK ISLANDS

Tuamotu Islands

Tahiti

Rarotonga

P A C I F I C

O C E A N

Final Voyage of the Sofia

chapter 1

Joining the *Sofia* for Her Second Circumnavigation

Floating in Boston

One doesn't discover new lands without consenting to lose sight of the shore for a very long time.

—ANDRE GIDE

Boston Harbor
October 25, 1978
Early Dawn

"Ahoy, mates, hands off your cocks and on your socks!" This raunchy charge is the rude awakening delivered by our ever-ebullient skipper. Although not an entirely appropriate command because women make up half the crew, we all leap from our bunks, infused with the captain's enthusiasm. This morning we go to sea. Casting off from Boston's tired old Lincoln Wharf and its relative comforts and securities, we will sever our ties to our past and to any certain future. The United States will drop away in our wake as we leave behind everything familiar. In a most profound sense today we are leaving home.

During the rare moments of calm that invade the manic atmosphere of readying the ship for departure, it occurs to me to marvel at what we are undertaking. The dank, metallic gray of a late autumn New England dawn lies heavily over the harbor; it is the kind of gray you can feel in your teeth. An impatient North Atlantic sucks and drags at our ship's massive hull, trying to draw her out. The proud sixty-year-old, 123-foot, three-masted gaff-topsail schooner *Sofia* answers the sea with an almost palpable yearning as she groans against her moorings, leaning her topmasts toward open water. She has been a long time in port, a thorough and extensive refit. According to those most knowledgeable, the *Sofia* is strong and seaworthy. The ship is ready. I wonder, "Am I?" and how is it that I am here?

INTRODUCTION

The early spring of 1978 found me living a blissfully landlubbing existence, hunkered down in my cabin atop an unbridled meadow on the property for which I was caretaker. As resident naturalist for forty acres of a 180-acre nature and wildlife preserve in northern California, my daily preoccupations concerned controlling the prolific growth of scotch broom and gorse, appeasing loggers, coexisting with farmers, and struggling to ensure that the property could support itself financially. From my lofty crib atop a curiously lush and fertile million-year-old sand dune, the landscape ambled down a lazy, terrestrial staircase to the sea five miles below. Great stands of ancient redwoods shuffled between layers of pygmy forest as the earth wound its way down to meet the retreating ocean.

Because the income generated by classes and tours proved insufficient, the land's stewards implored me to figure out how to bring in more money. I wrote a grant proposal for an outdoor education program that would target the youth of local schools who were struggling in a traditional classroom setting. And in fact we got the grant, under the Comprehensive Employment Training Act (CETA). Teachers throughout the area began to identify students who would be good candidates for the classes, while I busily began setting up shop on the property. However, California abruptly and systematically started shutting down its government-funded programs, and those funded by CETA grants were among the first to go. No grant, no money, no preserve. I would soon be homeless and unemployed. Foundering and in need of a new direction, I was leafing halfheartedly through the current edition of an alternative lifestyle publication entitled *Co-Evolution Quarterly* when I found one.

Being in my late twenties during the late 1970s provided me with plenty of opportunity for radical change. Here's what jumped out from the classifieds: "Tall ship Sofia, cooperatively owned and operated 60-year-old schooner, returns to America to enlist crew for her second circumnavigation." According to the ad, $2,800 would ensure part ownership and afford a vehicle by which one could endlessly travel the great oceans of the world. My resolve to become a part of the capricious history and evolving odyssey of the *Sofia* would ultimately prove to be one of the most profound and precipitous of my life. I adhere to this certainty today despite what happened, or, more accurately, because of it.

⌒

February 23, 1982
1:30 A.M.
Tasman Sea
Off the North Cape of New Zealand

Soaked, shivering, inert, I lie inside my body immersed in fatigue. Like the broken lens of a camera, my eyes stare straight up, frozen in incognizance. Something has changed. *Look.* For more than three years the *Sofia* has been my home. She has carried me across half the planet, cradled me through sweeping calms, raging gales, fair winds and following seas, a hurricane. But not this. Never before have I had this feeling. The metallic grinding of the chronometer gears pierces the thick cabin air. It is dark, feels heavy. I adjust to see the clock face. Impossibly hard. I am straining to roll onto my side, turning up a steep incline. Gripping the edge of the bunk with both hands, I flex and lock my muscles to hold steady. *Listen.* Sounds too deep. The wash of the sea beside my head resonates bass, hollow. Not the familiar swish, the rhythmical surge, but a drone, as though from a gully, vacant and sepulchral. I blink, cold water dripping down my face. From where? With bewildered eyes I follow its trajectory across the cabin to the open porthole set high, so high, on the weather bulkhead. The sea climbing the hull, gaining the quarterdeck, bursting through *that* porthole? Unfathomable. Never before. In all weather the *Sofia* maintains a cadence, a motion that is uniquely hers. She owns it. A torsional roll, a serpentine dip, a shush, and then a lift, countering her balance, revolving with a centrifugal grace. This is a dance now more familiar to me than my own because I adjusted to her step years ago. She leads, perpetually fluid, light and wispy, strong and controlled. Always. Always before. *Feel.* This night the *Sofia* lumbers drunkenly, obese. She is wallowing, careening, struggling to regain her elegant meter, her convoluted rotation. Something is terribly wrong.

   Oh, God. Oh, no. Get up. Go on deck. You know what's up there. You know. Move. I press my hand to my chest. *Breathe.* My heart slams against my fingers with the force of a train racing out of control. THRUMB, THRUMB, THRUMB. *But I already know.*

∾

September 1978
Boston, Mass.

PUMP, PUMP, PUMP. As I lean my bicycle into a sharp turn, weaving my way through the cobblestone streets of Boston's North End, once again I hear, "Hey, lady, shave ya' legs!" I'm late for work. I have a reprieve from the drudgery of manual labor aboard a tall ship so that I can report to my job as clerk and nutritional guru at a local health food store, and this hiatus is pure joy. Suffering the harmless taunts of the local hoodlums en route is small price to pay and one I'm getting damn used to coughing up. But, boy, do I ever know that I'm back East. In blissful rural northern California, where I spent the past several years, a razor was as much an oddity as a debutante. Local men there had long resisted trimming their beards. Women didn't bother to shave their legs. Everyone was loathe to shear their armpits. With smug superiority we proclaimed that we had evolved beyond the foolish need for such artificial beauty treatments. Our clan was sanctimoniously au naturel and proud of it. For this bohemian, coming to New England to join the crew of the tall ship *Sofia* was pure culture shock. Returning to the East is literally like going back in time. I had forgotten that the United States of the 1970s still harbored cretins who would bother to comment on another's personal expression.

"Get a job, you slimy lowlife!" I bellow back, discovering a spark of my old, unevolved self skulking surprisingly close to the surface. Well, in any event, this is not an appropriate time for me to revisit my Lady Schick days. I have been informed that freshwater stores aboard the *Sofia* will be used exclusively for cooking and drinking, because water is a true survival commodity at sea. Bathing with it will not be allowed. Using it for shaving one's legs, I gather, will be entirely out of the question. I'm advised that a healthy squirt from a bottle of Joy dishwashing liquid into a bucket of seawater will lather up quite adequately, facilitating a proper bath. But shaving with it? Not bloody likely. Salting one's wounds won't be a facet of the tough-guy sailor persona we're expected to adopt while on board. For now the YWCA a few blocks up the wharf provides shower facilities, and, yes, ostensibly we could also shave there, but why postpone the inevitable? Those who are still hopelessly attached to their razors will be required to relinquish them sooner or later. For my part, I'm well ahead of the game. I've already groomed a fine coating of soft fuzz that will soon be coveted by the bristled newly unshaven aboard the *Sofia*. So my

transformation to shipboard life, at least in this one respect, is less prob-
lematic than for many of the other new recruits. But in other respects, it
is decidedly more troublesome.

I am having serious difficulty adjusting to the sprawling mob of bodies
taking up residence in the limited space available on this funky old sailing vessel. In recent years I catered only to my own particular whims where
home and hearth were concerned. I cozied right in to the self-indulgence
of attending purely to my needs, those of my dog, and those of the intermittent human visitors or occasional farm animals. In Mendocino I
floated in an herbal broth of delicious simplicity, compulsive neatness,
and immense clarity. On board the *Sofia* my space is fermenting compost.
All my physical and psychological bits are scattering helter-skelter to the
four winds.

My dog, a great gentle bear of an Airedale, cannot go to sea with me.
He'll be taking care of my parents and vice versa until I return. I feel lost
without him. I have abandoned the generous, demonstrative attitude of the
pastoral Pacific Northwesterner. Now I endure the stolid angry reserve of
the New England city dweller. Nobody hugged me when I got to Boston.
I have traded the clean open spaces of the Mendocino countryside for the
sour crud of Boston's port district. And, last, I have forfeited my raptur-
ous solitude for the communal throng of an ancient tall ship.

Tom, the skipper, comes to the *Sofia* with eminent qualifications. He
exudes confidence. Good thing too, as his appearance might belie his credentials. He comes off more like an overgrown, overzealous, swashbuckling kid. Tom replaced Brad, who piloted the *Sofia* through much of her
first circumnavigation but jumped ship here on the eastern seaboard to set
out in search of "a boat of my own." Many old Sofians on board sit
around discussing doing much the same thing, far too much for my comfort. I find it disconcerting. It dredges up old insecurities, the ones best
voiced by Groucho Marx as he wondered whether he really wanted to join
a club that would consider having him as a member. I sense that the veterans toy with the notion of striking out independently whenever the *Sofia*
falls into one of her lean periods of regrouping and redefinition. It must
be mostly hot air, though, as many of the old crew are still hanging around.

Evan, the first mate, is one of these old-timers. He's been with the *Sofia*
for several years and even made a bid for captain when the position opened
up, but the resident crew soundly rejected his offer. I wasn't around during the process of his elimination, and I don't pay too much attention to
the random snippets of gossip that float about the vessel, but I gather that

the bulk of the resistance was rooted deep in clashes of personality. Not surprising. Evan is subdued and shrouds himself in mystery. He retires frequently to the relative privacy of his exclusive aft cabin, where he will deign to entertain the bevy of young women that follows him around. Also not surprising. Evan is the epitome of tall, dark, and handsome. With his curly hair, bushy mustache, lean muscular physique, Errol Flynn shirts, and large broad knife belted at the waist, he fits the image of the gallant, traditional sailor of a tall ship.

Norman, the Sofian of longest standing on board, is a funny duck. Thin, lanky, and sparse of head hair, he sports a neatly cropped full beard and rubber bands the mousy fringe of remaining hair near his ears into a tight little knot of a ponytail that sticks straight out from the nape of his long neck. His face is normally pinched into a stiff grin, and his laugh ejects like a high-pitched rat-a-tat of forced air; it causes his arms to jerk and his body to bob with the effort. It always startles me a little. Norman is highly accessible but seems constantly tense, never angry but often frustrated. He is a wealth of useful information, everything from the fine points of the *Sofia's* functioning to an interesting and knowledgeable critique of her history and evolution. Nonetheless, I am confounded whenever I solicit instruction or advice from him. As Norman speaks to me, I stare hard into his earnest face, intent on understanding. Instead, I sink into a thick mire, a drone of meaningless sounds. Eventually, I become so lost and uncomfortable that I utter a dismissive "uh-huh" and just wander off. I'm baffled as to why this occurs, but I'd sure like to sort it out. I detect in Norman a fine man whom I could trust and respect if I could just figure out what the hell he's saying. He's a veritable encyclopedia—ask him where the used diesel goes and you get a dissertation on the chemical breakdown of petroleum. Fail to move on and away fast enough, and you will be buried in a master's thesis on the politics of oil as well.

Mother Boats, the *Sofia's* radio operator and boatswain (the sailor responsible for maintaining the ship's rigging) is an absolute sideshow. He is large, loud, a little doughy, and a lot flouncy. In contrast to Evan, Boats could be the poster child for old queens who go down to the sea in ships. The guy is obviously a top-notch, marlinspike sailing veteran, but he is equally obviously gayer than springtime. He makes no attempt to hide either of these seemingly opposite aspects of his character. Offering a limp-wrist handshake, accompanied by his own trademark moronic giggle, he introduces himself straightaway as Mother Boats but announces that he will also answer to Boats, Mama, Mother, and, when he is feeling particularly exotic, Mama de Bateau. The women on board use all his aliases, but the guys refer to him only as Boats. There's just so much of his affect that the fellas are willing to buy into or admit that they accept. He doesn't seem perturbed. Boats dances on over however he's hailed, bouncing on the balls of his wide feet, his toes perpetually pointed skyward as if the nails have just been painted and are still a little tacky.

Davey, the ship's chief engineer, is a South African from a middle-class white family that he claims to have abandoned in order to avoid being drafted into the military. Where he stands on apartheid is unclear to me, but I'm interested to learn the perspective of one whose life has been so altered by the revolution in his native land. I'm not certain when Davey hooked up with the *Sofia*, but he already appears at home here. He is a hairy little man with wise twinkling eyes and a button nose that pokes through a shag of dark, unkempt full beard. His feet point left and right and look just like Fred Flintstone's. His front teeth and fingertips are discolored with the burnt yellowish stain of a long-time stogy smoker. But when Davey speaks, what comes out is at odds with this hobo-ish appearance. His accent is elegant. Obviously well educated, he comes off as self-possessed, even aristocratic, without a hint of self-deprecation in the way that he handles his diminutive elfish frame. In fact, he exudes dignity and immediately elicits respect. I get the distinct impression that this guy knows exactly what he wants and gets precisely what he's after.

These five fellows are the *Sofia's* resident elders, but a few other mates among us possess substantial sailing credentials as well. Patrick is a professional sailmaker, originally from England and presently employed in a highly reputable sail loft in Boston. He has quite a bit of sailing experience and has offered to stitch up some new sails for the *Sofia* in exchange for passage to Martinique. Patrick has been formally trained in British seamanship. I'm curious to observe how his strict background will blend with the *Sofia's* more relaxed style of sailing. He'll put on the happy-go-lucky-young-man-in-a-commune hat and almost make it look like a believable fit. However, I suspect that it's a superficial cover, because I've already witnessed his haughty edginess. When things are not done "right and proper," Patrick reacts as though he's been slapped in the face. Once, when I was told to perform a particularly distasteful task, the rudiments of which were not made anywhere near clear enough to me, I whined, "Oh, why me?" Patrick got right up in my face, fixed me with an icy glare, and spit out, "A sailor does not ask why. A sailor does as he is told!" Scowling, I reminded him that I had yet to be a sailor and that, as a rather

reluctant resident swabbie, I felt justified in asking for an explanation.
Patrick visibly shook off his arrogance, forced a grin, and nodded with
resignation. He is definitely still bound by some damned straight laces.
There's evidence of an overly large male ego buried just beneath his acqui-
escent shrug, and I can't help but wonder what might happen if it ever
busts fully loose.

Anders is a young Swede who has already garnered an impressive raft
of sailing experience for his tender years. He has traveled with the *Sofia* in
the past and is so appreciative of the opportunity that she affords him
that he reciprocates lavishly. At present our ship is the grateful beneficiary
of his extensive electronic expertise. I accompanied Anders to an abandoned airfield where the broken shell of an old plane lay crumpled and
forgotten on the weed-blown tarmac of a deserted runway. Anders ostensibly had obtained permission to salvage any parts from the wreckage
that he reckoned he could refashion into something useful for the *Sofia*. I
watched enthralled as he meticulously unraveled a web of tangled wires
and detached the aircraft's main control panel intact. He was later able
to mount this bright shiny plate on the *Sofia's* shabby saloon bulkhead,
connect the various toggles and switches to an elaborate jury-rigged stereo
and cassette complex, and produce some remarkable tones. Thanks to a
maze of leads that Anders then ran throughout the ship to an assortment
of ancient speakers positioned just so for optimum acoustics, our traditional sailing vessel has become the residence of a high-tech sound system. I gather that this is considered a basic necessity on board, something
on the order of the archaic refrigerator, which looms like a ridiculously
misplaced monolith in the middle of the *Sofia's* saloon. The sole purposes
of the fridge are to manufacture a daily supply of minute misshapen ice
cubes and to keep the skipper's gin and olives properly chilled. The *Sofia*
has neither running water nor bathrooms, but can she boast fine tunes and
a passable wet bar? Oh, you betcha!

Linda has the fresh young face of a high school cheerleader, is in her
early twenties, and also possesses an impressive sailing résumé. She and
Captain Tom share some vague history and even now appear to be something of an item. Linda is into this venture big time, gung-ho to get the
work done and get going. She portrays herself as an accomplished tall-
ship sailor, bustin'-a-gut eager to get back out to sea and demonstrate her
abilities.

Martina and Kathy joined the *Sofia* at around the same time and apparently buddied-up quickly, as they already seem to enjoy a well-established

mutual support system. Kathy is blond and stout, a farm girl from Vermont, as I recall. I can see that she is cautiously reserving judgment, observing and evaluating rather than wholly buying into this venture. Kathy hasn't got a lot of sailing experience, but I credit her with the strength and intelligence to appraise this situation soundly. If she chooses to commit, I'll lay odds that she'll rise to the top of the *Sofia*'s hazy hierarchy and grab hold of this experience with both hands. But my guess is that if she cannot achieve this, she'll humbly take her leave.

Martina impresses me as the more passive of the pair; she is lithe and pretty, with a cosmopolitan sophistication beyond her twenty-one years but somehow repressed and emotionally dependent. She even looks out of place here—too refined, too soft, too vulnerable for the *Sofia*'s rough edges. I've heard that she met the ship several months ago in New York, where the *Sofia* was still hanging out after participating in the bicentennial tall-ship parade two years ago. Rumor has it that she and Evan struck up a romance back then. There are inklings of an on-again, off-again relationship between them even now but nothing clear-cut. (I have yet to discover much of anything on board the *Sofia* that is.) However, for the time being, Martina is a pleasant addition to the crew's social complement.

Then there's Barney. If ever there was a living, breathing person who inhabits the stereotype of a dude from Bakersfield, California (his hometown), it's him. Actually, Barney both looks and moves like the "keep on truckin'" figure portrayed on bumper stickers all up and down the West Coast. He is the proud owner of a "fully developed sense of humor," which he exercises freely. But within his personality also lies a great heart; his warmth spills over through puppy-dog eyes and gentle mannerisms. Barney's real name is Tom, which he obviously prefers, but he has agreed to allow us to call him a bastardized version of his last name in order to avoid confusion with the captain. "Barney" suits him. He grudgingly concedes this, although he's not thrilled about it. He just shrugs, cooperates, and with an endearing smile voices one of the more descriptive of a litany of already-famous Barneyisms—"Oh, well . . ."

Barney is a closet public relations man, masterful in the arts of sarcasm and subtle irony to get his point across or sometimes just to ease the atmosphere on board. During a recent meal, when a heated argument erupted about the questionable quality of the dry goods that were being laid in, someone pointed to Barney. He was sitting quietly at the end of the saloon table. He had methodically separated his dinner into two heaping mounds—one of beans and one of bugs. The bean pile was larger but only just. Recognizing with an expert's sense of timing that he now had everyone's attention, Barney glanced up, shrugged an "Oh, well," and smiled placidly into the horrified faces of his crewmates. Point made. Point well taken. Barney is here on a more substantive mission than most. He's confided to me that he and his big brother had always dreamed of sailing around the world together. His brother died, and Barney is fulfilling the promise.

The last of the new crew to join the *Sofia* here in Boston is Karen, and what an odd creature she is to find in our midst. Karen looks far more like a country schoolmarm than a tall-ship sailor. She dresses daily in dowdy knee-length skirts and old-fashioned blouses—attire wholly incongruous with the setting. I've witnessed several casual observers do a double take when, while scanning the work in progress on a normal *Sofia* day, they spot Karen—dressed much more appropriately for a Friday night barn dance—vigorously sanding a rail or slapping a coat of paint on a mast. Karen's personality, however, suits her strange appearance. She is effusive in her down-to-earth, homespun openness. To my knowledge she has no sailing experience whatsoever, but she is simply as excited as a small child to travel and to see the world. Karen is devoid of sophistication or affectation, and in this alien arena in which we all now find ourselves sparring, her presence is as refreshing as a prairie breeze after a summer rain. I like her immensely, but I am concerned about how well she'll weather this experience. She is clearly not representative of the *Sofia's* crew at large. In fact, if there was a single classification into which I might bundle the rest of us, it would be that we are all, well, nothing at all like Karen. I don't think she is a stranger to this distinction, though, and the strong will and fierce determination that come from experience are evidenced in her refusal to be intimidated. For instance, during meetings, when the debate concerns our proposed ports-of-call, she announces her agenda. And she doesn't hold back—quite the opposite, actually—when we are discussing sensitive issues regarding shipboard behavior. Karen is absolutely rigid in certain moral and ethical respects and completely dogmatic when defending her peculiar pet peeves. No one has openly rebuked her yet. However, I have observed enough exasperated smirks and vaguely veiled sardonic responses to suggest that it won't be long before someone challenges her. I fully expect to see the day when Karen will have to measure the strength of her convictions against the vacillating value systems of the *Sofia's* volatile crew. She just might surprise us all by hanging in here, though. This gal's got some grit.

The Varmit! Varmit is the Sofian of longest standing and hands-down the most fascinating. The Varmit holds the lofty position of ship's mascot. He is a coatimundi, a rodent-like creature indigenous to the jungles of Mexico and Central and South America. Coatis resemble raccoons in size and coloring. They're about two and a half feet long with a brownish coat and black mask, but they have a long, semi-prehensile bushy tail. The Varmit's nose is also much longer than a raccoon's, more along the lines of an anteater's. His feet have slender, tapered toes with razor-sharp claws. A coati's teeth also are longer and sharper than a raccoon's, more suited for ripping into the insects and tearing apart the reptiles that make up the bulk of its diet in the wild. Our Varmit weighs in at an impressive 10 pounds of either cuddly cuteness or pure orneriness, depending upon whether you're in his good graces at the time. He was acquired by the crew six years ago when the *Sofia* was sailing around Costa Rica. A local marketplace was selling him and his siblings as food, when an outraged crew member hid him in a stalk of bananas. Varmit was just a pup then. He has lived his entire adult life on board the *Sofia*.

Varmit's seniority stands him in good stead with the revolving cast of characters who enter his domain unprepared to cohabit. Our mascot doesn't know that he's a critter, and he definitely doesn't acknowledge that he is not in charge. In fact, I'm discovering that he is in charge. Anyone brave or foolish enough to take issue with this will soon regret it. The Varmit has a violent temper and an uncanny memory. His spitefulness is both painful and personal. A Varmit vendetta should never, ever be taken lightly, lest one cares to have one's sheets soiled, toiletries tampered with, or ankles gnawed upon. Among Varmit's less-than-endearing qualities is his unabashed love of anything that smells sweet—toothpaste, perfume, soap, shampoo, and the like. He will pursue these items shamelessly, sniffing out their whereabouts from the most clever and obscure hiding places, and then with amorous ardor swabbing them all over his tail and pretty much all over the entire surrounding area as well. Our little Varmit leaves absolutely no doubt that he has come a-calling.

Another of our mascot's more irksome idiosyncrasies is his bestial reaction to the tones created by the jangling of metal against metal. Varmit might be elusive—not spotted much for hours or even days at a time—but should someone casually rattle a row of wrenches or shake a sack of shackles, our amazing coati will materialize out of nowhere, single-mindedly launching the frenzied assault of a fierce hunter. Actually, Varmit waddles like an overfed house pet, and his claws tend to slip around ridiculously

on the varnished cabin sole, but do not be fooled. He can still be light-
ning fast and deadly serious. The high-decibeled screech of metal irritates
a particularly raw nerve in the Varmit, and it isn't soothed until he can
sink his rotten, razor-sharp teeth into soft flesh. Now here is the uncanny
part—only the flesh of an avowed enemy will do. In one instance Mother
Boats accidentally dropped an entire tray of knives, forks, and spoons. Varmit came galumphing madly into the galley, instantly came upon his
beloved Boats frozen ankle-deep in the offending silverware, promptly
spun about, scanned the saloon, spotted a terrified Anders perched high
on the tabletop, raced over, and bit him soundly on the leg. Anders, a card-
carrying critter hater, was positively furious and in intense pain, but he
still knew better than to retaliate. At least, as far as he knew, his bunk was
as yet unsullied.

    No one wins an argument with the Varmit. The futility of trying was
made clear by Evan recently as he lectured on ship handling. He was discussing working aloft in the rigging while the *Sofia* is under way—a topic
of particular interest and no little concern to many of us new recruits.
Evan emphasized that were we at any time to lose our grip, we should try
to fall down onto the deck rather than off into the sea. This sounded
patently absurd to me until he elaborated, explaining that the ocean has
an eerie way of quickly swallowing any and all evidence of an object that's
gone adrift upon it. For example, during the previous circumnavigation a
crew member became so incensed with some especially vile shenanigans of
the Varmit that the mate, in a fit of blind rage, snatched the Varmit up and
flung him overboard. The Sofians witnessing this ghastly act descended
upon the perpetrator with merciless admonitions. Immediately feeling
remorse, the guilty sot leaped over the side himself to rescue his victim.
By the time the ship could alter course to try to retrieve the pair, their
two bobbing forms were completely lost from sight, buried in the swells.
After several hours of searching, they were finally spotted and rescued. The
Varmit, who is by no means a water creature, was in surprisingly good nick.
The sailor, an excellent swimmer, was a bloody horror. When his assailant
reached him, the Varmit reckoned that to survive he needed to gain higher
and dryer ground, so he scampered to safety atop his savior's head. When
the ship found the duo, the brave rescuer (or shameless evildoer, depending upon where you've come into the tale) had been clawed to shreds by
those stiletto-like nails. Evan concluded dramatically: *Lesson No. 1*—Falling
overboard means a serious risk of being lost at sea. *Lesson No. 2*—Don't
mess with the Varmit. In my own mind I carefully reversed these two good
lessons in order of priority.

I've resisted introducing the crew members who soon will be leaving us because I hate to have my questions about them left unanswered. They'll leave the *Sofia* here in Boston. At some point they'll gain the stature of local folk heroes in *Sofia* history, a chronicle painstakingly recorded and preserved in the ship's archives. I'm told they'll eventually become the stuff of legend. Katy is a crusty Australian who boarded the *Sofia* three years ago with her then-two-year-old daughter, Sephra. Even with my limited exposure to the ship, it feels like one of the worst environments a parent might choose for raising a small child. But Sephra, to all outward appearances at any rate, seems to have fared quite well. She is a sharp, spunky, lively little mite who has obviously delighted in a plenitude of love and affection from many of the adults in her midst. But it's certain that she has also been subjected to the inconsistent discipline and cold indifference of others on board. Even her mom has a raw edge to her that I imagine is at least due in part to her *Sofia* sojourn, and I wonder what elements here could be responsible for so hardening a young woman. For me, Katy will remain a fascinating enigma. The only mystery about little Sephra, however, will be her future. She comes like a wide-open book whose single unknown is the ending, and she will take with her a bit of the sun when she leaves. Sephra is a joy—a sweet, innocent, small fluff of a girl with a mop of bouncy blond curls, a trickling laugh, and a pathetically lonely, lazy eye. Her bright, exuberant greeting, "Hey, you silly billies!" can engender feelings of warmth in even the most austere on board. I'll bet she has been quite therapeutic for the crew, but I'm far less certain of how positive an effect this lifestyle has had on her. Although I will miss this pair, I do wish for them a more secure and safe life ashore. No one could deny that these two remarkable females are a team and that they will undoubtedly carry on with some measure of success, if not convention, in the future.

Since coming aboard I've noticed that the *Sofia* has engendered much local curiosity. Boston's harbor ferries have recently included us on their tours. "Old Ironsides," the original USS *Constitution,* is tied up just one wharf over, to a much more respectable dock I might add, and I've learned that, of the two, the *Sofia* is the more popular point of interest. The ferry operators have played right into their passengers' curiosity, elaborating (and embellishing, I'm sure) on the more controversial and renegade aspects of the *Sofia's* colorful history and aberrant lifestyle. Many visitors have wandered our way after completing one of these tours, needing to satisfy for themselves that the rumors are either awesome fact or fanciful fiction. They rarely leave disillusioned. Here are some of the queries we hear most often:

"A floating nudist colony is what we were told. Oh, not quite, huh? But
    sometimes?"

"Hear you've got a dangerous wild animal on board. Omigod! There
    he is!"

"So, do you actually go up there, out on those flimsy ropes, in a storm?
    Damn!"

"Hey, think you'll get as far as Tahiti? Boy, I'd sure like to go there.
    'Course, I have responsibilities. Um, when might you be heading
    there . . . ?"

"What are those fuzzy balls up there? Poodles! Oh, 'baggy' what? Baggy
    wrinkles? Uh-huh, chafing gear. Ha ha. I get it. Sure do look like
    poodles."

"Listen, what do you need? I mean, I can't go along and all, but what can
    I do? I'd like to help out, be a part of it somehow, you know? Just tell
    me what you need, OK?"

"Does your mother know that you're doing this?"

"Say, could I use your bathroom? None? Hmmm."

Several publications have nosed around, soliciting stories and interviews.
Us magazine came and took some great action shots and is planning to
run a full photo layout with an informative article in its November 1978
issue. Here is how the reporter, Roger Vaughan, described the *Sofia*: "*Sofia*
doesn't have a schedule. She's not a cruise ship, a research or charter vessel,
a school or a floating extension of an organization's plan for world peace.
Sofia is her own woman; she's a lifestyle."

That does pretty well cover it. *Soundings*, a sailing magazine, also came
over, and Joel Avni wrote up a lengthy piece on the *Sofia*, which appeared
in the October 1978 issue:

With each crew change, the ship assumes a new character, but so far they
have always managed to keep the flag flying. Differences do arise, but they
are either cleared by discussion, resolved at the frequent crew meetings, or
simmer away until a crew change or time makes them meaningless.
    But the ship sails on.

Yep, no one is misled here. No punches are pulled and no lilies gilded.
Ultimately, there is nothing to be gained by misrepresenting the *Sofia*—
and a great deal to be lost. Even with wide-open eyes we are probably not
adequately prepared for what we might encounter. It is imperative, from

the ship's standpoint, at least, that everyone knows what she or he is getting into—theoretically and hypothetically speaking, of course.

The *Sofia* began as a Baltic trader; she was built in Pukavik, Sweden, in 1921. In the 1960s a group of weekend sailors from an Oregon university got together to purchase an old ship, and their search led them to the more notable wooden boat graveyards of the world. In Kalmar, Sweden, they found an aged, retired Baltic trader that promised to suit their purposes quite nicely. They bought her for $7,000 and christened her the *Sofia*, after a former queen of that country (or so the story goes; the queen probably was Sophia of Denmark or the Netherlands, not Sweden). The following winter found our enterprising young lads moored, gratis, in an ice-encrusted harbor area that Copenhagen had set aside expressly for the renovation of traditional romantic, historical vessels. There, the *Sofia's* rebirth began in earnest.

They poured several tons of concrete ballast into her substantial bilges to give her stability. Her cargo hold became a makeshift saloon with some roughed-out sleeping accommodations. They leveled the top-heavy, unsightly aft pilothouse and returned the engine to marginal functionality. With an exuberant fistful of crew, the ship was then able to transit the Kiev Canal to Portsmouth, England. From there the *Sofia* slogged over to the famous wooden boatyards of Spain and Portugal where her masts were fashioned and stepped, yards for square sails welded up and rigged, broken frames repaired, and rustic cabins constructed. The *Sofia* was emerging as a viable floating vessel once again, but she still needed a character, a classification—a sail plan.

The records of the *Sofia's* original rig were lost years earlier in a fire that totally destroyed the boatyard in Sweden where she had first been built, so the 1960s crew made for England, the land of some of the most renowned sailmakers and designers in the world. There they bought half her total complement of fore and aft sails and laid in the material and blueprints for stitching up the remainder. The *Sofia* was reborn as a gaff-topsail schooner, an honorable rig for a proud sailing ship.

Over the course of the next several years and nautical miles, the *Sofia*—destined to perpetually be a cost-plus operation—would continue to be repaired, renewed, upgraded, and maintained as funds and manpower would allow. It was slow, grueling going at times, but the miles kept ticking off, the scenery was constantly changing, a succession of exotic ports-of-call were recorded in the ship's log, and an intensely heterogeneous, outrageously intriguing amalgamation of multinational crew came and went along the equatorial trade routes of the world. The social structure of the minisociety afloat varied with the passage of time. Trial and error, proving nearly fatal at times but producing a tough scar tissue that ultimately helped to strengthen the fiber of the adventure, was standard operating procedure. The *Sofia* was being created on the go, in every sense of the word.

So her devotees lumbered on: soliciting crew, marketing goods, hauling cargo, bartering for bare necessities, sailing, sailing, always keeping the old girl afloat and sailing, often on an uncharted course heading for a destination unknown. The crew, which could roll with the social, emotional, and physical punches, hung in, sometimes for years at a time. But the vast majority of those who signed on for short stints upon the *Sofia*'s decks would jump off as sprightly and vigorously as they had once stepped on. The ship's annals are full of these short-termers. In fact, in retrospect it might have been the energy generated by the constant rotation of bodies that supplied the primary juice that kept the *Sofia* going.

The goal for reconstructing the *Sofia* always was to establish her as simple and traditional. Certainly, the rigging was done appropriately, with a few grudging concessions, for example, using synthetic, longer-lasting materials rather than natural, traditional, and short-lived ones. But still, the *Sofia* may best be characterized by what she does not possess: satellite navigation systems, Loran, WeatherFax, anemometer, winches, electric windlass, auto pilot, depth sounder, propane, inboard 110-volt electrical system, private staterooms, hot water—heck, running water at all—showers, heads, heat, air conditioners—well, I guess the list could be endless. In fact, many of these amenities are now commonplace on all manner of sailing craft. But the *Sofia* is not all manner of sailing craft. Something else that she does not have is perhaps what best defines her. The *Sofia* continues to resist activating a chain of command.

Her early architects struggled mightily to design and maintain the lofty ideal of a true sailing cooperative that would function successfully with no internal hierarchy. It was a noble experiment. But it was marred from the moment of inception because of its intrinsic dependency upon the concept of the great collective "we." "We" are merely human. At first the fellas who conceived the *Sofia* attempted to institute a captain-for-a-day format. The ideal of equality afloat soon dissolved into the reality of chaos on the high seas. Although high-minded in theory, its application proved to be self-destructive, naive folly in practice. So a more orthodox version of a captain was adopted. A skipper was appointed, the one who in true democratic fashion was most qualified, most supported, and most willing. Beneath him, the hierarchy remained more relaxed. Longevity seemed to be the most important criterion for qualifying for a position of responsibility or authority on board (it absolutely determined who got first dibs on what bunks). Short of that, one needed only to be eager. Period. This trend continues in full force today, and I'm thrilled to report that I've discovered a fertile pod of zealots germinating within our ranks. Why, we seem to be developing an enthusiasm that borders on reckless abandon.

Our crew probably averages thirty years of age and oddly now possesses and has begun to exhibit the explosive energy of a gang of teenagers. Evidently, we are not so old that we can't remember how lusciously intoxicating the teen years were. Nor are we distant enough from the boardrooms, PTA meetings, and office cubicles of our future not to recognize that we have been handed a new lease on a carefree life—one that we find ourselves diving into headlong with the passion of our youth. Like sixteen-year-olds, we see our bodies as golden once again, our minds wide open. Boundaries are nonexistent, possibilities limitless. We are like adolescents, our adventure aboard the *Sofia* the ultimate breaking away.

As we set our sails for this passage, we are exuberant juveniles defying the laws of gravity, thumbing our noses at propriety, rejecting conformity. With the cavalier aplomb of our more miraculous immature selves, we dare to do this wild thing. But how far will we actually go? Will we risk being weird and outlandish? With all of us running our high beams once again, will we glow brilliantly and be fully alive?

This is the dream. This is the promise we cannot resist. Hell, we're already hooked. But are we doomed to suffer the pitfalls that accompany any vice? Will devastating lows follow glorious highs? Personalities are certain to clash. Egos are destined to crumble. Foundations will be tested. Lives will be threatened. Heroes may emerge. So may villains. A sound sense of ourselves will become essential. Fortitude will be absolutely mandatory. Dare we really go out there? Yes. Yes! Here we go. Out to the very edge. Out and away. Here I go!

The author at the helm of the *Sofia*

chapter 2

Into the Teeth of Hurricane Kendra

My Maiden Voyage

Being in a ship is being in a jail, with the chance of being drowned.

—SAMUEL JOHNSON

INTRODUCTION

I boarded the tall ship in Boston on August 20, 1978. We left the harbor bound for the Caribbean in the early dawn of October 25, marking the beginning of my maiden voyage aboard the *Sofia*. Those introductory months in port had proved interesting if not illuminating, productive without the benefit of certainty. I was there, but I did not yet belong. Had I not spent so much of my early life marching chin high, shoulders squared through unfamiliar territory in which I felt no semblance of belonging, I might have bolted for somewhere safe and something accustomed. But as before, the magnetic attraction of the unknown ignited my resolve to face that interminable feeling of aloneness. I embraced the awkward, stumbling persona of the novice that I had chosen to assume time and again. She was an old friend with whom I had nowhere to go but up. So I continued apace. I was going somewhere I hadn't yet been and that was sufficient fuel to fire my persistence while I confronted my own inadequacies.

Once, while slogging away at the *Sofia*'s galley dishes with Katy, the Australian single mom who'd just completed half a circumnavigation with her young daughter in tow, I wondered aloud when I might feel as though I knew what the hell I was doing. The old sage cocked a savvy eyebrow in my direction and replied that it would happen the moment someone came on board who knew less than I did. Well, no matter what we as a crew knew or didn't know on that late October morning in New England, we were going sailing. Hurricane season had "effectively" ended, the refit was "effectively" complete, and we had made arrangements to haul the ship out of the water in Martinique to do the work on her under body.

It would be hammered into me that the *Sofia*'s sailing schedule would be dictated by her physical status, as well as by conditions of weather and sea. This was not to be taken lightly, ever. In a pinch, however, a veteran core crew of only four or five sailors would be expected to command a green band of eager swabbies through just about anything.

Before the sun had cleared the grimy rooftops of the tired old brick buildings cluttering Boston's Italian North End, we had cast off. Motoring out of the harbor, which was bustling even at that early hour, we were soon able to cut the diesel-fume-spewing, serene-sunrise-shattering cylinders of our ancient 1935 Jüne Munktell engine. We had sufficient wind to commence setting the schooner's more than five thousand square feet of sail. It had been predetermined that we would be standing three-hour watches, with three crew members to a watch plus Tom, the skipper, and Evan, the first mate, alternating four-hour stints as watch captains. Regardless of the schedule, on that first day everyone was on deck. This was an event, one many of us had worked for and dreamed of during those long servile days in port. Ordinarily, everyone except the captain was supposed to take his or her turn at watch every day—except on the day that crew member was scheduled to cook. Our departure fell on my galley day, but I did not intend to miss any of the action, so I had prepared the midday meal the night before and had only to set it out on the saloon table below. My first official watch at sea was to begin at noon.

I recall that the wind was fresh, the weather fair, and the seas calm— optimum conditions for setting the sails. *Sofia*'s were massively weighty, controlled only by traditional block and tackle. There were no wimpy, "yachty" winches on our salty old girl. It was time to go to work, and we were ready. Initially, we reported to our designated sail stations, but soon we disintegrated into a single enthusiastic herd, gleefully stampeding from halyard to halyard. It was still fun at this point. The *Sofia*'s fore, main, and mizzen sails were gaff rigged, meaning they were large rectangular-cut sails attached to spars, both along the foot and the head. The upper spar, the gaff, had to be sent aloft with the sail, an exercise requiring finesse, strength, and spot-on teamwork. The two opposing ends of the gaff needed to be raised independently yet simultaneously, parallel to the deck. If the outermost peak dipped too low or arched too high at any point in its ascent, the gaff jaws at the innermost throat would be jammed into the mast, abruptly terminating the procedure until the proper balance was regained.

Crew members clustered on both port and starboard quarterdecks at the cap rails to tend lines. The groups splintered off into four tangled companies, adopting the splay-legged, set-spine stance of a tug-of-war team at the ready. The heftier bunch grappled for handholds to "sweat up" the coarse, inch-thick, three-stranded laid line of the throat and peak halyards, while the stragglers took up slack on the "tail." Dozens of white-knuckled fingers braided along stiff rope; bodies, arms, and hands swung rhythmically as the great sail filled with wind. A sea chantey frequently accompanied the exertion, both lifting the spirits and maintaining a delicate meter, "sweaters" in unison, "tailers" a half-staccato beat behind. Still more eager hands would be tending a variety of other lines as the canvas stretched skyward. The vang, a line controlling the wildly pitching tip of the gaff, would be held taut but fed out judiciously as the spar rose. At some point, depending on the tack of the ship and the point of sail (the direction of the wind upon the vessel), we would have to use a series of sturdily built blocks and tackle—as well as the sheets, topping-lifts, and preventers (the lines for raising, and controlling, and determining the angle of the boom)— to lift the enormous boom from its crutch.

Once the gaff sail was properly set and lines made fast on belay pins at the rail, the topsail was sent aloft. A member of the crew would accompany this sail by scrambling up the ratlines to the hounds, wedging between the rigging cable and feeding the unwieldy rectangular wad of lines, gaskets, and canvas into position while keeping it free from fouling in the mangle of rigging aloft. The clew line, which attached the outermost tip of the sail to the aftermost end of the gaff, would need to be reeved, or fed through manually. I was instructed early on in this exercise and learned that it was potentially the most dangerous maneuver a sailor might have to perform aboard the *Sofia*. Consequently, it was strictly voluntary. No one would ever be commanded to attempt so dicey a task. In carrying out this awesome piece of work, a sailor would climb to where the gaff jaws encircle the mast and would take up position well above the web of rigging that provided a network of lifesaving handholds. Here, it became pure circus act—no net. With clew line clamped fiercely in her teeth, the sailor gamely straddled the gaff. Gripping the spar with the entire length of her torso, she'd shinny out to the tip and feed the line through the block, sending it snaking to the deck far below. All this as the ship was pitching and rolling violently, the spar maniacally stabbing and flailing. The lines could

effect only a certain measure of control on the gaff's peak in this position, so the spar had a tendency to whip, slash, and lurch, creating the perfect action for catapulting an unwary volunteer off into space—and onto
the ocean's surface or upon the ship's decks several stories below.

So once the topsail was secure, the spunky volunteer repeated her aerial feat—in reverse—shakily regaining the deck and grinning ear to ear,
struggling mightily to keep down her breakfast. She'd grab one solidify-
ing lung full of hearty sea air, salt spray prickling her ruddy cheeks, before
scampering off to aid in a replay of this exercise, until the appropriate sails
(the *Sofia* had sixteen in all) were set and trimmed, lines belayed and neatly
coiled down, gaskets and sail covers properly stowed, windward hatches
battened, portholes dogged down, gear relashed and secured, course set,
departure logged, and watch team in motion. As the sailors gazed aloft,
proudly surveying their work, they would gingerly flex their raw, blistered
hands. We virgin crew would find ourselves teetering about the decks like
awestruck toddlers, experimenting with the delicious sensation of moving
inside the ship's motion—apprehensively fluid, tentatively self-assured,
shyly flirting with actually being OK out there.

I remember rushing below to lay the lunch out on the gargantuan
slab of timber that served as our saloon table and then excitedly reporting to the helm for my watch. Some time later, about midafternoon of
that maiden day of our maiden voyage, all hell began to break loose. Fingers of the cold North Atlantic were insidiously penetrating the tepid
waters of the Gulf Stream. A late bloomer was being conceived. A monster threatened to emerge. Hurricane Kendra would be born. Our ship
was scheduled to collide with a nemesis possessing a blind fury far greater
than anything she had ever encountered before. *Sofia* and Kendra would
have it out. We rookie crew were destined to become old salts long before
our time.

❧

JOURNAL ENTRY
Hamilton
Bermuda
November 1978

In Boston I sacrificed comfort and privacy for warmth and protection
from the elements. I had to abandon my burrow of cozy sleeping bags on
the foredeck as the season's first New England frost hit. A series of frigid

blustery nights finally chased me below with the rest of the swabbies into the dreaded forward cabin. Positioned just beyond the main saloon in the direction of the forepeak, the main cabin houses the most bunks of any single compartment of the *Sofia*. Eight tightly stacked berths press into the bulkheads encircling a clearing that is overwhelmed by the great fat stick of foremast that juts through its middle—as fitting a centerpiece as any for a boudoir on a tall ship, I suppose. I cannot begin to count the number of times I have collided with this beast while semiconsciously feeling my way toward my bed. Never do I retire to the forward cabin fully alert. It is far too depressing to contemplate in an awake state. So I sleepily stumble through each night and thunk! Invariably, I lunge headlong into the mast. Recovering slightly, I reel to the left, feel for the upper platform, stick my feet in the face of the poor sot on the lower bunk, and launch myself up and in. Fending off the hull with one hand while jerking my superfluous curtain shut with the other, I take a deep breath, relax, and somehow find peace. Everything beyond my six-by-three-foot cave—except the smell—disappears and I sink into blessed sleep.

Being in the forward cabin is like being entombed. I came to this ship after years spent blissfully in virtual self-imposed hermitage. Previously, I had chosen my circumstances carefully, always giving priority to solitude, an abundance of elbow room, and a wide expanse of clean, open, natural surroundings. The accommodations might be spartan. I had lived one winter in a tent deep in the New Hampshire woods; when I lived in California, I fashioned a one-room cabin in an isolated stand of soggy, northern redwood before moving up to a tiny crib overlooking a grand spread of meadow. Of course, during these times I worked, socialized, and generally interacted quite appropriately and productively but always on my own terms and at my own initiative. Whenever I wanted to be alone, seclusion was ever at my fingertips . . . until now.

Enter the *Sofia*—123 feet of damp, cloying, cramped space stuffed with the necessities to sustain life for herself and a couple dozen anonymous bodies for an indeterminate period at sea. Now, all the "stuff" doesn't bother me so much. I find I'm pretty fascinated by it, curious to learn what everything is and does. But the "bodies" represent for me an odd conundrum. For better or worse, this bunch are my new buddies, my mates. Initially, I am fairly terrified at the prospect of getting chummy with the likes of many of them. But, alas, it is unavoidable on some level, and, as it turns out, we all share this same wariness. Why, we do have something in common, after all.

We each tiptoe cautiously around one another, prudent not to disclose anything vital, certain we don't want to learn too much. We all sense that it will be open season on whatever we toss out there that is of a personal nature, and none of us is eager to be identified just yet. We new recruits are still sizing up the elders of the group—feint and parry, parry and feint, trying somehow to level the playing field. Boats is, hands down, the most "out there." (Or so it seems at first glance.) We just sit back and enjoy the ongoing "Mother Boats Review." Evan is by turns taciturn and on the make. The guys vie for his respect. The gals try to remain guarded and discreet. Norman is immediately strange, curiously uneasy in his own skin, impaired in his tireless attempts at socializing. The guys quickly dismiss him as a nonforce. The women openly befriend him with a mind toward establishing clear boundaries within the relationship. Captain Tom is a luminary. Everyone instantly warms to him, attracted by his charisma. In essence, he is the embodiment of promise for so many of the new crew—perhaps for the old as well. Each new phase for the *Sofia* seems to require redefinition. Weighty expectation falls upon Tom for this most questionable of ventures, and he rises high to the occasion. But many others are like me, simply feeling around in the dark. Clearly, we are an interesting bunch, but time and circumstance will have to reveal the particulars. At this juncture we are still window dressing, disqualified from playing an integral part.

On the morning that we set out from Boston, our collection of cooperative members has not yet coalesced. But we are game to give it a go and eager to begin. Tom bursts into the dungeon of the forward cabin before dawn and shakes us awake with great jubilation and a distinctly male call-to-arms. The theme from the musical *The Rocky Horror Picture Show* is blasting top-volume from the stereo speakers. (I can only guess what the little old Italian bakers in the cannoli shop across the way are thinking.) The aroma of strong coffee and sweet odor of some unidentifiable gruel wafts into our cabin and momentarily pierces its ever-sour stench.

It is bitter cold in New England this late October, and the *Sofia* has to be pretty well sealed up against the elements. Hatch boards are securely in place, portholes dogged down, skylights battened shut. Our mammoth cast-iron diesel oven provides our only heat below. When it is fully cranking, it gives off a wealth of warmth, but it also emits a pall of diesel fumes that, without proper ventilation, swarms below like a venomous smog cloud. The *Sofia* sports a lofty Charley Noble, the chimney fitted to the deck to carry away galley smoke. However, the draft necessary for sucking

up the exhaust is often insufficient or negligible alongside the wharf. At
low tide the *Sofia* can lie as much as eighteen feet below the docks, with a
veritable airless wall of pilings rising abreast of her. Consequently, the
diesel fumes, combined with the pervasive effluvia of dirty laundry, damp
bedclothes, and sweaty bodies, transforms our captain's crude wake-up call
into a welcome rescue. The crisp, relatively clean air of the *Sofia*'s decks
beckons us. We fly from our bunks, prepared to get ourselves and the *Sofia*
finally underway.

In the frenzy of getting the ship squared away for departure, we give
little consideration to anything else. Not until the *Sofia* has cleared the jetty
and set sail do I pause to reflect on my surroundings. I inhale a briny
breath and spin full around. The ship's canvas, wood, and steel separate
me from my past. She is now my whole world. Behind me, Boston's skyline is a hazy distant mirage, like the faint glimmer of a dream just
interrupted. Before me, over *Sofia*'s bow, which is finally unleashed and biting into the waves with a voracious hunger—charumph! charumph!—lies
the far horizon that promises my future. It looks soft and summoning. I
feel marvelously empowered and rarin' to go.

We had cautiously waited out the hurricane season, dallying in port
much longer than was either comfortable or convenient for us. We carefully monitored each successive summer storm as we tried to discern a
pattern while the winds pounded away at the Gulf, the Caribbean, and the
eastern seaboard. The seasons ultimately offered us our most valuable clue.
Historically, it's warm weather that breeds hurricanes. Well, it was pretty
bloody cold by then and there hadn't been a storm of note in weeks. We'd
already extended our margin of safety far in excess of that proscribed by
even the most conservative seamen. By all accounts, it was time to go.

Setting the sails is a kick! We practiced our duties at our specified stations ad infinitum, ad nauseam while moored to the dock. But at sea the
tedium of the drills takes on all the glamour and spectacle of a live stage
production on opening night. To an outsider, we might look like a polished chorus line, our bodies moving gracefully across the stage from mark
to mark as the great bundles of canvas rise methodically and majestically,
filling with impeccable purpose. What wouldn't be obvious are the desperate whispers shot with furtive glances between us green sailors, who are,
in truth, being physically corralled from one halyard to the next. "Psst!
What is a topsail brail?" "Hey, where is the course sheet?" "Oh, shit, what
pin does this go on?" "Um, have you gone aloft yet? Will they make *me*?"
"Jesus, my hands ache!" "Uh, you don't look so good. Are you going to

puke?" "Yeeeessss. Please, which side do I go to?" "Not to windward, for crissakes!" "Which way is windward?" "Oh, man . . ."

Comic relief and patient leadership buoy us along. By midday we have already been up for hours. The sails are set, there is no land in sight, lunch is on the saloon table, and I am reporting to the helm for my first official watch at sea. I find this too to be quite a bit harder than I had imagined. Reading the compass, holding the course, and monitoring all the moving parts of the vessel are nothing at all like driving a car, as I have been so flippantly misinformed. I discover that because I am so short, I have to stand down on deck with my nose to the compass and rotate the wheel with my arms behind me, holding it in place with my butt. I can't see the ship as well from this vantage point as I might from up on the raised quarter-deck behind the wheel mount, but I don't know what the hell I'm supposed to be looking for anyway. Keeping my eyes trained tightly on the quivering compass needle is what I can handle at this point. I single-mindedly lock my eyes on the course setting and my hands and butt on the wheel.

Each member of the watch team is to take the helm for an hour. When one sailor hands over the wheel to the next, he announces the course in a sharp command and then waits for confirmation from his relief. For example: "Hold course two-three-zero, south by southwest!" "Two-three-zero, south by southwest. Aye, Aye!" I get that part down without a hitch. Someone else will just have to manage the actual sailing of the ship, right? Wrong. It is the helm's duty to steer. This necessitates my factoring in the proper set of each sail and calculating the true versus the apparent wind (the direction from which and speed at which the wind only appears to be blowing, taking into account the motion of the boat through the water). How is this accomplished? Why, by using a telltale. And what's that? An old piece of cassette tape. No kidding. Sofians have found that an eight- or ten-inch section of this discarded filament tied approximately fifteen feet up on the aftershrouds is beautifully suited to the purpose of providing the helmsman with a telltale by which he is able to astutely determine the apparent wind. I am instructed that while at the helm I should try to keep the telltale blowing at my shoulder. Yeah, right. I am also assured that eventually a sailor will develop a sixth sense, a savvy by which all the subtle and mysterious computations come through automatically. OK. Well, since I am not quite yet one with the ship, I have my work cut out for me. Setting the sails is a snap compared to this "driving the boat" exercise. I am sweating cannon balls by the end of my hour. With obvious relief I hand over the helm to my watch mate.

"Hey, what's the course?" he inquires indignantly, insisting on playing his debut part precisely as rehearsed, voicing all his allotted lines.

"Uh, jeez . . . two-thirty?" I offer limply.

"You mean two-three-zero," he yaps back at me.

"Uh-huh, south by southwest, I think. See, it shows it right here," I volunteer, gesturing toward the compass face.

"South by southwest! Aye-aye!" he shouts at me, causing me to stumble backward. I frown disapprovingly back up at him. Giggling moronically, Mother Boats intervenes before my mate and I come to blows. Boats protectively leads me below to the chart room for my next lesson.

"Man, that was stressful," I sigh.

"Really?" he teases. "Now all you have to do is mark your hour on the chart and log it in the book." I grab his sleeve viciously and growl, "Don't you dare leave me, Boats!" I was taught this procedure and had practiced it with great self-discipline while bobbing idly, tied to Lincoln Wharf. But this is the real deal, and I don't want to risk making a mistake. Besides, at the moment I'm a little rattled, to say the least. Boats watches over my shoulder as I carefully calculate our speed, distance, and direction and plot them on the chart. Then I read the chronometer (a twenty-four-hour clock based on Greenwich Mean Time—the time at Greenwich, England, the location of zero meridian), read the barometer (an instrument that measures atmospheric pressure), locate our position in terms of degrees of latitude and longitude, and record all this information in the ship's log. As is customary, I add a visual appraisal of the wind, sea, and sky and conclude with a poignantly emotional account of my experience. Boats begins howling again, obviously approving my choice of colorful language to describe my first hour at sea at the helm of a great tall ship. At least I can cuss like a proper sailor. And so we sail on.

The dawn of our third day at sea creeps over us like the hollow of a bad dream. If we thought the previous twenty-four hours were rough, the sunrise manages to confirm our worst suspicions and cements our most dreaded fears. We are embroiled in a tempest. The maelstrom is everywhere: cold, bottomless, endless, merciless, furious ocean, wind, and sky. No land is visible in any direction, as though none has ever existed. And for the crew of the *Sofia*, in effect, none does.

Boats has been steadfastly monitoring the radio communications. The weather system—the one we are in the throes of—is building. We can feel this well before he informs us. Even those of us who have not yet

developed a weather eye or a sea sense know. We can read the hard white
sheet of anxiety breaking through the thin veneer of calm and confidence
plastered on the faces of those most knowledgeable. This isn't going away;
the sky will not lift, the wind abate, or the sea relax. We have given up
any hope of our maiden voyage's magically transforming into the idyll that
we naively envisioned. At best, we reckon that we are in for a confrontation. At worst . . . we don't even know how to define *worst* out here. So
we are cautioned to stay alert, to pay attention, and to do as we are told.
We are also strongly advised to maintain tight control of the only thing
over which we still might be able to exercise any real control—ourselves.
Ultimately, this last task becomes the most vital.

As the weather worsens, the tone of the reports coming in becomes
more urgent. Mother Boats sits constant vigil at the radio. I hover over
him expectantly whenever I can. Boats isn't prone to lying. He'd be really
lousy at it if he tried, and he knows it. What I'm thinking is this: "What
is happening? A storm? A gale? Surely not a hurricane! It's nearly November, for crissakes! We did this right, didn't we? Weren't we so careful? I
trusted you guys, goddammit!" Yet I still manage to ask calmly, "So, where
do we go? What do we do?" Boats just chuckles and continues making his
notes, charting the course of the storm, reporting the *Sofia*'s position.

Out of New England, our radio contact is Coast Guard Group Boston—
Communication Center. As the *Sofia* gets blown farther south, we're contacted by the Coast Guard Weather Service out of New York and then
Delaware. By the time Boats is frantically piecing together the fragmented
weather accounts sent out by Coast Guard Group Maryland, the gale has
developed into a full-blown hurricane. It is official. They have given it a
name—Kendra. Over the course of this week and a half, we judiciously
alter our heading as we are instructed, first trying to avoid the storm that
Boston fears is brewing off the coast, then attempting to escape the gale
that New York suspects is building in the North Atlantic, and finally trying to run like hell from the hurricane that Maryland confirms has developed in the Caribbean. Before we lose contact for good with the Eastern
Seaboard Marine Weather Service, Coast Guard Search and Rescue obtains
one final position for the *Sofia* from Mother Boats. After reporting our longitude and latitude and receiving confirmation that they have been recorded,
Boats leans into the radio well and asks softly, with uncharacteristic resignation, "What is your recommendation?" Bathed in a surreal calm, I
listen as the staticky voice on the other end of the broken frequency quietly requests the full names of the *Sofia*'s crew and their next of kin.

"What?" I stutter. "Boats? What?" My fingers are digging into his shoulders. He won't look up at me. He can't lie. He does let a little giggle escape, though, just as an "all hands" is called up on deck. We both respond immediately.

The wind has reached gale force. It threatens to shred the sails and carry away the rigging. The effort of the storm upon the ship is too great, daring to shatter her to bits. We can no longer risk using the wind's awesome power to facilitate our escape. The skipper commands us to furl all sail and run under bare poles. Often the ship still sails on because the masts and rigging provide windage, or surface area for the wind to act upon. Under bare poles the *Sofia* will still make a remarkable eight knots.

Although sail has already been significantly reduced, the last remnants of canvas now need to be muscled in, and every strip of line and sail has to be lashed down. We move across the ship in a huddled mass like a chain gang bent against the onslaught of the slashing rain and blasting wind. To secure the ship requires the collective eyes, hands, brute strength, and know-how of the entire crew, progressing from station to station. No sooner is a line lifted from a belay pin than the sail detonates with the force of the gale. Lines whip frenetically, slicing hands and searing rails. Deadly heavy blocks slingshot wildly in a lethal dance at eye level. For a moment we have lost all control. Then our bodies launch upon the belly of the canvas, tackling it, and knocking it to the deck. Aching arms wrestle to enfold the luff, dragging the angry sail into the spar, rendering it breathless and inert. Bloody hands grasp to break coarse lines that run insanely free, burning through timber and flesh.

The headsails were furled hours ago (or is it days? seems like years) but have broken free of their gaskets and are flailing violently. To venture out into the bow net under these circumstances seems a ridiculous act of supreme self-destruction. Yet out we crawl on swollen hands and bruised knees, gripping the netting with bloodless fingers as our bodies are flung and twisted like lifeless forms. With each pitch and roll the bowsprit plunges into the crest of a wave and emerges through its back on the other side. Should the netting break apart or our hands, wrapped like a rider's on a bucking bronco's saddle horn, come loose, we'll vanish into the foam without a trace, swallowed up by the churning madness that is this ocean. When we finally regain the relative safety of the foredeck, I breathe purposefully, trying to find a rhythm, concentrating on quieting the deafening screeching in my head that I feel certain is the sound of my own brain reeling in abject panic. But the thunder is external. It's all around me. Every fiber of the *Sofia* is roaring in a cacophony of protest—her wood, steel, hemp, and canvas are grinding, groaning, pealing, piercing the storm's fury with their own staunch resistance. The ship feels completely organic to me at this moment, a vital force, vivifying, like my own life's blood. I somehow know that if I can remain with her, she will protect me, carry me through. The *Sofia* is now the sum total of my existence. She *is* life. Everything around her is its dissolution.

Mother Boats approaches from behind and urges me around, directing my gaze toward the yards above us. His smirk says, "We aren't done yet, not by a long shot." We had furled and gasketed the square sails in the storm last night. Now they are coming away, threatening to break loose altogether.

"Well, mate, let's go. Whaddaya say?" he urges. The prospect of going aloft in this weather is patently unthinkable, so I try not to think. I'm green. Maybe it isn't all as bad as it seems. Maybe this is sailing? All I can do is nod as Boats escorts me to the forward shrouds. To ascend the ratlines one first has to climb up onto the cap rail, the outer perimeter of the ship. The *Sofia* is rolling so severely that with each successive jolt, her entire six feet of freeboard (the distance between the water and the deck) lie nearly flat at sea level, and her rail teasingly laps at the surface. Then the counterroll abruptly flings her back, and she rockets straight skyward. The vessel's motion at the peak of each dip and thrust is pure propulsion. During these whirlwinds Boats and I hug the stays with all our strength, willing our bodies to melt into the rigging. At the righting moments between the pinnacles of each pitch and reel is a blessed vortex, a flash of dreamlike calm when, for a few precious seconds, the ship slips into complete harmony with the forces around her, floating serenely, almost weightlessly. During these pauses we climb, one rung at a time, frantically regaining our fierce hold before the bottom drops out again.

And so we scale the ship, me ahead, Boats just behind, overlapping my legs with his arms, encasing me in a pocket of his upper body. When we reach the yards, we slither out along the foot ropes that are strung beneath the teetering spars. These bounce with the same random spasms of the ratlines, only not just up and down but port to starboard, bow to stern, as well. We have absolutely nothing to grab hold of out here. Our legs split out, our feet press down hard on the thin ropes, our torsos fold over the yard, simulating the catch-and-release-like grip of a loop encircling a toggle. We tussle in the ballooning canvas with one arm while slapping a lashing around it with the other. I have an eerie sensation as we inch along out there. From my aerial viewpoint the monster surrounding me changes form. There is no distinguishing feature that separates sea and sky. The ocean tumults upward in a swirling mist that joins in midair with the cascading rain. Seventy feet below me I see the whole of the *Sofia* clearly, as if I'm disembodied from her. She's caught in the whirlpool, spinning out of control. I hang there, watching, as she suddenly shudders awake at the brink of each breach into the black hole and regains her valiant stand. My ship is defying this freakish assault of nature, daring it to defeat her.

Mother Boats is never farther from me than arm's reach, and he never stops talking (even though I cannot recall a complete sentence—not one cohesive thought, I swear to God!). His voice is the only constant other than the storm, the ship, and my terror. He jabbers on, his tone light and whimsical, peppered with high-pitched tittering and saucy expletives. I swear we've been aloft for hours. When we finally do regain the deck, my knees buckle under me. My muscles are Jell-O. Mama grabs me and guffaws mightily. I think he is proud of me. I think I am going to throw up. But I manage to grin back at him. Then I allow myself to fully embrace the resolve that has been born in me while struggling aloft, high in the storm-torn upper reaches of my venerable ship, the *Sofia*. "Next of kin, my ass!" I hiss out loud. We are going to make it.

The next several days have no form to them, no routines to mark their passing. It is one cataclysm after another until they are the routine. Karen becomes totally wasted by seasickness. She has to take to her bunk early in the storm and remains there, moaning in a semiconscious state, for the duration. At one point the ship pitches so violently that she is ejected from her berth in the forward cabin and flung face first into the infamous foremast. Her nose is bashed and bloody, and her eyes blacken immediately. She looks a horror. I am quite concerned about her and check on her regularly. While leaning over her, peering into her swollen puffy face and shaking my head in disgust, I mutter under my breath, "Jesus, Karen, you are really a mess." She startles me by having a spontaneously lucid moment and responding, "Pam, I don't care. I really don't. I'm just so sick, I want to die." Karen is not prone to hyperbole. She isn't that sophisticated. She means it, and I know it.

Although a tad eccentric, with some pretty extreme philosophical viewpoints that she'll readily expound on, Karen is one of the most genuinely honest people that I have ever met. Her open and unguarded sincerity is almost childlike. Without knowing me well enough to take the risk, she once revealed to me an aspect of her self-image that seemed as fragile as an adolescent's. "You know, Pam, there are days when I wake up in the morning and look at myself in the mirror and think to myself, 'I am really pretty. My hair is pretty and I have a very nice smile.' But on other days I look in that same mirror and think, 'I have crooked teeth and glasses, and I am such a homely woman.' I'll feel either happy or sad each day, depending on how I look to myself in that silly mirror." It is an absolute truth, one most of us are subject to but few will acknowledge.

The *Sofia* is now running under bare poles. We need venture on deck only for emergencies, whether of a personal or nautical nature. Lifelines have been strung fore and aft, port to starboard, for such times. The ship's motion is so haphazard, the seas so unpredictable, that someone who is not hanging on will be whisked overboard in an instant. We also string lifelines below to make transiting the main saloon less hazardous, but these ropes soon become useless as handholds, because they have quickly been transformed into laundry lines instead. Sopping-wet clothing, bedding, and foul weather gear are draped in sodden mounds over every available inch.

The *Sofia* is leaking. Her decks, portholes, hatches, and bulkheads either ooze, drip, or pour water outright, nonstop. Her hull, "working" as it is designed to—plank grinding against plank, oakum shrinking and swelling, pitch expanding and contracting—is working overtime. She reminds me of a great loaf of sponge that is being saturated, squeezed, and released, over and over again. Many of the *Sofia's* seams have opened up, and seawater is spilling in from above decks and gushing through from below her waterline. A thick scum of water constantly sloshes above the bilge boards (the removable planks on the cabin sole, or floor, that allow access to the bilges).

Davey is never far from our engine's side. He needs to keep it going so that Evan and Tom at the helm can maintain some semblance of steerageway. Without it, a rogue wave could catch the *Sofia* on her beam-end (broadside) and lift her like a piece of driftwood, lay her over, and leave her capsized. The auxiliary bilge pump runs off the generator, and it is running incessantly. We might be able to control the amount of water that the *Sofia* is taking on by using her manual pumps, but that would require our being on deck around the clock. That is far too dangerous now. Without the electric pump we are literally sunk. At least once a day, though, the ship drops into a particularly steep roll, causing the pump to lose its prime and stall out. Whenever this occurs, the whole of *Sofia's* crew freezes, instantly attuned, alert, alarmed. Davey suddenly materializes and within seconds has the pump primed and beating rhythmically again. Our demise is right here, courting us each time, and each time Davey flatly rejects it, denying it its due.

I have taken to sleeping—a dreary blend of startled wakefulness and feverish nightmares—in the antique converted dentist's chair that is mounted at the head of the saloon table. It's bolted down, stationary, has high padded arms, a padded seat and headrest, and an adjustable footrest. It affords me as much comfort and security as I'll find anywhere on the ship. I squeeze in, wearing all my clothes—I haven't changed in days, not even out of my foul weather gear—and am relatively well buffeted against the vessel's erratic seizures.

Scrunching there sometime in the middle of the onslaught, I look down and casually observe a large clump of what appears to be wet grass floating lazily past me and on through the saloon, meandering toward the forward cabin. Davey emerges from the engine room, ever-present cigar butt protruding from his woolly face, and announces, "Yep, mates, the old girl has opened up a seam so wide somewhere that hunks of Sargasso seaweed are passing clear through." We are traversing waters that are fed by the Sargasso Sea, so I suppose I shouldn't be surprised. And, truth be told, I'm not. Everyone who is anyone on board the *Sofia* seems to be taking it all in stride. The veteran sailors stay on top of every imminent disaster. They exercise great caution, exhibit awesome feats of seamanship as though they are business as usual, and never give in to panic. We new recruits follow their lead. We don't know any better. (Is this sailing?) Boats, Tom, Norm, Evan, and Davey are the mainstays. They carry on. The rest of us are carried along.

Mother Boats, never one to miss a meal under any circumstances, keeps our big diesel oven running full bore to warm the cabin and provide a steaming kettle and a pot of something sustaining. While he's nonchalantly frying up a little snack, the ship suddenly does a particularly acrobatic leap. Hot oil flies from the pan and splatters everywhere in the immediate periphery—on the companionway ladder, the mast, the bulkheads, the cabin sole. Startled awake, Anders comes hurtling naked out of the bleakness of the forward cabin and at a full clip hits the thin layer of oil slick that's coating the seawater on the floorboards. Balancing on a single bare foot in an arabesque, he slides gracefully across the saloon. I scrunch in my dentist's chair, watching attentively as he grapples with the mast—also slippery with oil—executes a perfect 180-degree loop, and smacks solidly into the heavy frames of the stairs leading up to the deck. Anders crumbles to the sole like a glob of wet tissue. Leaning over the arm of my seat, I look down at his pathetic heap just in time to see him retch volumes into his lap. With a huge sigh he very carefully stands up, smiles blearily, shrugs apologetically, and proceeds to mop up the floor with some of the drenched bedding hanging on the line. I think I chuckle a little. I think I muse to myself, "Wow, how strange and unreal this all is." I think I notice that he is using my sheets.

At one point the constant tension peaks at a slightly greater elevation than usual. At the time I'm squatting on deck with my arms tightly wrapped around the stanchion of a fife rail (the waist-high rail encircling a mast on large sailing vessels)—peeing. I have long since given up my usual practice of hoisting my bum over the taffrail. The taffrail is the rail around the stern of a ship. On the *Sofia* it is a length of raised, varnished planking that is thirteen feet long and three feet deep, abaft (aft of, or behind) the helm and extending high out over the rudder. This usually serves quite nicely as our crew's restroom. With the ship's frenetic motion, however, I simply have not been able to relax my urethra sufficiently to pee without risking getting bucked off the stern in the process. I try to isolate and relax one single muscle in my body while every other one is tensed to the max. It ain't happening. Besides, I envision a rather grander epitaph for myself than "She was last seen sitting hunched, waaaaay back aft. Her trousers were down around her knees. On her face she wore an odd mixture of concentration, consternation, and constipation. And then, WHOOSH, she was just—gone." Lately, I've taken to clawing my way forward along the lifelines, finding a deserted spot in the lee of a bulwark, bracing myself against the pitch and the roll, dropping my drawers, and finding myself blessedly able to pee. The ocean offers a ready bidet. A cleansing wave crashes over the bow every few minutes, washing away all evidence of my indiscretion.

So it is while I'm up on the foredeck, hunkered down fairly comfortably, emptying my spasming bladder, that I feel the *Sofia* shudder. The deck visibly scoots out from under me, and the whole body of the ship bellows with a deep low groan, as if she's splitting apart. Everything is suddenly altered; the rigging sags, the masts grind painfully in their steps, the *Sofia* feels . . . loose. Bundled crew are urgently making their way forward along the lifelines. I yank up my pants and join in the rush to the bow. Tom is the first to get there. He leans way over the rail and then shouts out into the raging storm, "Bloody hell! The bobstay has come away." The *Sofia's* bobstay is a massively bulky length of chain that leads from the tip of the bowsprit and attaches to the stem of the ship at the cutwater by way of a two-inch-thick through-bolt and shackle. This shackle has, amazingly enough, chafed clean through. A bowsprit is the spar that projects outward from the forwardmost point on a vessel. Its purpose is to provide support for and to counteract the tremendous effort of the wind upon the ship's lines, stays, and masts. The stem is the forwardmost upright timber in the vessel's framework to which all her hull planks are fixed. As the bobstay snaps, the *Sofia* loses her ability to remain erect. In an instant her muscles are rendered flaccid, causing her appendages to waggle limply at the pummeling gale.

Captain Tom turns toward his horror-struck gaggle of sailors and, pointing an authoritative finger high in the air, proclaims "I'm goin' in!" Boats runs to fetch a boatswain's chair, while Evan attaches a line to the samson post, the sturdy block of lumber used to secure the heavy tackle necessary for raising and lowering our gigantic anchors. Today it will facilitate the raising and lowering of our skipper. Armed with a monkey wrench the size of an axle iron and a shackle as wide as his fist, Tom squirms onto the wooden slat that serves as our boatswain's chair, weaves one arm through the support ropes, and with the other arm motions to be lowered away.

The *Sofia* is just barely outside the reach of Kendra's deadly grip. She is full on in the gale, and the winds are blowing like stink. The seas are crashing, the hull is gyrating, the rigging is screaming. The crew in desperation is hanging on. So, we pray, is the captain. With each successive wave the *Sofia's* bow rises on the crest and then hangs there, suspended on a breath, until the weight of her body catches up with her, driving her nose first into the deep trough between the swells. Her entire forward section is consumed by the oncoming wave until it peaks and shoots her like a missile into open air again.

Over and over, as each wave drums the ship, Tom rides the bow. When the *Sofia* dips, he's gone, sometimes for whole minutes at a time. When she rises, he emerges, arms and hands working furiously, shaggy head shaking off the sea like a wet dog. Each time he goes under, we half-expect to see the chair reappear without him. I can't fathom how he hangs on but he does. Once he has the bobstay reattached, he gives us the thumbs up, and we hoist him back on board. He wedges himself out of the chair and stretches tall. Facing his adoring crew, he sets his legs, tenses his arms, throws back his head, and yowls like a banshee. I don't quite know what to make of these tall-ship sailors. Ships of wood, men of steel? Well, I'll swear to it this day.

At another point—and I'm not sure if it's days or hours later—the seven-hundred-pound fisherman anchor, which is catted to the *Sofia*'s outboard starboard bow, breaks free. It is mercilessly ramming its iron flukes into the *Sofia*'s hull. We have to duplicate much the same operation as with the bobstay, but it doesn't seem quite so enormous a task this time. Catastrophic occurrences are becoming rather commonplace out here in the Atlantic as we run from this hurricane. We deal with each as it presents itself and then stand fast, anticipating the next one with ever-growing confidence. If it is possible to feel omnipotent in the face of disaster, we do. The sea and the storm are clearly in charge. This is indisputable. But our ship is holding her own against all odds, and so are we. Cold, wet, exhausted, scared, puking on our boots, no end to the misery in sight. And still we persevere. Why? Because we have no real choice? Because this *is* sailing? And because, finally, we can? Yes, I believe so. And yet I acknowledge that to your run-of-the-mill sedentary landlubber, this doesn't explain a damn thing.

When we eventually limp into Bermuda, ten grueling days out of Boston, we are hundreds of miles from our intended destination. Before we left the States, we had debated hotly and often where our first landfall should be. A small camp was vocally in favor of making for the Azores— clean across the Atlantic. The vote swung instead for the warm, tropical climes. We now reckon that at one point during our recent mad chase around the ocean, we were actually almost half the bloody distance to the Azores, and those who pushed for Martinique are sure to hear about it.

We have had the crap beaten out of us by Kendra and her team of peripheral assailants, but we have all survived. The ship is a sorry wreck, as are we. Although there's a stack of repairs to attend to before we can contemplate getting underway again, the crew sorely needs a spot of R&R. We enter Bermuda at Hamilton Harbor and are instructed to raft-up (tie beam-to-beam), as sick irony would have it, next to the *Sofia*'s sister ship, the *Lindö*, which just happens to be here at the same time. Sister ships are vessels of similar dimension and specification, often built at about the same time and in the same shipyard. The *Lindö* is owned and run by a wealthy European charter company, and she is kept shipshape in Bristol fashion, neat, tidy, shiny—perfect. The *Sofia* looks like the poor relative. Our crew's appearance only reinforces this image, as if we don't feel bad enough already. The folks of the *Lindö* are nonetheless exaggeratedly kind to us and hardly a bit condescending. We have just been through a hurricane and all.

We Sofians exchange the requisite niceties and then anxiously make for shore in search of phones, food, drinks, laundries, warm beaches, safe havens, anything that even remotely smacks of civilization and/or—dare we hope?—paradise. Well, we don't get far. Bermuda is a very uptight little place. It is snobby and proper, pretending to be a class act. Anders goes ashore in the only clean, dry clothes he has left—a Speedo and a tank top. He is briskly escorted back to the ship by the local gendarmes, who point smugly at their pleated and pressed khakis and inform us with icy indifference that the island has a strict dress code. We have just nearly been lost at sea and still we are not going to be allowed ashore without first donning Bermuda shorts? Right-o, then!

It takes most of us the remainder of that first day to piece together appropriate attire. When we each finally do venture out, off and away from the *Sofia*, a strange thing happens. The solidarity born of the storm begins to dissipate. We have just been engaged in a single, desperate, all-consuming struggle to save our ship, to save our lives. We have been literally inseparable, completely interdependent, a monistic universe unto ourselves. Once this critical element is eliminated, we fall apart. Some allow themselves to confront their anger. "What the hell was that? Nobody told me we would be battling fucking hurricanes! I did not sign up for this, I can tell you!" Others, by dint of their experience, feel that the ship should be the priority, requiring everyone's immediate energy and attention. "Don't you realize what could have happened out there? The *Sofia* saved our lives. There's never more than her thin sheath of hull separating us from the ocean floor. We must attend to her!" And still others (I am solidly in this third group) just need a breather, a chance to be away, alone, warm, dry, comfortable, safe. I need to both process and reevaluate. "Yeah, yeah, right. Sure. OK! Just give me a minute. Jesus," adding barely under my breath, "We *definitely* should have gone to the Azores."

Each person who makes a choice and takes a stand, then has to deal with the subsequent wrath of the others. Bad vibes abound. As if the physical conditions on the *Sofia* aren't dreadful enough, the social tension makes the atmosphere unbearable. In the dark alley of the storm, a single throbbing heartbeat distinguished one vital pulse. Suddenly relieved of the need to fight or concede, sink or swim, live or die, we no longer know what we are meant to feel or where we are destined to go. We balk at following even the most basic shipboard routines of galley days and anchor watches. It's too soon. The risk of committing is too great. Does acquiescence define us, label us, assign us to a particular faction? Are we in, or are we out? Few seem ready or able to make this promise.

For the remainder of our stay in Bermuda, the crew muddles along. While readying the ship in Boston, we had tolerated a formidable period of grueling work under less-than-perfect conditions. But the prospects had still been bright then, with a warm tropical light beckoning at the end of our labors. We were going sailing on a circumnavigating tall ship, paradise bound. The recent storm's hard knocks, which we had expected at some point in our journey, had come much too early and had packed far too great a wallop. Had any of us been in need of a wake-up call, Kendra delivered it. Now, with forced enlightenment, each of us has to decide all over again whether to stick with the adventure.

I take some time to reconsider. Boston was hard, my maiden voyage abominable, but I have endured. Were I to believe for a single moment, though, that the past few months are the rule rather than the exception, I'd be hoppin' the next stage out of Dodge. I keep reminding myself that I have seen the pictures, heard the stories, read countless books. There is an exotic world out there comprised of brilliant wonders and fascinating cultures, promising endless horizons and illuminating adventures, seducing me with wholly unique challenges, and daring me to accomplish awesome personal leaps of faith. The *Sofia* is my ticket. I have no doubt that I can suffer the intermittent hardships and transient disappointments now so obviously inherent in the voyage. But more important, something else is occurring that I wasn't prepared for. The *Sofia* is sinking her hooks into me. The ship herself—not a relationship on board, a history to retreat from, or the allure of a distant never-never land—is binding me to the venture. My burgeoning allegiance is to the schooner *Sofia*. Whether she personifies something buried deep in my own murky psyche is not a notion I'm equipped to examine at the moment. What I can say with absolute certainty, however, is that the *Sofia* is special and that the opportunities for me on board are exemplary and unparalleled. She not only epitomizes the road less taken but the road upon which a screeching halt and abrupt U-turn are often made. I consider that great privilege may then be awarded to those who do manage to persevere. Yes, I will play out this hand. I still have far too many places to travel, so much more to see and experience, volumes to learn. Besides, it can only get better, right?

A view from aloft on *Sofia*.

chapter 3

Too Much Rum,
Too Many Steel Drums

Too Long a Stay in the Windward Islands

He who would learn to fly one day must first learn to stand and walk and
run and climb and dance; one cannot fly into flying.

—FRIEDRICH NIETZCHE

INTRODUCTION

We had already spent nine long months in the Caribbean, and that period
certainly was not what I'd anticipated or could have imagined—light years
from it, actually. My initial stirrings of doubt and discomfort in Boston
proved to be much more prophetic than I'd realized at the time. I was woefully incomplete in my new identity. At each new intersection I could have
taken the road back. Dozens of prospective crew members already had. In
my private resolve, however, I understood that I was paying the requisite
dues to earn a place on the ship, in the world, for myself. These were all
now somehow interconnected. In fact, I was moving forward down the
right road. The sailing adventure rang true for me even when it was
absurdly hard. Sure, the *Sofia* was a work in progress. But so was I. Experiences, good and bad, ebbed and flowed like the tides. And we remained
afloat, my ship and I. Somehow that was enough to keep us both trudging forward.

∿

Just signed off from a phone patch to home and family. Here we lie at anchor in the Lesser Antilles, a Windward Island group in the Caribbean, and I'm lounging about the aft cabin speaking to folks in Michigan! With the exception of learning to master the unfamiliar two-way radio choreography—button up, button down, talk, listen, "Roger, roger," and so on—it's just like phoning from next door. Of course, there is a vague concern for the lack of privacy, as an anonymous assortment of helpful ham operators scattered around the world can be privy to every intimate detail of any crew member's on-board transmission. But of a more immediate concern, so can Mother Boats. He fancies his role as radioman extraordinaire, facilitating each communication while monitoring every item of personal business and reveling in his unique access to "all the dirt," as he calls it.

This is yet another aspect of Boats's character that exasperates his crewmates. He is an admitted gossipmonger and information whore, groveling for any insight into our private lives. For what it's worth, however, he does reciprocate. If you stay within earshot of him for more than a few moments at a stretch, you're force-fed juicy tidbits from his own autobiography. I particularly enjoy standing night watches with Boats. The hours fly by, dissolving into "raves"—long, nonstop monologues that are maniacally disjointed, hilariously insane, poignantly pathetic, foaming at the mouth with self-indulgence, and unbridled in their prurient nature. On one 3 to 6 A.M. watch down from Bermuda, I learned that Boats hails from an affluent, high-profile family. His affinity for sailing sprouted as a young boy, when his parents enlisted him in the Sea Scouts, and developed as he grew, launching him into a stint in the U.S. Navy's submarine program. With Mother Boats the tales become so outrageous that I wonder what is fact and what is fiction, but they are nothing if not entertaining. What he told me that night was that while he was stationed aboard a sub, either he figured out that he was gay or the sub's commander did. Suffice it to say, Mother Boats and the navy soon parted ways. Chortling like an idiot as he told this story, Boats went on to describe how his parents fought to hold the Department of the Navy responsible for turning their son into a homosexual. Despite Mother Boats's self-deprecating humor, he does harbor a deep affection for his family and a sincere desire not to hurt or embarrass them.

Although flamboyantly uncloseted by the time I met him in Boston, Boats doesn't at first glance appear effeminate. When he tries to—and he does—it's quite comical. This is largely because he's a beefy, burly guy, sporting a rugged handsomeness that he successfully masks beneath a shroud of slovenly unkemptness that he has perfected to the level of fine art. Though his well-honed eccentric affect puts many crew members off at first, they soon overlook it. Sofians are an assemblage of peculiar characters, all with some streak of the maverick. So we cut each other slack and fall back on our common threads, the most obvious being the *Sofia*. We are all . . . here.

Mother Boats has been on board for years. His ties to the tall ship are venerable and strong. At present he is instructing me in the time-honored craft of marlinspike seamanship. As the *Sofia*'s boatswain, his knowledge is extensive. He can do it all, from tying the full repertoire of sailors' knots in his sleep or half-drunk to swinging happily from a boatswain's chair a hundred feet above the deck, liberally applying a lifesaving coating of pine-tar slush to our steel rigging for hours or even days at a time. Mother Boats also is a capable teacher: patient, encouraging, and not a smidgen sexist or condescending. I like him, and I trust him. And although I think he considers me a compatriot, we have a wary friendship. His most unguarded encounters come while he's manning the radio controls. Here he is faceless, not subjected to rolled eyes, tsk-tsks, and self-righteous rejections. It's evident that his quirky but genuine affection for the other crew members is deeply rooted in the fact that we help enable a seagoing lifestyle that works for him. The *Sofia* is the rare niche where Boats is comfortable, successful, and almost happy. He acknowledges that he is a societal misfit, but he bundles his crewmates into his exclusive clique. He reckons that the *Sofia* is one beamy bucket filled with an assortment of elite square pegs, floating about in a decidedly round world. He may well be right.

I've stitched up my own ditty bag, which now contains a boatswain's knife, stone, palm, fid, twine, leather, grease, wax, needles, and tape. This is the gear of a true marlinspike sailor and I must look the part. Motoring into the harbor at Martinique, my new image was put to the test. We were chugging along at 5 knots on our approach to the anchorage, when our view of the entrance became eclipsed by a veritable wall of polished chrome and bright white steel. A hundred meters broad off our starboard bow, a huge cruise ship was altering course. Giving way, she was allowing us to approach on her port beam. Someone on board recognized her as the *Queen Elizabeth II*, on one of her regularly scheduled tours of these islands. We were so absorbed with the meticulous threading of the *Sofia's* sloppy steerageway between the channel markers and the substantial incoming and outgoing traffic that we were abreast of the *QE II* before we noticed that she was listing to port, over in our direction. Her nearly full complement of passengers, gathered gaily on deck for their arrival in port, was crowding the aft quarter rail in an attempt to get a good look—at us. And not just our schooner but *Sofia's* helmsman herself was attracting a fair bit of attention. I was so focused—gripping the helm, holding my course, and keeping my eye on the narrow entrance to the harbor—that we were abeam of the luxury liner before I realized that I was the object of many salutations arising from the crowd. I apparently was quite a sight, with a wild halo of sun-bleached blond curls crowning my bronzed cheeks and peeling nose, a pareu draped and belted at the waist with a large, sheathed boatswain's knife. Once we were into the bay and the hook was set, our captain came aft and ruffled my hair. "Guess you've arrived!" he commended me.

It is lovely here in Martinique. Maybe this will be my first real experience of tropical island paradise. Bermuda doesn't count—too cold, too stodgy, and too close to home. Today, though, we are disappointed to learn that the likelihood of hauling the boat here is nil. The cost is prohibitive. I wonder why we didn't know this beforehand. Couldn't we have just called up before we left the States to get an estimate? But this is how it works, I'm told. Part of the program is being able to let go of schedules, pat answers, guarantees, expectations. An obsessive-compulsive would surely go all the way nuts on board the *Sofia*. When things don't work out as planned, we're expected to shrug it off, make an alternate plan, and carry on—and on, again and again.

The whole bloody island of Martinique is expensive. We Sofians are finding that we are not equipped to be tourists here. The merchants are neither friendly nor courteous to our ragtag multinational crew of men and women. That we are thrilled to see, do, learn, and experience while visiting their island matters not in the least. We approach like giddy schoolchildren bounding out onto the playground, ingratiating in our desire to be accepted. Most often we are ignored. Should we (could we?) flash some cash, we can expect treatment that is cordial at best but could hardly be considered kind. It's snotty here, all right, but maybe we do frighten the merchants a little. We are not from a flashy yacht. We don't wear "outfits," and we present as slap-dash packs rather than manageable couples or families. But we are harmless (I think). Anyway, we're only a day sail or two from many of the smaller, less pretentious islands in the group, and soon we'll take the opportunity to visit most of them. Dominique, Bequia, St. Vincent, all parts and ports unknown. Still looking for paradise. Roger, that.

But back to the passage down from Bermuda. What a relief—so pleasant, so comfortable, so not life-threatening. What about ships of wood, men (and women) of steel? Personally, I could do without any more hurricanes for awhile. Just some gentle communing with the sea, the ship, and my shipmates under less-than-dire circumstances will suit me. The sail down to Martinique fit the bill. A handful of rain-spit days, then fine weather. Sailing clear out of the fetch of the storm into the blessing of fair winds and following seas, we were entertained most of the way by an ocean transformed into a wonderland of bioluminescence. Buckets hauled topside to wet down decks explode in flashes of color. Streams tossed onto the planks take on a rippled texture, thick and sticky-looking with brilliantly variegated hues. Baths topside, no longer erotic because of the inevitable necessity of nakedness, become psychedelic light shows. Audiences gather, far more enraptured by the electric, fluid organisms' glittery descent over flesh than by the flesh itself. Suspicions of whales and dolphins in escort are borne out by the laserlike reams that illuminate the surface tension of the water as it rips over dorsal fins and breaching backs and gushes from blowholes in an eruption of iridescence.

As the colors gradually fade with the subsiding Gulf Stream, we're greeted by yet another odd manifestation of nature. Whole schools of flying fish appear out of nowhere, and we are in their way. For a few days we have to be on our guard—at the helm, pumping the bilges, napping on the coach roof, peeing off the taffrail—wherever we find ourselves on deck. Should our vessel interrupt the route of flying fish, we are bombarded by scaly, alien creatures, slamming into us at an impressive velocity. Anders, our big blond Swede, reckons to make use of this gift from the sea and scampers nimbly about the deck, deftly outmaneuvering his foe, the Varmit, to collect armfuls of fallen fish carcasses. These he delivers to the galley to be fried up whole. Anders doesn't cook them himself. He's sulking, having recently received a round of criticism for loading a fresh fruit salad with raw onion—skin and all. He assures us that Swedish mothers never intended that their sons should cook, so they didn't teach them. How convenient. The crew's self-preservation wins out, and we assign Anders to be the assistant on all his future galley days. Today someone else grabs a pan and some grease and soon a tasty snack is enjoyed by anyone with the patience and the stomach to pick around bones, scales, fins, and eyeballs. Protein is generally so scarce at sea that few mind making the effort.

Our next eventful encounter comes the day before Thanksgiving and is so special that it merits careful documentation. For me this represents one of the first in what promises to be a long succession of scavenging adventures on board the *Sofia*.

∽

JOURNAL ENTRY
Early afternoon
Thanksgiving 1978
Somewhere in the Atlantic

Well off the port bow we sight a freighter flying the French flag. Being the chat junkie that he is, Mother Boats races below to shout the French crew up on the radio. After exchanging formalities and moving on to pleasantries, Boats learns that the freighter is carrying a cargo of frozen meat. He laments that we are attempting to celebrate an important American holiday—our first Thanksgiving at sea—and, alas, we have no main dish around which to build the traditional feast. Following a short conference with his skipper, the French radio operator informs Boats that the ships crew will drop a package in the water for us. It is determined that two of *Sofia*'s crew will go fetch it. I volunteer. Anders, known on board as "the Electric Viking," offers to come along. For some obscure reason we each grab surfboards and leap over the side. Why we don't launch a shore boat is a mystery. This is a transfer of goods between two mighty vessels in the middle of the Atlantic Ocean. What are we thinking?

The freighter has to make a couple of carefully orchestrated passes in order to get near enough to keep both her off-loading cargo and Anders and me in her lee (the side protected from the wind). During one pass we glance up from our deliberate stroking and there she is, a dozen or so meters abreast of us, and closing fast. Without warning there we go, surfing, as the bow's wake combines with the wash from the freighter's hull to propel us on a four-foot cresting wave at breakneck speed straight at the ship's still-rotating propellers. I feel the blades shudder to a grinding halt just beneath me as I concentrate frantically on clinging to my board and fending off the ship's rapidly encroaching topsides. Anders has managed to shoot out one long, lanky arm and snatch the line with the crate attached to it. I am useless to him at this point, having already been whizzed well past the hull and left lying winded behind the stern. Helpless, I gurgle enthusiastic encouragement to Anders as he struggles to untie the line while balancing his body and the crate on a bobbing board in the substantial surf. "Attaboy, Undish! [the Swedish pronunciation of his name.]" "Good catch there, matey!" "Way to go, me bucko! Need any help?" Turning my attention to the ship's quarterdeck, which is about thirty feet overhead, I remember to acknowledge the crew and to show my sincere appreciation. I am surprised to find that they are the ones who are acting appreciative. The rail is a clot of French seamen exclaiming "merci beaucoup!" and blowing kisses. Kisses? I realize then that Anders and I had neglected to dress for our excursion. We are buck naked. That probably explains why they came so bloody close to us.

It's the norm for Sofians to spend most of their days at sea in warm climates, in the buff or nearly in the buff. This is far more of a practicality than a social statement, as clothes rinsed in saltwater cling to hot, sticky skin. Also, because clothes wear out more quickly at sea, they become a commodity, used sparingly so that we might be presentable at anchorages and for outings ashore. Already, looking at each other's bodies has become almost as commonplace as staring out at sea, a sea that normally is devoid of anyone who might take offense at our nakedness. This particular meeting is an unlikely occasion, and the French sailors are clearly not offended. I blow back kisses as best I can and holler up a heartfelt "Vive la France!" As I pivot around to rejoin Anders, I spot the *Sofia* off in the distance, alone on the horizon, still and silent, a "painted ship upon a painted ocean." I have never before seen my ship like this, and I am profoundly touched by her majesty. There she is, poised under a full set of sail, floating in the middle of an endless ocean—and very, very far away. Sighing, I shake off my reverie and begin the long paddle back.

The entire way, I'm jabbering excitedly at Anders, who chokes out his responses in the form of grunts, reminding me that he is holding the crate with his teeth and balancing it on the nose of his board so that his arms are free to paddle. "Undish, we don't have any clothes on. God, how rude. Do you believe how dangerous that was? I think I actually saw the propellers stop spinning. Wasn't it fun, though? Undish, doesn't *Sofia* look beautiful? But, man, I do not remember paddling this far!" At one point I try to tow him but quickly give up as I'm having my own share of problems. Before I went over the side, I'd been oiling a section of pin rail and really getting into my work. So I too am well oiled, slick from stem to stern. As a result, I am sliding all over my damn board. We are a pair, Anders and I, foundering, squealing, and batting away flying fish. And we are exhausted. It is taking soooo long.

The winds are gentle, the seas calm, the swells running five to seven feet. We can make out the *Sofia* in great detail. A full complement of sails is set, with crew adorning the rigging like tinsel on a Christmas tree; bodies are aloft at the topmasts, swaying on foot ropes out along the yards, stacked up the ratlines, clinging to the net under the bowsprit, and even balancing along the massive mizzen boom with their backs braced against the taut sail. Strange. We paddle on. Arching my neck for a momentary position and direction check, I witness the *Sofia* in the midst of a full and violent jibe, potentially one of the most dangerous operations on a fore-and-aft–rigged sailing vessel. Jibing consists of taking the wind onto the other side of the mainsails. This must be done in an extremely controlled fashion or the wind will snap the sail across with such tremendous force that lines can split apart, blocks disintegrate under the pressure, spars snap—in a really bad situation, that includes the mast—or the vessel could capsize from the thrust, the very worst case scenario. This final possibility is a long shot on the *Sofia*, because she possesses a mammoth full keel that affords her a substantial righting moment. Every ship has a moment at which she cannot recover from a roll. On smaller vessels a jibe can often flirt with this dangerous degree of heel, or lean to one side. But with her round bilge, six-foot topsides, and four-foot bulwark (the wall built around the edge of a ship's upper deck), I have never known the *Sofia* even to bury a rail (dipping her cap rail into the sea, allowing blue water to spill onto the decks). Nonetheless, a jibe aboard the *Sofia* is not meant to occur accidentally, is never attempted casually, and always is orchestrated with full crew at the ready and the utmost control. Yet as I watch incredulously from my perspective, floating atop the surface of the ocean hundreds of meters away, I both see and hear the *Sofia* jibe. The crash, slap, and crunch of sail, spar, and rigging resound across the sea like a thunderclap. Most bodies aloft have disappeared, apparently to facilitate the risky maneuver. But I watch as the brave (or foolish) few who remain in the rigging are flung about like rag dolls, clinging to gear literally with tooth and nail.

Within a few short minutes the *Sofia* is upon us and we're whisked up from the Atlantic. Breathless and clueless, we glance about at our fellow crew members' haggard faces. Only after we are safely back aboard are we let in on the whole drama. Sometime during Anders' and my frolic, the *Sofia* was blown well downwind and lost sight of us. We were obscured by the swells, in effect lost to the *Sofia*, save a relative bearing on the position where we went over the side. Boats maintained constant radio communication with the French freighter, imploring it to stick around to retrieve us if need be. I'm told that the French crew offered to take the "mademoiselle" in trade for the meat. I assume that they were joking, but I'm thankful that, for whatever reason, they didn't forsake us out there. Another element of our escapade of which we are only now made aware is equally alarming in retrospect. The freighter had dual watches posted on deck—one to keep a fix and report on our position, another on shark alert. Unbeknown to Anders and me, in the commotion and the confusion of the exchange, the crate was damaged and the spoils were spoiling. A dull and deepening red smear was befouling an ever-widening swath of ocean in our wake, just beneath the surface.

After rehashing our respective versions of the caper, we turn our attention to the treasure. We hack open the case and rip into the package, and we soon have lying on the main deck before us twenty pounds of New Zealand lamb, purported to be the best in the world. As I am the only practicing vegetarian on board, I sit to the side, rethinking the day's events as the ecstatic crew debates how best to transform the gift into a proper Thanksgiving Day feast. I am struck by how in an unconventional existence, the outrageous becomes commonplace. Adventures stockpile and are neatly managed.

Thanksgiving is the first in a series of four glorious days of silken calm on a glass-flat ocean beneath a crystal, sun-gorged sky. The holiday dinner, served on deck at midafternoon, becomes a repast that lingers long and lazy over the next few days. We celebrate, taking advantage of a hiatus from sailing the ship to instead explore her ample and diverse playground facilities. Crew members swing from lines attached to the outer ends of the yardarms and accomplish impressive aerial feats by bouncing the jib boom like a diving board. This enables the spar to propel a body twenty feet into the air before delivering it slickly into a sea whose mirrored image of the heavens is so impeccable that one has the momentary sensation of piercing a fluid sky. We drag from the ever-present man-overboard line that trails the stern, like limp bait trawling for some imaginary sea monster. Rum-fueled contests to see who can leap out from the highest ratline batten produce some impressive records as well as a few gnarly bruises. While drifting about in Lake Atlantic, or the Pond, we read, sleep, sunbathe, even do some cosmetic touch-ups on the ship. Everyone gives quiet thanks for the inverter that a helpful young cadet liberated for us from the Coast Guard base in Boston. Its sole function is to run the freezer compartment of the antiquated refrigerator scavenged from a barn in New Hampshire. Consequently, we are able to keep cranking out a steady supply of itty-bitty ice cubes for the myriad strange and wonderful alcohol-rich concoctions that we mix up during these bountiful, becalmed, balmy, besotted days.

The second night of serenity holds yet another implausible encounter. Around midnight the watch spots the running lights of a small vessel approaching from astern. Soon the thirty-six-foot ketch comes alongside and requests permission to raft up on our port beam. We toss fenders over the rail and tie the yacht off the *Sofia's* midships. Then we welcome the ketch's crew aboard. We are drifting in the middle of an ocean, several days' sail from the nearest landfall. The odds against such a chance meeting are monumental. Yet no one appears even mildly ruffled.

The *Sofia's* sleeping residents emerge from their bunks to greet the visitors. The vessel turns out to be French registered, skippered by a feisty woman in her forties. She's one hot ticket, having absconded with the boat and her two young children in the midst of a nasty divorce settlement. By her account the sweet little ketch is all she wants from the ill-fated marriage, and it is destined to go to her ex. Also on board are three fellas who signed on as crew to help the distressed damsel make her getaway. I cannot imagine where she dredged up these characters, but they don't appear to know a lick about sailing. One is wearing skin-tight fuscia bell-bottom trousers with a matching long-sleeved, collared, polyester shirt. The other two look even less nautical, if possible. Maybe they're the nannies. Between their attempts at tangled English and our marginally conversant French, we begin to put the picture into focus.

"La voile [sail], she is broke," announces the gentleman in the disco ensemble.

"Voile?" we all echo in patient oblivion.

"Oui, oui, la voile," he repeats, becoming mildly frantic.

"Merde [shit]," moans the captain, in obvious exasperation. "The jib, they have blown it out."

"Ah," we chime in unison.

"Oui, oui," she sighs.

"Non, non eau [no water]!" the crewman continues with excited gesticulations.

"Oh?" we urge, expectantly.

"Merde," the skipper shrieks, hands in the air, eyes ablaze with pent-up frustration. "Water! Eau! Seventy gallons—out the spout!"

"Oh!" we nod as a group. "Non eau. Oh, no!"

"And no food," she shrugs. "Like gluttons, they eat while we sleep. Merde!"

"Oui, oui," we shake our heads conciliatorily.

"Merde," we repeat. (We just like the word.)

Needless to say, they are all thirsty, hungry, and tired. Patrick goes right to work, repairing their headsail. While some of us prepare a meal and entertain the children, others restock their craft with food and water. Dawn is eager to break upon one more fantastic day when we load the wayward French onto their refurbished vessel and say au revoir, waving from the rail as the ketch slowly dissolves into the brightening horizon. A strange and dreamlike encounter, oui.

The third day of calm finds us boarded once again, this time by a flock of off-course cliff swallows. They are so fatigued by the time they find sanctuary on the deck of the *Sofia* that we are able to urge them into our hands as we stroke their feathers. Despite our efforts to sustain them, the birds die, one by one. The old Varmit, who has never had to worry where his next meal is coming from, surprises us by becoming an exuberant stalker. For days we stumble upon caches of ratty little beaks, feathers, and feet. When we do have wind during this passage, the sailing is sublime. I'm learning more each day and feeling increasingly comfortable in this element. I'm also feeling much more in command of my own condition. The painful blisters on my hands have hardened to calluses. My back, arms, and shoulders are getting stronger. These are the badges that go with the territory, and this is a territory that I am growing to love.

෴

JOURNAL ENTRY
Fort-de-France
Martinique
West Indies

Lying at anchor just behind the cruise ship mooring, I have a panoramic view of the Baie de Fort-de-France, a concourse of yachts representing a league of nations. I love this perspective. When in port the *Sofia* sets her hook well off-shore, usually as the most outlying ship in the harbor. This allows us ample room to swing on the substantial amount of scope required for us to anchor securely. Scope is the length of cable (heavy chain in our case, although smaller vessels frequently use line) connecting a ship to her anchor. The scope roughly defines the arc of a circle in which an anchored vessel can swing if pushed by wind or tide. Normally, on yachts the scope should be at least three times the water's depth. On the *Sofia*, though, because of her weight, windage, and less-than-high-tech anchor package, we adhere to a more conservative formula. In a protected harbor with a good bottom and a gentle tidal flow, we are able to pay out five meters of cable for each meter of depth. In a dicey anchorage a ratio of 7 to 1, in conjunction with our standard twenty-four-hour anchor watch, allows us even more breathing room.

Another important consideration when anchoring well out is privacy. A great deal of shipboard life on the *Sofia* takes place above deck: work, play, baths, and the like. Also, because of our formidable crew complement and the constant stream of visitors that we attract, we are often anything but quiet or low profile. We are more like a floating suburb. Consequently, our more reclusive position in port meets with the approval of the majority of boats making up any given anchorage. Plus, most yachts don't have a crew large enough to allow a full-time watch. The *Sofia* has and does. On more than one occasion we have rescued yachts dragging their anchors, either drifting out to sea or on a collision course with another yacht in the harbor. We have also served as "neighborhood watch," discouraging unwelcome visitors from trespassing aboard temporarily vacant vessels.

Being well outside the hub of traffic and activity in port has many advantages, but it also has some drawbacks. From shore it makes us less accessible, even to ourselves. We are often as much as a couple hundred yards from the nearest dinghy landing. As a result, I have perfected my whistle so that it reaches the volume of an air raid signal. When I was ten, my dad taught me to place two fingers on my tongue, pucker, and deliver a mighty blow. I can call in a shore boat from a quarter mile. I've become a proficient rower as well, often volunteering to take the *Salty Dog*, our larger shore boat, or *Jonah*, the smaller one, ashore to deliver or collect crew. I love weaving my way through the busy harbor, waving, chatting, rubbernecking, further exercising my new and improved upper body.

I've been using some of my free time to observe Patrick. As resident sailmaker, he brings with him sterling qualifications. A true professional trained by the best both stateside and abroad, what this man can fashion from cloth, twine, needles, shears, yardstick, and chalk is remarkable. If the *Sofia*'s hull represents her metaphorical body, then her sails become her wings, and our mighty ship flies high, thanks to Patrick's capable hands. Today he and I spent the morning rowing around our floating community soliciting work: sails to be sewn or mended, sail covers made, sun tarps fashioned, and so on. We hustled up a few days' work and began to make a name for ourselves as well. Word travels fast between islands—few of which support a local sailmaker. I'm learning that "yachties" often haven't the know-how, materials, time, or inclination to repair their own vessels. On a cruising boat something always needs attention, and in harbor we Sofians are a pretty handy lot—well equipped, knowledgeable, ready to work, and happy to help out. At present our ship sports a sailmaker, electrician, diesel mechanic, fine carpenter, marine electronics specialist, boatswain (and his eager apprentice), a few sailors with a circumnavigation under their belt, and a whole slew of able bodies. In her engine room the *Sofia* has a huge workshop, complete with tools, paints, generators, welding apparatus, a full sail and boatswain's locker, and a lazarette (originally a place for the confinement of lepers, now a storeroom for supplies in the stern of a vessel) that is spilling over with spare and miscellaneous parts.

There is a tacit understanding that whatever a member of the crew earns while sailing on the *Sofia* is split down the middle—half goes into the pocket of the laborer and half to the ship's kitty. This delineation can be hazy, though, because the *Sofia* relies heavily on barter. We are as often paid in goods and services as we are in cash. It's a very hospitable way to do business. But no matter how little I make for myself, I come out ahead in the bargain. I'm exercising new skills, my ship is benefiting, and my private stash of such basic necessities as toothpaste, postage stamps, and cold beer is ample. I view it all as an investment in my future.

The interaction among our crew continues to be dynamic and interesting. It also appears to be the primary factor that will make or break the experience for many on board. Whenever I see egos collide, I'm thankful that I found the *Sofia* at this juncture in my life because my sense of self is strong. I wear my experience like armor, my years like insulation. I know better than to indulge in petty game-playing. Yet I see crew members, in the throes of self-doubt, erupt with such naked emotion that they're often left with no choice afterward but to abandon the journey. It is so very fragile out here. I can't afford to take my eyes off my goals. I focus hard on my direction, holding fast and fiercely protecting myself. For me now there is no copilot, no one else to whom I can assign blame or credit. It's a little scary out here all alone, teetering on the growing edge of myself.

But I find strength in knowing that *I* will make this adventure whatever it turns out to be in my life. There are the occasional wrinkles, sure, but they're wrinkles in rainbows. I mean, really, look at where I am!

Lately, I'm learning something about celestial navigation, the *Sofia's* only means of determining her position when out of sight of land. Coastal navigation, however, is a skill that I was required to cultivate straightaway. Beginning with my first watch at sea, I was responsible for marking our progress on the chart and noting our position in the ship's log—a procedure strictly followed on the hour, after each sailor's stand at the helm. Coastal navigation is concerned with keeping track of one's position while in sight of land by taking and calculating true, relative, and compass bearings. In simplistic terms it is strategic geometry, much like that used to aim a particular ball at a particular pocket in a game of pool, except that degrees of latitude and longitude on a chart replace eyeballing a point on the bumpers of a table. The watch captain and skipper oversee the calculations of novices on board, but they both assume and expect that each crew member will perform this duty with accuracy. It's interesting how I've risen to this occasion. Instead of breaking out in a cold sweat with a wall of incognizance rising before me, as I did throughout all my years of formal education whenever I faced any mathematical task, here I just do it.

Celestial navigation is the art of directing a vessel across unmarked open seas and ascertaining a position by observing the sun, moon, and stars. One calculates the angle of these heavenly bodies in relation to the horizon, the ship, and the time of the sighting by using an age-old sailor's tool, a sextant. The modern sextant is the most recent in a very long line of similar instruments. Their names reflect the size of the arc that they can measure: the quadrant, a fourth of a circle; the octant, an eighth; the quintant, a fifth, and the sextant, a sixth. Celestial navigation is a complicated exercise that follows an elaborate formula. I am thankful that many on board are able and willing to instruct and that we have a library full of texts on the subject. This is not a skill required of the crew at large. On the *Sofia* the skipper is responsible for taking the sights and plotting the ship's course. But anyone can learn. Avid students of this ancient art can practice with the several plastic sextants aboard. I'm practicing. The 3 to 6 A.M. watch is my favorite. Here I have it all: the quiet, the planetarium-like night sea sky, and the new breaking dawn. I'm told that celestial navigation uses about sixty stars and four planets for sighting, and most are visible at this time of year. Two days out of Martinique, just a blink before sunrise, I spotted the Southern Cross creeping over the horizon. This was a first for me, as I have lived my entire life beneath only the Northern Hemisphere's half of the constellations. I raced below, recorded the sighting in the log, initialed it to memorialize the event, and then made the rounds, waking the others who had, like me, awaited this most poetic of initiations to the southern latitudes.

Sometimes I awake in my bunk and go up on deck, just to reassure myself that I am where I am. The surreal enormity of the sea's night canopy never disappoints me. It is so busy, so animate. Sightings of shooting stars, satellites, brightly illuminated space debris, and unidentified, strangely lit objects are commonplace. Anyone who has ever spent any time at sea would have to at least entertain the possibility of extraterrestrial life.

I've been hearing a lot of jabber about something called the "green flash." I haven't seen it yet, so I'm not certain it isn't just some prank perpetrated on unsuspecting rookies by old salts (like the "sky hook" I searched for all one summer, as a young camp counselor-in-training). This flash is said to occur when the sun sets on the sea. It's a peculiar phenomenon, seen by only the most observant mariner. On a clear, calm evening as the sun descends, mere seconds after it dips its upper arc beneath the horizon, a tiny, brilliant, blue-green flare in the shape of a candle flame will flicker for just an instant, then die with the final remnants of the sun's halo. But you'll see it only if you have the self-discipline to gaze obliquely at the sunset. Should you look straight on, too soon, or too long, you'll miss its elusive brilliance. Still, there are trustworthy souls aboard who swear to the existence of the green flash. So I'll keep trying. At worst, I'm witnessing one magnificent sunset after another.

∽

JOURNAL ENTRY
Still in Martinique . . .
West Indies

This morning I'm writing from a small cafe on the picturesque waterfront of the bustling little town of Fort-de-France. The petite cups of thick, pitch-black French roast espresso, or demitasse, are so strong that I'm having trouble controlling the shaking of my pen. Joseph, a local cab driver, is sitting next to me with his head in his hands, bemoaning the day's developments. All the local banana trucks have gone on strike, and their belligerent drivers have dumped their large cargoes of heavily laden stalks in the middle of the narrow city streets. Traffic is blocked in every direction by the knee-deep barricade of fruit, which is fermenting in the tropical heat. Another cruise ship came into the harbor last night, and its excited visitors are all being methodically ferried in as Joseph and I watch from behind our steaming coffees. Poor Joseph is stymied. He can't get his cab to the landing, and he's certain the wealthy tourists have no way of getting to him. I try to commiserate with him, but actually I'm amused at how this stalemate affects me. I'm sitting here, dressed to the nines (or, more accurately, to the fours, as that's the limit of my formal *Sofia* wardrobe), and sweating like a pig. Last night we Sofians befriended one of the cruise ship's water taxi drivers in a local pub. We schemed to have him deliver our motley crew back out to the cruise ship today on the final leg of his circuit. As nearly all the passengers would be ashore, we reckoned that this would be the perfect opportunity for us to explore the liner's many luxurious compartments. Sofians have pulled this off in the past, I'm told, but it looks like I won't be finding out how, at least not today. I think I'll stick around and see how Joseph makes out, though. He is a friend. We met him a few days ago when a group of us were returning from a trek into the countryside. Each cab driver on the island owns his own vehicle and can do with it whatever he pleases. On this day it pleased Joseph, and the three local farmers he had along, to pick us all up, pile us into the car, and bump us along on a makeshift scenic tour of the island. We were treated to cucumbers, breadfruit, and a raucous concert of local music en route, before being deposited neatly at the dinghy landing several cheery hours later. The fare: two francs (50 cents) apiece.

ᥬ

JOURNAL ENTRY
The afternoon of the morning at the cafe . . .
Martinique
West Indies

Now I'm resting in the park across from the post office, waiting for the rain to stop. I had to forsake Joseph and the main thoroughfare around midday when the sun, the odor of rotting bananas, and the accompanying swarm of mosquitoes became too much to bear. As I gingerly weaved my way among the bruised banana stalks, which were settling into a rancid sludge, I noticed a line-dance of grinning tourists maneuvering toward me in much the same fashion. Nothing was going to deter the cruise ship passengers from enjoying their Martinique experience. This was one of those "island-a-day" trips—you snooze, you could lose an entire culture.

From my bench seat in the park I can engage in some serious people watching. The locals are very striking, a lovely mix of French, Indian, and Creole. Even the men are beautiful, with their milk chocolate skin and large sparkling eyes. In terms of friendliness the local men are the exception here, being overtly familiar and often crass in their suggestiveness. I'm starting to wonder whether wearing this flower in my hair is a symbol of open invitation.

Last night we received a radio transmission from the States: San Francisco's mayor, George Moscone, was shot to death. Some of our crew members took this news hard. One in particular had come to the *Sofia* fresh from Gov. Jerry Brown's staff. She knew Moscone personally. At the cafe this morning I leafed through a discarded issue of *Time*. The pages were plastered with photographs of a yard cluttered with dead bodies, the result of a horrendous mass cult suicide in Guyana. Placed among the bodies—it almost seemed protectively—were the small crumpled forms of children. I hear the squeal of a child's laughter as he splashes through the puddles in the park. Dozens of hummingbirds flit about the tropical flowers in the garden where I sit writing. The heavy puffs of trade-wind clouds overhead squeeze out their last spritz of rain as the sun's rays refract in an eye-squinting dance upon the bay. This too is real. "I am happy," I say to myself. "And it's OK."

∾

JOURNAL ENTRY
Bequia, St. Vincent
West Indies

It's early morning as I sit up on deck feeling the wind and the approaching dawn. My arm, hand, and ribs are losing the ache and relaxing from the rigidity of the night. I can finally take a deep breath without pain and write without grimacing. This injury, the result of stumbling into a three-foot-deep cement ditch on New Year's Eve, is the only real physical damage I've suffered since going to sea. I guess I could dream up a better story, like I fell out of the rigging in a storm or was wrestling a shark or beating off pirates. But, no, an inebriated somersault into a drainage pipe will have to do. In fact, accidents involving injury while sailing aboard the *Sofia* are rare. Whenever ship handling is the order of business, people pay attention. The *Sofia* is intimidating. Images of catastrophes are easy to envision and not invited. It's when we let our guard (or our hair) down that we slip up: a party on board, recreational play in the rigging, a disaster in our marginal and highly combustible galley, a celebration ashore. After my slip the local doc taped, slung, and medicated me. I returned to the ship and promptly untaped, unslung, and unmedicated myself. With one functional arm, no lungs, and sloppy on muscle relaxants, I was a mishap waiting to happen. I'm managing fine now, but it's clear that daily life on board requires all one's limbs and most of one's faculties.

Patrick is also up early. I can hear him down below, stitching out a jib to rig on *Jonah*, our smaller launch, so that he and Evan can enter the regular Sunday dinghy race held here on the island. It begins in just a few hours. Some yachts are game enough to enter their sail-rigged tenders, but the race is run almost entirely by locals in their sweet, hand-made double-enders (hulls that are pointy at bow and stern). The Bequians, I've discovered, are renowned masters of fine wooden boat building. A miniature shipyard here, right on the beach, directs all its energies toward assembling one privately commissioned boat at a time, start to finish. Rumor has it that the half-completed forty-five-footer now occupying the slipway is being custom built for Bob Dylan. Probably true. We already share most harbors with the lovely *Raglan*, another classic wooden schooner, owned by Neil Young. I need only to do a studied sweep of the island's beachfronts to realize that I am in the company of master craftsmen. Graceful dories litter the shore amid a clutter of jeweled sea shells and fallen palm fronds, all tossed like so many discarded gifts from nature. Art, elegant and harmonious, casually scattered across the sand. Needless to say, the locals always win the races, but they appreciate any attempt by visitors to compete, and the locals play with unbridled enthusiasm to an audience. We'll all hike to the reef at the south end of the island to meet the boats as they sail in.

Bequia is proving to be a haven for us. It just feels like a *Sofia* kind of place. We have been well received and incorporated into the docile flow of life on the island. It's a comfortable fit. I've made friends with a local gentleman who is part of Bequia's character and history. Sydney hails from the wealthy, elite, white segment of the Bequian population, whereas the less affluent locals live more modestly. In fact, all the folks on the island complement one another, like the bass and trebles of a soft reggae rhythm. Everyone here is content. Everyone is living a supreme quality of life that isn't affected by an excess of material goods. Bequia has more than enough beach, ocean, sun, and sky for all its diverse population to enjoy. And well they do.

Sydney, still quite a dandy at seventy (or thereabouts), has written a book of poems—memoirs, more accurately—in which he describes some of his wilder, gayer times. His reflection upon his youthful escapades is insightful and touching. Although his book is for sale in the local shops, almost everyone I run into on Bequia is the proud owner of an auto-graphed copy, which the author has presented as a gift. I too have been so honored. Inside the cover of my volume Sydney's inscription reads: "To Pam. The secret anniversaries of my heart, now shared with you." This lyrical collection of vignettes and musings is a treasure that I will protect and preserve. Sydney is someone I will remember.

∿

JOURNAL ENTRY
Still Bequia, St. Vincent
West Indies

Seems we're going to be here longer than planned—an old story on the *Sofia*. We make a day sail to the neighboring island of St. Vincent, treat-ing many locals and friends to a tall ship experience. They get what they come for all right—very stiff winds that allow the *Sofia* to really kick up her heels but result in a fractured mizzen gaff. Now we have to find a replacement piece of wood large enough and suitable for shaping. As there are no spruce forests in these islands, our work is cut out for us. But by golly, it is a glorious sail.

The decks are a confusion of bodies, everyone eager to have hands on a line. We drive the *Sofia* and her passengers hard through every point of sail, out into open ocean and back again. Night has fallen by the time we find ourselves tacking back into the harbor. Coming sharp about in the congested anchorage, our substantial leeway (the distance a vessel skids sideways when attempting to sail straight ahead) is sliding us straight toward a great fancy yacht—something on the order of an Onassis toy. Foreseeing imminent disaster, we of course turn to our skipper, who responds by commanding, "Prepare to wear ship." This is a complicated operation in which the vessel is turned in such a way that the wind is brought across one side of her to the opposite side, from astern. It's a piece of work to accomplish in optimum conditions. Conditions now are any-thing but optimum, but we have to rescue the *Sofia* from her soon-to-be calamitous slide. The crew scrambles, sweating and heaving lines with a fury. The captain bellows a hearty "Helms a-lee!" from back aft as we, in the heat of our Herculean labors, feel the *Sofia* swing trimly about, scudding spitting distance from the yacht's amidships boat boom. Our overwhelmed passengers, who have tucked in all along the bulwarks, bracing for certain collision, poke out their heads and recommence breathing. The fine yacht's nattily uniformed crew has also been busy racing around the deck, crashing into each other like Keystone Kops. Our ever-confident captain snaps to attention, throws the slumped and slack-jawed yacht crew a sharp salute, and quips briskly, "'Evening, gentlemen." They are so relieved that they just gape and, with practiced politeness, deliver a half-mast mechanical wave in response.

Never have our guests had such a sail. They all stay, eating, drinking, and talking, puffed with a new salty pride as they recount the day's events while showing off their blistered sailors' hands. Aaarrrggghhh, mateys! A day that began at 5 A.M. winds down into the early morning hours of the next day. As I lie in my bunk listening to the few remaining stragglers reluctantly boarding shore boats for home, I find myself grinning like an imbecile. God, I feel proud! Proud of myself. Proud of my skipper. Proud of my shipmates. Proud of my ship. Sixteen sails, all 123 feet of her, and she can maneuver like a sports car under the expert command of a damn good leader and the knowledgeable handling of a united crew. It's been a helluva day.

∿

JOURNAL ENTRY
A few days later
Bequia
West Indies
Caribbean

I am becoming aware that the *Sofia* is part of something much grander than she. We now recognize many vessels from sea or other ports. Several have crew who have become our friends and with whom we reunite at each successive island. Scanning the anchorage, I see the *Lily*, a Swedish Baltic trader like the *Sofia*, only smaller. She runs charter in these islands. The *Ariadne*, a huge old charter boat from Germany, broad off our port quarter, is a hulking monstrosity. A member of her crew, Martin, jumped ship in Martinique to join us. While here in Bequia, Oliver and Willy followed suit. They were all unhappy aboard the *Ariadne*. Needless to say, the *Ariadne*'s captain is not always glad to see us. Off our bow lies the *Norwind*, also out of Germany, with our friend Frity among the crew. The *Tontra Schooner*, hailing from South Carolina with her family—Iris, Leed, and pretty little eighteen-month-old Viva—is also here. *La Ami* is well off our starboard quarter, also a Baltic but from Denmark. She is a flashy charter yacht—a real beauty. The *Tannequill*, owned by a family from New Jersey, is anchored in close to shore. The *Sub Sea* is here too. She's another German-registered charter vessel and a bit of an old barge. *God's Bread* rests softly in the tide several meters off our bow. Americans Buck, Becky, and their dog call her home. Then there is the smattering of big and small yachts—boats we see all over and with whom we share an unspoken acknowledgment of fraternity. With them, we go our separate ways, together. Everyone is out here doing something, going someplace.

A Swedish naval training ship has come in. Anders, our resident Swede, escorts a group of us over for a visit. The crew is kind enough to grant us permission to come aboard and we jump at the chance. What an impressive vessel—270 men and six thousand tons of steel! We get the grand tour, culminating in the officers' wardroom for cocktails. "La-di-fucking-da," says Mother Boats. He accompanies us, and though in heaven because he is surrounded by handsome young men, his seaman's curiosity wins out and he manages to behave. He is so interested in the workings of the ship that he keeps himself appropriately occupied by conversing about numerous complicated aspects of her operation. The *Sofia* is now called on regularly by the ship's young cadets, who opt to spend their shore leave with us. We all agree that we prefer their company to the officers'. The cadets relax, take their shirts off, ask to hear reggae, trade their pressed khaki shorts for worn dungarees, and openly relish the female company. They all speak perfect English and they impress me as so young. But rather than identifying with them or being attracted to them when I'm with them, I'm flooded with nostalgia. Am I gettin' old? They don't seem to think so.

∽

JOURNAL ENTRY
Bequia, St. Vincent
West Indies
Caribbean

It's now two weeks since I last wrote. I've been out working charter on the seventy-foot English schooner *New Freedom*. I hustled up the stewarding job (maid, bartender, and general bearer of good cheer when not sail handling) while at a party ashore. The yacht was setting sail at six the next morning, so I only had time to hop aboard the *Sofia*, toss a few things in a duffel bag, slap a scribbled note on the chart table explaining my sudden disappearance, and shoot off again. It was good to be away for awhile. We sailed south through the Grenadines, a string of a dozen or so gorgeous islands surrounded by a shallow coral reef that makes it too hazardous for the *Sofia* to traverse. I worked really hard and loved most of it. The entire crew consisted of the captain and his girlfriend, who was the chef, a local island boy who was sixteen, and me. The boy and I shared two bunks and a head in the forecastle. The captain and mate had the aft cabin suite. On either side of the substantial midships area below were scattered private cabins with twin bunks and heads with showers. It was plush, with a few more amenities than I'd been used to of late (although by the end of the trip, I'd long for the *Sofia*'s good old taffrail).

Everyone on board was nice enough, but the folks chartering the trip really made the experience special for me. They were a wonderful couple from the States who'd decided to spend their fortieth wedding anniversary with their three children and respective spouses aboard a schooner in the Caribbean. What a close happy family they were, and they drew us all right in. I found myself becoming reacquainted with an aspect of my identity that had lain dormant since joining the *Sofia*. They gave me the opportunity to participate in a safe, honest interchange, and I dived right in, immersing myself in the warmth.

The Grenadines were a pleasure, isolated and serene—that is, until we reached Grenada, at the foot of the string of tiny islands. We'd heard radio reports that Grenada was experiencing some political unrest, but as it was on the tour, everyone thought we ought to at least give it a go. Upon our arrival a heated coup was reaching a rolling boil. No sooner did we drop anchor than we had to hoist it back on board and make a hasty retreat. It tickled me no end to watch our oh-so-charming and debonair captain turn positively pale and not regain his ruddy color until Grenada was out of sight and well out of sound. The machine-gun fire from the jungle was loud, steady, and way too close for comfort at our little anchorage off the normally peaceful St. George's.

On our return leg we made only short recreational stops at some bays and beaches that we had especially fancied on the outbound trip. At one such anchorage the captain and his girlfriend went ashore, invited out to a meal by their grateful guests. The boy and I were of course also invited, but someone had to stay with the yacht. And, besides, didn't we have work to do?

By this time I was so sick of cleaning the heads that I could literally puke. Whoever designed the *Sofia* and left out the bathrooms did not make a mistake. Toilets don't belong on boats. They become clogged, stink, and break down mercilessly. Even the most seasoned vacationing families know the ever-present evil threat of diarrhea and general intestinal malaise. As the steward, alias maid, on a packed yacht out for a two-week charter, these ailments were not my friends. I found myself slogging from one cute, shiny little head to the next each morning, unclogging, dismantling, rebuilding, disinfecting, and finally renewing to its original and cruelly deceptive pristine form each and every misrepresented commode on the yacht. The *Sofia's* simple lavatory system blossomed in my regard. With each successive morning spent trapped in *New Freedom's* water closets, I found the *Sofia's* versatile taffrail taking on the dimensions of a sensible, civilized, and highly efficient stroke of genius.

Once our chores were completed and the guests still hadn't returned, my little buddy and I were free agents. He suggested that I take a wee holiday and give the yacht's windsurfer a try. He was already a veteran of several charters, so I naturally assumed that his offer was kosher, that we swabbies were allowed to play with the boat's toys too. He rigged the board and sail, and I innocently ventured off. Soon I was several hundred meters downwind and being carried out to sea with the tide. "Ah," it occurred to me somewhere just beyond the protective reef, "I don't know *how* to windsurf." I saw my gallant rescuer approaching fast, aboard our yacht's motorized inflatable tender. With one hand on the bowline, like Ben Hur driving his trusty chariot, and the other making a tight fist and bulging bicep, he was striking a perfect "I'll save you, Nell" pose. So I proceeded to drop the sail. Dudley Do Right ran over it with the outboard. Sulking, we towed the damaged goods back to the boat, returning just in time to be hailed from the beach by our unsuspecting shore party.

After displaying the tattered sail, the deckhand and I hunched before the boss like errant children awaiting a scolding. And the captain was posturing a pretty fair outraged father impersonation too, until the chartering family chimed in, defending us and refusing to allow the skipper to further rebuke "these two fine young people"! Although the skipper did deduct the repairs from our salaries, the family, anticipating this, more than made up for it in our tips. They really did like us best. Promising to call my family in the States and tell them how much we had enjoyed each other, and to report that I was fine—save a constantly sunburned, peeling nose that they lectured me about for the entire two weeks—the happy charter group disembarked with hugs and tears.

I return to the *Sofia* to discover that the work projects progressed while I was away. Shortly after we arrived in Bequia, we engaged an old gentleman named Esau, a professional caulker from the island who descends from a long line of Bequian traditional boat craftsmen. The arm in which he wields his caulking mallet is easily twice the size of his other arm. Before I left for the Grenadines, I spent many hours watching him and learning. Caulking means filling the gaps between the planks of a wooden vessel. First, all the old caulking must be reamed out. Then the seam must be dried. A layer of a soft filigree-type material, such as unwoven cotton, is embedded in the bottom of the seam. On top of this, pieces of oakum, tarred fibers of hemp, are driven into the seams with a caulking iron and mallet. Finally, hot pitch, a mixture of tar and resin, is ladled over the oakum, providing a waterproof seal for the crack. It is methodical, repetitive work that I personally find very satisfying and meditative. The rhythmical "tink-tunk, tink-tunk" of the mallet head against iron is like a mantra. Not only can it be heard each day, echoing all across the island of Bequia, but one can let one's mind drift and imagine the same familiar sound filling the smoky air of boatyards and ship landings around the world, hundreds of years past.

Esau has almost completed the caulking of the *Sofia's* decks. And our Barney has finished laying a new foredeck, complete with a shiny new monkey forecastle, an area of raised deck, just afore the windlass. Barney, an experienced master craftsman and fine carpenter himself, has done so fine a job that it would well suit a much fancier yacht. The crew also has found timber appropriate for a new mizzen gaff. Evan is busy shaping it to precise specification as it hangs, strung between the fore and the main masts, across the main deck. The ship is getting shipshape.

❧

JOURNAL ENTRY
A few more days later
Bequia
West Indies
Caribbean

Today Linda will be leaving us. As one of the most experienced sailors on the *Sofia*—she even racked up a semester of college credit aboard a proper sail-training vessel out of Massachusetts—Linda hopes to make sailing her life's work. The *Sofia* is way too avocational for people focused on a career goal. Our ship more appropriately fits the classification of a lifestyle that just happens to move by virtue of the wind and sea. So Linda is signing on to a "sailing oriented" vessel that will cover sea miles faster and allow her to establish a bona fide reputation and résumé. In the beginning Linda was an energetic, motivated addition to the crew. We came through the hurricane together, and I will always remember her as able, willing, and even heroic. I don't blame her for quitting the tedium of the *Sofia*'s "chip, scrape, and paint" routine for a chance to swing from some other ship's foot ropes, fly loftier sails, visit more exotic ports of call, log greater watch hours, see more sea time, maybe even battle fiercer gales. None of this is on the *Sofia*'s immediate docket. I think that Linda will be happier elsewhere. Her spark of late has visibly dimmed aboard the *Sofia*. I will miss her. So, I'm guessin', will Captain Tom. Not much about their relationship has been left to the imagination.

It's almost inherent in the *Sofia*'s mode of survival that the crew will, for a wide variety of reasons, become disillusioned and leave. Since I've been on board, we've lost a dozen or so sailors, including, yep, Kathy. And I've just learned that Anders is planning to leave too, "just for a few months," to sail the Mediterranean aboard the swank Panamanian charter boat *Zolana*, where he'll act as chief engineer. On the other hand, though, we also keep getting new blood, even though we presently sport a stable crew of only ten. I find that the comings and goings don't have a substantial effect on me. My interests and expertise continue to evolve. My vistas loom soft, warm, colorful, and melodious. My direction remains unaltered. Perhaps I'm an example of the communal living phenomenon. Because we are forced to live in such close quarters, I maintain emotional separation to try to strike a balance. More and more, I find myself stepping back to observe as some individuals react to group interplay with a pretty extreme range of responses. Usually, I remain quietly apart amid exhibitions of frustration, anger, dissatisfaction, rivalry, knock-down-drag-outs, and full-blown cat fights. These explosive displays, by the way, are much more prevalent in port than at sea. Long stretches of time at anchor aren't good for anyone on board the *Sofia*. They contribute to an inertia of body, mind, and spirit; we are dead in the water in more ways than one. But when we are sailing, the pressure is off. And when major safety and financial concerns no longer hold us in port, we again become masters of our own collaborative destiny, explorers in search of paradise. In the meantime, however, I'm still garnering benefits: learning a hell of a lot about ship's carpentry, engineering, and hull construction, shipwright work, wooden boat maintenance, sailmaking, how to be a boatswain, local culture, history, social drama, my fellow crew members, and me. It's all growth. But I feel in my gut that we need to get sailing again and *soon*.

JOURNAL ENTRY
Later still
Still Bequia
West Indies
Caribbean

We may sail within the week. We're tidying up loose ends (does a ship have them?), and readying for our passage to Barbados. Since joining the ship in Boston, I've taken on the job of buying the stores for the galley. As fresh produce makes up the bulk of my vegetarian diet, I have a vested interest in this area. Despite our location amid these tropical latitudes, where fruit and vegetables should be bountiful, they are in fact scarce or too pricey for our budget. So our shipboard diet has had to be heavily supplemented with carbohydrates and fats. We eat loads of breads, cakes, and "dough bombs," an infamous *Sofia* filler made of deep-fried dough balls. These get slathered with peanut butter, molasses, or a thick, waxy yellow paste that comes in a gallon can and is called Mantécca. Mantécca, I'm convinced, has no food value whatsoever, as even our cheeky, ravenous cockroaches won't touch it.

I'm preparing a list for what I expect will be the last of my regular weekly shopping excursions to the neighboring island of St. Vincent. This trip is an experience worth committing to print. A forty-foot wooden double-ender, driven by an asthmatic outboard and a single, decrepit steadying sail, departs from the Bequia dock one morning each week. Her rows of benches, chock-a-block under a threadbare, faded sun tarp, are always crowded with local women toting an array of sacks, plastic containers, and small squirmy brown children. A few yachties and I ride along. We are all making the weekly pilgrimage to shop in St. Vincent's open marketplace.

The distance between the Port Elizabeth landing in Bequia and St. Vincent's bustling port capital of Kingston is about twelve nautical miles. Our tiny ferry has neither the time nor the fuel capacity to head outside the rim of groundswell for the journey, so we make a straight shot between two points, throwing caution and any hope for a smooth ride to the perpetually brisk onshore wind. Caution, though, is the least of what gets thrown along the way. Spaced beneath each seat throughout the passenger area is a collection of old pails and buckets. On my first trip I made curious note of them and wondered whether we were all expected to bail. Nothing quite so pleasant, I soon discovered, was related to the intended use for this odd conglomeration of receptacles. No sooner had we cleared the cut and made a sharp right turn into the choppy surf than I observed every local, without exception, reach down between her legs and bring a basin up onto her lap: uh-oh. Then a disorienting fog crept over me as that familiar twinge stabbed at the base of my skull and sour saliva began curdling up my esophagus. Heavy seas bashed against the small craft's beam. Suddenly, our motion made no sense. I felt like a poor victim thrust into a ring of bullies who were heaving and shoving me at random in all directions, or a pinball being propelled off whatever paddle or bank it fell against. On the foredeck a wrinkled old man with splayed bare feet was hoisting the solitary sail. "Well, thank God," I gasped. "That'll steady her." No such luck. We were beating into the wind and the sea, and if the sail had any effect, I was too absorbed to notice as I battled my own all-consuming urge to retch. Women and children all around me were upchucking in their pans, calm as you please. It hardly interrupted their ongoing conversations. I, on the other hand, was interrupted repeatedly. Not wanting to miss any of the scenery, I had chosen a "window seat," and consequently a bucket brigade of revolting vomit was being passed my way to be dumped over the side. On the *Sofia* these days I pride myself on my well-conditioned iron stomach. "No, I do not get seasick," I assert whenever asked. Well, here I was subjected to extreme conditions. More extreme than a hurricane? Hell, yes! This was cruel and unusual punishment and I was succumbing to it. Wave after stuporous wave of nausea hit me, as wave after breaking wave of water hit the boat, as wave after putrid wave of puke was shuffled down the aisle. The murky tea and pasty "dough bombs" of my breakfast were launching a violent attack on my intestinal tract, threatening to break free and eject on a sled of Mantécca.

My iron will proved stronger than my iron stomach and allowed me to keep my breakfast down, or somewhere between down and out, but it was the last time I'd eat before boarding the ferry. It was also the last time I'd sit on the benches. The old deckhand is a kind, easygoing fellow, and having no Coast Guard safety rules or insurance waivers to contend with (we really are far from the United States), he welcomes me up on the foredeck. On all subsequent trips I take my place beside him at the mast, helping with the sail and the mooring lines. He seems impressed with my courage as I crouch beside him beneath the rail, smiling as we're assailed by the heavy seas breaking over the dory's proud bow. Hah! I happen to know that this is nothing compared to what I'd have to endure if I dared venture back aft.

Once ashore in Kingston, the marketplace is just a short walk up a steep gravel path that leads into the main street. The market is a pretty shoddy operation, by all appearances. Piles of trash litter the road, a constant peal of excited haggling pierces the steamy, heavy air. Swarms of bugs are everywhere: on the fruit, on the fish, on the animals, in our mouths, ears, and hair. The thoroughfare is a maze of stands, shacks, and carts, all run by merchants peddling their wares with shrill and forceful voices. The *Sofia* can't afford for me to give in to impulse buying or high-pressure tactics, so I consult my list and proceed systematically from booth to booth, purchasing only that for which I have the allotted funds.

After filling several huge sacks and baskets, I submit to the insistent demands of one of the local urchins blocking my retreat. His hand is in my face, his eyes are ablaze with angry urgency: "You go *me!* You go *me!*" These are not like the joyous children who surround me in the village on Bequia. They are more like the boys I counseled years earlier, who were fencing stolen goods on the streets of Boston's poorer suburbs. These local island lads are making a living, helping to support their families, who like so many others have gambled, giving up fishing and farming to provide goods and services to wealthy tourists. I think they made a bad bet. The children look unhealthy and unkempt. They are not smiling. And they are working very hard.

After loading my purchases into one of the children's rickety carts, I follow behind as a small boy assumes the round-shouldered, bent-head position meant for a mule trudging between the splintery staves of his wagon. I am not permitted to help. When we reach the landing, I unload my bundles and fish in my pack for my own money, which I always bring now for the express purpose of tipping the youngsters. They are not begging. With hands straight out, eyes unaverted, revealing neither shame nor submission, they confront me with firm, hard stares. They work, I pay. Then, without thanking me, off they race up the steep path for their next fare.

The return trip to Bequia—thank heaven for small favors—is always easier. We still have the swells on the beam, but at least the wind and seas are following, and the launch rides much more comfortably. I hope my next journal entry will be from some port in Barbados. We are on track to leave within the week. I've just learned that our passage should take us much less time than the week of hard sailing that was first estimated. Rather than beating the entire ninety miles (having to travel as close to the wind as possible, tacking back and forth, following a tight, zigzag course with the wind blowing on alternating sides of the vessel), we've been told of a handy alternative. Our friend John, the captain of an old cargo trading vessel, the Brigsom trawler *Diligenke*, tells us that if we hit the right wind shifts in the exact spots at the proscribed times, why, he reckons, we ought to be able to make the crossing in thirty hours.

❧

JOURNAL ENTRY
Barbados
West Indies
Caribbean

Well . . . here we are in Barbados, one aborted departure (due to one harbor collision), six days, and 380 nautical miles later. So much for hitting those elusive wind shifts. But, golly, it was good to be sailing again! We had really heavy seas, a hard beat, and lots of uncomfortable motion. A half-dozen crew were overcome with seasickness, either groaning in their bunks or rolling semiconscious in their own vomit in the scuppers—not a pretty sight. As I was one of a small group of sailors who remained functional, I was able to exercise my growing aptitude and self-assuredness as a tall ship sailor. Other than having to step around gross, debilitated bodies, nothing terribly momentous happened during this passage. We danced with some more porpoises and did have to alter course one night, to avoid being run over by a large cargo ship.

As a vessel under sail, we have the right of way over a vessel that is motoring, but adhering to this rule applies only if *they* see *us*. My watch spots a freighter off in the distance and takes regular relative bearings of its progress until it becomes clear that it is on a collision course with the *Sofia*. After several futile attempts to raise the freighter on the radio, we wake Tom and Evan. Shaking off sleep pretty darn fast, they dive into the depths of a cluttered lazarette and emerge with a massive searchlight. Our captain and mate muscle it onto the starboard quarter rail and begin directing its laserlike beam up onto the giant wall of white created by our fore and aft sails. It is impressive, making the canvas look like a jumbo television screen that has just been switched to pure static. I think, "Whoa, what a wake-up call. Hey, big tanker, in case you haven't noticed, we're here." They don't notice, and our stirring light show is lost on the huge ship powering toward us. It neither acknowledges us nor alters course. We move on to Plan B. "Well, then, we'll just prepare to come about," our indignant skipper shrugs from the helm. Within minutes we are sailing the *Sofia* on a parallel heading with the cargo ship and out of harm's way.

I am told by the experienced open-ocean sailors aboard that it is not at all uncommon to encounter vessels at sea that are relying solely on an electronic autopilot to keep their ship on course through the night—no alert helmsman, no lookout on the bridge, no radio operator at the controls, no nothin'. What an eerie thought, all these bulky masses crisscrossing the vast oceans like so many ghost ships, passing (one might hope) anonymously in the darkness.

Good weather and steady breezes finally carry us into the anchorage at Bridgetown on the island of Barbados at 2 A.M. As I am up to my ears in my most recent apprenticeship, I'm not on deck for our arrival. Rather, I'm pumpin' and grindin' in the greasy bowels of the ship under the watchful eye of Davey, the chief engineer, whom we affectionately refer to as the "Poison Dwarf." (I have no idea why everyone on board is assigned a nickname. They call me "Rosy," by the way.) My mentor has been tutoring me in the strange and mysterious workings of our auxiliary engine, an ancient and trusty 1935 Jüne-Munktell two-cylinder Swedish diesel chugger that is more jury-rigged than original in form. (We call her "Juni Baby.") There are a dozen delicate steps that need to be followed in proper succession to get her fired up. I want to detail this operation, but it deserves much more attention and concentration than I'm able to muster tonight. For now, suffice it to say that the term *grease monkey* aptly applies to anyone who ventures to dabble in our diesel's unique intricacies. I enjoy it, though. It's a nice diversification, and I'd like to feel competent in each aspect of the workings of the *Sofia* while I'm aboard. She protects and carries me. Can I in clear conscience do less than reciprocate?

∽

JOURNAL ENTRY
Some time later
Barbados
West Indies
Caribbean

In Bridgetown Harbor we are awakened by a raucous fleet of obnoxious day charter boats known as the *Jolly Roger*. This questionable armada is made up of old barges dressed in decorative tall ship rigging. The flotilla, however, is totally bogus. The rigging is window dressing, and the vessels are not capable of doing much more than they do. They motor their inebriated tourists in circles about the anchorage. The exuberant guests appear not to care a snip that their ship is a sham. Liquor flows from dawn to dusk, while the decks rebound with spastic dancers reeling to the on-board steel drum bands.

Although the *Sofia* lies well outside the glut of yachts anchored in the basin, the *Jolly Roger*'s skippers have taken it upon themselves to extend their parade route beyond the far perimeter of the anchorage, to include our noble and solitary schooner. They are probably trying to claim some misguided tall ship fraternity. We don't buy into it, but nonetheless twice daily we're subjected to this charade—every bloody day. Being the good sports that we are, though, we try hard to refrain from appearing rude or offensive. So we wave, pitch salty salutes, stick knives in our teeth, snarl, and even join the ferried hoard in a toast by tossing back a few swigs of rum ourselves.

Ahhh yesss . . . the rum. Mount Gay is the local hooch of choice. Now here is a rum of note, what I expect all rums would someday want to grow up to be. A thick, syrupy spirit the deep amber of aged clover honey, it is meant to be swilled neat. Smooth as old chamois on the tongue, it caresses all the way down, settling into a hot pool in the belly. Yep, we like it—a lot. At 50 cents a bottle, each member of the crew can manage to keep a private stash. The ship too has invested in several cases of this exceptional commodity, which are stored away to be kept for trade. This store does get dipped into on occasion. For example, a few lusty guzzles of Mount Gay make palatable the twice-daily intrusion of the *Jolly Roger* into our otherwise-sequestered existence. Why, I dare say, some of our crew have even grown to look forward to the armada's arrival. The shout,

"Here they come again!" is answered by the obligatory curse "Oh, bloody hell!" and then the resigned shrug, "Oh, well . . ." Finally, someone will blurt out an almost believable hail of, "Ahoy there, mateys!" Then they'll run for one of our bottles and pass it around as we return as many toasts from the *Jolly Roger*'s crowd as we can and still be sober enough to manage the business of our day.

Ah . . . it seems that we've come to some fateful times here. The imminent appointment to haul *Sofia* out at the boatyard—looks like it's really going to happen—is not the least of the precipitous events, but others are packing a much greater punch. Patrick will be leaving us this week, flying home to job commitments and a final attempt at saving a failing marriage. He met his original obligation to the ship months ago, but had he his druthers, he says, he'd never leave—there is no place on Earth he'd rather be. We all care about and respect him. He will be missed. He hopes to rejoin us in six months, maybe eight, twelve on the outside. I can't help but think, however, that we exist as a kind of *Brigadoon* to those who lose us for a time to another reality. I wonder whether they will ever be able to find us again, not so much in physical terms but in the sense that the *Sofia* functions as an ethereal presence in an otherwise certain world. I hope I'm wrong, because we're also facing the impending departure of our captain, and this is truly shivering our timbers. Tom has been the consistent, high-energy, bright beacon for a foundering gaggle of would-be sailors to follow; his humor has been unfailing, his instruction invaluable. But he hails from the old school of traditional sailing routine and regimentation. His skills haven't been fully exercised here, his hopes for the *Sofia* remain unrealized, and his tireless efforts and noble ambitions have been frustrated. He does love the *Sofia* for what she is. But what she is is not for him. He leaves us to command and refit the *Dwynwyn*. It is owned by the present captain of the *Zolana*, who once skippered the famous *America*, on which Tom sailed as a teenager in the Seychelles. At sea vast life cycles reduce to concentric circles, each spinning within the other. The constant static electricity of connections is fascinating. It is also reassuring.

Evan, the mate, will assume command. On board his appointment has engendered serious discomfort. Reservations abound, primarily those stemming from personal conflicts. Evan's seamanship can hardly be questioned, however, and he has sailed the *Sofia* for the past four years. Unlike 'most anyone else on board, his life is this ship. We'll work out the social tribulations, I trust.

∾

The reports are in. It'll be at least another two weeks before we can even get up on the boatyard's slipway, to say nothing of how long we'll have to remain up, once we've surveyed the extent of the worm damage below the waterline. The Toredo worm, which thrives in warm tropical waters by feeding off submerged timber, is the evil nemesis of wooden boats. Unchecked, the parasites can eat their way to the very core of a ship's hull, doing massive damage that can condemn an older wooden vessel. Toxic bottom paint is applied to a ship's underbelly to inhibit these creatures from taking up residence in the planking. Our paint, the soft, sloughing variety that allows the hull to "work," or move against itself without chipping and cracking an otherwise hardened coating, requires reapplication annually. However, on a ship of the *Sofia*'s rough type and obvious antiquity, we adhere strictly to a twice-yearly haul-out regime. Our exhaustive logistical maneuverings to locate yards around the world that are both large enough to haul the *Sofia* and fit within our tight budget, followed by day after labor-intensive day in dry dock, are a fact of our life. These are the insurance premiums that we are ever willing to pay. And we crew members do all the work ourselves: recaulking spit oakum, replacing disintegrated fastenings, scarfing in new planking, chiseling off corroded zincs, overhauling through-hull fittings, grinding the propeller, burning out worm, digging out rot . . . staving off doom. We slap on at least two coats of bottom paint, brush on a waterline that would please the most discriminating artist's eye, and gently redeposit the *Sofia* into the sea, monitoring her oozing bilges 'round the clock until her dried-out planks swell tight again. It's a one- to two-week marathon that goes far toward cementing an intimate relationship between ship and crew. There are always the "knowns" to be concerned about on a seasoned old girl like the *Sofia*. And even they can be the stuff of nightmares. But it's the unknowns, those things that we cannot see or touch and may never know for certain, that strike pure white terror into the hearts of even the saltiest sailors. It is with each successive haul-out that we attempt to minimize the deadly impact of these unknowns.

So we wait. It feels like we've been cursed. Nothing is happening when or how it's supposed to. Everyone is getting burned out with the delays.

Chris, a veteran of only six weeks on board, is jumping ship. He's signed on to a cargo vessel, bound for Trinidad, and plans to weave his way home to New England from there. He and I found some common ground, a similarity in how we had been accustomed to relating and interacting with people, before the *Sofia*. But for him, the social struggle on board is not worth the effort. Lately, whenever I lose a comrade, a soul mate, I do find myself examining my own position, and I do now acknowledge having serious doubts. So many times it would have been such a relief to just say the hell with it and return to the States. And yet I stay. I must be after something, and the opportunity to get it—whatever *it* is—must outweigh the onslaught of negatives. Each successive extended period spent languishing in port tips the scales, though, and threatens to spill out the entire crew. I try to be patient and positive, but all too often I'm made aware of the gargantuan risk that I am taking to get somewhere without being sure it's where I even want to go. However, I do believe that time will tell me, if I listen very, very carefully. And then, of course, there are always those good times, those golden memories that I cling to like lifelines. Here's a critique of some past good experiences not yet chronicled.

After we left Martinique the first time, we sailed over to Ille de Saints to investigate a report of a slipway. This is my first experience with an authentic, unspoiled tropical paradise. The locals are a blend of West Indian and French. They aren't wealthy, and they rely on a very small scale fishing industry to support themselves. But I recognize none of the trappings of poverty as we've come to identify them in the United States. We have a wonderful time there, hiking and exploring. The most vivid event in my recollection of Ille de Saintes is the festival.

A small open fishing dory—it looked like the launches strung from the davits of old whaling ships and was loaded with local men—motored alongside the *Sofia* to invite us to their tiny sister island where a festival was in full swing. Mother Boats wasted no time in bounding over the rail to join the gleeful group. Anders and I followed. What a ride—wet, rollicking, resounding with uproarious singing, and rocking with athletic dancing. I soon began to regret my eager leap into the merriment as we were "gunwales" (the topmost rail on the side of a vessel) three inches from the tide with thirty bodies packed like sardines and gyrating like Mexican jumping beans. Our inebriated helmsman ran the dinghy right up onto the beach full bore, tossing us tumbling into one another, over the bow and onto the sand. Once there, we found the entire island soaked in celebration. Men, women, and children, all dancing and singing—in the streets, on the beach, in the shops. A narrow trail slithering up into the jungle was lit with a string of Christmas lights. We followed it, en masse, receiving warm hugs of welcome from the locals, who made up a steady procession all up and down the slope.

At the top of the island, the hub of the activity, the gala had already reached a fever pitch. Every modest home, shed, barn, even the church, had been converted into a bar or a ballroom. People were everywhere, moving, swaying, some in costume, all immersed in jubilation. One fella, a vigorous chap well known by everyone we encountered, liberated me from my escorts early on and led me from dance hall to dance hall. He was exceedingly proud of his ability to perform all the American dance steps and insisted that he required a partner up to his speed. Well, I did win the dance contest at my senior prom. So my new friend and I did the mashed potato, the jerk, the monkey, and twisted the night away.

I was having so much fun that I neglected to notice that my companion's amorousness was on the rise. By dawn it was evident that although the festivities were winding down, my date was not. I flashed back to those booze-hazy bashes in college when, after my friends had disappeared, one by one, behind anonymous bedroom doors, I'd find myself sitting and staring into the beseeching eyes of some guy toward whom I usually felt zero romantic inclination. The problem on "de Sainters," however, was . . . well, there were actually many. I was very far from home. I didn't speak the language. And except for the persistent companionship of the village "ladies' man," I was on my own. After lengthy discussion, comprised of two opposing dialects and positions colliding in a tiresome performance of my batting away his wandering hands, my adversary and I reached a shaky understanding. He had assumed that I *wanted* to repay his hospitality. I discovered that he was laboring under the misconception (at least I hoped it was a misconception!) shared by most island men in this part of the world. They believe that American women come down here for the express purpose of "having themselves a West Indian man." My buddy— we were both calm by then—saw himself as the answer to my prayers, or at least to my several thousand sea-mile search. I let him down as gently as I could, finally admitting that, so sorry, but I have this nasty little sexually transmitted disease (a tiny white lie). Now this he accepted without objection. Apparently, this was also an integral part of the West Indian male's stereotypical view of American females. So we parted ways on civil terms.

As I made my way down to the beach, wondering how the hell I was going to get home to the *Sofia*, I spotted Anders and Mama sleeping under a coconut palm. They hadn't gotten lucky. No one propositioned either one of them. So there we sat, chins in palms, contemplating our predicament, when, to our relief, the owner of the boat that had ferried us over the previous evening appeared, putt-putt-putting up the coast. He searched us out, pulled into our inlet, motioned for us to climb aboard, and with no more than tired smiles exchanged among us, drove us back to our ship. I guess we were his responsibility, start to finish.

The rumored slip never materialized on Ille de Saintes, so the *Sofia* crew decided to power over to the nearby island of Dominica. We had been regaled with tales of its verdant tropical rain forest. The first day there we awakened to the sight of dozens of banana boxes floating past the ship on their way out to sea. Someone on board initiated an all-crew ocean rescue. We took to the water in dinghies, on surfboards, or swimming, rounding up all we could haul, float, or shove. By the time we dragged ourselves back on the ship, the main deck of the *Sofia* was full to overflowing. Later that morning we were informed that the Geesh boats, the cargo haulers for all the bananas throughout the West Indies, identified these stalks as being too ripe to make it to market, so they chucked 'em. Never ones to pass up a gift from the sea, we of the *Sofia's* crew found ourselves mellow in yellow. For weeks the primary responsibility of the person on galley duty was to dream up some creative slant on any palatable variation of a banana recipe. An unenforceable quota was also put in place, requiring every member of the crew to consume a half-dozen bananas a day—above and beyond those incorporated into the meals, of course. From shore the *Sofia* looked like she was dressed in some curious camouflage. Stalks of bananas at varying stages of maturity hung like ornaments from masts and rigging, forming a sweet-smelling awning from bow to stern.

We anchored away from the main ports and cities in a quiet bay on the lee side of the island, facing a mountain of dense jungle that ascends through a ring of misty clouds and emerges as a peak of towering rain forest. The young local boys of the nearby village ventured out to the *Sofia* almost before the hook was set. Few boats visit this particular anchorage, which made our being there somewhat of a happening. But, of course, we are also the *Sofia*. We are a happening-and-a-half! Handmade outriggers are to the local youngsters what bicycles are to American kids. Soon our perimeter was a veritable boardwalk of boats swinging softly in the tide. A tattered array of painters (bowlines on small boats) were tied off all along our port and starboard rails. The children spent whole days and nights on board. They helped us with simple chores, swung from the rigging, showed us how to prepare local foods, laughed, sang, danced, and played. Among other things, they taught us where to dive for conch and how to clean, tenderize, marinate, and cook them. Quite a process!

Within a couple hundred square meters of the ship were several reefs with nests of the tasty shellfish just a few feet below the surface, shallow enough for free diving. The shells themselves are quite large, some the size of soccer balls. The "foot," or part of the strong muscle that attaches to a piece of rock or coral, is extremely difficult to dislodge. We had to use chisels, screw drivers, and caulking irons. Once the conch was farmed and brought back on deck, we faced the mighty task of opening the shells. It is some muscle, and we were never successful in prying it apart without smashing the shell to smithereens and having to pick the shredded meat out of the shattered bits. But the native children are masters at it. They squeeze a drop of lime into the vice-grip-like mouth, position the tip of an awl on some ancient secret point on the shell and, voilá, it yawns open like a trap door, exposing an intact iridescent fleshy pink glob of almost pure protein. The meat that the boys extract is also surprisingly tender. We reckoned the kids know some kind of magic, until one of their mothers confessed that if the conch dies in a state of tension (being whacked to death with a belay pin probably does the trick), it will not only lock its shell shut and hang on by its tensed foot for dear life but prodigious pounding will be required to tenderize the meat. What great fun, though! We all, Sofians and locals alike, benefited from our shared experience.

Of course, our trip to Dominica wouldn't have been complete without a venture into the jungle to visit the rain forest. A local family invited some of us along on a truck tour of the higher elevations. These folks cautioned us that the trails are untenable by foot and that we would get lost in the jungle on our own. I had never been in a live, tropical rain forest and it was mystical. On the drive up, we were treated to the daylight's disco ball effect as the sun's rays slanted through the jungle's canopy. Soon we noticed the darkness closing in (even though it was only midday) and the air becoming heavy and dank. It pressed down on us like a broad hand, making us feel sluggish in the simple act of straightening our shoulders or raising our heads. Moments later the sky opened and torrents of rain came down. Here we were forced to retreat, certain that the road ahead would be washed out. No sooner did we begin our descent than the downpour abated, the sun peeked through, and the air thinned. What a strange and wonderful ecosystem.

Once back at sea level, we treated our guides to cold drinks at the village shop. The jolly proprietor spoke some conversational English, so she engaged us in friendly banter.

"Why you so faaht?" she asked, singling me out. All the West Indians speak with a melodious tone that lilts airily upward at the last syllable of each sentence.

"So faaht?" I echoed, confused, trying to mimic the lilt.

"Faaht," she boomed.

I figured that although the word sounded ever-so-slightly familiar, a little like the English word *fat*, it must certainly have some other connotation in the islands, like happy, rich, or maybe cute? She answered my puzzled stare with a gigantic guffaw.

"Faaht!" she hollered, pushing her stomach forward, with her arms forming a big circle in front of her middle.

I looked down at my once-lithe frame, now a little puffy, sure, under its beautiful bronze sheen. But "faaht"? Damn! I realized that she was right. Without the benefit of my accustomed measures of weight gain and loss—the fit of clothes (don't wear any), full-length mirrors (don't have any), a bathroom scale (yeah, right), I'd forgotten to be aware of my shape. I guess all those dough bombs took their toll. I returned to the *Sofia* committed to more than meet my quota by vowing to subsist on bananas until I could no longer be considered "faaht" by anyone's standards.

The next day we returned to Martinique. By this time Martinique epitomized all the big-city money, people, pollution, hassle, and headaches that we'd set sail to escape. Nonetheless, Christmas was around the corner, we expected mail from home, and we had work to do on the ship. We discovered a secluded little bay tucked in back of the lee of Martinique that suited our needs. Just a handful of small boats was anchored off shore, and the beachfront was empty and inviting. A couple of bars peeked out of the palms—sand floors, thatched roofs, lift your feet when the swells hit the beach, cold local beer. Our interim here was one long party. Everyone from shore, as well as our fellow boaters, congregated as usual on board the *Sofia*. For a few days we worked and celebrated any number of things. Then we faced the inevitable serious business at hand. Sailing back around to the commercial shipyard, the one that we couldn't afford, we acquiesced to at least get our waterline attended to before setting out again on our search for the illusory slip. Tom and Evan put their heads together and dreamed up a scheme for careening the ship against the dock (tipping *Sofia* slightly over to each side). It was an ambitious idea—an experiment, really, as nothing of the kind had ever before been attempted with the *Sofia*. But the guys were enthusiastic about it.

"Hey, in theory it should work," they crowed. So we rigged our thickest hawser from the main topmast to a sturdy pole about thirty yards inland. Then we lowered our larger shore boat, *Salty Dog*, from its davits, brought it up off the bow next to the dock abreast of the foremast, attached it to the dockside course yardarm, and proceeded to fill and sink the *Dog* in an attempt to tilt the *Sofia* enough to raise her outboard waterline just above the surface. Our crew, accompanied by a smattering of game fellow cruisers and all the locals within shouting distance, then lined up along the length of the hawser and heaved with a might, droning in unison the chant of the Volga boatmen. We managed to wrench the *Sofia's* outboard waterline six inches above the surface, made off the line, raced around, mounted surfboards, chipped, scraped, and painted the exposed waterline, raced back to the hawser, lowered her away, swung the *Sofia* around, repositioned the *Salty Dog* on the opposite yard, hauled away, and repeated the process again until both the port and starboard waterlines were renewed. Everyone in the boatyard suspended their duties and stood observing us, shaking their heads, never for a moment believing that we could pull it off. But by the end of the twelve hours that the entire production took, the gallery was cheering us on, so impressed that they didn't even charge us the dockage fee. It was all captured on film for our archives. A *Sofia* first! Except for a cracked yard (spar) from the weight of the *Salty Dog*, the *Sofia*, her crew, and the shipyard emerged unscathed.

෴

JOURNAL ENTRY
Barbados, West Indies

We share this anchorage in Bridgetown, commonly referred to as the careenage, with other memorable vessels. The 110-year-old *Anne Khristine* proudly graces our starboard view. She's a stately schooner-rigged Baltic owned and run by George, a Swede, and his English wife, Lilly. Although both are capable sailors, the pair felt that they might benefit from having a couple of deckhands aboard for their Atlantic crossing. I can't imagine that ships find it difficult to recruit experienced sailors in these parts. Yet we repeatedly run into situations where cruising vessels solicit, encourage, or endure totally unskilled labor.

For example, Lilly and George had enlisted the aid of two young Englishwomen for their Atlantic crossing. These lasses had never been to sea nor had they ever stepped even a pointed toe aboard a sailboat. In the middle of the Atlantic something vital broke loose on the topmast. With Lilly at the helm George informed the women that they would have to hoist him aloft in a boatswain's chair so that he could survey and repair the damage. They did manage to get him up the mast—no small miracle—but in so doing they exhausted what little sea sense they had acquired. Swinging at the hounds (shoulders formed at the top of a mast that support the shrouds or rigging that hold the mast to the sides of a ship), George hollered down for them to "make fast." This is a positively elementary sailing term that means to securely tie off a line. The women, gazing aloft, their pensive faces the picture of blank slates, had no idea what they were now expected to do. They conferred: "Well, we've got 'im as 'igh as 'e can go. 'E's bellerin' fer us to do some'fin, 'fast.' Reckon 'e means fer us to get 'im down in a 'urry, aye?" So "our lovely lollies from Liverpool," as George refers to them, slacked off the line that they were holding and proceeded to lower away. In so doing, they nearly jolted the unsuspecting George out of his perch. He screamed down again, more emphatically this time, "Make fast! Make fast!" "Don't you dare yell at us, George, 'cause we're goin' as fast as we can," the indignant swabbies shouted back as they further accelerated their efforts. The line ran too quickly, burning their hands, so they let go and leaped back away from the anticipated thud as George found himself hurtling downward. As luck would have it—a sailor's luck to be sure—the line fouled in the block, whiplashing George and his seat into a dead halt mere inches from the deck. Bouncing like a two-year-old in a baby swing, George fixed his deckhands with an incredulous stare. They glared back, mad as hell, hands on hips, eyelids batting, the epitome of righteous indignation. "Are you fixin' to break me bleedin' skull?" he inquired as delicately as he could. Insulted, the women turned on their heels and stomped off down the deck, flinging back over their shoulders, "Well, George, if 'at weren't fast enuf fer ya, ya can bloody well do it yerself next time." By the time we meet up with the *Anne Khristine* here, all has been forgiven and the story is already being told with equal portions of good humor by owners and deckhands alike. Sadly, the *Anne Khristine's* sister ship has long been ensconced in a maritime museum in San Francisco, but the *Anne Kristine* is still out here having adventures.

Off our port bow lies the lovely *Karin,* another old wooden vessel. She's a double-ender, beamy and cutter rigged (sporting a single mast with two head stays). San Francisco Charlie and Inga out of Denmark own and operate her. Below decks she's fitted out like a snug rustic mountain cabin, complete with wood-burning stove, kerosene lamps, and a wealth of hand-made articles. Inga is a weaver by trade, Charlie a woodworker. Their boat is a floating manifestation of what they do and what they love.

The *Tyele,* before she weighed anchor and headed home to the States, lay well into the shallows with easy beach access. This giant trimaran—a three-pontooned multihull drawing less than a foot and therefore needing very little water beneath her—was built and sailed by Barbara and Martin Breheny and their four boys, three of whom—fifteen-year-old Donald, eighteen-year-old Dave, and twenty-one-year-old Dan—were on board. We were told that the eldest boy, Brian, had fallen in love while the boat was in Australia and had jumped ship there. This family had already been cruising for three years, and the *Sofia* was not unknown to them. They'd read about her in the logs—really ambitious guest books—kept by various yacht clubs, pubs, and land-locked old salts in all manner of shore hang-outs the world over. These books invite visiting vessels to document their sojourn in them. Aside from being a crackerjack way of chasing down a boat that may have gone missing, the entries are an invaluable opportunity for independent cruisers to somehow feel connected as they scatter across the world's oceans. All through the South Pacific the Brehenys had followed the colorful *Sofia* paper trail from her first circumnavigation. We were some-what of a legend to them, and they were thrilled to finally meet up with us. The two younger boys, Don and Dave, became regulars aboard the *Sofia* and even moved in to help with the haul-out. We couldn't have done it without them. When we finally did manage to haul the boat, we had fewer crew than ever to work on the slipway, and we still got more accomplished than in any other single haul-out to date. Quite a feat. I really thought I knew what to expect, but I could not have possibly anticipated what haul-ing the *Sofia* entailed.

Straightaway, we have to dive in the putrid waters of the careenage and follow our ship underwater as she's winched out onto the Bajans' (the locals' slang term for themselves) antiquated slipway. Along the route we have to manually position her bilge blocks to ensure that her arthritic keel is sup-ported. The boatyard employs several barrel-chested little men whose job is to dive and set these wooden wedges themselves while lying on their backs, forcing the blocks in with their powerful legs. Nevertheless, we feel we can't trust the *Sofia's* unique physique to even their capable hands and feet. Once up on the boatyard's rusty old rails, we construct a maze of makeshift scaffolding that encircles the hull. Next, up go the lights. The project is taking on all the appearances of a long succession of all-nighters. Then the work list is tacked to the saloon bulkhead, confirming my worst suspicions. Caulk. Burn. Grind. Paint. Mix. Build. Weld. Chip. Scrape. Clean. Cook. Oil. Grease. On and on—three long pages of projects. We each do a bit of everything, and one after the other the jobs get checked off. We are out of the water for more than a week, but the work has been performed in double time because we are paying by the day, in more ways than one. Each day out takes a hefty chunk from our cruising kitty and compounds a critical problem once the ship goes back into the water. A wooden hull dries out, planks shrink, caulking cracks, oakum spits out, water oozes in. Every day that our hull is out of the water means paying that much more attention to the bilges once she goes back in. Until the wood swells and the seams reseal, we pump 'round the clock. I don't remember ever being as fatigued or as filthy or as proud as I am after this long-awaited episode on the "hard," a sea-bum's all-to-appropriate nickname for a slipway.

With the *Sofia* we have weathered a hurricane and survived, but she has taken some brutal blows. On the hard we are able to salve her wounds, close her lesions, refortify her constitution, make her whole again. Although exhausting, it is a labor of love and gratitude and faith.

Dave Breheny will accompany the *Sofia* when she departs Barbados. His family plans to head home to the States from here, and he's not quite ready yet to swallow the anchor (leave the sea). He'll come aboard the *Sofia* with free passage to Panama—because he worked flat-out for us on the slip, because we could use his seasoned sailing skills, and mostly because he just wants to sail with us "more than anything!" His folks are fine with this, ready for a breather, I reckon. Barbara confided to me that her boys decided to see what it would be like to live like cavemen: no bathing, no eating with silverware, no washing clothing, none of the tiresome social niceties of civilization. Of course, they approached this purely as a scientific experiment. What a courageous mom! Most parents will confess that they simply try to survive their children's teenage years. But picture poor Martin and Barbara, sandwiched literally cheek-to-cheek on a small vessel at sea with their brood of boys for most of the lads' hormone-driven rebellious years. Yikes!

Not surprisingly, Mom and Dad say a temporary adios to Dave with visible glee. He no sooner tosses his duffel bag aboard the *Sofia* than he

strips right down and begins sauntering around his new digs buck naked.
We inform him that while, yes, Sofians are known to sail sans clothing—
as is consistent with all the stories he's heard—we do try to maintain some
level of decency and decorum while in port. David shrugs, grins his sheep-
ish man-child's grin, and consents to don a pair of old cutoffs while at
anchor. A strappy, happy-go-lucky fella, Dave is soon nicknamed "Packy,"
short for pachyderm. Because he is as strong as a young elephant and
overly eager to tackle any job requiring pure muscle, it suits him.

Well, it doesn't take Packy long to realize what he's let himself in for.
If the haul-out hasn't scared him away, though, it is a safe bet that nothing
else the *Sofia* can dish out will, either. But test him we do. We are the *Sofia*,
where outrageous and unconventional experiences lurk around every bend.
I get to witness Packy as he tries to process his introduction to Juni Baby,
our engine.

As our departure from Barbados and the West Indies grows imminent,
all that remain of our crew out of Boston are Evan, Norman, Mother
Boats, Karen, and me. Barney needed to get away for awhile, to home and
family. Kathy just plain got discouraged, fed up with the delays, disappointed in the crew, depressed by the unstable atmosphere. Another two of
the "old guard," Davey and Martina, departed a few weeks ago. Martina
left to try her hand at modeling in New York City. Davey left because
Martina left.

Davey's absence leaves the *Sofia* minus her chief engineer and me minus
my diesel mechanics instructor. Norman and Evan, of course, both know
the rudiments of the engine, but when motoring in and out of these over-
crowded Caribbean obstacle courses, Evan takes the helm and Norm stands
as lookout. Boats is on the "horn," or radio, following the instructions
of port authorities. Karen, who still wears a skirt most days, insists that
the engine room is not her domain. That leaves yours truly holding the
"grease ball" in my pathetically inexperienced hands. When Australian Katy
promised me that I'd feel like I knew what I was doing as soon as someone came along who knew less than I did, she forgot to add that I'd also
find myself doing all sorts of stuff I don't know how to do, because there'd
be no one else around to do it. This is how I become the engineer of our
ancient tall ship. Both in and out of Barbados's boatyard, I am left with
the responsibility of operating Juni.

First, I flick the switch on the Deutz generator to begin the warm-up
of the cylinders. Then I check the prop pitch to make sure it's in neutral.
After a proscribed period—ten to twenty minutes—I open the forced air

pressure and cooling seawater cocks by rotating large wheels at the pipes on the overhead of the engine room. Then I insert a six-foot steel pole into one of the holes on the outer edge of the giant flywheel and bear down on it with all my weight. I have to jump in the air and ride the stick down to get the wheel to rotate. And then I have to yank that ol' pipe out again just before it hits the casing. Once the flywheel is rocking on its own, I take up the engineer's position astraddle the torso of the behemoth. I pump the two fuel handles in and out, in and out, as if I am performing an overzealous bust-enhancing exercise, all the while craning around the cylinders to watch the flywheel to ensure that the pumping coordinates with the forward and not the reverse rock of the wheel—"fump, fump, fump." Pump, pump, pump—faster and harder until Juni engages and is running on her own. Squeezing out from behind the guts of the motor, I jump to tighten back down on the air valve and carefully race around the flywheel to switch off the heaters. Ascending the step to the aft cabin, I take up my position at the prop pitch and grin up at the helm while I await my next command. All the while Juni is vibrating like something alive and about to burst. Her rhythm can be felt in every fiber of the ship. Crew members cha-cha to her beat as they move about the deck.

Coming down off the slipway in Bridgetown, I assume my position next to the engine. Once I get the go-ahead to start her up, I begin the now-accustomed series of steps; switch, crank, stick, lurch, run, squat, pump . . . pump . . . pump . . . Shit! Juni is firing from only one cylinder, not nearly enough oomph to make her turn over.

"Start her up," the skipper calmly commands from the helm. "We're nearly away."

"Um, Evan, she's firing from only one cylinder," I shout back, my confidence beginning to falter just a tad.

Not quite so calmly, he replies, "Engage the damn engine, Pam. We're drifting out into the careenage."

It is normal for us to run mooring lines and maintain a dockside tie for warping-to (moving a ship in harbor by means of ropes or hawsers). However, the careenage in Barbados is not normal. It is a schizophrenic, crushing, thronging, howling, vile cul-de-sac foaming with a rabid herd of immobile barges, flash yachts, manic runabouts, local kids diving frantically for tossed coins, and at the moment a one-hundred-ton tall ship splashing in, stern first and utterly out of control.

"Use the flares!" Evan squeaks. Oh, I remember: "Trouble-Shooting Lesson 101"—When the cylinders are too cool to ignite the pistons, you can light flares and drop them down into the four-foot silolike chambers, providing an instant shot of super heat. Just as I am completing this emergency phase, while squatting with my fingers in my ears awaiting the imminent explosion, I notice young Packy staring dumbstruck from the engine room passageway. He's come to the *Sofia*, which he calls the Incredible Hulk, straight from a handy dandy, modern yacht, where pressing a clean, white, disembodied button in the cockpit engages the engine. Packy stands there frozen, mouth agape, eyes bugged out, hands on his heart, muttering, "Lordy, Lordy, Lordy. They start their motor with firecrackers."

Juni finally fires, engages, and idles patiently as I fly through the final stages of her operation. Squealing with laughter, I grab Packy's hand and drag him up on deck just in time to hear Juni let loose a powerful belch and blast a huge ball of carbon out her exhaust pipe, which does look rather like a howitzer. The shot sails clear across the careenage and hits squarely on the beam of a large, funky, garlic-hauling freighter. Packy closes his eyes, hangs his head, and groans, "Oh, God, now they've attacked the *Margita*." Then he and I together jump down into the aft cabin and, per Evan's orders, yank the prop pitch into one-and-a-half reverse and then, straight away, lay her over to one ahead. The *Sofia* pivots like a ballet dancer, clearing the myriad boats and children in the shallows, and glides back out to the far end of the *Jolly Roger's* parade route.

In anticipation of our impending departure from the West Indies, our crew complement is swelling. Another young'un, Dan, a seventeen-year old runaway from Denmark, has just consented to become a Sofian. He had been hanging out alone on the island when he was mugged and robbed. Broke and homeless, he found his way to us. Dan is a sullen, slight, and very white boy. Seeking sanctuary within the safe surroundings of our ever-accepting cooperative seems an auspicious choice for him at the moment. He has no money so we are giving him free passage as working crew. He'll be good company for Packy. As the youngest member of our group, we nickname him "the Kid." Christy, an old friend of Evan's from San Francisco, flew down and helped on the haul-out. She'll remain aboard for a few months of—it is hoped—sailing. Ronda, fresh from a stint in the Peace Corps, worked on the hard and has also opted to accompany us for a short bit. Anyone who puts in time on the slipway is entitled to time sailing. Fair enough! So we are heading out with a crew of nine. Not much experience on board, but with downwind runs on short hops within one hundred miles of land for the foreseeable future, we reckon we'll mostly be fine.

Here I am, a veteran of several months on board, much of which has been spent languishing in a variety of harbors, and, voilà, I'm considered one of the "old crew." I have learned a great deal, have often had to use my knowledge before it has gelled, and I've discovered that I even possess some natural sea sense. So the jobs are getting done right and proper, and we are still afloat.

Scuttlebutt has it that some time before we set out across the Pacific, a number of former crew members will rejoin us. Barney sent word that he'll be coming down from California. Anders plans to return from the Mediterranean, and Patrick has just written that he'll be flying over from Boston, loaded to the gills with sailmaking materials and a whole new set of sails. What a windfall—for the *Sofia*, that is. His marriage wasn't as lucky. Oh, well . . . Go sailing! We hope everyone will regroup in time for the next haul-out in Puntarenas, Costa Rica, the one that will prepare the *Sofia* for the South Pacific passage. We'll need all the help we can rustle up to ensure that the ship will be ready for the long crossing. We don't plan to haul the *Sofia* again until New Zealand, many, many months and many more nautical miles around the globe.

I can't deny that we have had some hoary moments when it felt like this whole venture might all come down around our ears. And I expect that there will be more of these episodes in our future. We seem to maintain a tenuous balance on the ball of a great pendulum as it sketches its arc wide across destiny. The *Sofia* continues to remain viable, however, and will so long as she doesn't stop swinging altogether.

I shouldn't close the book on Barbados without acknowledging what far and away was the most outstanding aspect of our stay here. We will long remember our association with the inimitable Dick LaRoche, U.S. consul general in the West Indies. Dick heard about us from his young colleague Tim Foster, the U.S. vice consul based in Martinique.

In all of her questionable affect and enterprise, *Sofia* remains the stuff of fantasy. Folks from every slice of society are drawn to her, and rarely does she disappoint. Our crew always has a wayward representative or two from the upper class who can hobnob with the hoi-polloi. The remaining crew provide interesting company and often pure unadulterated entertainment. When you're aboard the *Sofia*, the facades fall fast. The hair comes down. The uniforms come off. The inner child sneaks out. It's gotta be a kick to be in our midst if most of your days are spent being prim and proper. The pervasive theme on board the *Sofia* is come as you are. No judgment will be delivered, no obligation required. You don't have to buy in to the ideology or sign on for the duration. You are free to refresh your spirit with a quick dip in our nonconforming medium. Those who do stay have, like most of us, chosen the wild side and walk that fine line between what intoxicates and what disturbs, what soothes and what scares the hell outta most people. It won't always be secure, but it's guaranteed to be challenging and life altering. Folks love just dabbling in our delicious lifestyle. They come in awe and often out of an intense curiosity. And they usually conclude their visit with smiles, memories secreted away to savor later, decorum preserved, and impulses held vigorously in check.

Tim, the vice consul, had become smitten with a member of the *Sofia*'s crew during our layover in Martinique. Pamela (not me) was an old flame of Evan's—they do keep popping up everywhere, like dandelions. She had not been on board long enough to refrain from referring to "upstairs" and "downstairs" instead of "on deck" and "down below." It always gave us a chuckle. We reckon she gave young Tim more than a chuckle because he courted her with persistent vigor while we were there. As a result, he was on board a great deal. Before we set sail, he wanted to reciprocate, or perhaps he was showing off a bit—not that it mattered in the least to any of us—by hosting a lavish dinner party at his opulent waterfront condo. *Sofia*'s crew was not shy about doing justice to the gourmet meal and well-stocked bar. Long before Martinique's steamy apricot sun had plunged into the cool cobalt-blue sea, we were engaged in one raucous celebration. Our sloshed skipper, Tom, was dirty dancing with an ecstatic Mother Boats. The female vice consul in charge of visas, who was dressed in a chic evening gown, was chugging Dominican rum from the kerosene jug that the *Sofia* had contributed to the festivities. Barney was cozying up to said vice consul and vice versa. Suffice it to say, we all enjoyed the extravagant affair. It was an exemplary farewell party.

Word travels faster than the *Sofia*—not a huge accomplishment—and our very first morning in Bridgetown Harbor, Barbados, found us acknowledging the decidedly American voice that was greeting us from the water. Dick LaRoche had swum out to welcome the famed *Sofia*, about which his Martinique colleague had already briefed him in vivid detail. While treading water, he requested permission to come aboard in a polite and formal tone. Clad only in sporty swim trunks and with twinkling eyes framed by a disarmingly open face, Dick hopped on deck and was instantly at ease. This small handsome man in his early forties was no stranger to diplomacy. His office obligated him to meet us, and meet us he did—but on our terms. We all liked him immensely, straightaway.

Dick ends up sharing many felicitous occasions with us, both on board the *Sofia* and at his spacious hilltop villa. He opens his home to the entire crew. We spend many a long lazy weekend relaxing with him there, gorging on his hospitality—hot showers, big clean beds, fine wine, and athletic romps with his German shepherd, Ringo. Before leaving the island, we want to show our profound gratitude for Dick's gracious cordiality, so we arrange to host a slide show in his home for him and his invited guests. We find ourselves playing to standing room only because Dick wants to share us with his entire general constituency. The crew prepares a wonderful dinner, which is capped off with a couple of hours of the *Sofia*'s best slides. We add a running, animated commentary and historical critique. The audience, to a Bajan, is rapt. At the end of the long, lovely evening, the crew presents Dick with two eight-by-eleven color photos of the *Sofia* racing under full sail with her sister ship, the *Lindö*, in the Seychelles. Although anxious to leave Barbados the following day we do have one regret—that it will be a very long time before we will be able to renew our bond with our dear friend Dick LaRoche.

On deck later, the same night as Dick's farewell bash, as we are seeing to the last-minute details of squaring the ship away for departure, we each remark on the odd hue of the sky. Hovering overhead is a single, massive, inky, dense cloud, eerie and ominous. Nonetheless, the barometer holds steady, the winds are gentle, and the seas swell with reassuring rhythm. All is calm. As we drift down below to go over the morning "getting underway" routine one last time, Mother Boats comes tripping down the companionway. He is flouncing, frothing, and shrieking like a madman, but no one takes much notice. Mama has been imbibing a touch and is in general prone to theatrics and mock hysterics. We ignore him and go on with what we are doing, so he bounds back up on deck, but we can still hear him ranting and prancing around up there. Gazing distractedly up in his direction, our patronizing grins fade as we become aware that the open hatches and skylight are emitting no light—none at all. The masthead light is obscured, as is the bright glow of the night's full moon. Mother Boats pokes his head down the hatchway in one last, valiant, histrionic attempt to get our attention, and this time he manages to formulate a complete, albeit expletive-rich, sentence: "Fuck me dead, mates! We're being covered in vol-fucking-canic fallout!"

Incapable of dismissing him any longer and curious about the unsettling darkness enveloping the ship, we all respond to Boats's desperate cry for attention.

It is Friday, April 13, and as we gain the main deck, we find ourselves gathering in spooky silence and the total absence of light. Here we lie, swinging at anchor in Bridgetown Harbor, Barbados, ninety miles east of the island of St. Vincent, and we are ankle deep in thick, powdery, volcanic ash. A steady flurry of dingy flakes snows down out of a slate black sky. It falls all night, and by morning the *Sofia* and several other ships in the harbor have drifts eighteen inches deep on deck. Mount Soufrière, the live but normally quiet volcano at the peak of the island of St. Vincent, has erupted in all its fiery glory. The ash shot twenty thousand feet into the air and got caught up in a high easterly wind as it crept out to sea. But the weight of the debris caused it to drop down to where the trade winds snatched it and tossed it for one hundred square miles.

For several days afterward Mother Boats is transformed into the "Voice of the West Indies." He is in his element. He becomes the base of operations, manning the radio controls 'round the clock—receiving data, disseminating news, organizing rescue and evacuation teams. Mama Bateau becomes our own little Tokyo Rose, minus the propaganda but complete with darling kimono.

Dick gets a lift to St. Vincent and uses the *Sofia* as his communications link. We hear rumors that the Caribbean's whole volcanic chain might blow. Many a ship hoists anchor and makes for open water to ride out the expected tsunamis, but they don't happen. No Armageddon yet. We, of course, remain in Bridgetown and do what we can locally. And, anyway, it takes several days for us to clean all the ash off the ship.

Weeks later, when we are back out to sea and well on our way to the Panama Canal, we catch a stiff following breeze and are able to set our downwind square sails again. As I sidle out onto the foot ropes and release the gasket lashings, I stare entranced as the ash that has remained trapped and hidden in the folds of the canvas floats delicately down onto the breeze and is swept up into the lazy surface of the eastern Caribbean Sea, which we are finally leaving far behind.

I believe that I began this epic upon our arrival in Bequia, confident that I'd finish this installment there. Barbados was as good a place as any to put a lid on this episode. There aren't many sea stories to spice up these ramblings. But, then, this is part of the *Sofia* as well. Mundane realities pervade even the most romantic experiences. The *Sofia* isn't some fool's paradise run on pie-in-the-sky faith. She is a tangible web of wood, metal, cloth, and rope. She is a vessel. Only through our very human efforts does life get breathed into her. Her maintenance on all levels is crucial, in large part because of the fragile nature of her cargo. The *Sofia* carries the dreams that her sailors hope to realize through her. But, hell, if dreams can exist on the high seas, fueled by the forces of nature, then maybe mine are sleeping on the wind, blanketed by the sky, waiting for me on board the *Sofia*. I think I'll hang around to find out. Anyway, it's well after midnight on my watch, and I haven't given any attention to the bilges. I'll go pump for half an hour or so before waking the next duty. On board tonight is a quiet, a peace and a comfort for me, that I'm reluctant to put to rest. I sure hope I can still find it when the *Sofia* and I face tomorrow.

Esau caulking *Sofia*'s decks. Bequia, West Indies, Lesser Antilles, Caribbean.

chapter 4

Old World, Third World, Unspoiled World

The Dutch Antilles, Venezuela, the San Blas Archipelago

It takes a long time to become young.

—PABLO PICASSO

INTRODUCTION

Leaving the West Indies was therapeutic both for our ship and her dogged few remaining crew. We were a broken and battered vessel of foundering travelers amid islands full of affluent tourists and bitter locals. To this day, negative feelings checker my memories of this phase of our journey.

It was apparent that the inhabitants of these Windward Islands had once been content and self-sufficient. They had farmed the rich soil, fished their fruitful shores, and enjoyed the simple lifestyle of a care-free people. However, with the inevitable influx of a burgeoning tourist trade, the islanders grew more and more inclined to rely on the money they brought in from catering to wealthy visitors. Many stopped spending the time necessary to tend their fields and instead sold their land off to foreign developers. Their once-proud, hand-hewn native dories lay orphaned on the brilliant beach-fronts, while foreign commercial interests fished the prolific reefs. These islanders now occupied themselves elsewhere: in resorts and businesses that pampered the decadent whims of outsiders who, while boosting the local economy, were simultaneously eroding its culture and spirit. Children fetched and carried for the tourists, and a refusal to pony up their standard fee was not acceptable. Yachties learned to maintain twenty-four-hour anchor watches, lest they return from shore to find their dinghy, outboard motor, electronics, jewelry, or cash stolen in lieu of appropriate payment for the kids' services. As the islanders gave up their economic independence, they grew to need us, the vile foreigners. Many now hated us for it.

Aggravating this resentment was the all-too-pervasive attitude of superiority displayed by some foreigners. Far too many of us are products of a culture in which we are used to making demands and being indulged. Such arrogance is hard to disguise and of course evokes the term *ugly American*. But Americans do not, by any stretch of the imagination, have a corner on the market in rude and boorish behavior. It is a disgrace not specific to any one nationality.

By and large, the *Sofia's* eclectic crew succeeded in convincing the locals of the ports at which we anchored that we were not there to take advantage of them. We had very little of monetary worth to offer. So the honest camaraderie and safe friendships that we were able to establish were based on what we did have to share: a meal, a bottle of rum, a day of swinging from the tall ship's rigging, music, stories, a heartfelt desire to learn and grow from the blending of our cultures. These represented our happiest times. But they were all too scarce in the Caribbean.

The physical and financial realities of the *Sofia* and her crew contributed largely to the melancholy that we experienced during this time. Our ship was poor, our crew transient and malcontented, our future uncertain. We carried a full bilge of our own foul baggage in those early days of the *Sofia's* second circumnavigation. Clearly, each member of our crew had personal issues festering just beneath the surface. And the ship's maintenance issues were a constant and unpleasant reminder that a day of reckoning was imminent. These two dynamics created the pervasive sense of being slightly off-kilter that hounded us during those long months in the eastern Caribbean. The *Sofia* was a proud sailing vessel. We on board were struggling to become sailors. For both ship and crew, that incessant freshman year was comprised of nearly terminal inertia and blessed little sea time. We were desperate to get underway.

In setting her sails the *Sofia* set life in motion. Kicking up her heels and shedding her root-bound ties to the West Indies, the *Sofia* left an area and an era far astern. We all felt it. Our hopes rose on the tide and a great weight—as of years—drifted away in the fading wake of our once-again noble schooner.

∾

JOURNAL ENTRY
Willemstad, Curaçao
Netherland Antilles
July 1979

My eyes squinch open and focus again this morning on placid rows of creamy Scandinavian faces with fine blue eyes and broad tranquil grins. The group that assembles daily is partially obstructed by a gauzy film of army surplus mosquito netting that drapes over the main boom. Although it affords us negligible privacy, it does give us our only protection from the quay's swarming gnat population. One by one, we crew of the *Sofia* begin to stir from our makeshift campground atop the main coach roof. We smile back at our audience and rouse ourselves for the day.

After we arrived at the entrance to Curaçao's harbor at Willemstad, the port captain escorted the *Sofia* to a convenient side tie along the crowded wharf that fringes the open marketplace. This location gives us easy access to the city's many amenities and lively attractions, but at the same time it deposits us smack dab in a dead-air environment that is hot, sticky, and devoid of even a whisper of a breeze. Below decks feels just like a Dutch oven. So we sprawl up top to find sleep, content with only a filmy green sheath separating us from the early morning hoard of curious shoppers.

Curaçao, Aruba, and Bonair are the three islands comprising the southern group of the Netherlands Antilles, which lie off the northern coast of Venezuela. Although too dry and barren to support a farming trade, both Curaçao and Aruba have established themselves as flourishing shipping centers. To port the *Sofia* is bordered by the quaint and bustling city center. Greeting us each dawn is a multicolored pastel pavilion of awnings stretched above the stands forming the marketplace, which traces the perimeter of Willemstad's main business district. Across the channel, standing in brazen contrast, we see the other businesses that provide valuable services for the myriad sailors who crew the steady stream of ships in the port. A faded, dilapidated three-story building with a lopsided sign reading "El Gato Negro" (The black cat) rises prominently amid the saloons and whorehouses that dominate this section of the city. The upper two levels of El Gato Negro have balconies off each bedroom, from which dusky animated women with greasy crimson lips shout salacious greetings to passersby. "Aeyee, pretty! 'Gwa hey' [go on ahead] come see me! Gwa hey!" The Laundromat that the crew of the *Sofia* patronizes is in this neighborhood, so we are often among the hapless recipients of good-natured catcalls from these gals.

The waterway separating these two mutually exclusive cultures is on our ship's starboard side. It sees a constant flow of merchant, commercial, and recreational vessels, all entering or exiting Willemstad's harbor. The heavy traffic is choreographed by a bridge the likes of which I have never before seen. It lies flat on the surface of the water, spanning a hefty chunk of ocean for several hundred feet between the two sections of the island. A tireless, stout little tugboat fastened to one end of this structure either pulls it open or pushes it shut, a mammoth jaw pivoting on its hinged joint.

In general, the people of Curaçao are very different from those native to the islands where we'd spent the past many months. The languages spoken here are English, Spanish, Dutch, and a melodic mixture of the three called Papiamento. Sophisticated and genteel, this society exudes an aura of wealth and refinement. The folks are obliging, exhibiting polished manners and charming customs. Waking here, despite the lack of privacy, feels welcoming and sedate—a far cry from our mornings in Barbados.

Young Dan's mother tracks him down and turns up in Willemstad to retrieve him. Dan makes clear, in no uncertain terms, that he has no intention of returning home with her. She doesn't appear surprised, only hurt. Seeing for herself that he is in good health and good hands, she is wise enough to recognize that supporting him in his efforts to attain some autonomy while crewing aboard the *Sofia* is the least of a multitude of possible evils. She pays his passage ($10 a day) to Panama, implores us with a painfully vulnerable modesty to please look after him, and then departs as quietly as she has appeared. I read the proud, masked heartache in Dan's mother's face and the confused torment in his own. This day, I do not wish to revisit seventeen. I remember it only too well.

Between Barbados and Curaçao we lay over for a short bit at Isla de Margarita, anchoring off Pompator, a small village a few miles from the main port of Porlamar. We are alone in this quiet harbor with the exception of a single other ship, the *Serbine,* a Danish carrier vessel. Members of her crew are so thankful for the company—specifically, the female company—that they make their ship and all her amenities available to us. We row over sometime in the early part of each day, use their washing machine and dryer, take showers, watch videos, drink their cold Danish beer, and share sea stories. The *Serbine*'s chief engineer and her first cook take a particular fancy to my hair. It has been a year since my last trim, and my coif has grown into a thick, sun-bleached mane of wild blond curls. By way of a thank-you, before the *Serbine* weighs anchor, I snip off a hefty corkscrew for each of my admirers. We Sofians don't have much, but, hey, we give what we can.

The tiny bay then becomes the *Sofia's* private sanctuary. For the next week we work on the ship by day, and by night we relax on deck. A festival taking place in the village provides us with evenings of a sky set ablaze with fireworks bursting to the accompaniment of chiming church bells. It could all have been staged for our benefit, as we occupy the best seats in the house, lounging on coach roofs, swaying in hammocks, cuddling in furled sails, enjoying the show, sipping from our cups of contraband rum. Yep. We still have rum.

The customs officials, as anticipated, board the *Sofia* when we enter the harbor. And, as usual, they make a melodramatic production of checking us over. But also as usual we understand the ransacking to be cursory. In each successive port of entry, whenever officers come below on the *Sofia*, the first thing they see is the saloon table festooned with an innocuous array of top-ten cassette tapes, cartons of American cigarettes, stacks of *Playboy* magazines, and a bottle or two of good liquor. The agents proceed unfettered through the ship, performing their duties. Then, as they leave, the saloon table is left as clean as *Sofia's* unblemished record. We aren't doing anything illegal. No bribes are openly offered or accepted. No deals are struck. Nothing incriminating has transpired. In fact, this is just the way it's done out here. It's appropriate and expected. In Porlamar did we, in fact, have anything to hide? Were we, in this case, carrying a large surplus of unbonded rum? Yes—in fact, you couldn't have opened a locker or shaken a sail cover without a bottle or two rolling out. But is this uncommon? Of course not. I'm learning that few vessels ever declare their "goods." Every day all manner of stuff is smuggled from island to island, port to port, across oceans covering the globe.

On a ship the entire bulk of your existence rests within the confines of a compact and fragile hull. At worst, you are prepared to protect it with your life. At best, you do not volunteer to relinquish any part or parcel of it. This applies to everything from a pistol to a couple of joints. Forfeiting the contraband does not mean that you will be home free. More than likely, it means that you'll not only never see it again but that you'll also be leaving yourself wide open to a world of grief from unscrupulous agents who regard you as an easy mark. So many of these small islands are a revolution-waiting-to-happen. Their officers are working dirt cheap for a corrupt administration (or uncle or cousin, etc.) in a miasma of unstable politics and confused government policies. Whatever booty they acquire, whether openly volunteered or circumspectly left on the table, is considered to be their well-earned perk. This is the unwritten law of the land. The sooner you learn it, the easier you go. If our table is cleared during a routine customs inspection, we reckon we have some friends in the castle and will enjoy a hassle-free visit. If our table is left untouched—which almost never happens—we scramble to clean up our act as best we can and brace for discord. And in the spirit of the gray shades of law enforcement practiced in many of these questionable republics, all flavors of aggravation and agitation can and should be anticipated.

The *Sofia*, I find, is pretty darn correct but she ain't lily white. This, once again, is a direct function of the ever-fluctuating complement of her crew. I'm beginning to wonder whether *cooperative* isn't synonymous with *anarchy*. But on an even grander scale, I wonder whose show it is out here. The rules keep changing. As soon as I feel like I'm on solid ground, the foundation crumbles beneath me like so many dried seashells. So I tiptoe that very fine line. Long internalized values, morals, and ethics sway squeamishly with the ship as she crosses boundaries and moves beyond limits. The parameters of behavior are not firmly established here, and if they are, I don't always know how to recognize them or how to respond. However, as I identify each new framework, and I eventually do, why, that fine line magically becomes as wide and solid as a honking city block. And that, I guess, is life on the *Sofia* in a nutshell. We gently press the confines, careful not to break them. We are stalwart as we gain the thresholds but cautious not to teeter over the rim. We pose questions. We remind ourselves that if we hadn't questioned something initially, we wouldn't be out here at all.

JOURNAL ENTRY
Puerto La Cruz, Venezuela

From Curaçao we sail back over the top of South America to putrid Puerto La Cruz. En route we travel with a steady stream of oil tankers— a very bad sign—through a sea that becomes a swill of grease and slime. For solace I train my eyes to the heavens, up where the winged painters of the sky have changed from the Caribbean's strange, prehistoric-looking frigate birds to the Americas' stately flocks of huge pelicans flying in perfect formation. I sense that spring has ended and summer has burst forth

in my hometown in the Midwest. Wherever I travel, I still feel the old familiar shifts of season. On the passage out of the West Indies, the majestic
pelicans become my messengers of rebirth. It does feel as if an interminable phase, like a long hard winter, is behind us. And Panama, our gateway
to the South Pacific, with all its mythical, tropical promise, stretches before
us. But first we have to transit these residual foul waters and make a grudging yet mandatory layover in a bona fide Third World setting.

Scuttlebutt has it that the diesel fuel in Venezuela is selling for a whopping 13 cents a gallon. Our budget almost sighs aloud with relief. The
Sofia's thousand-gallon fuel capacity has dwindled to coagulating dregs. We
have already accomplished some ill-advised maneuvering under sail in way-
too-tight spots and floated aimlessly about in way-too-protracted calms,
in a futile attempt to ration the *Sofia's* last remaining diesel. In Puerto La
Cruz we look forward to simply filling 'er up.

Puerto La Cruz is a sewer. We are ordered to anchor in the scummy,
congested commercial basin off the city's choked industrial center. This
is as near to the fuel docks as we are allowed to bring the *Sofia*. We're
informed that because of strict regulations controlling the transfer of fuel
(the *Sofia* is apparently a million laughable miles from meeting the requirements), we are not permitted to tie up to the quay. I reckon we just can't
afford to slip the pump jockeys the requisite fee for turning their well-
exercised blind eye.

After meeting with the authorities at the dock, Evan returns to the ship
and informs the crew of the lively challenge he now perceives us to be facing. "We have to refuel, gang, no doubt about it," he shrugs. If the *Sofia*
had a gas gauge, which of course she doesn't, it would likely read somewhere between "running on fumes" and "get out and swim."

"So how we gonna do it?" we inquire, a touch deflated at the prospect
of not being able to just fill our tanks and beat it out of this pit, pronto.

Here, Evan, shifting way out of character, becomes animated. He explains: "First, we launch *Salty Dog*, off-load our best fifty-five-gallon drum
into her, place our stoutest rowers at her oarlocks, and scull to the wharf!"
The audience begins to sag, our faces turning from brightly curious to
dimly wary. "Then we tie up to the dock, stick the spout in the drum,
and fill it," he continues, excited as a young sprite.

"Uh-huh. But . . . how do we get the fuel from our drum in the *Dog*
on the water to our fill pipe in the deck feeding the tanks?" Somehow we
know we aren't going to like the answer. Evan looks a little scary at this
point. He can't quite control the quivering grin tugging at the corners of

his mouth. If the task is a simple one, anybody can be expected to accomplish it, right? Well, Evan is not an anybody. He is a veteran tall ship sailor and not the sort to back down from a challenge—quite the opposite—and I have to admit that I've observed that this particular personality trait of his usually has a positive effect on most members of the crew. It inspires a steady confidence and a newly awakened sense of gumption in most. However, there are always those who cannot or will not share his enthusiasm. Typically they have no choice but to go along, wondering in despair why they ever left home. In the more outrageous circumstances they wonder whether they are destined to ever return.

So we wait for the punch line. Evan's eyes are glowing. He resumes the detailed explanation, a diagram of diabolical genius, a blueprint of enormous enterprise, a plan among plans: "When the drum is filled, we row back out to the ship. Now, this will be a tad dicey. The basin here has a hefty swell running through it, and the anchorage is lousy with traffic. The filled drum will make our shore boat top-heavy and unstable."

"Yup!" we chirp in, not certain whether we should be laughing dismissively or appearing concerned. (What are the rules? Where are those undulating parameters?)

"Then we tie *Salty Dog*'s bow and stern to the aft quarter, grab a length of hose, and siphon the fuel into our own tanks," he asserts. His eyes are still playful, but his jaw is set. In an instant, we all understand that this *is* going to happen and happen just as Evan has described it: twenty nerve-tweaking trips back and forth, twenty foul-reeking drums sucked and drained until the *Sofia*'s tanks are topped off.

The entire operation is completed in a couple of days. It is a small miracle. We all have to take our turns at "sucker," because the inevitable swallowed dribbles from the less-than–high-tech siphoning process would soon prove lethal for any single martyred crew member. The fumes alone make it a struggle for a mate to stand fast and just maintain control of all the moving parts—the ship, the launch, the drum, the hose, the valiant sucker. Exacerbated by the tropical heat and humidity, the atmosphere surrounding the refueling project gets wonky fast, so we have to institute a mandatory rotation. Nevertheless, before we are finished, the bad taste left in all of our mouths by the port of Puerto La Cruz is carcinogenically tangible.

As horrendous and unpleasant as this improbable feat is, it is also accomplished, as are all the improbable feats that the *Sofia* and her crew undertake. In the wake of each success we feel renewed pride, a reinforced sense of self-reliance, and a grander boldness of spirit. *We* are making this incredible thing happen—maybe not fast, easy, or by the book, and almost never without a hearty helping of chutzpah. But if our ultimate accomplishments continue to offset what we must endure to achieve them, then we stay. We are Sofians. We accept that what we will have to do will often be over the top. So we reserve passing judgment on those who choose to chuck it all and leave. I'd like to think that they don't judge those of us who choose to remain, either, but I rather doubt it. Cognitive dissonance being what it is and all, folks rationalize and support their own choices to resist appearing absurd to themselves. In a somewhat pathological sense, those of us who stay accept this same premise, but we wear the allocated absurdity with dignity and distinction. Square pegs in a round world? Who can say? But for now I stay.

Puerto La Cruz is a compromise stop for the *Sofia*. We have been advised by fellow cruisers to stay well clear of Cartagena, where we had intended to refuel. The high incidence of drug-related piracy visited upon the hapless boating population in the Colombian waters is a great big red flag for the *Sofia*. Not that we're fast enough to be of much practical use as an abducted drug-running vessel, but neither are we fast enough to outrun any pilfering brigand with burglary on his mind. Caracas is a viable option, but tales of its being a hectic, sordid, corrupt city lead us to backtrack to Puerto La Cruz. Maybe I should be glad that we're here, then, but it's sure hard to imagine that this is the lesser of any evils.

We'll be stuck here with official business for several more days, so some of the crew are planning an escape. A few of the more adventurous and financially solvent in the group are organizing a trek down the Orinoco. They hope to get as far as the fabled Angel Falls, the highest waterfall in the world. En route, they plan to visit a couple of legendary Indian villages tucked away in the jungle. Sounds exciting, but I have neither the cash to participate nor the naive belief that these esoteric South American jungle tribes will be quite as thrilled by an impromptu little get-together as our gleeful band of wayward travelers anticipates. I just hope that everyone makes it back safely. We can't sail out of here without them. Besides, I'm actually growing fond of them. For better or worse, we are all family now.

As a veteran crew member, now adept in all aspects of the *Sofia*'s functioning, I feel I have a responsibility to remain on board here in port (as good an excuse as any to explain my reticence to jump on the overland bandwagon). And although the scenery here is more dreary than the verdant rain forest, the newfound peace and relative privacy aboard ship in my mates' absence will be a very welcome respite. A bitter residue of dissatisfaction and uncertainty still lingers from the *Sofia's* recent socioeconomic and logistical hardships. Some thinly mask their continued resistance to Evan's command. In their view any and all ills befalling the ship are attributable to his leadership or perceived lack thereof. When our microsociety is riddled with deep-seated resentments and failed expectations, even an undersized crew can create an oppressive environment. It feels tight, as though we're bumping into symbolic walls of one kind or another at every turn. But when a ship's crew, even a big one, is content, the space on board expands like magic, allowing for everyone's personal expression. It's not the bodies that press in and down, it's the spirits. With a few of these unhappy campers off on walkabout, I expect the *Sofia* will become a more joyous place to be, and I look forward to the recess.

While the crew is away, I'll assume many of their shipboard responsibilities, including my old role as food purchaser. With my Spanish-English dictionary in hand and three years of high school Spanish under my belt, I reckon I can handle myself ashore, even though my initial interaction is a rude awakening. Jumping into a taxi, I slowly piece together my request. Imploring the driver to please forgive my poor pronunciation, I ask to be delivered to the local shopping district. Without even turning his head, he barks back, "No comprendo English, Señorita!" Swell. I thought I was speaking Spanish. Daily, I make such faux pas as asking, "Can I buy your bathroom?" or idly inquiring, "Where is my boat going?" or apologizing by saying, "I'm sorry, but you don't speak good Spanish." Finally resorting to hand signals, athletic gestures, and exasperated smiles and shrugs, I'm getting by.

While shopping in what I suppose is Venezuela's answer to a supermarket, I have a disturbing encounter. Perusing rows of unfamiliar cans and jars, concentrating on the pictures on the labels to try to identify the contents, I stumble upon a woman in a nurse's uniform whose starched, pressed whites are a stark contrast to the faded, ragged clothing worn by the vast majority of shoppers in the market. Women dressed just like her are posted at the intersection of each aisle, and they are handing out free samples of infant formula to the pregnant and nursing women who are present in startling numbers.

I think to myself, this can't be—a living example of lying capitalism straight off the pages of one of the radical *Shopping for a Better World* publications that I subscribed to while still living in Mendocino? I confront one impostor who, thank God, speaks some English. As I suspect, not one single member of her team has ever so much as seen the inside of a nursing school. They are convinced, however, and damned successful at convincing the cluster of oh-so-appreciative young mothers, that their formula is far superior to breast milk—and that it is what all the modern Western and European women are using today.

I am dumbstruck. I mean, even in my most ardent antiestablishment phases, whenever I would devour yet another article on the horrors that corporate America was visiting upon the underprivileged of the world, in my heart of hearts I still harbored an overriding belief in the inherent goodness of people, an inkling of doubt that so malicious and heinous an act could ever be perpetrated upon other human beings. Oh, well . . . live and learn. Because I was educated in northern California's counterculture classrooms of the seventies, I know how this sad story ends. The naive mothers, desperate to be "modern" and to provide the best possible care for their children, will accept the free samples. The samples contain just enough formula to ensure that by the time it runs out, the mother's milk has probably dried up as well. Worse, very few families have the money to keep buying the now-required formula. Even if they do, they don't have the potable water that they need for mixing the powder, causing the babies to fall violently ill from the tainted water they do use. The infant mortality rate from epidemic levels of childhood dysentery is sky high in areas where these methods are being practiced. The parent company of the subsidiary that makes this particular formula is well known to me and to most American consumers. I've been boycotting it for years, purely because of what I read. To witness it in person feels like being punched in the stomach, and a sick hopelessness creeps up into my new consciousness.

This is the downside of travel. To see and to experience firsthand can be rewarding or appalling. In either case, we hope we are changed for the better. Or, in a more perfect world, we commit to effecting change and to improving our expanding reality. I find myself struggling with this dilemma time and again, even now as the fresh bile from this most recent revelation churns in my gut.

৩

JOURNAL ENTRY
Golfo de San Blas

The sail from Puerto La Cruz, Venezuela, to Carti in the Gulf of San Blas, is a mix of sensations. On this leg of our journey the welcoming seas offer sanctuary and the busy skies are threatening. Before we weigh anchor, the crew is all present and accounted for. The brave little tour group didn't make it as far as Angel Falls but didn't disappear in the jungle, either. I consider that these travelers came out ahead. With a full complement of hands to manage the sailing on this passage, Dave and Dan are free to spend most of their off-watch time engaged in their latest avocation—fishing. Schools of dorado, known stateside as mahi mahi and often called dolfinfish in New Zealand, escort us out of the sludge of the Gulf of Venezuela and into the pale clear blue waters of the Gulf of San Blas. Packy and the Kid try, to no avail, to snare a dorado. Finally, they have to settle for stretching out in the bow net, watching the deep carpet of iridescent pinks and lavenders as the fishes' prismatic scales reflect the tropical sun's brassy-yellow glare. Sometimes the schools are so thick around the hull that it looks like the *Sofia* is smearing across an oil painting. The broad flat heads of the dorado just skim the surface, creating razor-sharp wakes like fingernails zigzagging over a wet canvas. This show creates for us a dreamy reverie that is, unfortunately, routinely shattered by the thrumming propellers of dozens of small menacing planes circling overhead.

A steady rotation of Piper Cubs buzzes our ship day and night. We are sailing through territory notorious for the trafficking of illegal substances. Drug runners, pirates, and *policía* are each in turn keeping a close eye on us. Many a vessel has come to a bad end in these waters, and, needless to say, the *Sofia* doesn't want to be here any more than she is wanted here. But we are sailing as fast as we can, and although that's not always saying much, in this instance we do have a fair bit of breeze to scoot us along. Juni Baby can push us at only five to six knots, max, but we take some deluded consolation in having ample fuel with which to run, if we need to. We do not discuss where in hell we think we'll go or what we'll do once we get there. We are in one of the unavoidable badlands of the cruising world, where no scenario short of getting through and getting out is promising. So on we sail, maintaining a twenty-four-hour watch and spending as much time observing our peaceful dorado entourage as paranoia will allow.

Finally making the Gulf of San Blas is a gigantic relief. Nothing could be further from the filth, poverty, and corruption of the South American coastal communities than the serene, primitive villages of the ancient Cuna Indians, long the sole residents of these islands. The Gulf of San Blas lies just beyond the Archipiélago de las Mulatas, a string of small islands off the spit of Panamanian coastline that extends northeast of the canal. To maneuver the *Sofia* in these waters is hazardous. There are abrupt shallows and jutting reefs everywhere, so we adopt a very conservative method of piloting our great hulking mass of a ship through the area.

When Evan is at the helm, he stations a crew member—some mindless lackey who can be trusted to respond without question to his command—at the prop pitch and throttle below in the chart room. The helm—wheel and compass—are mounted on deck. The engine controls are steps and leaps below. Their operator is blind to the deck, the sails, and the sea, deaf to all but the orders from the helm. I prefer this post to any other while conducting these dangerous maneuvers. Mindless? Perhaps. But I am confident that I can carry out my duties here with total reliability and accuracy, and this, aboard a ship like the *Sofia,* affords me an uncommon period of calm. I take these where I can get them. They help to keep afloat my own sometimes flagging self-esteem.

The crew member who for all practical purposes carries the weightiest liability while weaving a ship through this deadly maze is the con. *Con* is a seaman's term for lookout, or the person who guides the ship by sight. Quite logically, "to take the con" also means to take navigational control of a vessel. And so, poised as high as a body can balance, aloft on the upper topsail yard, astraddle the topmast, wearing a pair of shocking yellow Polaroids, stands our mighty con, Norman. Norman probably has as much sailing experience as Evan and even more time on board the *Sofia;* he is one of the original Sofians, a veteran of her first circumnavigation and maybe even was around at the time of her inception and rebirth as a sailing cooperative. He and Evan, however, mix like diesel oil and saltwater. From the first day that I boarded the *Sofia* back in Boston, productive dialogue between these two men has been nonexistent. And now that Evan has assumed command, when conversation does occur, the animosity is so thick you can cut it with a dull boatswain's knife.

While piloting the ship with a con, the "conversation" consists of sharp, directive gestures like those made by the guys who stand on landing strips motioning planes into position. Our con, by dint of the garish Polaroids, is able to see beneath the reflective surface of the water and detect the forbidding discoloration of breakers and eddies that signal shallows, sandbars, coral shelves, or reef—with any luck before the *Sofia* lands upon them. In addition to these gestures, Norman shouts down to a deckhand—who relays the information to Evan—the degrees to bear astern, ahead, to port, or starboard. If the lookout should see an obstruction dead ahead, for instance, the directive travels from the con to the deckhand to the helm and reaches me at the throttle, sounding like a crisp, "Full astern!" This command jets through my ears to my brain, down my spinal cord, out my taut arms, and on into my ready hands as I yank the lever back, hard. Although I'm certain I appear cool and robotic, my voice might give me away as I mutter, "Oh . . . shit. Oh shit. Ohhh shit!"

Everyone is well aware that Evan and Norman are fiercely distrusting of one another. So the job at hand is bound to be compromised sooner or later. We are all praying for later, but frustrations are mounting. Nerves are fraying. Voices are squeaking. Before disaster strikes, the two men have the good sense to dissolve their flawed partnership, and we, the nervous observing crew, all heave a giant sigh of relief—that is, until the *new* con is appointed. I am relieved of my comfortable position below and ordered to take Norman's spot. Like the mindless lackey that I am, I find myself ascending the ratlines, clammy plastic Polaroids clutched in my sweaty palm. I am scared, even before I get a good look at where we are. As I climb, my mantra begins to bubble out. "Oh . . . shit, oh shit, ohhh shit!" When I stick the glasses—too big, too greasy, too revealing—on my face, I can't see anything but reef and shallows—to port, to starboard, ahead, astern! What the hell are we doing here? "Ohhhh shit!"

We inch the *Sofia* along, me conning, Packy relaying, Evan steering. Mother Boats is at the throttle. Karen and Christy are standing ready to set backing headsails, if necessary. Dan, the Kid, is just standing there. Norman is on the foredeck, tossing the lead over and over as we creep along. This is an obsessive-compulsive behavior when performed correctly, and Norman is perfectly suited for it. Lead lines are the traditional means of determining the depth of the water. They've now been made virtually obsolete by electronic depth sounders, but the *Sofia* still relies solely on this ancient tool. The lead (pronounced like the element) is a rope with a large lead weight tied to the end and various markings along its length. The water's depth is ascertained by dropping the weight over the side and reading off the mark on the line to which the water rises, just like they did on the old river boats where Samuel Clemens got his pen name. The *Sofia's* lead line is a coil of about twenty-five fathoms, or 150 feet. Traversing the Gulf of San Blas, we are marking at between two and three fathoms— twelve to eighteen feet. The *Sofia* draws nine feet at bow and stern (*draw* refers to how deep a vessel's keel floats beneath the surface). In the Gulf of San Blas we are clearing mere inches beneath our keel. But our charts for this area are current and accurate, and they tell us that the *Sofia* can cruise these waters—very, very carefully.

We make it, and it is well worth the risk. This is not a place that I would want to miss. We enter the Gulf of San Blas at Porvenir and then settle in a clump of tiny islands known as the Carti Group. The surface area of the islands is almost entirely at sea level; from sea the only visible sign of land is palm fronds. As we approach to within a few hundred yards, through the mist we can make out the husky thatched roofs of a sprinkling of huts and the thin gray smoke trails from their flues. This entire group of islands has a pale, washed-out appearance. Shallow ponds in soft greens and powder blues encircle the taupe-colored beaches that fringe drab, grass-clotted patches of earth. On these mounds are the homes of the Cuna Indians, each identical to its neighboring hut, all with parched stalks supporting the dried palm-frond thatching of the roofs. The walls are open air. The floors are sand. The air hisses as a breeze reverberates through the withered landscape, creating an incessant hum of pure white noise.

Standing in bold contrast to this monochromatic environment are the Cuna people themselves. Their flesh is a sun-soaked, rich sienna. Their hair, inky, glossy black like polished glass, is thick and luxuriant. The women and adolescent girls all wear large gold rings looped through their noses and earlobes. Many women also paint their faces, sketching a long black line from their hairline to the tip of their nose, giving their nose a longer and, in their estimation, more aristocratic appearance. Tribal law has always prohibited intermarriage with white people, so the Indians' genealogy has remained nearly pure. They do, however, have the bizarre distinction of possessing the highest proportion of albino births in the world. This strange anomaly has long given rise to the myth that a secret tribe of "white Indians" exists somewhere in the jungles of Panama.

The unusual clothing of the Cunas is what catches the eye of any visitor and dots these islands with their rare, vibrant, primary colors. *Molas* are the decorative additions to the blouse of the Cuna Indian. They are made from great swatches of vividly colored cloth that is cut and then hand-stitched in progressive layers to form an intricately pieced-together mosaic. The more primitive and rudimentary of these designs are composed of an assemblage of geometric shapes tossed on the material in random profusion. Many *molas* also depict scenes from the Cunas' natural environment, concentrating on tropical birds, fish, and flowers as well as some designs comprised of gay stick figures dancing amid an array of simple handmade musical instruments. In recent years, as Western culture has found its way to these remote villages, the diagrams have taken on oddly familiar themes: two figures boxing, wearing gigantic gloves bearing ridiculous ghoulish faces; a television set with horns for antennae and a ridiculous ghoulish face on the screen; a childlike adaptation of an automobile, with bare feet for wheels and ridiculous scary faces where the windows would normally be. I detect a pattern. Whenever we inquire about the meaning of the decoration, the Indians jab furious fingers at the cloth, whispering "Diablo, Diablo!" Apparently, the villagers stumble upon photographs in American magazines or glom onto the logos plastered on the t-shirts worn by the now more frequent visitors and then incorporate them in their art. The Indians, of course, have no idea what they are copying. But since it's unfamiliar, foreign, and consequently probably evil, it is given a frightening visage and labeled a devil.

The variety of motifs represented in the art form proves limitless. And the caliber of the craftsmanship is consistently excellent. Minute, hand-drawn stitches in clean cuts of layered material culminating in an exquisite creation of color, texture, and theme are the trademark of Cuna Indian women. From the dignified, matriarchal great-grandmothers down to the prepubescent girls, Cuna females sew *molas*. Swinging in hammocks, squatting around hearth fires, clustered in small bunches under the shade of palm trees, laughing and socializing, the ladies crank out a rapid succession of squares to be stitched up as everyday wear or sold as wall art. The Cunas have not ignored the market potential of their labors. No sooner has the *Sofia* set her hook amid the reefs in the lee of the Carti Group than troops of natives descend upon us. They paddle out en masse in their handsome, hand-carved dugouts, called *kyukas*. Without waiting for an invitation, the Indians come alongside, toss up great bundles of cloth, and raise their arms to us, signaling that they are ready to be lifted on board. We toss our fenders—old tires wrapped in thick hemp—over the side to assist in the, thus far, comical onslaught of the Cunas upon our vessel. Balancing in their tippy canoes, they stretch their small frames the six long feet overhead to the cap rail and grasp at our extended, slippery arms and hands. Their bare, wet toes skid down the *Sofia's* slick topsides as they try to run up the hull. As many as not end up in the water, splashing around and giggling until it is their turn to try again.

Soon the entire surface area of the *Sofia's* decks and coach roofs is a veritable carpet of *molas*. The crew peruses, stooped over, moving from one square to the next. As we busy ourselves with the shopping, the women and children make themselves right at home. With unbridled curiosity they peek and poke into every mysterious nook and cranny of our floating community. Conspicuously absent from the entourage, however, are Cuna men. We soon learn that the women run the show in these islands. They are the dignitaries, the business handlers, the decision makers, and the order givers. The men of the villages have all left at dawn, as is their routine each day, to paddle up the rivers and veinlike tributaries deep into the Panamanian mainland. Here they farm their family's rice fields, harvest the ripe mangoes, bananas, and coconuts from their fruit tree groves, and haul home drinking water from the freshwater pools. Some Cuna men spend their days searching the fertile reefs for fish, but this task usually falls to the younger boys of the tribe. I have witnessed this exercise often and observe as much care-free swimming and playing as actual serious fishing. Given the opportunity, it seems boys will be boys wherever one travels. The Cunas are a self-sufficient people with a simple lifestyle, so they can afford to invest ample energy in just having fun. Laughing, in particular, might be a national pastime.

A rumor that filtered down to us while the *Sofia* was still in Boston has proved to be true here. We were advised to stock up on five- and ten-gallon plastic buckets to use as trade goods. I didn't really grasp the logic of this at the time, but as I was employed at that nearby bulk foods co-op in Copley Square while the ship was readying for sea, the buckets were easy for me to amass. The several dozen that I've managed to store on board end up being the one item that pushes the Cunas' bargaining button. I find that they are eager to trade me one *mola* per gallon—five *molas* for a five-gallon bucket and ten for the larger ones. The climate in the islands is dry, and the natural water sources are either salty or brackish. Other than that which they can haul from the mainland and ration, the Indians' drinking water is rainwater, which they have to catch and store. Squalls pass through often but quickly, so it is imperative to gather as much of the runoff as possible from each short downpour. When we venture ashore, we are delighted to recognize our buckets scattered everywhere throughout the villages, placed at each corner of the thatched huts, positioned for optimum drip potential. In a storm the villagers form bucket brigades and pass filled containers along to be dumped and held in fifty-five-gallon drums, then back again, ready to catch the next cloudburst. It is much like our procedure aboard ship. Our coach roofs and rain tarps are designed with a camber, or slope from the center, to a spout fitted into the side, which we rely on to catch rain to replenish our perpetually diminishing freshwater stores. In these tiny islands, as aboard a circumnavigating tall ship, great effort and enterprise go into obtaining and preserving scarce commodities—in the case of drinking water, a survival necessity.

Each small island group in the Gulf of San Blas has its own particular charm. Porvenir, where we enter, is the main stepping-off point. Customs, immigration, and a couple of rustic hotels are located in town. From
Porvenir you can catch a prop plane to Panama City for just $11. (Ronda
just boarded one, bidding farewell to the *Sofia* and beginning her long journey home.) Also, it's the one spot in these solitary islands where one might
happen upon another yacht. Here we meet Gary and Taffy, out of Texas
aboard their sloop the *Stormcloud*. And what a lucky find they chance to be
for the *Sofia*, even saving our bacon on one fateful dawn.

Our first morning after clearing customs finds the *Sofia*'s crew standing
an attentive twenty-four-hour anchor watch. I have the 3 to 6 A.M. shift
and spend most of it stretching my bare foot along a length of taut anchor
chain. The slightest vibration will signal movement of the anchor against
the bottom—urgent danger. The hook is meant to set, grab, and hold, and
during my watch I am convinced that it has done this. I back up my hunch
by taking regular cross bearings, the technique of sighting one's vessel
between two separate stationary objects ashore, in order to determine that
the ship is holding her position. Eyeballing each object in relation to myself
by placing a knife's edge in front of my nose and pinpointing the spot I
need to focus on directly behind each object is a safe way of detecting any
change in our position. So far, we are good. I retire at 6 A.M. and hand
over the duty. As I head below, I notice that other crew members are beginning to amble up on deck. The sun is just breaking the horizon when I
feel myself drift off to sleep, but I stir awake again as the "brrrr" of a
small outboard approaches the hull.

"Ahoy, the *Sofia*! You're dragging toward the reef!" hails Gary from the
Stormcloud's tender. Not a bloody budge all night! But with dawn comes
the wind, so soft and slithery that none of the sleepy crew on deck notice
that the *Sofia* has begun to inch astern. The ship immediately springs to
life. Taking a quick body count, we realize we have a total crew
complement of five: Evan, Norman, Christy, Karen, and me. Boats, Packy,
and the Kid rushed ashore the evening before to gorge on steaks and beer
and crashed for the night in the hammocks of the local pub on the beach.
It is looking pretty grisly for the few of us on board. We have no time
or room to pay out more cable in the hope that the anchor will regrab.
Another couple of fathoms (twelve feet) of scope will lay us squarely atop
the jagged shelf of coral directly off our transom. I dive into the engine
room to find Norman already there, lighting the flares. While he and I
race through Juni's quick-start procedure, Evan, Karen, and Christy begin

to set headsails, sheet them full out, and hope to break our sternway. But we all know at this point that Juni Baby is our only real hope.

Now, among her many other less-than-endearing qualities, Juni possesses one particularly inopportune quirk in her mechanism. Her flywheel will often fly backward. When this occurs, we have to shut everything down and begin the whole routine over again, until the fuel is juiced precisely when her behemoth of a wheel is balancing at a forward-rocking thrust. Then we pump like crazed fools. This morning, in these most compromising of circumstances, Norman and I have to perform this operation an unprecedented four full times before Juni cooperates. All this while Karen and Christy set sails and Evan sprints between the foredeck and aft companionway, punching his head into the engine room, and announcing with cold insistence, "Four more feet to go, gang. Three feet now and closing."

Juni cranks over, and I dash up and shove the throttle to full ahead before Norman even has her on an even chug. Then we all tear over to the windlass and begin the enormous task of bringing in the anchor. Splitting up two to a handle, we muscle the wheel that turns the drum, which winds the cable, which hauls in the hook, which drags on the bottom, which holds the reef just inches off the tender hindquarters of the ship that we built (rebuilt). We ride those long metal windlass arms like a makeshift teeter-totter, accelerating our rhythm to breakneck speed until the hook breaks the surface, freeing the *Sofia* to maneuver without risk of snagging and swinging into the teeth of yet another jagged, submerged coral head. Then, opting to cut our losses, we make a hasty retreat, motoring clean out of the cove in search of a more relaxing anchorage. En route we collect our boys—Mama, Packy, and the Kid—who have been shaken from their hammocked hangovers and ferried out to us by Gary and Taffy. Since the *Sofia* is underway anyhow, we shrug and decide, "Well, hell, let's make for the Cartis." As our rescuers prepare to take their leave, we blubber effusive thanks while trying to give them a couple bottles of rum. They adamantly refuse the grog, vowing rather to come back on board and drink them with us when the *Sofia* returns to Porvenir to clear customs before leaving the Mulatas.

A close call. It is not yet 9 A.M. and we have already saved the ship once this morning. The five of us are exhausted, but we feel splendid. Our bleary-eyed beach bums, on the other hand, are sorely compromised and useless for the remainder of the sail to the Carti Group but no matter. We don't need them. We can handle the *Sofia*. Haven't we just? We allow ourselves an extra measure of swagger on this day.

This morning, as we study the *molas* displayed on deck, the Cunas are distracted, alternately amused and terrified by the Varmit's antics. Today the Indians have made the grave error of bringing a pet parrot on board. Varmit takes no time hunting it down and attacking it, He's not as quick or as sure as he once was, and I am able to chase him off the loudly protesting fowl with a broom. The Indians are howling with laughter and scrambling up the ratlines like monkeys, thinking they'll be safe there. Hah! Our amazing Varmit surprises the gang by scampering right up after them and chomping down on several bare Cuna ankles before we can wrestle him away.

The natives are afraid of our critter, but they cannot resist following him about, and he seems to enjoy the attention. He pokes his long proboscis into everything, struts around hissing and squeaking, and accomplishes great macho aerial feats that appear to be purely for the entertainment of an audience that he can still both thrill and intimidate.

Our Varmit has come almost full circle now. When we reach Costa Rica he will be home, returning as a circumnavigating, salty old man to the same jungle he left seven years ago as a pup. If Barney, our resident artist and fervent Varmit devotee, were on board now, I imagine he would fashion a comic strip to commemorate the event, depicting a homecoming parade complete with brass band, ticker tape, and an adoring nubile coatimundi fan club. As I write, sitting here thinking of this and smiling, the Cuna women have gathered around me. They have turned their attention away from the Varmit and are oohing and aahing at my stationery. Its logo is the word *Sofia* with the S formed by two intersecting fish. I offer them a sheet, imagining myself returning here someday to find *molas* bearing the *Sofia* insignia—complete with ghoulish faces, of course.

I love looking at the Cunas. They are so pleasing to the eye; petite—most shorter than my lofty five-one frame—compact, and a warm blend of bold hues. The people are quite beautiful. The flamboyant dress of the women—batik wraparound skirts; colorful head scarves; shell, gold, or silver arm and leg bangles—complement the centerpiece of *mola* blouse worn by every adult Cuna woman. But their heavy gold nose rings and earrings are the pièces de résistance. When a Cuna girl begins menstruation, she is welcomed into the ranks of womanhood with ancient Indian ceremonial rites and rituals. Her hair is cropped into a short bowl cut, and her nose and ears are pierced with large gold loops. She is also allowed to wear face paint and to sketch that curious black mark along the bridge of her nose. The young women are very striking. Brilliant white teeth flash ready smiles from smooth, umber cheeks, which are often sculpted with deep, dark dimples. Their young eyes are soft and trusting, while the wizened eyes of the older women of the tribe twinkle with mischief through crinkly, timeworn laugh wrinkles. The men, as befits their stature in the community, are rather nondescript, often wearing a conglomeration of recycled American-type clothing—shorts, t-shirts, and the like. The teenage boys of the village, however, appear incongruous, bearing the telltale scars of Western influence. Many strut like urban adolescents. Their tank tops are emblazoned with the images of Bruce Lee or the Bionic Woman and on their feet are the laceless and pathetically inessential knockoffs of expensive brand-name sneakers. By all accounts, these boys have visited the city of Panama once too often. But, heck, how do you keep 'em down on the farm? This parental plight, I am learning, is universal.

The boys smoke the *dacca*, or *caya*, local euphemisms for marijuana, which exists in great abundance in this part of the world. Back in northern California, I remember hearing tales of the rare and much-coveted "Panama Red," a certain strain of marijuana known for its exemplary strength and purity. I guess I'm knee-deep in Panama Red country now and it's anything but rare. The Indian boys, however, have not yet acquired the hard-edged savvy of the street-smart city kid. Theirs is still a benign, mimicked act, bearing the underlying but still visible and shy naiveté of a life honed by generations of simple, honest pleasures.

A group of us row up the river to a semi-freshwater pool used for washing clothes. We accidentally stumble upon a funeral, which is in progress on the adjacent spit of land, which has been set aside as a cemetery. Embarrassed by and ashamed of our intrusion, we prepare to take our leave, but a very insistent local woman beckons for us to follow her. She leads us up the bank to the village's burial plots and ceremonial shelters. We proceed past the huts of several families in which tiny tufts of dried earth are mounded with what appear to be the belongings of the deceased. I notice that a few of the smaller hillocks are cluttered with children's toys. We are ushered to the hut where the funeral is taking place. Our guide is relentless; she seems to need us to participate. Urging us under the thatched roof, she pushes us toward a small hammock around which a half-dozen or so mourners are seated. There is a wee form in the hammock, wrapped in a white cloth decorated with gold and silver beads. I presume it is the body of a child but despite our persistent attendant, I respectfully refrain from going any closer. Cuna men and women with bowed, covered heads surround the body. The women wear their standard red scarfs, but the men have fashioned their head drapes from old towels and rags. They are all rocking, wailing, and chanting as the rest of the group stands behind them, slapping at the hammock with an assortment of cloths. Because of the Indians' obsession with the devil, I guess that this is a way of chasing out the evil spirits, but I'll never know for certain. I am an interloper. I want only to express my condolences in some way and leave. Not being able to converse in their language, I lay a hand softly on those nearest me and whisper "lo siento," the Spanish phrase for "I am sorry," and hope that they understand.

Shortly thereafter the *Sofia* moves on to the Holandas Cays, a more isolated island group that is virtually uninhabited because it is too far from the mainland for the Cunas to travel to tend their farms or collect freshwater. After not quite a year aboard the *Sofia*, it seems that I may finally have reached that dreamed-of, long-awaited, faraway, unpopulated, wild tropical paradise. The Cuna experience was an exceptional one and unique, but even it got old. The ever-presence of the villagers aboard ship began to grow oppressive. We couldn't, of course, deny them access without risking offending them. They did not refuse us entry into their village. In the Holandas, however, we are utterly free of visitors. These are a handful of small islands that offer bountiful diversions and a maze of reefs brimming with all manner of sea magic. Fan, stag, brain, and even the deadly fire coral abound in this group's pristine waters. We dive for conch and lobster in the deeper coves. On the shallower shelves we find live blue crabs, snappers, mollies, sea urchins, and a variety of shells housing sea clams and hermit crabs. Closer in toward shore, we can wade in the sea grass and flush baby rays out of the stalks, only to watch them flutter off lightly and settle again beneath a flurry of floury sand.

One of my greatest thrills occurs just moments after we anchor. Dropping the hook in a little less than four fathoms, Evan sends Dave over the side to check its lie. Dan and I grab masks and join him, just in time to catch him pointing excitedly at the bottom. Below him, a giant manta ray is idly feeding on the reef. Dave, an excellent free diver, doesn't hesitate for an instant. Down he swims. The water is so clear, warm, and still that as I scull a few feet below the surface, I can almost imagine that I am at home in my living room, watching a Jacques Cousteau documentary on television. Dave creeps up behind the ray and reaches out a tentative finger, touching its tail. The ray drifts away like a butterfly in slow motion as Dave follows in the fluid dance, stroke for graceful stroke. The manta ray is Dave's size, approximately six feet long, with an equivalent wing span.

They are a perfect match, lithe partners in a sea waltz. Swaying above, Dan and I follow the dance as they sashay across the ocean's floor. The elegant pair dip, swing, and twirl. The ray, capable of darting away in a flash, seems to sense that Dave is not a threat. The twosome are harmonious, whirling like mirrored images in a dream for just a moment, and then it is over. The ray vanishes without a trace or a ripple. I later dream that it is floating just beyond our range of visibility, stationary, calm, watching us for the remainder of our stay.

The islands themselves are a minijungle of coconut palms and mangrove swamps. Egrets, pipers, pelicans, killdeer, and enormous black crows swarm the skies overhead. Aggressive land crabs the size of house cats share the sandy beaches with fire ants. We even spot a boa constrictor, obscenely bloated from a recent meal. The reef sharks that frequent these waters curtail our otherwise care-free swimming excursions. Our young Dane has set himself one all-consuming goal since departing Denmark—he means to catch himself a shark. We on board all feel a little uneasy about this. The ocean is where we live now. It is also home to the shark, and he was here first. We just pray that the sharks will be gracious enough to allow us unharassed visitation. I reckon that if a shark doesn't bother us, we shouldn't be bothering the shark. This laissez-faire approach to life at sea seems auspicious at best. Quite simply, the sea in all her incumbent and embodied powers and prerogatives can have her way with us at will, so why test her?

But, then again, the *Sofia* is a cooperative. Our lifestyle does lend itself to personal caprice. Despite our counsel to the contrary, young Dan, the Kid, is allowed his individual expression in this regard. Each night while the *Sofia* swings serenely at anchor, Dan labors, setting his meticulous trap. He baits a hook the size of a man's open hand with the severed head of a large fresh fish. Then he lowers the hook over the side with a heavy nylon line that he has strung through the aftershrouds on the port quarter and then rigged to the ship's bell, which hangs from the davit above the *Sofia's* transom. As I've now moved up into the aft cabin, this entire apparatus is secured just outside the porthole to my new bunk.

It is nearly midnight at anchor in the Holandas Cays when I'm ripped from my sleep by the sound of thick nylon cord whizzing against rough, splintered wood. I leap from my bed and gain the deck before the bell even has a chance to toll. Norman is on anchor watch. Dan is asleep on deck—on shark watch, I guess. The three of us reach the cap rail simultaneously. Now the bell is clanging and donging up a storm. Evan and Dave also suddenly materialize. Norman grabs hold of the line, which is pulled taut astern. "Whoa, it's a big one!" he says as we all peer over the side, just in time to witness a ghostly gray shadow shoot by, inches beneath the surface. Norman, who is still holding the line, is spun 180 degrees on his heels and is now facing the bow. The nylon has cut clean into his leathery palms. We all scramble to help him tie the line off on a belay pin. After several hours of futile fighting, while the bell tolls an incessant death knell and I lie sleepless in my berth with useless pillows pressed against my ears, the great fish is dead of exhaustion. Dave and Dan gaff it and hang it by its tail over the side until morning.

At first light the boys are up examining their prize catch—a six-foot, one hundred plus–pound, mature black shark. Before filleting it, Dan wants a snapshot of his trophy. He uses every ounce of muscle in his slender frame to hoist the massive fish in his arms for a picture. He needn't have bothered with the camera, however, for he'll bear a memento of the shark he slayed for a long, long time to come. While Dan grips the once-mighty torso and poses for the photograph, the shark's razor-sharp skin, malevolent even in death, delivers the final blow. The Kid suffers deep lacerations on his chest, belly, arms, and hands. In the tropics wounds heal so slowly that scarring is a given. Dan will long remember this fish, all right. They try eating the meat—pretty gamy—and the jaw is extracted and rowed ashore. Dan buries it in the sand for the ants and crabs to pick clean. He plans to take it home and mount it on his bedroom wall.

The next day I escape to shore alone, find a secluded beach, and spend the entire day in total isolation. I need distance from my mates and the crazed hacking to bits of the shark. So I swim, read, dance, run, whoop, sleep, think pure and clear, feel free and light, make not one concession, do no cooperating. It is a therapeutic retreat, and I return to the *Sofia* with my spirit somewhat replenished.

A few days later Evan and Dave row the *Salty Dog* ashore to beach her and brush a coat of anti-fouling paint on her bottom, and they take Varmit along. Big mistake. "Varmit *never* leaves the ship!" He is allowed to sail the seas without having to submit to strict quarantine laws only because we are successful in convincing the immigration authorities of this. Well, in Evan and Dave's defense it didn't appear that anybody in the Holandas Cays would mind because it didn't appear that anybody was here.

Once on land Varmit is beside himself with feral excitement. He is a free coatimundi in his almost-natural habitat. He prods his nose into every one of the small island's orifices, chases frantic sand crabs, savagely attacks each fallen coconut, and just has himself an undomesticated heyday. When it is time to return to the *Sofia*, Evan and Dave discover that the Varmit is nowhere to be found. He has flown the coop. At dusk, after searching for hours and calling out his name (they must have been seriously desperate— Varmit never answers to his name), the guys return to the ship alone, and with agonized faces they give the rest of us the bad news. Mother Boats nearly has a coronary. We practically have to sedate him. He has a special affinity for the Varmit, and I believe it is reciprocated. Whenever our little furry mascot is missing, he'll often turn up somewhere in Mama's nesting area. I don't want to suggest that the Mama de Bateau is a slob, but Varmit feels right at home in his bunk. And, in truth, Varmit has evoked the blind rage of enough crew over the years that, were it not for Boats's protective devotion to the critter, I'm certain the Varm would have met a bad end long before now.

Suffice it to say, none of us sleeps very well. At dawn we are all ashore, perfuming the bushes, spraying deodorant on the trees, smearing the beach with toothpaste, and generally deploying all the catnip of a coatimundi but to no avail. We begin to fear that he may have come to harm at the hands of some neighboring Cuna hunting parties. One lone Indian in a *kyuka* paddled over to the *Sofia* the day before and informed us that our uninhabited little island getaway has been visited for four consecutive nights by a 350-pound *tortuga* (turtle) that is laying its annual load of eggs—hundreds of them. As these eggs supply a necessary supplement to the Cuna diet, to say nothing of the protein value of a few hundred pounds of turtle meat to a single village, a small band of Indians had been dispatched to monitor the turtle's behavior. They don't want to risk disturbing her routine before her final laying, but at the same time they want to be ready to capture her as soon as she is through. Knowing the Varmit's weakness for eggs and his uncanny ability to ferret them out of anywhere, we reckon he may already be simmering in the Indian patrol's stewpot. But it would appear that the Varmit has the luck of a sailor too. He emerges from the jungle late on the second day, just as we are resigned to returning without him. Our Varmit staggers out of the brush—bedraggled, hungry, thirsty, frantic, pitiful, and very glad to be leaving the wilds and heading home to the relative sanctuary of the *Sofia*.

Our lads, Dave and Dan, are fully using these lovely, uncultivated islands. They venture off each dawn to explore every reef, cove, and lagoon, returning at dark with lobster, crab, conch, or some variety of reef fish. Both boys are utterly happy and at ease. It is great sport for them and good eating for the crew. But, once again, the *Sofia* must move on.

Upon returning to Porvenir to clear customs before saying our sad fare-wells to these captivating islands and setting sail for the Panama Canal, we chance upon a fascinating group of people. On assignment for the Smithsonian Institution, these gifted scientists are studying the unusual reef formations specific to the Mulatas and the subsequent rare marine life that thrives within these islands. With them is a young woman from the University of California, Berkeley, who has lived among the Cunas for a full year. Although she came to study the Indian music, she has become a veritable wealth of information on the most intimate aspects of the Indians' lives. Over an infamous *Sofia* supper we are made privy to the exotic and more obscure details of the Cunas' culture and history and the vicissitudes of their familial, social, and political structure. I feel fortunate to have lucked upon people who can provide so edifying a finale to what has already been an intensely rich visual, physical, and emotional experience.

The Mulatas are the sweet, bright cherry atop the sometimes melted sundae that is my *Sofia* experience thus far. It serves as a fitting capstone to our nearly yearlong Caribbean interlude.

Molas, the Cuna Indian artwork, spread across *Sofia's* decks. San Blas Islands.

chapter 5

Great Escapes

The Trip Overland through Mexico and Central America

Since four of you are making the trip from California to Costa Rica, why
not drive? It will be less expensive and much more interesting.

—BERNARD SISMAN, M.D., MY FATHER

INTRODUCTION

I flew home from Panama, taking advantage of my proximity to family
and one last stab at earning U.S. dollars before cutting loose from the
Americas. For cruisers, crossing the Pacific represents establishing true
autonomy. The symbolic umbilical cord that attaches us to secure lives,
loving families, and valued careers is effectively severed by vast open ocean,
whereas coastal navigation, no matter for how long, still allows a sailor the
comfort of knowing that it is quite feasible to make landfall and simply
board a cheap bus, train, or plane for home. Even the ever-popular cruising
waters off the coast of Mexico and in the Caribbean afford a cruiser this
reassuring commuter quality, which may explain why these harbors are full-
to-busting with now sedentary yachts that were once readied for great
ocean passages. Making an actual "crossing," however, is making a commitment to be gone—very far away and for a very long time.

I had made this commitment, so I wanted to touch a close, safe, familiar base once more before sailing off. After about a month in the States,
I was ready to rejoin my ship. My old crewmate Barney was also planning
to rejoin the *Sofia* at this juncture. We were contacted by a young German
sailor traveling in United States and a brand new recruit, both of whom
were hoping to join the *Sofia* for the South Pacific run. It was at this point
that my father innocently suggested that we four make the trip together.
We naively jumped at the prospect.

❧

JOURNAL ENTRY
Golfito
Golfo Dulce
Costa Rica

Reconnoitering at Barney's house in Bakersfield, California, we plan our trip overland through Mexico and Central America. Our chariot is an old reconverted Volkswagen station wagon. The *Sofia* is waiting for us in the Golfo Dulce at Golfito, Costa Rica. We reckon we four will complete an interesting, inexpensive, and pleasant jaunt in a little more than a week. It turns out to be ten days. Interesting? Oh, yes. Inexpensive? Sure. Pleasant? Not even close. We should have taken a hint from our hellish twenty-four hours of staggering around Mexico City, trying to procure visas from the Central American embassies.

For a whopping $450 Barney purchases the automobile that is destined to transport us south through six separate countries. He then invests a significant amount of time and energy lying on his back beneath this vehicle, tweaking, fine-tuning, jury-rigging, and otherwise making it fit for travel. Oliver the German, Mikey the new guy, and I each kick in $150 to square the deal. Unbeknown to us (he insists to this day that the secrecy was for our own protection), old Barn is also doing a little extra diddling on the car, strictly in the interest of very private enterprise. He's already spent enough time cruising aboard the *Sofia* to have cultivated a pretty wizened scammer's eye, but all that we three anxious road-trippers see when we gaze at the automobile is a right nifty little hatchback into which we immediately proceed to pile an absurd amount of crap.

We contact the appropriate government agencies when we reach San Diego and request assistance in procuring visas for the Central American countries. They advise us that our best course of action will be to obtain the papers from their respective embassies once we arrive in Mexico City. We shrug agreeably, reckoning that these officials can certainly be trusted to know what they are talking about, and we prepare to head out. Barney, Mikey, and I are game, but Oliver seems ever-so-slightly reluctant to leave. It is clear that he is wary of cutting loose from the States without first having the necessary documents firmly in hand. Although only in his early twenties, Oliver is both an accomplished sailor and a veteran world traveler. He is also a paranoid foreigner. We Yanks, however, are easy. Heck, who are we to question the recommendation of our own local authorities?

This is their area of expertise, right? We three unite in an effort to cajole Oliver into going along with the plan so that we can leave.

Barney is still his pillowy, laid-back self, his grin and shrug tacitly reassuring. Mikey comes off as boisterous, obnoxious, and opinionated. I swear that I see Barney's hackles rise within minutes of meeting Mikey. Mike is flat out in favor of "gettin' the fuck goin'!" Me too, actually, as I am coming off a full month of peace, quiet, and complacency and am consequently in virtual adventure withdrawal. The accepted *Sofia* mode of travel has already been well integrated into my psyche—let go of schedules, forget guarantees and take care of business on the fly—so any tendency on my part to behave cautiously is long gone. We three Americans are hot-wired to hit the road. Soft-spoken, congenial, and truly very concerned, Oliver finally has no choice but to hop aboard and hope for the best. And so we are off. First stop: Mexico City. We cross the border into Mexico without incident.

Consulting our maps, we agree to take the quite civilized-sounding Pan American Highway down to the capital. From our topographical charts it appears to swirl like icing along the very tip of a range of high mountains that cut straight through the entire length of the country. In truth, it should never have been called a highway and doesn't nearly fit the description we Americans have come to rely on. Actually, it is a two-lane road, mostly paved, some dirt, lots of obstacles. It does reach an impressive elevation high up in the clouds, as a matter of fact. So we should anticipate some rain. But what we get is a monsoon.

Within a few short hours of our hitting the highway, we are slammed with a deluge so immense that mud slides start dribbling all up and down our already-marginal strip of asphalt. We are doing a decent job of skirting the minor slides when we come around one particularly severe switchback, where we can see that several hundred feet in front of us the oncoming traffic isn't moving. Barney quips sarcastically, "Hey, I guess that's where we're supposed to park," but he downshifts to a crawl and approaches the next turn with extreme caution. It is a darn good thing that we have been given this heads-up, because no sooner do we round the bend than we have to stomp on our brakes. Our tires skid on the wet scree, and the Volkswagen stutters to a stop within an inch of the rear bumper of a mammoth old green bus. Its front wheels are hovering and spinning in slow pointless rotations above an abyss several hundred feet deep. The road has disappeared. Gigantic boulders and great slabs of mud have come down the side of the cliff and obliterated the pavement. The bus apparently swerved to avoid the landslide and instead almost joined it on its rolling descent down the mountain. All the passengers have disembarked and are pressing against what is left of the bluff. They are clutching crying infants, squawking chickens, and an impressive array of frenzied livestock. Everyone is sweating profusely and genuflecting frantically.

We get out of our car and go over to survey the situation. Peering over the edge, we realize that they all almost bought it, all right. Across the crevasse we can see the folks on the other side, all of whom have abandoned their vehicles and are now standing there in the universal "What do we do now?" pose—shoulders raised, arms extended with palms up, eyebrows arched, jaws dropped. Mikey croaks, "Let's turn the car around!" Barney, Oliver, and I look at each other, look behind us, and emphatically shake our heads. No way can we retreat. It is still raining, hard. The baby slides that we traversed earlier by now probably are about the size of the behemoth we are facing. We know that behind us there is no more Pan American Highway. Way ahead however, at least as far as we can see, still lies relatively drivable road. So the four of us roll up our sleeves and our pants and begin shoveling mud and rocks over the side by the armload. Soon most of the bus's passengers, those who aren't busy herding the frightened children and animals, pitch in, while the folks across the way commence digging toward us.

It takes hours. The rain stops and the sun bursts through as a mixed blessing, hot, steamy, and glaring. Someone's transistor radio is whining out a manic stream of crackly mariachi music. The baby Jesus on the bus's dashboard is jiggling with each tremor. And we are slinging mud like we're steam shovels. It is dark by the time we finish clearing the road and heaving the bus back off the precipice. Drenched, mud-caked, sore, and happy, we set out again, picking our way around the subsequent mud slides and an alarming assortment of dead wildlife.

We make Mexico City in the middle of the night, and from what we can see it appears to be an impressive metropolis. The first order of business, however, is to find a cheap motel room, preferably one with a shower. Next we need to locate a garage. Our hearty little auto has taken some hard hits. So has Barney, who alone keeps squeezing under it to survey the damage. Barney will recover with a good rest. Our car absolutely will not. It is in desperate need of new shocks and requires a bona fide mechanic with a proper lift. Drained, we pull into the first joint we come to, and all agree that the car repairs will just have to wait until morning.

Morning comes, all right—like gangbusters. I'd heard that Mexico has lax noise and air pollution control standards, but I had no idea what effect this would have on a city the size and population density of Mexico's capital. I don't know if it is the roar of a thousand unmuffled engines or the wafting blanket of toxic fumes that wakes me first. I do know that well before I even open my eyes, a migraine of some note already has a lock on my skull. Once we are out on the street, it just gets worse—and worse. None of us speaks much Spanish, and what we do know we have to bellow out at the top of our strangled lungs. It is almost impossible to be heard over the unearthly screaming of the trucks and buses that are careening about the city like a pack of wild, crazed monsters, spewing a dusting of orangish-black exhaust that is so thick that it practically has to be chewed. We stumble erratically from curb to curb, desperate to avoid being run over. It is crystal clear that pedestrians do not have the right-of-way, nor does anyone else, for that matter. Each intersection resembles a kind of first-come, first-served operation that disintegrates into something on the insane order of speed-up-and-cut-off-first come. We just vault out of the way.

Our motel is only a block or two from a garage where we are told flatly that our vehicle is irreparable. The mechanic just happens to be of German descent, however, so Oliver is able to urge him into at least trying. The head honcho insists that we unload "all that sheet" first. We unlash our dozens of bags and pile them in a heap in a greasy corner of the garage. Then we bound off to get our visas. We are on foot, leaping for our lives, speaking *un pequeño Español*, and not in possession of a clue to where we are heading.

We eventually are advised that we'll have to report to each country's embassy in order to be granted its visa. "OK," we shrug, still ridiculously optimistic. "Just point us in the direction of the government buildings and we'll take it from there!" "Buildings? There are no buildings," our informant snickers. In fact, were we the least bit inclined to be deflated, we'd have gotten a clue when we couldn't get a single citizen to commit to providing us with one bit of usable information that might lead us to the agents of any of the Central American nations. One brave soul finally offers a nervous hunch as to where the Costa Rican embassy might be located, and from here things do become a touch clearer. While preparing our papers, the genteel Costa Rican officer warns us of rumblings of growing civil unrest down south. Consequently, the embassies in Mexico have to keep moving their locations "just in case," he advises. Should political dissidents be looking for them, the officials don't want to be too easy to locate. Well, I can personally attest to their success in this regard. The Nicaraguan embassy alone claims four separate addresses, and we hit each one before we are able to track these officials down in the back room of a little storefront way off the beaten path. The agents apologize for the inconvenience, explaining that rumors of revolution in their country warrant their exercising an extra measure of discretion. "Don chew know what is going on down dere?" they warn. No, we don. But we should.

It takes us a full twenty-four hours to get our visas and our vehicle in order, at the conclusion of which I am certain that I have grown a brain tumor the size and color of a ripe mango. We are not the least bit sorry to be getting out of town.

It is dark by the time we reach the border between Mexico and Guatemala. We didn't plan it this way. We are unexpectedly detained at a "checkpoint," which is identified as such solely by the presence of an army truck and a couple of armed soldiers blocking the road. It is raining for a change—pouring, in fact—when we arrive at the checkpoint. Despite the weather, the guards order us to unpack every single bag and bundle in and on our car—in the dark, in the rain, in the mud. We comply and the soldiers rummage through each bit of it until they are confident that everything is drenched. Then they demand that we load up and move on. "Oh, man," squeaks a bedraggled Barney. "Well, at least we have that out of the way," he sighs as he puts one final lashing on our oozing mound of stuff. We had started out of Bakersfield looking pretty sharp, tight, and aerodynamic, but I have to admit that our little bus is rapidly beginning to resemble a half-dead camel, all lumpy, soggy, and listing way to one side.

We trundle on down to the border, and it is of course closed. "Maybe these guys keep bankers' hours?" Oliver offers with hope. So we do an about-face and head back north to find another cheap motel so that we can get out of the rain. But first we have to again pass through that checkpoint. And the guard has changed. We are told by the new patrol on duty to unload everything all over again, in the dark, in the rain, in the mud.

Now, our Barney is generally a fairly mellow fellow, but this is preposterous, and he just ain't havin' it. So he proceeds to throw this really interesting tantrum. I guess between the rain, the landslides, the phantom embassies, and especially the endless car repairs, he just can't take any more. Barney alone has kept the Volkswagen running, and his efforts are Herculean. Nonetheless, it continues to break down, and I'll admit that some of us aren't handling it very well. I myself might occasionally be heard to scold, "Now, Barney, didn't you just fix that?" Mikey, though, will regularly berate him by saying, "Do you even know what the fuck you're doing?" (Mikey, of course, knows nothing.) Or, "*How* much did we pay for this piece of shit?" Only Oliver keeps quiet and tries to help, but it has been Barney's cross to bear up until now.

So we're at this checkpoint, for the second time, and Barney starts throwing this really fascinating fit, bouncing up and down, twitching around, and making all these wet, spitty, wheezy noises. Actually, he isn't very well equipped to intimidate convincingly, not with his laughing eyes, Bakersfield drawl, and sardonic grin. But he manages to make us just uncomfortable enough that we don't dare whine or resist. We simply unload, load up, and whisk our riled little buddy off to any roadside dive we can find; we are convinced this is decidedly better than any jail in Mexico.

The next morning the sun is out and again we approach the checkpoint, this time with renewed spirits and, more important, with a fat stack of Barney's *Playboy* magazines. And this time we are ushered right on through. When we reach the border, however, we are surprised to find that it is still closed, and no one feels the least bit obliged to explain why. After persistent pleas in deplorable Spanish, our inquiries are answered by a guard who happens to notice our Bakersfield license plate frame. "Bakersfield," he exclaims, "I know Bakersfield! I was once involved in a migrant worker exchange program there." He is bragging in near-perfect English, by the way. Then he proceeds to inform us that this particular border crossing will be closed for three days or a week, maybe longer. He suggests an alternate point at which we can cross, but it is accessible only by the dirt roads and mountains we've just come through and barely survived. But we have no other option.

More mud. More rain. More landslides. More washouts. By the time we do reach a viable point of departure from Mexico, our poor little hatchback has forded so many creeks and ponds that we've begun to think of it as an all-terrain vehicle. The flooded areas are so murky that we never know how deep each body of water will be. We boldly charge ahead anyway, reckoning that we'll either sink, float, or raft on through. We do a fair amount of each, keep on truckin', and make it. Of course by now it is dark. The guard at this border stop doesn't even bother to make us unpack. He just jabs his arm into the cab of the car, begins clawing around on the floorboards, and emerges with a fistful of the substantial amount of mud chunks we've accumulated en route.

"Hashish!" he accuses with slobbering melodrama.

"Mud!" we counter levelly and wait for the next round.

Truthfully, the guard doesn't even take himself seriously. He proceeds to make a theatrical, cursory tour of our vehicle, never even bothering to check the trunk because he doesn't seem to know that it's located in the front on a Volkswagen. Then he smirks in a pompous, princely manner and directs us to move along. We do not need to be asked twice. We are positively ecstatic to be leaving Mexico.

From here we drive straight through to Guatemala City, where we stop and spend the remainder of the night. We want to visit a marketplace we've heard wondrous tales about. Situated high in the mountains, it is run by a tribe of local Indians who are known for crafting exquisite, ethnic art pieces. We are not disappointed. By dawn, all across the broad open mesa, a blanket of multicolored rugs is strewn with the natives' handiwork, unique, rough-hewn, and full of mystery. Dreamy flute music lilts on the warm breeze, and native children flit about everywhere, all holding what at first appear to be small kites. Upon closer examination I am delighted to discover that the kites aren't kites at all but lengths of string fastened around the large, incandescent, green bodies of strange bugs the size of hummingbirds. Their black wings flutter effortlessly as they dive and spin through the air, high above the gleeful youths' outstretched hands. These are pets to the Guatemalan children, and this is how they "walk" them.

Guatemala is charming, but vague ripples of unrest do filter into our awareness during our short tour of the country. We are advised of recent conflict between the leftist and rightist factions. The remaining tension is still very much in evidence while we are there. However, it is nothing compared to what we are about to find in the neighboring Central American nations. It would be easy to avoid El Salvador altogether, if we knew that perhaps it should be avoided, but, alas, we don't. Besides, we have worked darn hard for our visas, and we do not care to skip an entire country for no apparent reason.

After shopping at the Guatemalan marketplace and stocking up on a ton of trade goods and souvenirs, we again get a later-than-planned start and again reach the border at dark. This is becoming our modus operandi, and although not advisable, it certainly contributes to the intrigue of these questionable tourist stops. Darkness makes everything more eerie, more uncertain. Darkness is like having two strikes against you. We pull up to the border with El Salvador in deep darkness.

The checkpoint is again identifiable only by the presence of two heavily armed guards. One motions with his enormous weapon for Barney and me to enter the dilapidated one-room shack, which we hope serves as the official headquarters. I am stuck to Barney like Velcro as he way-too-confidently saunters on through the squeaky screen door that hangs lopsided on a single rusty hinge. The instant we are inside Barney stops and lets out a long, low "Oooooh, maaaaan . . ." A dim, bare bulb is suspended over a filthy card table and two rickety wooden chairs. A solitary fly buzzes incessantly in jerky circles around the opaque light. We are directed by rifle muzzle to sit. It is all like a scene out of a bad "B" movie. None of the guards has yet uttered a sound. A soldier shoves papers toward us and raps a grimy finger on them. Barney hunches over and gapes at the forms. He looks really tense, like he is taking a college final for a class he's neglected to ever attend. I just sit there, trying to smile and make friendly eye contact. I heard somewhere that making friendly eye contact can be useful in humanizing a bad situation.

Oliver and Mikey are forced to stay with the car, which we naturally assume is being ransacked by the guard who's remained outside. Then, without warning, Mikey bursts through the door, all clumsy and fumbling, clutching his wallet in one hand and waving a twenty-dollar bill in the other. He yelps in a shrill, jarring bark, "Hey, where can I change this for, uh, what do you guys use down here?"

The guard who escorted us in and has since been standing silently with his weapon at the ready, whips out an arm and snatches the bill clean out of Mikey's fingers, almost before he completes his asinine query. Barney and I just gawk, not daring to even breathe. "Tweenty dollar to cross deese border at night, gringo," the guard growls. Barney pounces out of his seat and scribbles something on the paperwork. He and I then shuffle double time sideways out that squeaky door to our car and to Oliver. They have both been left amazingly intact. Mikey stomps out scowling with his fists crammed into his pockets. We pile in and speed off just as fast as our beat-up old chariot will carry us. Once on the road again our group roundly congratulates Mikey for his ingenuous intervention. Mikey responds by grumbling fussily, "What are you jerks blabbering about? I still got no El Salvadoran money and that bum took *my whole twenty!*" Mikey is clueless. We've warned him repeatedly about flashing his cash around the questionable agents of these questionable governments, but he doesn't learn. Like fools, we assume that he engineered the perfect bribe. He reckons we just stuck him with the check. All in all, we consider ourselves absurdly lucky, and we even lay off lecturing Mikey about his bourgeois behavior—for a little while.

By chance, Oliver is driving the night that we are passing through El Salvador. Mikey and I are asleep in the back. Barney is dozing at shotgun. When Oliver slows down and creaks the car to a stop, we rouse drowsily and gaze around us. We can barely make out the dull outlines of what appear to be deserted buildings and abandoned houses lining the narrow street. Then I see Barney shoot bolt upright, and I lunge forward to see what's caused him to react so violently. A deep, rough trench has been dug straight across the road just ahead of us. It is instantly apparent that we have driven smack dab into some kind of ambush. Oliver is perching in his seat, craning his long neck over the wheel with this sort of furrowed-brow, quizzical look on his face when Barney begins shrieking, "Back up! Back up! Back up!" Startled, Oliver slumps down, throws the car into reverse, spins around, and races down a side road, where within seconds he is hitting the brakes to avoid barreling into yet another barricade. At this blockade bed frames and miscellaneous debris are piled in a heap on the road. Peering around us, we spot the crouched figures of men with guns running from doorway to doorway. "Back up! Back up! Back up!" we all begin screaming at Oliver. The next road he tries is also blocked. There is no way out. Barney moans in desperation, "I can see the headlines now: 'Gringo *Idiotas* Caught in Deadly Crossfire.'"

Then a gunman approaches the vehicle and demands . . . something. We either can't understand him or are too frightened to try. This fellow is wearing what looks like an officer's uniform. He has apparently re-quested the passport of our driver, as Oliver frantically trying to comply, inserts his papers in the tiny crack he's cranked in the window. "Ah, German," the gunman nods with approval. Then he motions for Oliver to roll the glass all the way down. The officer bends over and leans well into the car to get a good look at the rest of us. I am furiously making friendly eye contact while praying silently that Mikey "please, oh please, oh please" keeps quiet for once. No one, thank gawd, utters a word. Then the sol-dier hands Oliver back his passport, moves the barricade aside, and waves us on through. We guess that Germans must still be in good favor in many of the revolution-torn Latin American nations, whereas Americans, it is safe to assume, are not. We are mindful of putting Oliver in the driver's seat for each subsequent border crossing.

We reach the city of San Salvador sometime during that same night and have to stop there. We are out of gas and have a couple of flat tires to boot, so we pull off onto the side of the road and semi-doze in the car until dawn. When we awake, we are shocked to find that we are sitting squarely in the center of what has been the site of heavy fighting some-time in the very recent past. The buildings are all shot up, the streets are littered with the tossed and abandoned debris of domestic life, and the town is deserted. Horror-struck, we scrounge some dirty gas, somehow rig patches for our pathetic tires, and bounce and wheeze our way out of that country, pronto.

We make the border with Honduras after dark, for a change, and once again spend a restless night sleeping in the car. Crossing into Honduras is peaceful enough, but even here everyone seems skittish and ill at ease. Despite this ominous undertone, we do enjoy the beautiful countryside, and it does feel immeasurably safer than El Salvador. However, we still have Nicaragua to traverse, a realm that is so notorious for political upheaval that even we are aware of it. We are extremely anxious to put that country safely behind us.

While motoring along, we feel a sudden jolt. Barney looks back just in time to see a giant blast of black soot jet out of our exhaust pipe. Our car proceeds to idle weakly for a few seconds and then dies out altogether, right on the side of the road, smack in the thick of war-torn Central America. "Oh, jeez," moans Barney, his arms hanging limp at his sides, his head drooped and wagging in defeat. He already knows what the problem is. The car has swum through so much mud and water that the fuel injec-tors are clogged beyond hope. We are clean out of spare parts, are certain not to find any down here, and are consequently really, really good and stuck. Oliver, an infinitely patient fellow, intervenes at this point and insists that he can repair the injectors if given the chance. Barney shrugs, "Hey, why not? We got nothin' to lose—but time, everything we own, our lives . . . Oh jeez, oh jeez, oh jeez." So Oliver sets to soaking, clean-ing, drying, and greasing the mechanisms until he is confident that he has bought them as much borrowed time as they can possibly have. It does take the better part of a day, but the time cannot be considered "lost." In fact, it is quite well spent. Somewhere back up in the mountains in one of the rains, in one of the jungles, the boys had come upon a clear, sparkling waterfall that they were convinced was clean enough to drink from. Against my earnest admonitions, they proceeded to gulp the water down. Their intestinal quakes began within a few short hours, and the to-be-expected eruptions followed in a steady stream of urgent pit stops, which have found one or all the fellows squatting and groaning in the bushes ever since. We have been, in effect, living in our car and the atmosphere has gotten pretty darn unpleasant. This one long day of relative freedom to hunker down in the roadside foliage and evacuate at will has allowed the guys a blessed opportunity to clean out their sorry systems.

Oliver's efforts are nothing less than heroic, and the results are nothing short of miraculous. He gets the old VW humming like a charm, and off we go, making the Nicaraguan border at, guess when . . . dark! It looks deserted so we sleep in our car again, as has become our practice. We are awakened by the incongruous sounds of a bustling mercantile center. While we are napping, dozens of trucks, carts, and buses converge at the border, off-load their wares, and set up shop. This appears to be a daily occurrence. As we are sitting in our filthy little bug, all rumbled and road weary right in the middle of the marketplace, a young boy rides up on a Stingray bicycle, complete with banana seat and wheelie bar, and begins to spin lazy donuts in the dust with his tires. He can't be more than twelve or thirteen, but his outfit belies his presumed immaturity. He is dressed in full camouflage fatigues, and slung over his shoulder is an automatic rifle that is as tall as he is. We smile and he approaches us unafraid. He speaks English, which he has been studying in school, he states with obvious pride, and so we chat. As he balances on the driver's side door, leaning over and amusedly taking in the whole of our little hovel, he explains that all his relatives were killed in Managua during the revolution. The Sandinistas adopted him. He is now no longer in school but in the army, and he has the honor of being posted as a border guard. This all sounds pretty shocking to us, but what makes an even greater impression is how unabashedly happy this boy is. We soon find that this affect is representative of the Nicaraguan people at large, at least those in the majority, who find themselves on the winning side of the coup.

The ruling junta in Nicaragua had been headed by the former Communist leader Somoza until he fled the country this past July and was recently assassinated in exile. We are traveling through the country shortly after the revolution. The Sandinista National Liberation Front has taken over the land, and the people are rejoicing. We bid farewell to our young army escort, but as we pass through the checkpoint, we notice an entire phalanx of these adolescent, armed patrolmen standing at attention with their chests out, bursting with pride as though they'd just won the spelling bee or a foot race. I mean, these are *children*. One lad takes my passport, purposefully flips it to page one, and with a victorious flair stamps the Sandinista emblem squarely over the official seal of the United States. Looking at the page, I know I am holding a unique and historically notable piece of memorabilia.

Once across the border, our first mission is again to exchange some cash and get some gas. Each one of these tiny nations uses its own currency, a detail that makes for no shortage of confusion and inconvenience for us as we struggle to venture through them. We set our course for the first large city en route, a town by the name of Esteli. Esteli, unbeknown to us, served as a rebel stronghold and the site of intense fighting just weeks earlier. We are not prepared for what we find when we arrive there. The streets are destroyed, dug or blown up. Buses and trucks are flipped onto their sides helter-skelter and riddled with bullet holes. The remnants of buildings stand abandoned with mounds of shattered glass and crumbling stucco scattered about their periphery. It has been a battleground. Now it is a wasteland. We search everywhere for any sign of life. We finally locate a *banco* where we pound on the door until a frightened little man nudges it open a sliver and hisses, "No money aquí!"

"Wait," we beg, "where can we get money? We are desperate."

"Go see the denteest," he whispers and then slams the door in our faces. We hear several locks and deadbolts fall into place and then a heavy scraping noise that sounds like furniture being shoved up against the door.

Mikey spins and faces us, his eyes as wide as the bullet holes in the wall behind him, and stutters, "The dentist! Do you think it's some kind of code name?" I expect we all have the same flashing image of Lawrence Olivier, who played the sadistic dentist in *Marathon Man*, and none of us is eager to play Dustin Hoffman's part—that of the unwilling patient. But who knows? And so what? We are stuck in Esteli, Nicaragua, on our way to Golfito, Costa Rica, and we have absolutely no choice. So we go in search of "the denteest" and find him in, of all places, his office. It is nestled in a quiet little courtyard that was probably at one time filled with flowers, children, and music but is now deserted and silent. He changes our money all right and then tells us to beat it, directing us to the shortest route out of the immediate area. There are many locals, he confides, who have not been friends of the Sandinistas, and they are all now running for their lives. We follow suit, although throughout the remainder of our journey in this newly liberated country we continue to be struck by the immense joy evident in these now-free people and their unmistakable pride in their reborn nation.

When we emerge in Costa Rica, I feel like Dorothy breaking through a violent storm to land safely in the glittery calm of Munchkinland. Costa Rica is a historically peaceful country of gentle people free from war, fear, or even the need for an army. The landscape is an ecological dream, protected as a nature preserve. The rain forests ring out with the soprano songs of hundreds of species of exotic birds, while the jungles thunder with the lionlike roars of choruses of howler monkeys. We learn that the citizens of this pragmatic country are as well taken care of by their government as is the environment. There is very little unemployment and to help ensure that the men don't drink away their earnings—consequently becoming malnourished and falling ill—their government institutes the wise practice of *bocas*. *Bocas* is the free food—rice, beans, tortillas, or fried fish—that is provided with each *cerveza* (beer), rum, or *guaro*, (a cheap, transparent liquid of nearly pure alcohol) that is purchased. This is the Costa Rican version of happy hour.

Our long overland adventure—six countries in ten days—culminates in the outlying jungles of the village of Golfito, in the dark in, yup, the middle of the night. There are no actual roads leading to the quiet pond where the *Sofia* lies at anchor, and our deflated vehicle gets stuck fast as we try to cross the marsh. Accepting that our homecoming will have to wait until daybreak, we drag ourselves to the nearest pub, where we agree to wait out the night perched on makeshift bar stools, drinking, eating *bocas,* and roosting until morning.

It is here that I first meet Emma, the madam of the local whorehouse and proprietor of the saloon at which we land that night. She will be one of the most captivating and delightful surprises of the trip, revealing herself during the next few months as an amazing woman as well as a trusted friend. We soon discover that we have been in the unwitting company of a "package" during our eventful drive south, one that could have neatly sealed our fate at any point along the way.

As Emma is making one of her regular patrols of her establishment, she notices our conspicuously out-of-place, scrubby, white group. Gathering us up with custodial care, she ushers Mikey, Barney, Oliver, and me into her private quarters above the saloon. Emma occupies a flat of four rooms— a kitchen, bedroom, bath, and living room—in the middle of a long corridor of doorways that are affixed with a colorful assortment of curtains, sheets, and blankets. "My girls," as she refers to them with obvious affection, are employed in these rooms by night. By day they eat, relax, are schooled, and in general live as a close family unit in Emma's home, where she assumes the role of doting matriarch. Emma professes to care deeply for the girls, and in fact her business is not conducted like any house of ill repute that I've ever imagined. All of Emma's employees appear to be clean, healthy, happy, and of legal age—as do their patrons, by the way.

Emma watches over her "family" like a mother hen, making certain that nothing untoward is going on that would in any way put any of her girls in jeopardy. And while we are guests of Emma's, this is the precise manner in which she looks after us. As we sit in her lovely bright kitchen, drinking mug after mug of robust Costa Rican coffee (which the *Sofia* will later purchase caseloads of), we can hear a vile stream of warnings being leveled at the vagrants who are salivating over our heaped-high, hot, dead car. It is protruding like a fat stuck pig from the thick welt of encroaching bush just outside Emma's place. Emma's girls alternate as security guards, hollering some pretty gnarly threats down from their bedroom windows. I feel certain that our vehicle will remain untouched until morning. I naturally assume that at first light, however, it and all our belongings will undergo yet one final, thorough ransacking at the hands of customs and immigration officials, who are posted in the little structure right next to where our car is sunk in the mud.

So we hunker down in Emma's neat-as-a-pin house and get to know one another. Emma, it turns out, is a miraculous woman. She is wise in the mysterious ways of her people's ancient customs and traditions. She is also surprisingly literate, well-read and self-educated, particularly in the areas of history, philosophy, and classical literature. She adores Shakespeare, she tells us, and asks if we by chance have any of his works, or any books at all for that matter, that she might borrow. During the next several weeks many of my happiest moments are spent in Emma's home as I bring over text after text from the *Sofia's* ample library for her to devour and for us to discuss at length. Her desire to learn is insatiable, and her delight in discovery is like that of an innocent, young child. Who would have ever guessed that I would stumble upon so unique a soul mate in so foreign a land, embodied in so strange and unusual a woman as Emma, the madam of Golfito?

At one point during that first night in Emma's kitchen, I remark that I think I feel the building shift. She advises us that although this area of Central America is known for having a fair amount of seismic activity, we can rest assured that we will not experience any earthquake without ample warning while we are in her domain. Emma is also the local seismologist. She claims that her scale is far superior to the one credited to that gringo Richter. Pointing out her window, she shows us how her house is built right into the side of a mountain, lying flush up against the lofty wall of a decidedly unstable cliff. Emma goes on to explain that she has picked this spot intentionally. She stands there nodding, with a faraway look in her eyes, like some ancient guru. The entire village relies on her to alert its residents to impending danger, she goes on to boast wistfully. We do not need to worry, she promises. She has never once failed them.

"Listen," Emma instructs us. "Even at night the birds sing here, the monkeys howl, the grasses swish softly with busy life. Hear?" And indeed we do. "When there will come a quake, my mountain falls quiet—not a sound, not a movement—and then I know. My mountain speaks to me. The crumbling earth has not taken a single soul in Golfito," she whispers, assuring us that we will be safe.

It must be near dawn when I briefly doze off with my head on my hands at Emma's kitchen table, because I recall light filtering like filigree strands of gold through the white doily curtains when I awake. I don't move, however; I just open my eyes in response to an overwhelming sense of doom, a breathless feeling of unmistakable terror. "It's happening," I gasp, my voice hoarse and raspy with a mixture of fatigue and fear.

"No, darlin'," Emma soothes, brushing back the hair from my face. "Hear the rhythm of life, the dance of morning? There will be no earth going down this day, my love."

"No, not the earth." I want to cry, but I realize that it has been a dream, and the words won't come. The sick apprehension of dread clings to me nonetheless, like a heavy black shroud that I cannot shrug off. It isn't the earth that is going down. "It is the *Sofia*," a small, frightened voice sobs inside of me, "it is the *Sofia*."

I am eager to go now, to see my ship again. So we quickly gather ourselves up and step out into a brilliant morning. Emma is already there, instructing Barney to go over to our car and collect something. He hesitates but she urges him on, assuring him that it is all right, that she has taken care of it. Mikey, Oliver, and I watch, puzzled, while Barney does as he is told. He ambles over to the customs house, tosses an awkward salute through the window, turns to us with a resigned, "Oh, well," and proceeds to climb back under the old Volkswagen one last time. He promptly dismantles the floorboards, emerges with a small handgun, sticks it in his day pack, and stands there grinning like the Cheshire Cat. At first we are astounded. Then we are mad as hell. We hadn't even suspected! And, in fact, this was Barney's plan. Had we known, he explains, we might have given ourselves away—which Barney considered a sure bet mere minutes after meeting Mikey. In retrospect, I have to agree.

Emma chuckles and hurries us along, leading us down the narrow winding path through the jungle to the pond. When we reach the clearing, Emma is standing there like a beacon, waving her arms in high, arcing circles. Off in the distance, on the glassy bay where the *Sofia* rests, her masthead light is bleak and only intermittently visible in the brightening dawn. I swim toward it.

A rare photograph of a Cuna Indian. San Blas Islands.

chapter 6

"¿Dónde Está American Embassy?"

What the Travel Brochures Don't Tell You:
Costa Rica, Panama, and the Galapagos

Politics. The diplomatic name for the law of the jungle.

—ELY CULBERTSON

INTRODUCTION

The *Sofia*, as I had known her, was about to change. We were on an approach to the Panama Canal, a major world port accessible and liberally trafficked by travelers from around the world. Most of our recent communications with prospective new crew members dealt with the logistics of meeting the ship there for her much-touted South Pacific crossing. We were expecting the arrival of about a dozen full-paying new crew in Panama and anticipating picking up several more hitchhiking future Sofians in the bargain. Young explorers would be congregating in this busy and fascinating hub. For many the Canal transit was a once-in-a-lifetime experience. For others Panama, a duty-free port, housed every imaginable decadence at a decidedly agreeable price. Needless to say, the Canal Zone was a veritable buzz of activity and energy.

In Panama the *Sofia* would find herself unwittingly enmeshed in the social and political ramifications of the effort by the United States to hand over control of the Canal to the Panamanians. Years earlier, in a college sociology class, I had learned that during a revolution, somewhere between the tearing down of the old order and the construction of a new one, there exists an inescapable interim period of total chaos. This aptly described our ship's Panamanian tour. The experience would segue neatly into the *Sofia*'s wholly unexpected "welcome" at her first landfall of the crossing—

the historic and renowned Galapagos Islands. Around this time I began
to accept the certainty that we of the schooner *Sofia* were existing in a very
separate reality.

∿

JOURNAL ENTRY
Archipiélago de Galapagos
Ecuador
Sud America
0° 54 S. 89° 30 W

I note the latitude and longitude because it is epic. Each lifetime has events
that mark a sterling accomplishment. For a sailor one such occasion is the
crossing of the equator. This journal entry is my first ever from the Southern Hemisphere. It's a moment worth recording, and our voyage into this
bottom half of the world is commemorated in time-honored tradition.

   We on the *Sofia* celebrate our crossing with the ceremonial "shellback"
initiation. Sailors crossing the equator for the first time are subjected to
an age-old ceremony that simulates prostrating oneself before the sea gods
and involves ridiculous and elaborate costumes and a litany of pompous
ramblings interspersed with theatrical blessings. This is all delivered in the
form of irreverent melodramatic soliloquies. There's always a handful of
brave souls who continue the tradition by christening their passage with
the piercing of an ear. In days of yore a solid gold ring dangling from a
lobe was not only recognized as the symbol of a veteran seaman but often
served as a sailor's best travel insurance as well. Once a seaman had crossed
into an unknown and presumably uncivilized area, the loop of precious
metal could serve as collateral or payment for a proper burial, if necessary.
Although most of us carry some cash and have secured proper documentation, many a Sofian still chooses to be so consecrated during the festivities. Our crew uses a cork, a sail needle, and a shot of tequila. Voyagers of
bygone days were resigned to putting their faith in charms and benedic-
tions to ensure safe passage. They had little else to rely on. We Sofians however, have already had our adventure lose this aspect of its foreign intrigue.

   In the past several months we have learned for ourselves one absolute
truth—nothing is certain out here. There are no hard and fast rules, no
guarantees, no sure-fire safeguards. Modern-day sailors possess no magic
talisman. But we reckon that we'd better not dare the omnipotent fates. So
we observe the protocol, perform the rite, and bow to superstition. We do

this while acknowledging that if we are successful in cajoling old King Neptune over to our side, he will likely be standing here alone. Apart from our own substantial guts and guile, the benevolent good graces of the sea spirits are now the best that we can hope to have in our corner. And that had damned well better be enough.

So far, so good. Getting by, however, has taken on a whole new meaning. The skin of our teeth is bristled raw, the seat of our pants worn clean through, and a wing and a prayer beaten and exhausted daily. To date, the romantic islands south of the equator have succeeded only in dishing out more trials and tribulations. As I write, the *Sofia* rests at anchor in what would appear to be a peaceful bay off one island in the Galapagos chain. And her entire noble crew is yet *again* under ship's arrest. No sooner had we dropped the hook and welcomed aboard the guardians of these lands of invaluable evolutionary information than our luck turned.

JOURNAL ENTRY
Fort Amador
Canal Zone
Central America

After leaving the San Blas Archipelago, the *Sofia* sails on to Panama, entering on the Atlantic side of the Canal at Cristóbal and anchoring in mud flats a few hundred yards off the commercial shipyard. We have ventured into a troubled region. The faces in this harbor are grim and uninviting. Eyes are averted beneath furrowed brows. Bent heads are tucked protectively into hunched shoulders. The atmosphere is thick with the quiet of caution.

We know that the treaty by which the United States is to hand over long-held control of the Canal to the Panamanians is in its final stages. We also know that the transition has not gone smoothly thus far. The full explosive potential of the situation is easy to imagine. But for now the conflict is still simmering on a slow boil . . . or so we believe.

As the final stipulations of the treaty are met, the United States is systematically demilitarizing the Zone. The steady withdrawal of American troops, long the only real bastions of law and order in and around Panama City, leaves a bustling world trade center in perilous disorder. We soon learn that dog-eat-dog has become an established means of survival. A slash, grab, and run scam is rampant—wear a backpack, risk becoming a victim in broad daylight, in the middle of a crowded thoroughfare. Dare to report the theft and prepare to be summarily dismissed. Panamanian authorities will flatly deny that the attack has been committed, even when presented with evidence of the fresh, ragged gashes left after backpack straps are sliced away. American authorities appear simply overwhelmed when confronted. They throw up their hands and raise their eyebrows in helpless frustration.

So once again we take the wayfarers' ancient and most reliable course of action. Word-of-mouth becomes our law, self-reliance our credo. "Carry all valuables deep in your pockets." "Travel only in groups." "Never leave your boat unattended." "Trust no one." And, last, "Well, you can bloody well forget about getting help from your nation's embassy!" Criminal acts have no apparent repercussions. There are no established guidelines for behavior or even a consensus on how the game is to be played. It is pure Jungle Ball—no rules, no fouls, no penalties. Uncivil disobedience is the order of the day in Panama City in the *Sofia* summer of '79.

I jumped ship in Cristóbal shortly after the *Sofia* was subjected to the umpteenth postponement of her passage through the Canal. I'd had it with the delays! I headed for my parents' home in the Midwest. Lucky for me, it was easy to find yachts whose owners were grateful for an extra mate to handle lines in the locks, so I didn't miss the Canal experience altogether. I had, however, already hung around Panama long enough to suspect that the country's present political and socioeconomic turmoil could easily turn cataclysmic.

So it was a relief to fly home to the small lakeside town in southern Michigan where I grew up. My father, when he established his practice, became the only pediatrician in the area. My mother became first and foremost a mom, the norm in those days. She gave birth to my two sisters, my brother, and me in five years, start to finish, and devoted herself entirely to family and to fulfilling the role of a prominent physician's wife in the community. My childhood was a time of Norman Rockwell innocence and Wonder Bread wholesomeness. Saturday mornings in the fall were one long succession of tailgate lunches and hot chocolate–filled thermoses at the University of Michigan football stadium.

Although (or because) my entire extended family for generations is crammed full of ardent U of M alums, I chose to attend Michigan State, which has an isolated campus upstate, deep in farm country in more ways than one. It was a pivotal error in judgment for this stubborn seventeen-year-old. I didn't belong there, never fit in, and in my hippy heart-of-hearts was the prodigal child of the thinking, feeling, searching radical that students at my relatives' alma mater epitomized in the sixties. Yet I found myself mired in a rah-rah cow college that, I was soon horrified to discover, the women of my day attended with the single-minded objective of snagging a husband, especially a premed or prelaw student. Many of those who were unsuccessful in this endeavor aspired to become airline attendants.

My parents, however, were determined never to let their children develop a small-town mentality. I was taught to believe that anything is possible and that the possibilities are potentially phenomenal. My folks exposed us to art, music, dance, diversity, and, yes, travel. We'd take what they called "mystery trips" several times a year. They'd load us into the station wagon with nothing but maps and secretly packed suitcases and then stage contests to figure out our destination. My father became president of the local school board and introduced travelogues (a precursor of the Discovery Channel) as part of the weekly evening activities at the high school. As I snuggled close to my dad in that dark auditorium, planet Earth, electrifying beyond my wildest dreams and magically attainable, extended a personal invitation to me. That was what sparked my wanderlust. I wanted desperately to go directly into the Peace Corps after graduation from high school but grudgingly consented to first give Michigan State the old college try.

After serving the requisite two years, I was done with pretending to be a good Spartan. The Vietnam War was raging, as was my altruistic desire to change the world for the better. I was the product of an exceptionally functional family and became committed to making less fortunate children's lives better. So I dropped out of college and ventured off first to work with seriously troubled youth in residential treatment centers in New England (which turned out to be a profoundly foreign land to me) and continued to devour whatever college courses were relevant or merely interesting at the time. My horizons expanded with my experience and education. I eventually followed the sun to northern California, the land of the proverbial alternative lifestyle, and then beyond.

Following a gratifying visit and enough time to earn some serious cruising cash, I rejoin the *Sofia* after she has departed Panama and is waiting in Costa Rica. I'd reconnected with my emotional roots in the states and I feel changed. I soon discover that in my absence the *Sofia* has also changed.

She rests softly at anchor in the Golfo Dulce on the southernmost tip of Costa Rica. The sleepy little picturesque village of Golfito, nestled between mill pond and looming jungle-encrusted mountains, is like Shangri-La to our ship's weary, veteran crew. I reboard my ship to find her occupied by many bright, expectant new faces as well. The atmosphere is light and contagiously enthusiastic. Of our original crew out of Boston, only Evan, Norman, and Karen have endured. Barney and I are returning. Patrick has found his way back. Mother Boats, however, is conspicuously absent. He bolted in Panama, because he needed to clear up some confusion regarding the authenticity of an Australian passport in his name. Ahhh . . . Boats. I trust he'll weasel his way out of his predicament and cut a path home to the *Sofia*. He always does.

So I am still an elder, but this time there is a distinct difference. My reputation has preceded me, and I find myself being presented as a sort of caricature of myself, one that has already been introduced into the minds and expectations of the new crew. While I was away, my image became inflated, as though I already held a prestigious place in the *Sofia*'s history. It's Evan's doing. He confides to me that he didn't think I'd come back. By jumping ship, I'd delivered the ultimate threat to the continued success of the venture. But by notifying him of my intent to return, I'd proved my allegiance. Stepping aboard, I consequently confront my new celebrity.

In retrospect, I see that throughout my earlier stay on board, I had been basically swept along, caught up in the all-consuming adventure. My persona as a Sofian had developed in ways both awesome and disconcerting. Initially, I bore very little resemblance to the part that I played. But I had been subtly evolving, and now I realize I have become that persona. These are the terms on which I greet my ship in Golfito. With bursting heart and savvy eye, I step aboard as a confident "knower" among anxious and adoring "know-nothings." I am a bona fide Sofian, and I am home at last.

Mornings in the Golfo Dulce are heralded by the deep roars of the howler monkeys. They shatter the still-life calm of the bay and awaken the tropical aviary. As the monkeys conclude reveille, the birds chime in with the sweet song of a new day. But with the sun comes the heat. Sultry waves evaporate the mist on the pond's surface and raise it like a curtain. Humidity closes in all around, increasing in density until afternoon, when it explodes in cascades of rain streaming down in thick, tepid skeins. We crew work all day.

By evening we retire to Golfito's unofficial yacht club. At the edge of the jungle on the fringe of the bay just outside town lies the home of Captain Tom. Tom is a jolly old one-legged sea dog who ran his ship aground here some years ago and decided as a result that it was a fine time to become a landlubber. He married a *tica* (a local's term for herself), bought some land, built a house, and proceeded to have a passel of babies. The remains of his boat, still visible at low water, lie just off the beachfront of his convivial open-air residence. Here the family serves up a steady menu of cold beer, jungle burgers (don't know what's in 'em and don't want to), and good company.

Costa Rica is home to an alarming number of expatriates who have purchased land, established flourishing *fincas* (farms), and are living a very comfortable, very economical, dreamlike existence. The town of Golfito itself has its fair share of these once-itinerant refugees.

We Sofians, the *ticas* and *ticos*, and landed immigrants alike all gather at Captain Tom's to collect our mail—his home is also the local post office—eat, drink, sing, celebrate, and just engage in quiet talk. I like the quiet talk best. Tom has more tales to tell than we have time to listen, but I never tire of them.

Behind his house Tom has dammed up a stream that runs down from the mountaintops, and he has rocked in a deep, cool pool, complete with waterfall. Here I've met the owners of the ketch that shares the *Sofia's* anchorage. They are Paul and Jane, out of New York. What a delightful pair. Paul is in his sixties. Jane is a decade or so behind him. Both left prestigious positions in highly respected academic institutions in the city, and both are having a grand old time cruising.

Paul is the seaman, experienced and capable. His ship is a utilitarian, no-nonsense vessel re-created in his own image. His pride in her and gratitude for the lifestyle that she affords him are apparent, as they are for Jane. Jane, it is clear, is here for Paul. Although giving it her all and having one hell of a good time in the process, she hasn't as yet been able to fully embrace the adventure. Jane has confided to me that she misses New York, almost grieves for the intellectual stimulation she left behind, and frankly gets a little tired of trying to prepare and eat meals while sitting braced on her galley's cabin sole. But this is Paul's dream. She loves him, so she is here. They are so full of life, such a joy to be around. The *Jane* will be going our way, and I find the thought of these two accompanying us along the great South Pacific highway somehow reassuring and reaffirming.

After an endless stream of goodbye parties and sad farewells, the *Sofia* sets sail for her haul-out in Puntarenas. Even with a full crew of twenty-one, we have only a handful of experienced sailors on board, so Evan, Norman, and I rotate as watch captains for the sail up the coast. It is expected to take three to five days. Instead, we suffer eleven days of miserable, cold, soggy sailing into heading winds, seas, currents, and squalls. The rain never lets up. The extra support panels that are stitched into the clews (the bottom corners) of all the headsails become so saturated they look like balloons. Mildewed canvas is splitting. Rotting lines are parting. We aren't able to stay on top of the repairs. One day we just say whoa and stop the boat. We furl sails, slap a lanyard on the helm, lash it into place, and just work for twenty-four hours straight—sewing, splicing, re-reeving. We affectionately refer to it as our Flat Tire Day. Despite the foul weather, everyone remains in fairly good spirits. Most don't know any better. "Is this sailing?" they ask, all bright-eyed and breathless. "Why, heck yes!" we assure them with a wink and a slap on the back.

There's a weather phenomenon that occurs in these latitudes that normally manifests in a three- or four-day stretch of variable winds and steady rain. These storms, known as *temporals,* are the rainy season's last hurrah and as such are generally tolerated quite well. But not this season. This year's siege, the worst in thirty cycles, begins without warning the day we leave Golfito and ends twelve unprecedented, marathon days later. True, the *Sofia* does have the reputation for unwittingly initiating new crew under extreme circumstances (boy, don't I know it!). In fact, it's become an inside joke. This particular passage, however, is more like a training drill in some evil tall ship captain's boat boot camp from hell: "Gaskets on. Gaskets off. Set the squares. Furl the squares. Sheet to port. Sheet to starboard. Trim the sails. Coil down the lines. Do it again. Do it again." Over and over, in the rain, in the cold, in heavy seas, with wet bunks, little rest, bad food, and a whole new slew of puking crew. Ahh . . . sailing!

We finally arrive intact and anchor off Hacienda Nicoyas, a short ferry hop from Puntarenas proper. This is such a magnificent spot that the grisly remnants of the sail soon dissolve into the unparalleled spectacle of the surroundings. This bay is encircled by mountains that peek through a lacy rim of cumulus clouds that are whipped like heavy cream by the upper air currents. The sky directly overhead, though, is crystal clear, day and night. At dawn, as the sun begins to crest over the mountains, its slashes of light filter through the border of clouds and strike the water in orange and gold shafts. At moonrise these same clouds are silhouetted on the mountainsides in eerie, wafting bodies reminiscent of the night sky in Disney's *Fantasia.* All day long the heat beats down a natural percussion of hot rhythm with the tempo steadily accelerating until midafternoon. Then the northerlies rush in and a crescendo of cloudburst reverberates. As the fat raindrops tap down on the thick jungle foliage, it sounds like a giant's sigh.

Each day after the storm I've taken to swimming the couple hundred meters around the peninsula into a protected cove that harbors the rustic, solitary Isla Jesusita Hotel. Here, I step out of the gentle surf onto the white sand beach and flop into a woven palm frond seat at the open-air bar. Palm trees festooned with the hotel's resident parrots and cockatoos shade the colorful, cool, hand-laid stone patio. An interesting American fellow by the name of Billy, who joined the *Sofia* in Panama, asks if he might accompany me on my happy hour jaunt. Billy is still timid and a bit circumspect. He hails from a small Midwestern town and a strict religious background, both of which he appears eager to put behind him. I don't detect in him either an abundant interest in sailing or in the fundamentals of the ship herself. He gets neither very involved in the work projects nor overly enthused during the decision-making process. Perhaps Billy is just along for the ride, going traveling, seeing the world on a shoestring. I wonder whether it even matters to him that the shoestring is attached to a high-maintenance, low-performance, beat-up old shoe of a ship. Billy seems oblivious. He remains disconnected, unconcerned. He neither competes with the guys nor vies for the gals. He is just here, smiling benignly and habitually twirling the ends of his heavy black mustache.

I welcome his company for the evening. Because Billy is a less-experienced swimmer, he hesitates to tackle the distance alone. He is also deathly afraid to go it blind. A nonchalant disregard for the substantial underwater activity is not something Billy has acquired yet. So I outfit him with mask, snorkel, and fins and warn him that he'll likely be more concerned by what he sees than by what he might imagine. These waters are rife with sand sharks, eels, crabs, and a variety of monstrous-looking fish. But the bay is so fertile, so rich with self-sustaining life, that nothing here poses an actual threat to anyone who doesn't threaten it. We are finally ready and waaaay beyond hot and thirsty, so I eagerly dive in and shout for Billy to follow. After a few short strokes I pause to check on him and notice that he is heading off in the opposite direction.

Now, I had previously observed that Billy walks with a slight limp. When I asked him about it, he told me that although he had been born with an abnormality in one foot, it had been corrected in infancy. I never gave it another thought—until now. When I reach Billy, I rap on the back of his head to get his attention and ask him why the hell he is paddling around in tiny circles in front of the ship. He grins sheepishly behind his silly mask and apologizes that his good leg has remained a bit stronger than his surgically repaired one. With his face frantically glued to the surface of the water so that he can scan the bottom for deadly predators, he doesn't realize that he isn't moving in a straight path. I smile, take his hand, and we swim side by side the rest of the way. It's like trying to maneuver one of those defective grocery store shopping carts with an infuriatingly stubborn, sticky wheel that keeps jolting you off to the side. We laugh about it for a long while, but Billy respectfully refrains from accompanying me on any more distance swims. What a shame. I think he'd have gotten the hang of it.

During a lull in the shipboard activities I give myself a little vacation and set out to visit Costa Rica's high country. Reports about the Cloud Forest, a renowned nature preserve high in the mountains, are too intoxicating for me to resist. I jump on a local bus and travel up to the Pensión Quetzal, a kind of youth hostel named for the national bird of Guatemala. An entire community of Quakers inhabits these mountains. They live a peaceful existence as dairy farmers, caretakers of the Cloud Forest, and managers of a chain of pensions where clean beds, hot showers, and three mountain-man-hearty homemade meals can be had for a mere $9 a day. From here I trek off each morning, following well-trod trails that meander through hillsides fat with psychedelically hued foliage. The air is thin and cool, infused with lilting, translucent butterflies and darting moths whose wings spread eight inches and are marked with a startling camouflage that looks just like two owl eyes. Iridescent frogs croak from furry ponds. Mud gushes up under a soggy blanket of ground cover. The moss on the trees is so thick that it swallows up a hand pressed into it. It is a paradise. Someone somewhere in the Costa Rican government has had a vision. The country has no armed military (and no need for one), no impoverished and ailing lower class, and 90 percent of its landscape is revered and protected as a nature and wildlife preserve. I am impressed. This is a country in which I feel I too could live quite happily. It is small wonder that these jungles have summoned folk from nations all around the globe.

I return to the *Sofia* for Thanksgiving, only to be informed that the shipyard in Puntarenas has balked at honoring its offer to haul us. Their story is that the *Sofia*'s crew, during her first circumnavigation, managed to make so unfavorable an impression that it has not been forgotten. That was seven long years ago, so that's some impression. We are never given the particulars—and decide not to delve too deeply—but all our attempts to persuade the yard to reconsider are to no avail. As I've already observed, the *Sofia* can and does redefine herself with each new crew complement.

But I am learning that she is also often made to suffer the repercussions of the actions taken by the architects of her past personalities.

The *Sofia* will not haul out in Costa Rica as we had planned and counted on for six months. Once again we have been led on a merry chase up, down, and around the ocean, in untenable weather conditions for weeks and months on end, to make our prescheduled appointment, which is critical to ensure the structural integrity of our vessel. And it has again been canceled at the last minute. We veteran Sofians are used to this runaround, but the new crew members are outraged. "What?" "What do you mean, they won't?" "This is simply unacceptable!" We just smirk and shrug. Nonetheless, the new folk are flat-out losing their senses of humor. A few of the Yanks, in true stereotypical form, are just not going to stand for it. They demand satisfaction and even threaten to call the American embassy. They haven't learned yet.

Some friends of Evan's, a couple from San Francisco, joined the *Sofia* in Costa Rica, expecting to accompany her into the South Pacific. They are frankly running out of vacation time, and they are not pleased. To make matters worse, they are experiencing some personal domestic troubles as well. Kathy, the female half of the twosome, is very well liked by everyone on board in general and attracts a fair bit of attention from the male population in particular. And Dale, her partner, is in an ornery snit about it. Actually, he's been in a snit about one thing or another pretty much the whole time he's been on board. He doesn't warm well to manual labor, for instance. And he positively hates rowing our shore boats, fussing constantly, "Why can't we have an outboard like all the other yachties?"

Dale is a character, all right. Shortly after boarding the *Sofia*, he announced to everyone that he and Kathy had an open relationship, the emancipating boundaries of which he planned to explore in full during his little sailing holiday. But, alas, he has been systematically rejected by each and every female member of the crew. Kathy, on the other hand, has enjoyed a steady stream of courters. Gosh, even old pal Evan gave her a tumble. It isn't really that surprising, though. Kathy is sweet, genuine, and in the end true blue. She and Dale will leave together, returning to the Bay Area to try to re-create their former reality and reestablish their injured romance. Too bad. Although I don't think anyone thought that Dale had much of a chance of surviving on board, we all had high hopes for Kathy.

Romantic relationships aboard the *Sofia* are enigmatic. Our mode of existence is too demanding to allow for much emotional availability. The crew complement is far too transient to promise stability. And the freewheeling aspect of our attitude would suggest that sentimental attachment is super-fluous. Yet, despite these inherent handicaps to involvement, relationships still perpetually form and disintegrate on the *Sofia*. Simply put, the basic human need to feel attached and significant supersedes rational behavior and interferes with the business at hand—namely, sailing around the world on a tall ship. Affairs of the heart abound on our ship despite the known risks, and often they turn our venture into a veritable war zone of collat-eral damage. Would-be circumnavigators are set emotionally adrift and foundering, time and again. On board the *Sofia*, love in the '70s is not free.

So the *Sofia* departs Puntarenas, retracing her steps to Panama, antici-pating a seven- to ten-day sail, which we expect will be as easy as the trip up was hard. Wrong! Wrong, wrong, wrong, wrong, wrong. After two full weeks at sea we are still nudging the southern tip of Costa Rica. Finally rounding into the Bay of Panama, our ship encounters light northerlies that are woefully ineffective at countering the infuriatingly stubborn three-knot current that is setting us astern. By the time everyone acknowledges that the conditions aren't going to magically break in our favor, we find ourselves almost abreast of the dreaded Colombian coastline. It is grudg-ingly agreed that we will take one final stab at making our course under sail without the aid of our engine. We hope to tap into the elusive on-and-off shore breezes reported to blow around Panama Bay's periphery. Wrong again. Two more weeks at sea. The pilot books have not adequately pre-pared us for this. We can't get a break. Frustrations on board are mounting. Accusations are flying. Camps form: those with Evan and those against him. Actually, no one is technically with Evan any longer in terms of his rigid commitment to pure sailing. We all think it propitious to crank up Juni to get us the hell out of the bay. But on principle alone, many of us are reluctant to stand against our stalwart skipper. Flirting with mutiny is a dicey precedent to set, especially for those whose plans don't include an imminent disembarking. We have, however, already set some precedents—180 miles of sternway. As a result of the strong current running against us, the *Sofia* is pointing north and being driven south, ridiculously butt first.

To make matters even worse fate throws some more spice into the mix. We are being blown to within shooting distance of the Perlas Islands where, unbeknown to us, the shah of Iran, who days ago fled his revolution-torn country, is now hiding out. The swankiest island of the group, Contadora, has given him sanctuary with open arms—loaded and ready to fire. At the moment these arms are being trained dead on our inconsequential, obliv-ious tall ship. We spot the phalanx of gunboats during one of our cursory lookout scans, suss out the full scoop from radio transmissions, and frantically make ready to *vamanos*. The small remaining clump of newbie crew members are now so horrified that they are practically blowing into our canvas themselves. Even *their* spirits are beginning to wilt. It isn't hard to understand. They've been rudely booted out of Puntarenas, shipped stern first back to godforsaken Panama, threatened at gunpoint by some refugee shah whom they never wanted to meet in the first place, and now a mutiny is promising to erupt aboard their very own little cruise ship over the disagreement with Evan about engaging the engine.

The wind does mercifully shift, just as Evan predicts it will (give or take a couple of weeks, a couple hundred nautical miles, and more than a couple brawls), and we sail on into safe harbor after twenty-three grueling days at sea. However, the monotony of this leg is broken up by a few captivating encounters as well.

Lolling about becalmed on Christmas morning, the *Sofia* bumps into a whole pod of pilot whales. The sea around our hull begins to boil in ripples and eddies of great gray-and-white speckled balls. Leaping over the side, Barney joins the gentle giants for a frolic. With bugged eyes grinning behind his mask, he reports to us on deck that it is like floating in midair with a bunch of Goodyear blimps. The whales and Barney tussle and nudge each other in slow motion and docile good humor.

Then New Year's Eve arrives with more foul weather and an excess of uneasy motion. Many take to their bunks as the '70s slip away and the '80s lumber in. Far be it for our nostalgic American contingent to let the era pass without due observance, however. As the *Sofia* is pecking forlornly at the Bay of Panama for the second time, we find ourselves within radio range of the "Free Zone," an area free of government interference that is piping music straight through from southern California. The Yanks on board gather back aft at the helm, arms draped over shoulders, damp cheeks pressed tight together, voices mingling in dreadful harmony, singing along to DJ Casey Kasem's top one hundred songs of the decade. We are the epitome of Americana at its drippiest, shaking our heads and recalling where and who we had been when we'd first heard each golden oldie. I glance around me, realizing that the *Sofia* has drawn to her a commune of aging flower children whose candles have not yet burned out and who have managed to still see the promised dream of the '60s and '70s through rose-colored sunglasses.

A few days later the *Sofia* has yet another of her improbable, chance meetings in open ocean. The *Daneca*, a Yugoslavian tuna trawler commissioned by Star-Kist, shouts us up on the radio. Its crew members spotted our blip on their radar, and their one U.S. passenger urged them to drop by for a visit. The American is a representative of the U.S. Marine Mammal Commission, a government-subsidized program designed to ensure the safety of dolphins from the threat of commercial gill nets. The *Daneca* is gigantic. Within minutes it is just abaft our stern, like a massive partition shutting off everything in our wake, and the crew is extending us an invitation to come aboard for dinner. Since we are dead in the water with no wind on the horizon, we determine that all save the skipper and watch crew will accept the offer. The *Daneca* lowers her twenty-foot motor launch into the sea—we were kind of hoping to be airlifted in its helicopter—and motors it alongside the *Sofia*. We board and are whisked over to the big ship faster than any of us has moved in many months. After being escorted into the dining room, we discover that a veritable feast has been laid out for us: fresh red snapper, pork chops with parsley garnish, fruits, cheeses, olives, crisp vegetables, sweet peas and tomatoes, watermelon, ice cream, fine wine, cold beer, good bourbon, and ice cubes! Following the meal, some Sofians settle in the crew's quarters to watch television. Others are welcomed into the projection room to view a movie. Our engineers are eager to examine the fine tunings of the big motors and, of course, the helicopter. For my part, I retire with my steaming cup of fresh-brewed coffee to the bridge, where the pilot instructs me on how to use the *Daneca's* high-tech electronics to obtain a bearing. He boasts that his modern equipment can guarantee our position anywhere in the world to within one hundred yards. I nod, impressed, and excuse myself in order to take advantage of the offer to indulge in a long, hot, private, freshwater bath. Total decadence! Come midnight the *Daneca's* skipper announces that the ship will have to be getting underway if it is to catch the dawn fish run down off Cocos Island. So we all congregate back aft for our lift home, only to discover that while the *Daneca* has held position, the *Sofia* has been carried way downwind. Our running lights are now just barely visible on the horizon. The *Daneca* powers over and quickly closes to within fifty yards of the *Sofia*. We then tumble into the launch for the remainder of the distance, but by this time the seas have kicked up a bit, most of us are juggling clumsy goody bags donated by the Yugoslavian crew, and we're three sheets to the wind, to boot.

Once back on board we all scatter to relieve the tired watch crew. Our mates initially are irked at having had to miss all the festivities and at being left alone so long with the drudgery of ship handling. But by morning they get the last laugh. Like kids in a candy store, we had all overindulged in the rich treats, and we are paying dearly for it. Dawn finds us all moaning, bent with one end or another over a rail. Nonetheless, not a one of us doubts for a moment that it was worth it. When I got back to the *Sofia*, I went straight down below to note the position that the *Daneca*'s pilot had for us, only to discover that the point at which Evan has the *Sofia*, using only dead reckoning and his trusty sextant, is spot-on the big ship's fancy-schmancy, instrumentally calculated position. Aaarrrggghhh, mateys!

Another engaging preoccupation for us during this long passage back to Panama is following the ongoing saga of a yacht in distress. We eagerly listen in on regular radio reports of its predicament. The crew is an older couple sailing alone. The wife has taken quite ill. Her husband is fighting exhaustion while trying to care for her, single-handing his yacht and radioing for help. The poor wife is seesawing between violent bouts of diarrhea and painful constipation. At first the husband radios for a 'copter to fly in an antidiuretic. Later he pleads for a dynamite laxative. Finally, an IV and rehydrating fluids are required. We follow the drama with intense interest, anxiously awaiting each new episode. They manage to crawl into Panama, and after a week in the local hospital both are cruising once again. It might have been a tragedy. Serious illness at sea is no laughing matter. So why is the rapt crew of the *Sofia* giggling and snickering as the story unfolds? Ironically, the yacht is named *Brown Palace*.

In the middle of a moonless night after a long passage, the *Sofia* sails into port off Taboga, one of Panama City's outlying coastal islands. Come daybreak, we want nothing more than to jump ashore and renew our land legs. Filling the *Salty Dog* to the gunwales with eager tourist wannabes, our skipper rows off, only to be halted at the jetty by a hostile guard who informs him that our papers are not in order. Not in order? They are in the same order that they were in during our previous visit just a few months earlier. To sort out the discrepancy, we are instructed to report to the headquarters at Flamingo Island, which is adjacent to the bustling new causeway. Because nothing else has been going according to schedule for us, we take this most recent wrinkle in stride. We aren't overly concerned, but we should be. Six months is a lifetime to a nation on the verge of revolution.

∿

JOURNAL ENTRY taken from the *Sofia's* Ship's Log
January 18, 1980
Bay of Panama
Flamingo Island
1730 hours (5:30 P.M.)

Everyone is ashore except a few of the fellas and me. I'm sitting at the chart table, sipping wine and writing letters, when I hear the muffled wheeze of a sickly outboard approaching from astern. I climb on deck and, with wine glass held delicately in one hand and pen poised in the other, I lean my elbows on the rail. I observe the funky fishing vessel that is stuttering over to the starboard quarter. The five stern-faced Panamanian men on board attempt to tie up to the *Sofia*. None is in uniform, the boat bears no official markings, and no one is speaking English. I shake my head slowly and refuse to take their bowline. They persist, shouting in Spanish. With passive resistance I put down my glass and my pen as I take one belay pin firmly in each hand. Still polite but unflinching, I then request, "I-den-ti-fi-ca-tion, por favor." Furious at having their authority questioned, the troops start fussing and throwing themselves around. One ratty little wild-eyed guy, who is holding a walkie-talkie, thrusts a Panama National Guard ID card in my face and stammers, "Capitán es en la policía estación!" Captain is in the police station? My captain? Uh-oh. I let the fellow with the ID approach. But in the direction of the others, I continue to wave my sturdy pins menacingly, belaying, avasting, and whatnot with attitude.

At this point the few remaining crew on board the *Sofia* begin to drift up on deck to see what the commotion is all about. Rick, a handsome happy-go-lucky American lad who joined the *Sofia* in Costa Rica, emerges from the galley attired in only an apron, baseball cap, and broad grin. He has been in the midst of a major bread-baking extravaganza and is covered head to toe with a light dusting of flour. Lars, a Swedish lawyer and veteran world traveler who stumbled upon the *Sofia* while touring in Panama, has been below taking a nap. He saunters up, cool and aristocratic, clad only in a dingy gray dish towel. Then Mikey, one and the same from the trip overland, stumbles up the companionway naked, does an immediate double take, retreats with classic Mikey buffoonery, and returns wearing some random swatch of material that he has hurriedly and inadequately fastened about his waist. Finally, Barney ambles over, unruffled and only mildly curious, novel in hand, clothed in—thank God for small favors—a completely intact and appropriate pair of gym shorts. He glances around, grins, and shrugs a "What the hey?"

Aside from being an accomplished attorney, Lars has studied in several countries and is fluent in five languages. Spanish happens to be one of them. He engages the "coastie," who has now been allowed on board, and learns that our ship and her crew are under arrest. The Sofians who are ashore are being systematically plucked up from the streets and deposited in a Panama City jail. We on board are being ordered to join them, straightaway. This does not sound good. I implore Lars to explain to the boarding party that at least three crew members must remain on the ship in case the *Sofia* drags her anchor. As he is translating this, I raise my eyebrows and point one of my belay pins in the direction of the very expensive, very fancy, very new causeway that is directly in the downwind path of our hulking mass of a vessel. The coastie's eyes flare wide with comprehension. He does not want that kind of mess on his hands. All right, he concedes, three can stay with the ship, but the remainder will have to accompany him pronto, and all our passports are to be relinquished. We still don't know what we've done wrong, but arguing about it is growing old. The boatmen are becoming enraged. And I think I smell Rick's bread burning. Convinced that we've won the first skirmish by being permitted to stay with the ship, I reckon I'll be able to just get on the radio and settle this misunderstanding once the vigilantes are gone.

So Rick, Lars, and I surrender our passports as Mikey and Barney dress for their arrest. As the fishing boat is preparing to leave with our guys, Lars requests permission to speak with our skipper via the coastie's walkie-talkie. This poor sot, who has so far been struggling to construct an official persona around his lame props, wilts and confesses that the walkie-talkie doesn't actually work. Besides, there is no system in place for communicating with the city jail, he tells Lars. It is smelling worse by the minute.

As the fishing boat prepares to shove off, its hapless crew members blow their departure by leaving one of their fellows hanging off the *Sofia*'s topsides. The scruffy old man at the helm screams that the young man dangling is his son. After several bungled attempts to retrieve him, they finally snatch him on the run and motor off into the sunset, ta-da! I can see Barney doubled over, laughing hysterically, as the vessel sputters away.

Rick races back below to try to salvage his burning bread as Lars and I make for the radio to enlist help. For the next several hours I sit with wine glass in hand and headphones on, shouting bloody-hell-all to a parade of operators in a futile attempt to find out who authorized the arrest of our ship and crew and why. Ultimately, I'm informed that because the *Sofia* neglected to hire an agent to facilitate our transmissions, none of my calls have been put through. What agent? Whose agent? So much for the radio free zone. The Panamanian operator at Flamingo headquarters manages a lame apology and admits that, yes, they have been less than forthcoming with pertinent information. He acquiesces to at least scout around for me to see what he can learn. When he calls me back, he has bad news. Neither the guard on duty at the causeway nor the bartender at the Balboa Yacht Club (strange combination of sources) has seen any evidence of the vessel that came and spirited our guys away.

∾

JOURNAL ENTRY taken from *Sofia*'s Ship's Log
January 18, 1980
Bay of Panama
Flamingo Island
2100 hours (9 P.M.)

The *Sofia*'s anchor light is switched on. Watch is set at ten-minute intervals to scan the shoreline in search of crew on the lam. Flamingo operator reports that he has reached immigration officials, who say they know nothing about our predicament (or will divulge nothing).

∾

LOG ENTRY
2245 hours (10:45 P.M.)

I sneak aboard our *Jonah*, and with the stealth of a secret agent I scull ashore to answer a flashing signal light. I discover a small handful of our crew who have managed to avoid the shore patrols. With the aid of a U.S. Marine, our "wanted men" have been able to slink back to the causeway. The marine confirms that Mikey, Barney, and Evan are in fact in jail. Given the numerous tales we've heard about the abusive treatment of foreigners by the Panama City police, we reckon we now have good reason to worry. Two of our crew, with the continued aid of the marine, creep back out into the city to try to contact the American embassy in the hope that U.S. officials will intervene and ensure the humane treatment of our incarcerated mates. I don't hold out much hope for this. I was put through to the embassy earlier in the evening, and I provided an in-depth account of our plight. The representative to whom I spoke responded by screeching, "Christ! Like I don't have enough to worry about!" and slamming down the receiver. I could hear the eavesdropping Flamingo operator chuckling under his breath.

∾

JOURNAL ENTRY taken from the *Sofia's* Ship's Log
January 19, 1980
Bay of Panama
Flamingo Island
0700 hours (7 A.M.)

Our three fellows have been released from jail, tired, dirty, hungry, and shaken up but otherwise unhurt and unhassled. They are able to piece together more information from inside than the rest of us managed to compile all night. Bottom line: The *Sofia* is being scapegoated because she is a U.S.-registered vessel. During the ongoing rift between Panama and the United States, no one has yet determined who will control what areas. In returning to Panama we acted precisely as we had previously. We checked in with the U.S. authorities and followed their instructions to the letter. "No, no," scold the Panamanians. It seems that the waters surrounding the causeway are one of those areas still in dispute. The locals are furious that we didn't secure permission from them. So they flexed some muscle and arrested us for unauthorized entry and international trespassing.

∾

JOURNAL ENTRY
January 19, 1980
Bay of Panama
Flamingo Island
1200 hours (Noon)

U.S. officials finally acknowledge that we have an actual "situation." They dispatch representatives to the *Sofia* to take our statements. All our crew are safely back on board, and our passports have all been returned. The U.S. agents photocopy my logbook accounts of the escapade in their entirety, rantings, ravings, blasphemes, and all. They plan to present them as evidence in an upcoming Senate subcommittee hearing on the Canal Zone.

We finally find out what happened here. In an attempt to determine which country has authority over certain areas, a joint commission has established preliminary boundaries. The bay off Flamingo Island has been temporarily split in two, half to be under U.S. and half under Panamanian jurisdiction. This is necessary so that both countries will have access to the causeway. However, some damn fool has delineated the division down the center of a chart by using a fat black marker pen. The width of the mark itself represents several hundred meters. The *Sofia* is anchored smack dab in the middle of it. The United States thinks we are legally in U.S. waters. Panama begs to differ. As a result, we are in limbo, and we aren't alone.

The following evening our old nemesis, the foul little fishing craft, attempts to force a similar power play on a million-dollar motor yacht that anchored near us earlier that afternoon. I am by now a carefree, pardoned sailor once again, placidly rowing the *Jonah* ashore to collect some crew members when I decide to sidle over near the yacht for a closer look. Those on board have been partying pretty hearty since their arrival, and I hope to get a gander at the gay frolickers. I am pulling gently and humming softly, "Row, row, row your boat" when I hear the familiar sputter of the approaching patrol vessel. Heck, the *Sofia* is clean and clear. No worries. "Gently down the stream." Is the pathetic little self-appointed police boat going to try to bully the expensive yacht too? Guess so, because they soon begin to blather orders at the yacht's crew through a broken megaphone and flick a weak flashlight beam in their direction. What a joke! I row on. "Merrily, merrily, merrily, merrily . . ." BOOM! WHIZ! ZING! "SHIT!" The fancy yacht has fired on the pushy patrol boat, and the *Jonah* and I are dead center between them. A company of inebriated and enraged older gentlemen has taken a shaky stand on the quarterdeck of the yacht. They are pelting the air and water all around me with a shower of bullets from the handguns each is firing. Then they switch on the searchlight mounted on their fly bridge and train it on the intruders, who are now silent and drifting in the tide. I am near enough to the fishing boat's greasy, cracked, pilothouse glass to notice that the original aggressors have lost a bit of their steam. In fact, they are crouched down and peeking out like frightened children, looking, for all the world, scared spitless.

So I'm floating there, glancing between the yacht and the boat, the boat and the yacht, the yacht and the boat, when it occurs to me that it might be a good idea to alert somebody to my presence. Just as I prepare to interject an "uh, excuse me," I hear a deep growl, slurred and threatening, emanate from a loudspeaker on the yacht, warning the posse, "I'm gonna count to ten and if I can still see ya, I'm gonna blow ya the fuck outta the water!" Not wasting time to make my little announcement, I duck, start my own countdown, and commence rowing like a maniac. "Onetwothreefourfive . . ." I am out of the line of fire pretty darn fast but not half as fast as the patrol boat. By the time I feel it is safe to stop rowing and look around, the fishing boat has hightailed it out of sight, and the dance music has resumed on the yacht. I shake my head and continue rowing ashore, now humming a tad more breathlessly and a mite less merrily, ". . . life is but a dream."

We later learn that the owner of the flashy yacht is a first cousin of President Carter's. Scuttlebutt has it that he charged into town the following morning and gave everyone a hefty piece of authentic southern hell. It is rumored that they even got old Jimmy on the phone. Needless to say, our little anchorage is unmolested for the remainder of our stay.

One day, while making my way down the causeway, I bump into an attractive, well-dressed Englishman who is eyeing the *Sofia* with obvious appreciation. Of course I invite him aboard. It proves an auspicious act of hospitality as we discover that he and our ship are in the unique position of being able to help each other out. The gentleman's name is Michael, and he tells us that he is an engineer from London who has been in Panama for the past four years, overseeing the construction of a new shipyard. The facility is now nearly complete, requiring only a game vessel to check out all the new equipment. The *Sofia* is nothing if not game. Also, she is in dire straits at the moment. So a symbiotic relationship is born over a bottle of rum and a handshake as we prepare to finally haul our ship in preparation for the long Pacific crossing.

Michael's state-of-the-art operation in Vacamonté, Panama, turns out to be quite a technological leap from the 1890s screw dock in Barbados where the *Sofia* last hauled. The ship, the slipway, and the crew all perform swimmingly, though, emerging unscathed, with the exception of a single unfortunate incident.

Among those who have recently joined the *Sofia* for the Pacific leg of her journey is a spunky redheaded American gal named Kathy. She has a potentially catastrophic mishap with my bicycle while the *Sofia* is on the slipway. As the amenities for the new yard are not yet complete, a block of makeshift toilets and showers has been erected for us at the far end of the jetty. This is just peachy, except when someone is in a rush to reach the toilets. It is on just such an occasion that Kathy blurts out, "Oh, golly, Pam, can I use your bike to ride down to the bathroom? I'll never make it otherwise!"

"Sure," I say. Why not? I have been keeping my bicycle parked at our end of the jetty, where it is conveniently located for daily jaunts into town. Kathy runs, hops on, and peddles off, making it neatly to the head in the necessary flash. The accident occurs on her unhurried return trip. Later Kathy will swear that she doesn't remember a thing. I guess we'll never know for certain what happened, as none of us becomes aware of the calamity until we hear the metal of my bike banging off the rocky slope of the jetty. I turn in the direction of the racket just in time to see Kathy's limp, rag doll frame somersaulting down the last twenty feet of the thirty-foot incline. The bike bounces down on its own, some yards away. Kathy's body kind of unravels the last few feet, landing in the water face down and motionless. I remember thinking, "Oh. She's dead." But I still climb down the ship's hull, dive into the bay, and swim toward her, fast, as though she might still be salvageable. When I reach her, I find her floating in a bloody puddle, still breathing and semiconscious. We are quickly joined by Barney and Andrea. Barney is his steadfast, composed self. Andrea, on the other hand, presents an additional problem, one we do not need at the moment. Andrea is another old flame of Evan's. She is very young, cute as a button, and highly excitable. The first thing Andrea does is start squealing at the top of her lungs, "OH, MY GOD! OH, MY GOD! KATHY, YOU ARE BLEEDING ALL OVER!" Frightened, Kathy reacts by moaning and thrashing around, splattering blood in all directions. Barney turns and, waggling his finger like some chiding kindergarten teacher, cautions Andrea to settle down. "Hey, Andrea, shut the fuck up, OK?"

Barney, Andrea, and I manage to haul Kathy's dead weight up to the outstretched arms of those who have by now climbed down the jetty to assist. In minutes an ambulance is there to whisk Kathy off to the hospital on the military base. She is lucky. She could have been killed. It was a vicious fall. After a few days in the hospital, however, she is able to return to the ship to complete her recuperation. The navy docs treated her for a severe concussion, multiple cuts, and bruises and sank several stitches into her skull. But by the time we say our thank-yous, sort out our documentation, and prepare to set off for the South Pacific, she is practically as good as new—and as eager as the rest of the *Sofia*'s dozen new crew members to get out there and get a taste of that elusive, beckoning, tropical paradise.

Working up on deck during our last evening in Panama, seeing to the final details before our early morning departure, we pause to watch the sun set one last time over the Atlantic. No, I haven't misspoken. The Atlantic mouth of the canal is actually eleven miles farther west than the Pacific entrance. Nowhere else in the world does the sun appear to rise in the west and set in the east. I'm happy to have something whimsical to say about this region, in closing. We certainly have had an enlightening experience here, all in all. And now we're off. Contrary to the rumors, we've been informed that we will in fact be allowed to call at the Archipiélago de Colón. South Pacific, here we come! First stop: the Galapagos.

 ᔑ

JOURNAL ENTRY
Archipiélago de Colón
Ecuador
Sud America
0° 54 S. 89° 30 W

Yeah. . . yeah . . . yeah.

. . . And so, here we are. Man, what a rude joke. The Galapagos couldn't be a sadder, more anticlimactic disappointment. The Ecuadoran government, which today holds these islands as protectorates, is a vile and corrupt lot. Ecuadoran officials brutishly shove their way on board, ignoring the optimistic looks on our faces and the goods on our saloon table. They then proceed to inform us that we have violated maritime law by raising our national flag over their courtesy flag as we enter their harbor. Uh-uh! In truth, we do have the flags accidentally juxtaposed at first, but we quickly recognize our error and repair it—*well* before we anchor. These guys are just looking for a bone to pick or, more accurately, to pick clean. Now this, sadly, is one rumor that is proving to be quite accurate. We heard a tale of a yachtie who was forced to pay exorbitant fees for bogus violations and still was threatened with imprisonment while visiting these islands several weeks earlier. But the *Sofia* sashays on over anyway.

The Ecuadoran officers decide to fine us—oh, say, U.S. $12,000—confiscate our passports, and place us all under strict ship's arrest. We are not even allowed to get in the water. Well, we reckon this is a fleece job if we've ever seen one, and, regrettably, we've seen our share in recent years. So first we try explaining to the constabulary that we didn't mean to do anything wrong and that if we've offended them, we are sorry. Sometimes this is all it takes—a little good old American bowing and scraping. Our sincere apology, however, falls on stone-deaf ears. Next, we assure the officers that we barely have two nickels to rub together, having just tapped our kitty dry in Panama while provisioning for the crossing. They aren't buying it. Last, we offer to bake them some pies, and we challenge them to a beach volleyball game—double or nothing. (It is all the same to us, as nothing is what we've got, although we do have some damn fine volleyball ringers.)

The officers remain unmoved and stubbornly turn on their heels, leaving us to stew in oblivion for several stifling, claustrophobic days. At one wit's-end point some of our crew members devise an elaborate plan to sabotage the solitary patrol boat in the bay and make a run for it in the night. We dismiss this idea pretty swiftly. The *Sofia* is no getaway vehicle. Instead, we amuse ourselves by getting really good at sneaking over the outboard side of the ship in the protective shadow of the hull for illicit brief, refreshing dips. After about a week of this stalemate, the Ecuadorans are resigned to the impossibility of extracting $12,000 from us, so they negotiate. The women on board are required to escort the local officials to a fancy dress ball. Afterward, we will all be allowed ashore for exactly twenty-four hours before being sent directly on our way. Hey, fine by us!

The party is actually a gas. The officers are perfect gentlemen, and the day ashore is interesting, to say the least. On the morning of our allotted shore leave, we Sofians all reconnoiter for a day hike up to the lake at the summit of the island. It is hot, dim, and dusty as we set out with our day packs. The Galapagos topography and climate are a zillion nautical miles from what I'd imagined they'd be. The landmasses are dry, rocky, gray, and barren. The air is biting, filled with tiny particles of dirt and sand that pepper the skin and irritate the nostrils and eyes. Our throats burn with the raspy breathing of the climb. We can't wait to reach the lake.

Giant tortoises, sea lions, and the famous huge iguanas do abound on the island, but they appear to be as exhausted and logy as the landscape itself. The beaches are bleached, the hillsides parched. The lake beckons. It promises relief and refreshment, but it delivers an example of the island's biodiversity that we aren't prepared for. When we reach the peak, we are halted dead in our tracks. The lake is here all right: cool, blue, inviting, just as we anticipated—almost. We had not counted on the great, bloated mass of deceased and decaying horse flesh that is twirling in small, dopey circles in the center of the pool. It is sending minute ripples outward to the shore and vaguely resembles a toy prize spilled from a child's cereal box left to float, forlorn and deserted, in the bowl.

This lake is the sole source of freshwater for the entire island. It irrigates the fields, feeds the streams where the fruits and vegetables grow, and provides all the drinking water. In one form or another it is running through the bloodstreams of each and every one of us. When we realize that the origin of the entire island's freshwater supply has been contaminated by the rotting, bacteria-ridden, lifeless creature bobbing in the lake, we know that without treatment a horrible disease will soon be visited upon us all. Oh, Lordy, Lordy, Lordy.

Distraught, we slog back down in the pounding heat and parade en masse into the village's unofficial apothecary. The American expatriate who runs the joint managed to make his presence known to us early on, just in case we were in need of any "medication" during our visit. This guy has a bloody pharmacy at his disposal, complete with all manner of drugs, and, boy, is he delighted to see us. Much to his chagrin, however, we Sofians are solely interested in whether he has anything in stock for treating the amoebic dysentery that it is now logical for us to expect. "But of course," he exclaims. "There is a dead horse in the lake, don't you know?" Now we do.

With our twenty-four-hour grace period expired, we reclaim our passports and set sail for the Marquesas, a passage expected to take anywhere from three to five weeks. We are advised by the druggist that common side-effects of Flagyl, the medication that we all have to take, are a slackness of muscle and a weak and wobbly sensation. We are also advised that this condition will persist for the full ten-day course of the treatment. We reckon that our wooziness will be a nuisance but manageable. What more concerns some of the crew is a particular counterindication of the drug. It is expressly not to be combined with alcohol. Ten days will be as much of a dry spell as a couple of our old salts have had to endure in quite some time. But they'll do it. Ships of wood, men of steel, and all that. Besides, our spirits are so naturally high at this juncture that no artificial mood elevators will be required. We are Sofians. We are resilient. We are not languishing in some foreign prison. We are not spewing uncontrollably from every orifice. We are on a fine, proud tall ship south of the equator, and we really, really, *really* are paradise bound, at long, long last.

The author as boatswain on *Sofia*'s deck.

chapter 7

The World's Longest Expanse of Uninterrupted Ocean

Crossing the South Pacific to the Marquesas

How beautiful it is to do nothing, and then rest afterward.

—SPANISH PROVERB

INTRODUCTION

For fifteen years my husband and I owned a fifty-foot brigantine. Our family spent the better part of this time living aboard her in a southern California marina. At the docks, we encountered hundreds of boaters coming and going; most either talking about, planning for, or actively engaging in cruising. The vast majority were of the talking and planning variety. Of the rare few who actually got underway, most would abort their trip sometime during those first difficult months. They'd find that their dream of cruising had become a nightmare. The boat would unceremoniously go on the market. *Cruising World* magazine was replaced by *Better Homes and Gardens* as the thwarted sailors instead began to devour real estate ads. They'd look askance at those of us who remained afloat. Either we represented a chafing testament to their failure or we were perceived as unenlightened lunatics.

While in the marina, *only* when asked, I'd encourage freshman passage makers to suspend any notions of idyllic cruising for at least one full year after they'd cast off. This has become my baseline period for grooming a happy sailor. Most people find that forfeiting house and land for boat and sea is as easy as finessing the toothpaste back into the tube. It is a colossal adjustment, for both body and spirit. Inaugural cruisers are also leaving behind dear friends and concerned family, braving life-threatening dangers, and facing ultimate self-reliance. And they are confronting the distinct probability of suffering relentless, all-consuming physical discomfort: being wet, seasick, claustrophobic, unwashed, unkempt, and unrested. All this will be accompanied by feeling bored, useless, inept, and resigned to their umpteenth consecutive meal of cold cereal because it's all they can face preparing or manage to keep down. They'll be incessantly repairing, rebuilding, and jury-rigging the multitude of time- and life-saving gear for which they have spared no expense to grossly overload their suddenly too tiny, too frail vessel. And in the end they might well find themselves cast utterly adrift and unavoidably attached to someone who will not fail to disappoint them time and again with myriad previously unrevealed and seriously alarming character flaws.

The weather will be inclement, anchorages untenable, customs officials unlawful, locals unfriendly, fellow cruisers immoral. There exists a vague community among seagoing travelers, a fraternity in which they will be automatic plebes. This is a society unlike any they've associated with before, and the rules change. The experience can be so disorienting that even the bright spots in those early tentative months go unrecognized or unappreciated amid the blur of despondency and alienation.

I caution the cruiser-wannabes to try to hang in there past the one-year mark. The payoff will come, I promise. Brilliant, golden moments will recur, clarifying progress and purpose. Emerging self-confidence and contentment will erode doubt and despair. Given the chance, confirmation will envelop a sailor like a soothing blanket. For me our twenty-eight–day passage from the Galapagos to the Marquesas was just such an epiphany.

This entry begins a journey that most non-comatose people dream about at one time or another. The Marquesas will be our first landfall along the great Pacific highway. Boats converging there will hail from nations around the globe. Most of these explorers will either be looking for or running from something. We will form a congregation that will continue to assemble religiously in each successive port along the way, usually at some raucous party aboard our ever-so-large and festive tall ship. And these folks will become our family.

∾

Hunkering down in the hush of a steamy, squally anchor watch from 3 to 6 A.M., I drift back over the details of the passage to and initial stopover in this remarkable island group. For a full twenty-eight days we barrel along a stretch of ocean void of any interruption in all its vast 360 degrees of horizon. It is glorious, offering me a kind of peacefulness I've never known. The *Sofia* moves as if in a trance: lifting, driving, in the groove, as though self-propelled and omniscient. This is the run she was created for, downwind before the trades with her powerful square sails pulling like a train. The ocean rolls beneath her as regular as a treadmill. We crew need only adjust her lines to avoid chafe and make subtle helm corrections to account for leeway.

The equatorial sun bathes us in buttery gold. The breeze is loyal, the barometer steady. The sky is too blue, too clear, too high. Trade-wind clouds dance around its periphery like dollops of ivory-colored meringue with crisp, burnt-black bottoms, escorting our commanding vessel and her deliriously contented crew. The nautical miles tick off, dissolving into a benevolent following sea.

Routine maintenance aboard ship is, as always, ongoing. But on this passage the almost mindless tasks of sanding, painting, and varnishing fall into sync with the *Sofia's* rhythm. Rebuilding, repairing, and overhauling match the pace of the ship's momentum and contribute to a great upwelling of progress and purpose. The physical confines and constraints of the vessel melt away. I have never before experienced such a profound sense of freedom. In any moment I can find solitude by disappearing into a novel or my journal or by spacing out to the zen monotony of moving a brush along a plank or a sanding block back and forth, back and forth over a rail. *Be the block. Feel the rail.* I can drop off to move with the music, sway hypnotically in the bow net, climb aloft to swing alone in the rigging, or lie apart in the sanctum sanctorum of my very own six feet of bunk space. Everyone aboard for this passage appears to be feeling this way. We travel with and past each other in a euphoric dream state. When we talk together, the conversations are quiet, meaningful, and revealing. It feels safe to share out here, and we grow closer.

During this voyage the night sky is a miracle in and of itself. In the complete absence of distortion from unnatural reflected light, the stars explode onto a slate black screen. There is no twilight in the open ocean. The sun's drop beneath the sea is followed by a brief splatter of psychedelic color dashed across the heavens and then SLAM—total darkness. The moon rises and the stars come out, as if they've been peeking from behind a heavy curtain asking, "Is it time?" Then the play begins. Constellations in precise astrological formation animate and collide, enlivening the stage with the quixotic mythological drama envisioned and given life centuries earlier by the ancient Greeks and Romans. Moon shadows of billowing sails and swaying lines waft across the deck in a ghostly tango. The evening is electrified by a subterranean hum of pure organic forces.

The mood that endures for the majority of the Sofia's South Pacific experience is born on this passage. Sadness, loneliness, insecurity, and powerlessness are markers that we've passed along the way. Now our direction is intuitive and our resolution affirmed. We will travel the world as sailors, as Sofians.

I am not eager to make landfall even after almost a month at sea. On the contrary, I feel that I can continue sailing on indefinitely. This sentiment is shared by most of the other crew members. It has been an extraordinarily heavenly passage. But, alas, our reverie will be interrupted in due time and quite auspiciously. On the dawn of a day marking the conclusion of our third week of the crossing, our endless vista is offensively obstructed by a flash of rugged, mist-enshrouded jagged peaks jutting out of a milky horizon far off in the distance. Still several days away, this blockade grows more ominous and imposing with each successive sunrise. Ua Pu, the nearest to us in the chain of Marquesas Islands, looms wild and foreboding like the mean monster's kingdom in a child's nightmare. The charts warn of a treacherous reef, and the pilot books describe an uninhabitable pile of rock. So we are content to scoot on by, shooting instead for a more hospitable anchorage on the island of Hiva Oa, another couple days' sail away.

We make our destination and enter a lovely bay off the village of Atuona, just two days shy of having spent a solid month at sea. The anchorage is occupied by a number of yachts, many already familiar to us. Anticipating seeing old friends again softens the blow of having to leave the serenity of the open ocean. Prominently positioned at the head of the inlet are our dear friends out of South Africa aboard their trimaran, the *Triad*. Two young, well-educated couples, along with their affable close friend and easy-going fifth wheel, Rupert, make up her crew. They motor over to greet us and inform us straightaway that the anchorage is "righteously wicked." The powerful winds and heavy swells, which are fueled by seas that have been rolling for three thousand uninterrupted miles, unleash all their fury on the first obstacle they meet—the Marquesas Islands. To better secure the ship, we follow the lead of every other boat in the harbor by undertaking the difficult job of setting both a bow and a stern anchor.

While concentrating on performing the elaborate choreography of this task, I am made aware of the changes in the atmosphere since we've left the open sea. Winds are shrieking down the canyons and through the valleys. Violent surf is pounding the shore. The *Sofia* is reeling on the swells. The crew is moving fast and furiously. My head begins to ache with the absence of peace and quiet. A high-pitched whine permeates the otherwise droning roar. A low drum beat hardens into a clash of cymbals as a wave trapped beneath a ledge gets squeezed through an opening in the reef's upper layer. Suddenly, white water bursts forty feet into the sky. The blow hole is just a handful of boatlengths off the *Sofia*'s stern, and as we work we are sprayed with the eruption's cool, feathery mist.

My other senses are also quickening. My nose twitches and my stomach turns. The wind is heavy with the cloying odor of copra, the drying meat of harvested coconuts. I have to take deep breaths as I struggle to acclimate. I am experiencing sensory overload. But a brand new world awaits me ashore, so as soon as the ship is secured, I hit the beach.

. . . Way, *way* easier said than done. Those same swells that are batter-ramming the *Sofia*, threatening to yank her loose from her moorings, are continuing right on past her in their inevitable assault upon the shore. The Atuona beachfront is minuscule, funneled between two swatches of stone jetty that cut out into the surf on either side of the shore. We have to approach stern-to, inching up on the swells and rowing back hard to fend off the rock wall, gauging the surge, riding the break, dumping crew members in waist-deep water with their packs held high over their heads. Then we pull with a will to slide back off the face of the wave before it breaks, capsizing our dinghy and slamming us ashore as well.

The tiny beach is littered with the debris of numerous such attempts gone wrong. Bits of smashed outboards, shards of fiberglass, tatters of torn and deflated inflatables, ragged splinters of bright-colored timber from once-sweet dories all serve as gory reminders of failed landings. Our enterprising crew, however, seeing scavenging potential in the remains of otherwise unfortunate mishaps, take to the surf and find a veritable treasure trove of articles gone missing in past spills. The churned ocean bottom just off the beach yields sunglasses, binoculars, and the scattered coins of a dozen nations. Of course, we return as much of this booty as we can to our fellow sailors, but most of the stuff has been ruefully abandoned by yachties now long gone. Whoever is willing to brave the dreaded rollers to retrieve it becomes its rightful owner.

Atuona is the largest village on the island. Its compact hub of resources includes a hotel, restaurant, school, Catholic mission, bank, post office, gendarmerie, two general stores, and a bakery. We know from the literature that we've devoured in preparation for this leg of our journey that the grave site of the renowned painter Paul Gauguin is somewhere on the outskirts of town. The village boasts one or two decrepit automobiles but little else that smacks of the ever-encroaching influence of European and American culture. And what evidence there is of our cultures has a distinctly Polynesian flavor. For instance, the single bank teller wears only shorts, a large tropical flower in his hair, and a wide benevolent grin. He sits with the proud authority that befits his station, atop an undersized wooden chair behind a long table in the center of the open room that also houses the post office and police station. The postman and local peace officer each also have a small wooden chair and large wooden table. Each wears the uniform of the banker and exudes the same kindly but imperious attitude.

The gang from the *Triad* tells us about a farm up the valley where we can purchase fresh fruit and vegetables. After a month at sea we Sofians are in produce withdrawal, so in no time flat we form a committee, don backpacks, and are off on the appointed trail. It turns out that the hike is a formidable one. Several miles of rugged overgrown pathway wind along the cliffs before descending into a distant canyon, which leads to a clearing that bursts clean out of the wild bush and soaring headlands. The farm is magnificent and prolific, without a hoed row in sight. Ripe fruits and vegetables tumble everywhere from thick tangles of vine and sagging plants. In this humid tropical climate everything germinates, blossoms, and grows like a hothouse gone mad.

The family that owns the farm runs out to greet us with hugs, kisses, and great dripping wedges of freshly chopped watermelon, which we launch into thirstily. Then the farm owners begin to load us up with melons, tomatoes, cucumbers, squash, cabbage, bananas, limes, papayas and mangoes, bunches of fresh flowers, and jugs of a rich and sludgy black honey.

It is tough going as we return to the ship with our weighty load but well worth the effort. Soon nets slung all across the saloon are heavy again with freshly harvested goods.

I return to the farm often during our stay on the island, and each time I make a point of visiting with the family. This seems much more important to these folks than money. Hands down, friendship is considered the greatest gift that can be given or received. On one occasion the family's teenage son insists on taking me to a shed where several intricate, hand-carved wooden saddles are hanging on the walls. When I comment on the fine workmanship, he puffs up proudly and leads me to a back room where he's working on his most prized pieces. I know I'm getting a private showing, and I prepare to behave in appropriate fashion. There, on a small table, very crude sculpting tools are laid in a neat row. Next to them on a bench is a collection of small, stocky, carved characters.

"Tiki?" I venture, pointing in disbelief at a statue.

"Oui, oui!" my friend nods with excitement, pleased that I know their proper name. Although I have done my reading and am well aware of the figures' historical importance, I did not expect that I would get to see any. Tikis are the ceremonial figures that represent the gods of the ancient Polynesian religion. Since the introduction of Catholicism, the natives, who want to be pious but without completely turning their backs on their heritage, have hidden away the large, venerable statues deep in the jungle. It has long been suspected that they still worship them in secret. Having gotten this far, I can't resist asking what he has used for his models, baiting him by saying that I thought the original tikis had all been destroyed long ago. It is obvious that his pride has gotten the better of him and that he now regrets his indiscreet disclosure. He lowers his eyes, shrugs, and turns away, putting an abrupt end to the discussion. I realize that although he no longer needs to fear repercussions from the church, he nonetheless senses that, in his youthful zeal to befriend and impress me, he has revealed too much. If I am fortunate enough to find original tikis, it will not be with his help. But I have opened the door.

I return to the *Sofia*, snatch down the book *Fatu Hiva*, by the famed author and adventurer Thor Heyerdahl, and flip to the page that I am looking for. As I stare at the sketches that the author made of the ancient tikis he discovered on this island many years earlier, I become convinced that they are identical in detail to the miniature carvings I just saw at the farm. I am awestruck. They do still exist, and I may actually have the opportunity to find them for myself.

I corral Lars, the young Swedish attorney who joined the *Sofia* in Panama. He is also an avid outdoorsman and fluent in French. Together we plan our trek. From what we can piece together from Heyerdahl's writings, charts of the island, and a little bit of folklore, gossip, and innuendo, we reckon that the original tikis might be somewhere in the island's Pau Mau Valley, roughly a twenty-six–mile hike overland from where the *Sofia* lies at anchor. The crew on board is large enough to manage the ship in our absence, so Lars and I feel justified in taking off for a spell. We load our packs and set out the following morning.

The hike is treacherous and brilliantly beautiful. When we get tired or thirsty, we stop and munch on the ripe mangoes and oranges that grow wild all along the trail. We gaze from atop the arched backbone of the island at the sweeping valleys, winding coastline, and endless ocean. It is as though we are standing on the top of the world.

By late afternoon Lars and I reach a fork in the road. Just as we are admitting that we have no idea which way to go and resigning ourselves to camping out right there until morning rather than risk stumbling around, lost in the dark, we hear an odd sound. The hacking cough of a gas engine is piercing the otherwise pure jungle melody. Within moments an antiquated jeep, more rust and dust than original form, spins into view and jolts to a stop mere inches from our bare toes. In perfect French Lars politely inquires which path leads the way to Pau Mau. The driver of the jeep points toward the trail that he has just come up on, clearly excited at the prospect of having company in his village. He says that only a handful of visitors ever ventures inland to reach the secluded hamlet. He assures Lars that it is just another twelve and a half miles, all downhill.

As Lars and I are struggling back into our heavy packs, the young Marquesan asks about our nationalities. I tell him I'm American. When Lars says that he's Swedish, the fellow chimes in that his father was Norwegian.

"Oh," says Lars, "then you must be of the family Lee." The other jeep passengers, who up until now have remained slumped in their seats listening impassively, perk up at Lars's observation and stare over at us. The jeep's driver thrusts out his hand and announces with obvious pride, "Oui, oui. I am Arthur Lee."

"Your father was Henri Lee, of course," Lars continues.

"Oui, oui," laughs Arthur. We shake hands all around, grinning and bowing. Then we say our au revoirs and continue on our separate ways.

I shoot a suspicious glance over at my partner and note his smug grin. Lars is an exceptional fellow in many respects, but telepathic powers are not among his talents. However, an impeccable memory for detail is. Like the majority of the *Sofia*'s crew, Lars has pored over our library's literature on the South Pacific. Prominent among the texts is, of course, *Fatu Hiva*. Lars recalled the author's mention of a family of Norwegian copra farmers who had befriended him on the neighboring island of Hiva Oa nearly a half-century earlier. It was logical to presume that Arthur Lee is a descendant of that same family.

As dusk encroaches, we find ourselves at the apex of the headlands where the trail turns to make its final steep descent the last six miles down to the valley floor. We weigh the relative merits of continuing on, exhausted and unable to see, or camping in the jungle with the wild boar, poisonous scorpions, and mosquitoes the size of barn swallows. We opt for camping—no contest. Even if the spirit is willing, the flesh is decidedly weak, particularly that which covers the soles of our feet. After months of barefoot shipboard life, wearing any type of shoe is pure torture. The lightest thong rubs and chafes, causing painful, oozing blisters that become infected and develop into the dreaded tropical ulcers we've read so much about. These sores don't dry and heal but instead grow lesions outward, becoming larger, deeper wounds that leave dreadful scars. The very bottoms of our feet, though, have become as tough and callused as shoe leather. We usually rely on them alone, and they hold up well against most surfaces. But the trail that Lars and I have just traveled for endless hours is no typical walking surface. It is ancient volcanic ash that has hardened into razor-sharp black gravel. By nightfall our bare feet feel as though they've spent the day dancing on a hot skillet. Our sorry human peds—evil jungle critters notwithstanding—demand a breather.

We are half-dozing on our bags when we again hear the incongruous bark of an engine. We can taste the dust being kicked up long before Arthur's jeep swings back into view. Returning home with his young son and his trusty vehicle packed to the hilt with provisions, he stomps on what is left of his marginal brakes and waves his arms, motioning for us to climb aboard. We pile in, reckoning that catching a lift on the overstuffed roller coaster is preferable to spending a sleepless night fending off bugs and beasts . . . but only just. The trail is horrendous, steep and overgrown. Our carriage has long since lost its headlights and apparently its first two gears as well. We are flying blind down an obstacle course of ruts, stumps, vines, and squashed mangoes. Arthur must drive it so often that he can do it on autopilot, because he appears to be quite relaxed. Lars and I, however, are clinging in desperation to whatever doesn't swing, bounce, or tear as every last ounce of remaining energy is thrashed out of us by the frenetic bouncing down the mountain. The whole way, Arthur's son squeals with laughter.

At one point Arthur hollers that he needs to make a quick stop at home to collect his wife and youngest son before continuing straight on to evening mass. This is Easter eve, and, as luck would have it, Arthur and his wife are the Protestant ministers of the village. When we try to quietly off-load with the provisions, graciously making room for the rest of the family, Arthur won't hear of it. The Marquesas Islands are predominantly Catholic. Arthur realizes, however, that because Lars is Protestant, as most Swedes are by birth, we will not want to miss his service. It is simply mandatory that we accompany the family members to church and return to their home as their guests for the holiday.

The very last flicker of daylight has extinguished as Arthur's trusty jeep rounds the final switchback into the valley. Below us a tiny vale dotted with small, candlelit structures sparkles in the moon's reflection off a velvety bay that licks sleepily at a perfect, crescent-shaped beachfront. We continue past the large imposing Catholic church compound and on into a grove that houses two tiny, cracker boxes. These constitute the whole of the Protestant properties.

Lars and I are instructed to wait on the front stoop of the smaller building with the two young Lee boys, Henri, named for his grandfather, and Olaf, named for a king of Norway. The boys tell us that it is the old pastor's house. It is the size of a walk-in closet. Arthur and his wife enter the other box, the church, with its peaked roof and makeshift steeple, and emerge with a giant conch shell. Positioning himself with much pomp and no shortage of circumstance, Arthur blows a golden blast into the shell to call the other Protestants to service. We learn that the village has about two hundred residents. Counting Lars and me, the total adult Protestant congregation numbers eleven.

We file in and split up, men on one side, women on the other, in narrow wooden pews. At the front of the church are two folding chairs and a card table covered with a lace cloth decorated with flower petals. The reverends Lee take their respective seats at the podium. She lifts a pile of hymnals from her bag, passes them around, and then signals for Arthur to begin. He explained to us earlier that because his wife is Tahitian, the service will be conducted in her native tongue. This poses no problem for the congregation because the inhabitants of the islands in these and neighboring groups are fluent in all the local dialects—Marquesan, Tuamotuan, Tahitian, as well as French, and a healthy smattering of English.

No problem for Lars and me, either, because we aren't listening. We are totally absorbed in our surroundings.

The women and girls are wearing dresses and colorful lace headscarfs. I remove the sweaty bandanna from around my neck and place it indelicately atop my unruly mass of curls. The men and boys are wearing a comical assortment of ill-fitting and mismatched long trousers and button-down shirts. I glance over and notice that Lars has turned his grimy t-shirt inside out in an attempt to clean up as best he can. We don't want to risk offending these folks, but our concern is unwarranted. Everyone appears exceedingly honored to have us among them.

Settling in, I turn my attention to the front of the church. I notice that Mrs. Lee's outfit is different from the other women's, befitting her elevated position, I presume. Instead of a scarf she wears a large woven hat with a broad brim that curls up at the edge. It is banded by a ring of live flowers and jangling shells. Arthur, I notice, has also changed into his formals. He is stuffed into a pair of slacks that don't fasten over his proud Polynesian paunch, a very tight collared shirt, and a white linen dinner jacket several sizes too small. He, like every man, woman, and child in attendance, is barefoot, and all wear flowers in their hair.

The service is short and lively. The Lees lead numerous rousing hymns and act out several folk stories that are accentuated with facial ticks and severe shifts in vocalization. At one point I look across the aisle and notice an elderly gentleman who is resting uneasily, with one grotesque, enlarged leg extended before him. This is my first encounter with acute elephantiasis. The affliction gets its name because the skin of the affected area becomes swollen and rough, resembling the hide of an elephant. The disease is caused by a worm carried by mosquitoes in the tropics. If it enters the lymph vessels, the affected areas remain painful and swollen for life. Although a vaccine introduced in the 1950s virtually eradicated new cases of the disease from these latitudes, gruesome reminders of its ravages still exist among the older members of the population.

As the service concludes, the women retire to the stoop of the old pastor's house and continue singing and dancing, while the men engage Lars in a heady discussion about the virtues of Protestantism versus Catholicism. Finally, the congregation breaks up, and we are ushered back into the jeep and whisked off to the Lees' house for supper.

Arthur is glowing with pride as he ushers us around his home, which is set in the middle of his sprawling copra plantation. He boasts that it is the original structure built by his father a half-century earlier. Arthur explains that he first met the Heyerdahls in this house, and he recalls spending many a happy evening in their company as a small boy. Then he shows Lars and me to our room, announcing that it is the same one that Thor and his wife had always occupied when visiting. The room is large, with a high bed made of layers of colored cloth stacked one atop the other. The walls are open, held up by ropes and pulleys, letting the breeze waft clean through. Our room even comes with its own bathroom, complete with toilet and shower. Now this is unexpected. As our tour concludes, I check my watch and see that it is nearly midnight. It feels later, much, much later. I long to be clean and cozy, nestled deep in my bright covers in "the Heyerdahl bedroom." But first, there is supper. Arthur insists.

A great table has been set, and Lars and I are ceremoniously led to our seats. Young Olaf is already sound asleep with his head in his plate. I eye him enviously. The Lees have us take particular note of the food. They have, in effect, broken out the fine china for us. The peoples of these islands are able to live abundantly well off the land and the sea, and this is what they normally do. But for us Arthur and his wife are showing off a bit. They have displayed quite a repast: The table before us is covered with tins of sweetened condensed milk, canned corned beef, English tea in bags, New Zealand butter, waxed paper packages of saltine crackers, and an assortment of obscenely irrelevant processed fruit juices in cans. We acknowledge all this with approval and appreciation, and the Lees beam.

Then we get to go to sleep. I don't remember another thing until Olaf is jumping on the bed, calling us to breakfast and the Easter sunrise mass. The morning meal and service are much the same as the night before. In church I find my attention wandering again. As we face the bay before entering the church that early dawn, we spot a tiny object far off on the horizon. Later, as I glance out the church doorway that opens onto the sea, I notice that the object is getting closer and that it is most definitely the fuzzy outline of a sailing ship. This is a highly unusual occurrence. A shallow reef makes entrance from the ocean extremely dangerous. Consequently, the people of the Pau Mau Valley, who rarely see visitors at all, virtually never have anyone approach by water. The children and I can hardly contain our excitement.

As I squirm around in my seat, captivated by the misty vision outside and boiling over with curiosity about the identity and the intentions of the brave or crazy interlopers, my attention is snapped back, front and center, to the podium of the church. A rapid skittering, like sharp nails clacking across linoleum, is piercing the soft tones of the hymns. A scorpion the size of a field mouse, bright yellow and orange with tail cocked and ready to fire, is racing across the floor in front of the pews, straight toward Mrs. Lee, who seems lost in song. I am about to holler out a warning when Arthur, hymnal protectively cradled in his arms, hooded eyes raised to the heavens, appearing also to be deep in prayer, stretches out one great spatulate bare foot and catches the demon dead on the run, squishing it flat between his toes. No one else in the church even misses a beat.

At the conclusion of the service we all scramble outside to see what vessel has risked being impaled on the deadly coral. Lars and I are delighted to see that the *Triad* is lying just inside the breakers. Only a multihull with a shallow draft of mere inches could have scooted over that reef and slipped inside to the flat water of the cove. As eager as we are to welcome them, my hiking buddy and I are otherwise engaged. We have traveled long, far, and hard to find the ancient tikis, and we feel certain we are close. The *Triad* will still be here when we return. We plan to have some fine stories to share with its crew then.

Thanking the Lees for their hospitality, we assure them that we will not forget their friendship and kindness. Then we bid farewell to the small cluster of congregants who've gathered for our departure. Once again Lars and I shoulder our heavy packs and walk off in the direction vaguely indicated by the villagers. No one seems overly eager to ensure that we'll find the tikis. Nor are they bent on deterring us. The Marquesans are comfortable in the knowledge that if we find the ancient relics, we are meant to. If we do not, so be it.

My trusty companion and I hike for hours, bushwhacking much of the way while being confounded by a dozen or more bejungled dead ends. We begin to nurture a vague suspicion that perhaps we have been misled, sent on a wild tiki chase, as it were. Midday finds us flopped down in a papaya grove, resting and reconsidering our limited options. A thrashing from the bush brings us back to our feet, prepared to fend off whatever is fixing to attack us. I fully expect a pack of wild territorial boar to come stampeding straight for us. Instead, out of the dense foliage, with machetes blazing and curses spitting, emerges a pack of stumbling yachties. It is the crew of the *Triad* with a half-dozen Sofians in tow, and they are completely flummoxed. Also in search of the elusive tiki, they have made it this far but are clueless about how to proceed. Feeling a might superior—we at least have an inkling of where we are heading—Lars and I reassure the motley crew that the statues are in fact just ahead, down the only trail that we have yet to try.

And, lo and behold, I'll be damned if that isn't right where we find them. Within the hour we are halted in a hushed semicircle before the entrance to the clearing that holds the ancient artifacts. They stand half-shrouded in vines and leaves, mute, powerful, eerie. The brush that tangles about them is unkempt and has been undisturbed for a very long time. The statues are unadorned, simple, and natural, like the Marquesan people themselves. I hope that they will be there, just so, for all eternity. Feeling like trespassers, we step gingerly around the figures without touching them or even speaking. Then we retreat, leaving them as we found them. They do exist. We have seen them. That is enough, more than enough. It is a precious gift. Their mysteries will remain undisclosed. They will be left alone, and we will be left with a sense of awe and wonder.

On the hike back to the village, we learn that the trimaran made the sail over by night and is planning to return to Atuona when evening falls. Lars and I are invited to come aboard. It is a much more appealing scenario than the return trek overland or—perish the thought—a jeep ride back to town. A sumptuous Easter dinner is prepared on board and consumed by all the *Triad* crew and ravenous *Sofia* tagalongs alike. Then we each curl up in whatever space we can find and nap until moonrise, our estimated departure time. I will soon be glad that I grabbed a few delicious winks, because this is a sail that I would not have wished to sleep through. The multihull is able to hug the shoreline so tightly that we can see the magnificent island by moon glow. We are so close that at times it seems as though I can reach out and brush the cliff's rugged face with my hand.

The *Triad* crew is full of avid anglers, always trailing a line, generally with great success. On the night that we accompany them, they nab a large tuna. As Rupert is reeling it in, he begins to strain and sweat disproportionately to the fish's apparent size and strength. We all gather around to root him on. As the leader clears the surface, we spy not a tuna but a nine-foot blue shark caught fast on the hook. It has found the snared tuna easy prey and has gotten itself snatched in the process. Small wonder that Rupert has to work so hard. It is a massively powerful fish. The shark has also tired from the struggle, so it tucks between the pontoons to ride the wash and regain its strength. I lie down on the netting stretched between the hulls, just inches above the surface, and watch the beast swim. Its dorsal fin slices back and forth as it moves without a sound, without a ripple. He is as graceful as a ballerina but as deadly as a depth charge, and I know it. At one point he slides over onto his flank and fixes a steely eye dead on me. My breath solidifies in my chest. Then he rolls back to continue his effortless progress. Soon bored with the game, the shark shifts into hyperspeed, breaking the hundred-pound test line as if it were spittle, and shoots like a rocket down into the deep, oily blackness. I remember a statistic from the Heyerdahls' book—the largest man-eating blue sharks in the world cruise the coastal waters of the Marquesas Islands. We just met a mere whipper-snapper.

We reenter Atuona bay at dawn and are surprised to find the anchorage now cluttered with boats. The *Osprey, Hard Rock, Jane,* and a dozen other yachts have arrived in our absence. It is, as always, a joy to see them and to know that they've landed safely, but it is crowded. After hosting a festive reunion, the *Sofia* crew sets to planning our departure for the historic neighboring island of Fatu Hiva. First, some of our more financially strapped members have to complete a scam they've recently embarked upon. Scuttlebutt has it that the local beer, Hinano, made in Tahiti and sold in quarts throughout the South Pacific, carries a forty-cent deposit on its bottles. Four of our fellows have spent the last few days scouring the local dump for empties. This is how they've chosen to spend their vacation in paradise, but their labors are fruitful. They have amassed a cache of one thousand, give or take, which they plan to flog off in Papeete for free brew. They stow the bottles in the saloon, which now smells just like the local dump.

We sail overnight, drifting silently past the forbidding islands of Tahuata and Mohotani. These are too wild, too reef blown, and too uninhabitable. At daybreak we sight Fatu Hiva, and it is a vision of staggering majesty. Our approach into Hanavave Bay reveals the cliff and valley formation just as Heyerdahl described it. He did not exaggerate. Pointy fingers of rock poke through a layer of soapy clouds. Mist sweeps down the emerald valleys, spilling out into the inlet. No other boats are in the bay. It appears completely untamed, as though we are its first explorers, a brave expedition of insane adventurers and incorrigible dreamers. Steep walls arch straight up in stone wedges with cleavages that ooze mossy green patches that dip down to spread out onto the tiny droplet of white sand beach leaking into the Pacific. We anticipate confronting another dicey landing here. We do not anticipate our welcoming committee.

While setting the anchors and squaring away the ship, we crew of the *Sofia* become aware that we are, in fact, not alone. Dozens of small, shiny, brown figures lace the steep walls of the entrance to the bay. These sheer rock faces are dotted with tight clusters of native children, who have been here watching and waiting for us since before dawn. Suddenly, at some obscure signal, they begin to leap out from the slippery ledges and sixty-foot precipices surrounding us. They plop into the surf, expertly gauging the swells to avoid being crushed on the shallow submerged rocks. Disappearing beneath the foam, they reemerge several yards away, closer to shore. Here the children bob to the surface like buoyant charcoal bits, grapple for floating copra, and gamely pin one under each arm in a novel, natural takeoff on water wings. Then they ride the surge in to the beach, scramble out, and scamper back up the cliffs to jump all over again. As I watch, obsessing fitfully about where the hell these kids' mothers are, I hear a familiar "whoopee!" from somewhere overhead. I glance up just in time to see our own Billy in midair, legs going like pinwheels, one hand pinching his nose while the other clutches his crotch.

Once the rest of us make it ashore, we find ourselves in a pleasant little village where friendly natives greet us with armloads of lemons, oranges, bananas, papaya, coconut, and a sweet grapefruit that they call by its French name, *pamplemousse*. We soon discover that this soccer-sized citrus has a decidedly nasty effect on the lower intestinal tract. Shortly after consumption it causes an eruption in the bowels of gas so malodorous that it sends anyone within thirty feet downwind gagging and gasping for fresh air. A crew member who has recently digested one of these hazardous fruits is not permitted below decks for at least an hour.

We know that Fatu Hiva is recognized as one of the world's few remaining spots where tapa cloth is still made in the traditional fashion. It has been worn here as clothing by the natives for many generations, ever since the Christian missionaries first condemned and prohibited bare decorated skin. Shortly after coming ashore, I inquire where I might find tapa. I am told to head for the island's Omoa Valley, way over the mountain range and back down to a valley three miles farther up the coastline. This village is also unapproachable by ship, as the surrounding horseshoe-shaped reef in its bay is shallow and treacherous. The overland route, our only option, is reported to be dazzling. It takes Lars and me, now veteran South Pacific Island trekkers, no time at all to decide to strike out together once again.

This hike is intense. It is as physically demanding as it is breathtakingly beautiful. A single trail has been used almost exclusively by the natives for more than a hundred years as they travel between villages. One might expect, then, that it would be clear and well marked, but the tropical jungle is as voracious as it is prolific. The overgrowth is almost instantaneous. We find ourselves beating through an almost impenetrable snarl of vines

and weeds. It is a steamy, thirsty climb, but our route is rich with pamplemousse trees. Lars and I devour the juicy treat and rumble our way to the
top of the island side by side. The vista is again a knockout. To the west
the Pacific spreads out like an infinite sheet of blue ice. A series of valleys
dotted with waterfalls undulates in rolls and tucks to the east. Unscalable,
shardlike peaks rise to the north. To the south our trail continues down
through an expanse of central valley that resembles a soft, rumpled quilt
soaked in spilled paint. Lusty primary colors explode beneath us in a visual
feast, and we dive right in.

By late afternoon, as we near Omoa, we can hear the lilting song of a
child resonating in the jungle canopy. We stop to look around and spot
a small boy perched high overhead in the branches of a pistache tree. He
has harvested a large bundle of the tree's tart purple fruit, which he tosses
down with a wave and a violet-smeared grin. What a savory climax to our
day's diet of pamplemousse and wild cashews.

Our approach to the town takes us along a stream and past a natural
swimming hole where a dozen or so children are playing and sailing tiny
boats with nutshell hulls and broad leaf sails. They squeal with excitement
when they see us, leap out of the way, and offer up their pool. We cool
off and clean up as best we can and then continue on into the village like
pied pipers, with the gleeful parade of youngsters following behind. The
villagers come out to greet us—bowing, touching, bearing gifts. We are
being treated like royalty. We later learn that these isolated natives see only
one or two white people a year. Although it has been an arduous climb,
we are still surprised to find out that visitors are so rare. Lars's command
of a common language proves invaluable once again, and we are escorted
to the home where the best tapa cloth can be found. Here we are introduced to the Motes, a family of undisputed local masters of the art.

The process of making tapa cloth begins by stripping sections of inner
bark from either the paper mulberry tree or the banyan tree, which is
called the hiapo in Marquesan. The soft bark of the breadfruit, or mei,
tree is also often used to make lighter-colored cloth. The quite rare, very
white cloth tapas are fashioned from the branches of the mulberry, or ute,
tree. These barks are soaked, then pounded with a wooden mallet upon a
log or stone, and hung to dry. This procedure is repeated several times as
the fibers separate and the cloth becomes wispy, thinner, softer, and more
malleable. Individual pieces can be glued together using a paste made from
arrowroot or the tapioca plant. Natural dyes made from native plants are
then used to decorate the cloth. A crude brush is fashioned from coarse

human or animal hair, and a design is chosen for the decoration. The tapa markings will almost always imitate the figures that Marquesans historically use for tattoos; these depict their revered and beloved tiki gods. Although the tapa had a functional application initially—to cover the natives' naked bodies—today the cloths are kept for ceremonies and only rarely sold or given as gifts.

Lars and I hope to be among those select few outsiders who will be allowed to possess tapa. Before such a transaction can even be considered, however, we are implored to accept the Mote family's offer of friendship and hospitality. Once we have consented to be guests of the Motes for a few days, they relax and promise to show us their work. We settle down for the evening meal before going on an odd excursion into the village to view a film that is being shown that evening. Everyone, we are told, will be there, and the Motes can't wait to show us off.

The film is a monthly event. It is shown in the meetinghouse, a cavernous cement structure in the center of the village. Omoa owns this one reel and replays it over and over. The movie is a classic, an old black-and-white John Wayne western, complete with daring rescue and cliché line: "You may not know it yet, little lady, but you're gonna marry me." The audio is of course in English and meaningless to the locals. But the dialogue is lost on Lars and me as well, as the entire packed assembly cheers, boos, and acts out all the shootouts at top volume, from opening scene to final credits.

Afterward, Lars and I wait for Isadore, the eighteen-year-old grandson in the Mote family who has acted as projectionist for the evening. What a fine young man he is and how oddly familiar he seems to us. Later, as we gather in our hosts' home, Grandmother Mote asks whether Lars and I have ever heard of Thor Heyerdahl. "Of course," we reply. She rises heavily and crosses over to a crude bookshelf propped against the far wall. She returns with a French copy of *Fatu Hiva*. With evident pride she opens the worn text to the page that holds a picture of Tioti, the young man who first befriended the Heyerdahls when they took refuge in this valley forty years earlier. Lars and I look from the photograph over to Isadore, who is smiling shyly. He is the spitting image of the fellow in the book. The ancient grandmother chuckles at her good joke, her whole body bouncing with merriment. Then she waggles a chubby finger toward the old man who has been sitting quietly in the corner since we arrived. Lars and I rise simultaneously, walk across the small room, and shake the hand of old Tioti himself. We sit cross-legged at his feet, listening raptly into the wee hours as Tioti recalls his adventures as a young Marquesan who once had a dear friend named Thor Heyerdahl, who came from a faraway land.

As we leaf through his copy of the book, Tioti stops us at the page where Thor describes a young native child who, for him, epitomized the character of the island—her unbounded joy, natural beauty, and pure lifestyle. Tioti's eyes sparkle with mischief as he leans over and whispers that this same little princess is now the wife of the town's mayor. He adds that she is also now old, fat, and toothless, and he assures us that we will meet her ourselves, as all guests in the village are expected to pay the mayor the courtesy of a personal visit. Tioti warns, however, that we should not make mention of her being in the book. Giggling, he explains that she sobs whenever someone reminds her of her youthful beauty. He is, however, quick to assert that she still possesses her true splendor beneath her weathered exterior in much the same manner as he still wears his tattoos beneath his clothing. With this remark, he pulls up his shirt and displays a magnificently illustrated torso.

We spend the following day relaxing with the family. Amanda and Tioti are the grandparents and true patriarch and matriarch of the clan. Margoline, Isadore, and Lewis are their grandchildren, and Isabella is the infant daughter of Margoline. Margoline shows us how to prepare fei bananas, the small, hard, bitter fruit that needs to be cooked in order to be digestible. Amanda, whom we are expected to address as "Grandmother," tries to help me make *umu hei,* a small bundle of fragrant flowers banded together with a strand of banana leaf frond and worn in one's hair. My attempt is a disaster, so she gives me hers, promising that I will smell luscious for days, attracting many men like bees to pollen. Tioti teaches Lars how to cook breadfruit in the open pit behind the house where the embers are covered and the fire is never allowed to die out. Although the village has the means for starting a fire anew each day, we are told that each home has such a fire pit in honor of the time in their people's history when keeping the flame alive ensured life and allowing it to die meant certain death. Lars and I both learn to grate the meat of the coconut on a traditional rake made of a scallop shell affixed to a long stick of wood. We are directed to sit on a stone and straddle the stick between our legs while rotating the coconut over the sharpened shell's edges extended before us. The grated meat falls into a fine cloth, which is then twisted until all the cream is extracted. This thick, sweet liquid is used in the preparation of many traditional Marquesan dishes. My favorite is *poisson cru,* a mixture of wild onion and raw fish swimming in coconut cream.

Next, Lars and I are allowed to attend the daily communal tapa-making gathering. The bulk of the town's population gathers in the center of the village for this very social event. The men cut the bark, while the young daughters soak and dry it. The adult women wield the heavy mallets, pounding the fibers and laughing and chattering like a group of good friends at a quilting bee. We try to perform all the various tasks, but we are clumsy and inept. Our efforts make for wonderful entertainment for the locals, though. At the conclusion of the session, Lars and I are granted the rare and distinct honor of being allowed to view and then choose from the village's most prized pieces. I choose my tapas carefully, paying particular attention to the quality of the cloth—unblemished, unbroken, uniform in consistency. I also want designs representative of the most traditional art, or tattoos on bark, as it were. My thoughtful perusal is met with obvious approval by the villagers. They are clearly very proud of their work.

Lars chooses a classic design depicting a full-size native man with a complete complement of battle tattoos, the image of the Marquesan warrior. I am fascinated by the familiar stance of the painted figure. I mention to Grandmother that the stance is easily recognizable to anyone in my country who has ever visited a doctor's office and seen an anatomical poster on the wall—the figure of a man with arms at his sides and palms open, feet slightly apart. Upon hearing this, she dispatches Isadore to the house to retrieve something. He soon returns with another text from his family's impressive library—*Gray's Anatomy*. The source of the model for Lars's tapa and the anatomical poster are one and the same.

We are not permitted to purchase our tapas; rather, they are gifts given to us by our new friends. In return, we follow suit and make them gifts of whatever we have. Later, wandering about the tiny village, I hardly meet a man, woman, or child who is not adorned in a necklace, earring, t-shirt, or scarf that I have given to them. Here we are, so very far from home in such a strange and uncommon land, and yet we have been accepted and taken in as family.

We meet a man in town who is reported to be the only resident descendant of a tribe that still occupies a hidden valley on the forbidden north side of the island. Rumors are that whatever flesh eaters remain in the Marquesas are secreted away in this distant valley. He offers to take Lars and me across the mountains with him the next day when he goes to harvest his coconuts. It will be a three-day trip, he warns, and we can expect the villagers on that side of the island to be far less hospitable. As it is a highly ill-advised trek to tackle unescorted, Lars leaps at the opportunity to go with a personal guide. No one he knows or has ever heard of has ventured into this taboo territory. I, on the other hand, decline. I am eager to get my tapas back on board intact, am feeling negligent with respect to my shipboard responsibilities, and am frankly physically done in. I do not in any way, for any reason, relish yet another overland hike. While helping Lars provision for his venture, I recognize a family in the local shop. They are the first folks I met back in Hanavave. They have come over by outrigger, and when they offer to take me back with them, I accept.

Jock, Felicita, their daughter Augustina, and I are soon lined up at the shore, facing the daunting surf. The breakers are running ten to twelve feet. A treacherous hike into cannibal country suddenly doesn't seem so bad. Jock insists that I get into the little canoe at the beach. As I have no experience in this exercise, he reasons that I'll be a liability. The timing has to be perfect or we'll get swamped or catch a wave abeam and be smashed onto the rocks. Jock and the women position themselves at the crossbar, holding steady, knee-deep in the shallows as they wait for the exact moment. We have been waiting for half an hour when Jock suddenly whoops, and he and his family start running, shoving the tiny boat out into the turbulent tide. I sit bolt upright, stunned and horrified. There is no way, I am certain, that it is possible to ascend the wall of white water charging down on us. These thirty minutes of careful observation, however, have not been lost on Jock. He has been counting the waves, timing the sets, waiting for the perfect groundswell mighty enough to lift us out, up, and over the onslaught. The little family pushes for several yards and then, just as the outrigger begins to rise straight up, bow to the sky, the three of them hoist themselves in and began to paddle in what seems to be one single, powerful, fluid motion. As we crest the wave, they dig their paddles in hard and tip us just over the peak. We ride down the back of the monstrous coil of furious sea and slide sleekly into the calm just outside the rim of reef.

I am reminded of the lessons from my oceanography class. A wave is a great circle with half its arc above and the other half below the surface. It is a gentle roller until the ring is disturbed. If broken by an abrupt shelf of coral, for instance, the vault of water in the submerged crescent of the wave is punctured, causing the upper half to collapse into a shattering, crashing avalanche of cascading foam. Yet just beyond the reef, the sea continues to roll on unbroken, in and out, like a gentle undulating pond.

Jock's family and I have attacked the demon and been spit out into the calm in little more than a heartbeat. Floating in the slack water behind the shelf, we can see the waves arch their backs, but we can only hear their assault upon the shoals beyond. I am panting like I've run a marathon, but I only sat rigid, white knuckles gripping the thin gunwales of the handmade outrigger's narrow canoe. Jock, Felicita, and Augustina, on the other hand, are quite relaxed. They have completed this operation numerous times, as have their relatives for generations before them. What this family does next—and their ancestors probably did not do—is stop their paddling and, in perfect unison, genuflect while chanting a prayer. The prayer, Augustina assures me, has been recited all throughout Marquesan history. No one dreams of putting to sea without paying homage to the gods, asking to be delivered across the waters and returned home safely. The prayer is the original, unchanged for hundreds of years. The genuflection, she confesses, is somewhat of a modern-day safeguard—a touching of all the bases.

We paddle close in along the coast for the better part of the day. It is an exceedingly brilliant and wet ride. Grandma Mote must have anticipated this, as she wrapped my tapas in three layers of oilcloth. They are the only articles not drenched clean through when we arrive. Augustina acts as my tour guide for the trip. This is her backyard and she knows it intimately. She points out many uncharted landmarks. When we pass close to the obscured entrance of a small cave, she whispers that a lovely freshwater lake lies hidden just beyond it and that it is accessible only by diving deep, swimming under the ledge, and reemerging on the other side, several yards inland. I remember reading about such a cavern in Thor Heyerdahl's book and am able to direct some of the *Sofia*'s heartier divers to it once I'm back on board. A small contingency braves the rocks, swells, and cold shark-infested darkness to explore the cave's mysteries a few days later. They return with cuts, bruises, and tales of dangerous adventure and unspeakable beauty.

Shortly after my return Lars strolls in, looking irritatingly fresh and unmauled. He has had a fine time, seen country that few white men ever have or will, and has not once been threatened with being the main course. He feels certain that the tribe had been put on its best behavior, as had he. He remains troubled, nonetheless, by the strong suspicion that earlier interlopers were less fortunate.

☙

We set sail for Nuku Hiva, the third and final island that we hope to visit in this group. As we scud away, I stare back at the Fatu Hiva skyline as it sinks beneath the ocean's surface. I know in my heart that I will never again encounter so wild, fascinating, and unspoiled a place or a people. The memory of my time here will stand alone, stellar in my life's experience.

Nuku Hiva is the center of the northern Marquesas group. While here we plan to see to the intermittent mundane personal chores that we usually can do nothing about. We have international phone calls to make, doctors to see, mail to send and collect. The passage is again a short one, and we are soon setting the *Sofia's* trusty hook in the bustling Taiohae Bay, which fronts the island's main village. Our first stop ashore is Maurice's shop. Evan knows it well. He spent a good bit of time here during his travels aboard the tall ship *Regina Maris* some years earlier and has stayed in touch with the proprietor ever since. Old Maurice runs a little general store that is equipped with a phone and mail drop. He is the best local service for cheap cold beer, bulk wine, general information, and good cheer. Maurice's has been here forever, serving as the unofficial yacht club of the Marquesas. He has a guest book older than I am. Within its pages is the history of hundreds of boats recorded in pictures, quotes, quips, and newspaper articles that tell the stories of a thousand lives passing through and passing away. The *Sofia* is commemorated in it twice, once during her first circumnavigation and since then in a grim litany of her sinking. In our travels we've run into sailors who have received and subsequently passed along this dreadful news, and we are quick and furious to dispel the rumor. Maurice's illustrative and venerable logbook is the unwitting culprit in disseminating much of this misinformation. But it isn't his fault. He tried to convince passers-by that it isn't—couldn't be—true, but he himself had begun to be worn down by the adamant and incessant repetition of the tale.

Needless to say, he is overjoyed to see us. We clear up the misunderstanding right and proper. Evan inserts into the book photographs of the *Sofia* and personal declarations by several members of the crew. He closes with our own ship's seal, stamped, dated, and signed. Maurice is proud to act as notary, as he has done in his neck of the Pacific for dozens of years past, and will, God willing, for many more years to come.

Nuku Hiva is far less dramatic than its island neighbors in terms of gorgeous scenery, but it offers other, less ethereal attractions. It has a local hotel run by a Yankee couple, Frank and Rose. They serve up a twice-weekly all-you-can-eat spaghetti dinner that is descended upon by the entire flock of yachties in the harbor. These yachties also offer a pleasant diversion. The *Sofia* has been rather reclusive for the better part of the past few months, choosing to discover the breadth and depth of her island paradise experience independent of the trans-Pacific caravan of yachts. In Nuku Hiva we are reunited with old friends once again, maybe for the last time until mid-July when we all plan to congregate in Papeete for the Bastille Day celebration. So we are primed to make the most of it. It is an ideal occasion for another famous *Sofia* get-together. Billy, formerly a reserved and timid fellow, now is our resident social director and good-time party boy. He announces that he would like to host the affair on his next galley day. He formalizes his proposal by waking at 3 A.M. on the day of the big event and baking mountainous batches of his beloved sticky buns. Then he rows to each and every boat in the harbor—at least two dozen—to extend his personal invitation with a special delivery order of hot cinnamon rolls.

The anchorage is quite a sight, with sleepy heads popping out of hatches and companionways like roused gophers out of holes, eyes barely open, excited noses twitching, homing in on the luscious aroma wafting across the bay. Every vessel has eager diners perched on deck, awaiting their turn to be visited and breakfasted by Billy. All that day the buzz never dies down, and the *Sofia* ends up having one of her all-time best turnouts and most successful parties. The celebration, start to finish, is recorded in Maurice's book. We are approached for months afterward by wandering sailors who request just one taste of *Sofia* Billy's world-famous sticky buns.

Among the hoard of yachts in the harbor at this stopover are a few that merit particular mention. Al and Ruth are here aboard their tiny double-ender, the *Myonie*. They've been cruising for twenty years and have circum-navigated four times. The conclusion of each round-the-globe trip finds Ruth pining for land and a home where the bilges don't need pumping. With a wink and a sigh Al complies, moves them home to Florida, settles them in a house for a bit, and waits patiently for Ruth to get the old itch. Before long she'll be yearning for the sea and her beloved old leaky *Myonie*.

Soon they'll pick up and set out once again for the open ocean and the world that awaits them.

The *Triad*, of course, is here, and the *Hard Rock*, the *Zenny P.*, the *Brown Palace*, and a ramshackle trimaran called the *Strata*. On board this unlikely passage maker are three fellas out of southern California, and they have some story to tell. Two of the guys on board had been partners in a bar in southern California. The third was their lawyer. It seems that they had jointly come into a large sum of money through, shall we say, unorthodox means and reckoned it might be an opportune time to buy a yacht and get lost for a few years. That not a one knew the first thing about boats or sailing was no deterrent. The team set out from Mexico, planning to head nonstop for Nuku Hiva. They were so deathly afraid of "tipping over," however, that they sailed the entire three thousand nautical miles at one-third the optimum speed of the vessel. They had reduced their sail area by an absurd two-thirds by reefing, or rolling in and tying down most of the canvas of their mainsail. What a pathetic waste of good wind and water. Not only that but they somehow manage to go up on a shallow bank just east of the Marquesas—the only obstruction in the largest expanse of uninterrupted open ocean in the world.

We on board the *Sofia* have taken particular note of them because they are so inept. They rarely manage to get in or out of their dinghy without one or all falling into the water. They're like the Three Stooges afloat. I'll be damned if they aren't somehow succeeding, though. They are determined to reach the Fete (Bastille Day celebration) in Tahiti—the party of the Pacific. This intriguing threesome is a fun-loving, less-than-kosher gaggle of likable dudes, and we're betting they will make it.

The sea has an uncanny way of forgiving blind, stupid, naive gumption. I've witnessed it on several occasions, and it never ceases to amaze me. Take all the navigation courses offered. Learn the full ropes of ship handling. Outfit yourself with the sturdiest craft and the most high-tech equipment. Lay in every safety device known to modernity. And you'll still find yourself out there, time and again, neck and neck with some hapless buffoon who didn't have the brains to stay home on the farm, who is sailing along on some lame, leaky little vessel that by all rights never should have left the boatyard, and who's as secure and content as a pig in shit. Even I am so taken with the charmed existence of the *Strata* crew that I consent to do these guys a favor that I will long regret. But I'll go into that later. First, I should introduce the most venerable occupant of the harbor and our most honored guest for the party that evening.

His name is Sid. He is an elderly retired British naval officer who was urged back to sea by loneliness following the death of his wife. Sid is single-handing his salty sloop. We first met him in Panama when some of our crew had occasion to assist him in transiting the canal. What a fine, accomplished gentleman he is and so dear. As so often happens among boat folk, Sid's saga preceded him to Nuku Hiva. When we arrive, we find him worn and woeful and his ship a crippled shadow of her former sturdy self. Sid's self-steering mechanism—an absolute necessity for a single-hander—packed in during the long passage, requiring the old man to stand at the helm 'round the clock for days on end. On the verge of exhaustion he was forced to heave-to (head up into the wind) and hold steady for a few desperate hours each night so that he could rest. He would carry out this complicated maneuver at his wit's end every twenty hours, swallow something to nourish himself, try to sleep, and pray for calm. Each dawn he'd round his boat back off the wind and sail on.

During one of these demanding exercises he got caught in a squall that blew out his mainsail. Although his vessel was severely handicapped—a sloop's only muscle is in her mainsail—Sid still managed to make safe landfall on Nuku Hiva. It is a feat only a seaman with fierce determination and abundant experience could have accomplished. Yet when we find Sid in Nuku Hiva, his spirit is nearly broken. His ship's damages are extensive and his available resources for repairs are nonexistent—that is, until the *Sofia* sails into port. Well, Lordy, our crew takes one look and turns to for that old cavalier with so profound a commitment that even the crustiest old salts are brought to tears.

Sid's story warms and tugs Patrick's patriotic English heartstrings. He vows to do everything in his power to return the proud vessel and her worthy captain to sailing readiness. We are all deeply touched by this old man's struggle, alone against the fates that seek to drive him from the only home he has left, the only home he any longer recognizes, the sea.

Our crew hauls the disabled sloop over and ties her alongside the *Sofia*. For two days and nights we work. Patrick mends her tattered sails, while Oliver and Anders devise a way to repair the delicate, sophisticated self-steering system. With no spare parts available, they have to rebuild the intricate mechanism from parts that they fashion themselves. Our deck torches burn all night, illuminating the hunched figures poring over diagrams, wielding welding torches, manufacturing tiny working parts on the tar-sealed, soft pine decks of our old wooden tall ship. We work on as the small but stalwart *Doreen Beatrice*, named for Sid's wife, is hugged in close, tucked in safe under the protective shadow of the *Sofia*'s mighty yardarms.

Sid oversees everything, working side by side, step by step, with the laborers. He pats their shoulders and shakes his head in amazed appreciation at the crew's genius and generosity. He shamelessly brushes away tears every time their grimy faces, aglow with each new success, lift up to him. Sid takes his meals with us. Our admiration for him grows, and our conviction in our efforts is fortified as he shares stories from his past and dreams for his future.

On the morning of the third day we all watch Evan, Patrick, and Sid sail the *Doreen Beatrice* out the cut for a trial run. Mission accomplished! She handles like a dream, graceful as her namesake and as strong once again as her skipper. The entire anchorage heaves a sigh of relief. For the remainder of our stay on the island, the crew of the *Sofia* is showered with praise and gratitude from the other cruisers, as well as from all those ashore who have ever been to sea. We humble sailors accept any and all gifts that the four winds see fit to blow our way. In Nuku Hiva the *Sofia* has been such a gift and she does the honor proud.

While the welders and sail menders are hard at work on board, I become embroiled in a benevolent though somewhat less glamorous labor of my own. The crew of the *Strata* left the States with every stitch of clothing they own and have since worn and soiled every stitch of cloth they brought. In Nuku Hiva they are hell-bent on finding someone to do their laundry. They haven't a clue how to tackle it themselves and less desire to learn. What they do have, however, is ready cash. We strike a bargain—for $25 and a dinner out, they can engage my services. They are ecstatic. Now, I can't for the life of me imagine what possible use these fellas found for all this stuff in the middle of the ocean, but they have managed to amass six large, bulging bundles of dirty clothes, sheets, and towels. The boys allow me to briefly scold them for their decadent, unseamanlike behavior before they cast me off to my labors. Then they bounce up and down with infantile joy, waving merrily as they watch me haul their heaps of smelly wash far downwind. I spend the day just inside the jetty in a large cement tub, which has a freshwater tap and makes an ideal makeshift laundry facility. The entire process—washing, rinsing, ferrying the sacks back out to *Sofia*, and hanging the wet stuff all over in the rigging—takes me a total of eight hours. As their clothes dry in the breeze, the boys take turns leaping to attention, naked on the deck of their tri, saluting their underwear flying high over Taiohae Bay.

Between working and partying, I do find some time to explore the island. The Catholic church is the most impressive sight I see here. As the local bishop lives on the island, a good deal of "holy monies" are available.

However, any wealth on Nuku Hiva seems evident only in the ostentatious church itself, and it is an incongruous blend of old and new art motifs. The grounds and structures are the result of modern architectural ingenuity, but the heart and the spirit of the Marquesan people are still apparent in the extensive, intricate woodworking by local carvers. Every bit of decoration in the church is sculpted wood, even the twelve stations of the cross. There isn't a single painting or a strip of plastic in sight. The atmosphere within the church isn't garishly heavy but rather clean and open, as befits the climate and the people. And even so, it seems to be more than what's needed. The strong, honest stone frame and wood sculpture would be enough. The modern application of design is for someone else. God? I think not. It is more likely to impress the French politicians who make weekly pilgrimages to the village.

The *Sofia* weighs anchor in Taiohae Bay and says farewell to the Marquesas, setting out for the stretch of coral atolls known as the Tuamotu Archipelago. Just outside the cut, we spot a school of sharks circling at the surface. These demons are no longer an unusual or particularly panic-inducing sight for us. Two hammerheads have made their home in the bay for years and have coexisted peacefully with the locals and cruisers alike. A couple of times I've even seen native children haul up onto the beach and play with a young shark who's wandered in too close to the shallows.

As we get wind in our canvas and blue water beneath our keel, my melancholy at leaving the Marquesas in our wake is soon evaporated by the pure rapture I feel at being out at sea once again. I have grown to so love sailing on the *Sofia*. While short overnight jaunts are fine, the prospect of the whole week that the next passage should take fills me with joy. I expect to feel increasingly fine as the land continues to fade behind us, but instead I find that I am not. In fact, I am beginning to feel pretty bloody lousy. By nightfall it is evident that I am quite ill. I begin to realize that I received more than I bargained for during my short stint as a laundress. We had all been forewarned about the bugs on Nuku Hiva. These tiny, swarming, almost invisible gnats known as "no-no's" carry a miserable disease that has been plaguing the islands this season. The insects like to cluster about in damp, stagnant areas near the shore—rather like the tub where I spent several airless hours doing the *Strata's* dirty work. By the time I finished my washing chores, my back and arms were covered with bites. I thought little of it except for the itch, that is, until we were back at sea. Before submitting and burying myself in my bunk to ride out the ravages of the disease, I inform Evan of my self-diagnosis. I am certain that I have contracted the dengue fever.

The Merck Manual from our ship's library informs me in cold, clinical terminology that I will experience a sudden headache, followed by a very high fever, combined with extreme joint and muscle pain and severe prostration. I can also expect to break out in a pink, macular rash. However, this scientific description of the symptoms pales in comparison to the careening Mack truck that hits me head-on in the middle of the Pacific. With the slightest movement, excruciating pain detonates behind my eyes. My head feels like a lit cherry bomb. Somehow, a solid, white-hot steel rod has been inserted into my spinal cord, rendering my limbs frozen into a paralyzing ache. I am desperate to vomit, but I can't organize the muscles required to carry out the deed. My ears have locked shut and a steady, screaming buzz throbs inside my skull.

I remember few details of that six-day passage. When the fever is at its peak, I am in a semiconscious state, delirious and confused. I'm told that I crawl up on deck and warn the watch crew to avoid the large rocks dead ahead, the ones only I can see. I holler for someone to get the Varmit the hell out of the radio controls as he is causing them to emit a torturous static, one that only I can hear. My crewmates try to reassure me. Mostly, the insensitive louts snicker at my delusional outbursts. I come out of the fever on the morning of the day we spot the first sign of the atolls. Were this sighting not confirmed by the lookout on the yard, I'd be certain it was another of my fanciful, fever-fueled visions. Can anything be so radiant? It looks as if someone dug up the bright green and blue, papier-mâché island that I made in third grade and skipped it out across a still pool. The Tuamotus, the gateway to the Society Islands, drifts before us, lovely, isolated, and as enchanting as a flower lei tossed from some distant shore, intoxicating with its mysteries waiting to be revealed.

View aloft from the main deck of the *Sofia*.

chapter 8

The Most Beautiful Islands
in the World

The Societies

Nothing ever tasted any better than a cold beer on a beautiful afternoon with
nothing to look forward to but more of the same.

—HUGH HOOD

INTRODUCTION

As I recall this next phase of the *Sofia*'s Pacific crossing, I am revisiting a
magical period. Waves of sun-drenched images wash over me. This was an
interlude forever set to music, a spell that swayed in gentle tempo with the
blissful throngs that congregated in what the travelogues designate as "the
most beautiful islands in the world."

The *Sofia* followed the sun along its equatorial path. Consequently, those
aboard were able to create an illusion of perpetual summer, ignoring the
passage of time. Not since childhood had I stood on the brink of a world
brimming with such secret promise. The *Sofia* was a downwind ship on her
best heading when following the trade routes about the belly of the planet.
All seemed right, deliciously youthful and rapturously exclusive.

The Society Islands live in my memory as a dream, out of place and out
of time. The landscape was sumptuous, the climate forgiving. Our sailors
numbered many, and they were ecstatic. The ship arrived in good shape,
physically and financially. The necessary repairs and routine maintenance
promised to be quite manageable in the affluent, cosmopolitan port of
Papeete, Tahiti. In contrast, the lavish sprinkling of outlying islands and
motus (Polynesian reefs with vegetation) assured any Sofian weary of the
activity aboard ship an alternative of relative isolation and anonymity. The
only matter of any concern for us was hurricane season. We planned to

ride it out in safe harbor in French Polynesia in the glorious summer of
1980, during the most festive of celebrations in all the South Pacific.

◆

The Tuamotus are our gateway to the Societies. This arch of dazzlingly
beautiful atolls that borders the famed islands of Tahiti, Mooréa, Bora
Bora, and a smattering of smaller, lesser-known islands, serves as an appropriate foyer for the grandeur that lies beyond. Atolls are circular bands
that rise just above sea level in the open ocean and are found primarily
in the Pacific. They are either built up on a submerged bank or formed
on the crater edge of a volcano that is resting just beneath the surface of
the sea. Microscopic animals take up residence on the ridge, constructing
homes of living coral that break through the surface to combine with the
tropical sun and moist air. This fertile union begets a landmass that sits
smack dab at sea level and extends only twenty to thirty feet up, to the
tops of the loftiest palm trees. That's it—no soaring mountain peaks to
snatch passing weather systems, so there are no clouds. No bloated water-
ways stream down cliffs and through valleys, amassing mud, silt, and other
organic debris to be deposited into the ocean and thereby creating murky,
turbid shallows. The water is utterly transparent. Visibility on all fronts
is sublime. Pink coral, blue sea, green palms, white sand, purple lagoon—
tropical colors fitting together like pieces of a jigsaw puzzle yet in startling contrast to one another. The Tuamotus are warm, breezy, clear, sunny,
and perfect, perfect, perfect.

Our port of call in the archipelago is Rangiroa, the largest atoll of the
group. The *Sofia* rides in on a cresting wave that has been barreling along
unharnessed and unobstructed for thousands of miles. We just have to hang
on as the beast gushes through one of only a handful of channels carved
through the reef by eons of battering torrents of water. All *Sofia's* 123 feet
of tall ship shush through a cut so narrow that great slabs of cobalt blue
sea—from the wedge she slices out of the wave—rise in rooster tails above
her cap rails. We slalom between jagged flanges of coral before being
slickly deposited onto a still, velvet-green lagoon. As though we've slipped
through the looking glass, the raging ocean is transformed into a tranquil

pool. The roar of massive breaking seas is muted to an echo, a hollow drum of distant thunder that resonates somewhere in our bellies and mimics the numb, mumbled *whooshing* sound that you hear when pressing a seashell to your ear.

Inside the lagoon, we anchor off the Kao Ora Village Hotel. Here the benevolent proprietor offers our crew the use of a vacant bungalow where we can shower and from which we have easy access to town, as well as to the best diving sites. The village is small and neat, but unlike those in the Marquesas, the natives enjoy more modern amenities. Their homes are similar to those in a modest, middle-class American subdivision, all one story but outfitted with glass windows, framed doors, upholstered furniture, and even drapes. The children appear healthy and well fed. Most speed about the well-maintained roadways on shiny bicycles. Although we are still several nautical miles away, it is evident that we are in fact in the suburbs of the booming cosmopolitan center of the South Pacific, Papeete, Tahiti.

Meandering around town on my first day ashore, I come upon the island's Catholic church. It is of medium size, with an unpretentious exterior, but inside a marvelous surprise awaits me. As I enter, I'm swallowed up in a world of rainbows. The brilliant morning sun refracts through hundreds of miniature stained-glass windows that run the length of the building on both sides. This creates a prism effect, filling the church with fluid bars of light that billow along the walls, over the pews, up into the cathedral ceiling, and out across the floor, finally ascending the altar. I draw in my breath and whisper, "Oh, rainbows!" and all around me in soft stereo I hear "bows . . . bows . . . bows . . . bows." Settling into a pew, I sit very still, smiling like an idiot for the longest while. Every now and again I murmur a hushed "rainbows" just to hear the church sigh back to me. It does, each time.

Our crew for this leg is well stocked with licensed divers and avid snorkelers, and for good reason. The Tuamotus are reported to have some of the most exciting diving in the world. According to the travel books as well as scuttlebutt, the best dive spots are on the outer face of the reef. This means going back through the cut. The first diving expedition is attended by Lars, Barney, Pere-Axel, and myself. Axel, as he is known, is a long gawky drink of sweet Swede who joined the *Sofia* at the relentless insistence of his old pal Anders. The four of us load the *Salty Dog* with air tanks, masks, snorkels, fins, weight belts, spear guns, juice, and cookies. After affixing to the *Dog's* transom the old three-horsepower Evinrude that Barney found and reconditioned, we set out early in the morning.

We are able to float through on the narrow ribbon of slack water at the outer edge of the cut, where the submerged reef is just inches below our dinghy's shallow draft. Once outside, we have to anchor our tiny craft in open ocean, deep enough that we can ride the swells well clear of where the waves begin to break but close enough to shore that our anchor won't dangle hundreds of feet above the ocean's floor. Lars and Barney strap on their tanks and belts, dive in, and swim away. Axel and I slip on snorkeling gear. We've agreed to stay near the dinghy in case the anchor breaks free, allowing our shore boat to be carried off and leaving us stranded in open ocean. As we place our masked faces on the surface, we can see that the hook is caught fast on a coral ledge forty-five feet down. The visibility is extraordinary. We swim down twenty feet or so and invert our bodies to face the glassy surface. The water around us becomes scored by bolts of bright yellow light that appear to pierce the surface and plunge upward into a domed delft sky.

A large shark lolls several yards off, paying us only enough attention to satisfy his idle curiosity. Axel and I hold hands, drifting with the current as in a dream, rocked by the swells, immersed in an aquarium of living reef through which a confetti of sea life swirls, reflecting colors that defy duplication by brush and pallet. Just as I begin to realize that the motion is making me nauseous, Barney and Lars reemerge with their tanks empty but their eyes full of wonder. They report that it has been a phenomenal dive.

As we ready the *Salty Dog,* the guys rattle on nonstop about their adventure . . . until it occurs to us to wonder at the absurdity of what we are about to attempt. Do we hope to ride our tiny dinghy down the foaming wall of white water that is cresting ahead of us? It is a patently insane prospect, but by this time we are committed. The swell is lifting us up its vertical fifteen-foot humps. We have to row furiously, surf our boat down the curl, and guide her over to the calm peripheral strip of flat water by which we'd exited the lagoon that morning. Once we stem the tide, we reckon that we can just scurry on through the cut, much as we had earlier in the day. Instead, we find ourselves stuck dead in the water with monstrous breakers mere yards to port and knife-edged coral heads erupting to starboard. We are caught fast in a torpedoing rip current that is threatening to spit us straight back out to sea. The sum total of our combined efforts is just enough to hold our position—for the moment—but we know we won't be able to hold it for long. Feeling like simpletons, we realize that not one of us had thought to consult the tide table. We will later learn that the tide runs into the lagoon at this particular cut for only three hours each day. Just before and just after that interval, the current relaxes for thirty to forty-five minutes before changing its direction. It is the only time that a small craft can safely maneuver through, and we aren't lucky enough to have hit that window.

With no forward motion we also have no steerageway. It is all we can do to keep the *Dog* from yawing over to the certain disaster awaiting us on one side or the other. Nearly out of fuel, strength, daylight, food, and water, we realize that we are just going to have to muscle our way back in against the tide and against all odds. By now, being challenged by improbable feats requiring superhuman wit and will has become commonplace. I don't think we doubt for a moment that we'll make it. With a bare minimum of conversation, we set to trying.

Barney and Lars each mount a thwart (the seat in a rowboat), wrap their hands around a heavy oar, dig in their heels, and pull. Axel prods the outboard to produce just enough oomph to hold us but not so much that it'll overheat and conk out. I perch on the bow to scan for reef shallows and to direct our course, such as it is. It takes us more than an hour to make fifty yards. It feels like we're dredging through thick sludge, but we inch along. At the edge of nightfall we slip through. Only on the way home along the silent lagoon do we allow ourselves to ruminate about what it might have been like to spend the night at sea in a small craft with no shelter, juice, or cookies. All of us are much relieved that we did not have to find out today.

The diving is so phenomenal in these waters that despite the inherent dangers, we can't resist making one more trip to the outer reef. On the second occasion we are careful to coordinate our comings and goings with the tides. Motoring through the lagoon, we take a short detour to explore a cove where we've heard that commercial traps have been set to catch rare tropical fish that are shipped to fish fanciers all over the world. As we dive down, we see that the cages are a simple system of underwater fences with mesh tunnels through which all manner of sea life can enter but not exit. We tread water with our faces pressed against the screen, nose to nose with the most diverse and unearthly collection of creatures I've ever encountered. It's like visiting some futuristic, alien fish zoo. As we stare, hypnotized by the bizarrely costumed specimens, a pair of giant manta rays swoop in to check us out. These mighty inhabitants of the sea aren't about to be captured. Rather, they are like noble space-age guardians, cloaked in jet black capes and prominent metallic silver masks, patrolling the ocean depths. Strange and powerful as they are, they have an aura of eerie omniscience, and it feels comforting having them near.

Once out the cut again, our divers, more daring on their second attempt, prepare to go much deeper than they had previously. We watch from a few yards beneath the surface as they climb headfirst down the wall of coral until they are swallowed up by the darkness one hundred feet below. Axel and I monitor them until their saberlike torch beams dim to nothing and they are enveloped by tons of endless ocean. When they return to the surface, I ask if they had been at all frightened down there, so far and so alone. "No," they reply as if in a trance. "The two rays were there by our side the entire time," they say, "guiding, protecting, and urging us on."

The Tuamotus in their entirety are magical and glorious. Each new experience we have here seems better than the last. The archipelago is an embarrassment of riches. Its reef is vibrantly alive with multicolored microorganisms. The lagoon, with the exception of the traps, of course, is a veritable tropical fish sanctuary, and the coral arch's outer perimeter opens a doorway into the endless mysteries of the vast Pacific. By the time the Sofia is ready to depart, my senses almost ache from the succulence of this paradise.

We expect to arrive in Tahiti around July 14, Bastille Day. We are planning to hook up with many old cruising mates for the occasion. The celebration is expected to consume the better part of the summer and encompass most of the outlying islands as well. In anticipation of the gala our crew devotes its final days in the Tuamotus to sprucing up our weathered gal. The Sofia has a reputation (several, actually) to uphold among the elite fraternity of traditional sailing vessels. Her crew is famed for knowing how to properly maintain a strong, working tall ship. The Sofia is old, but we keep her proud. We fully intend to sail her into the party looking sharp, shiny, and shipshape. Even our resident goldbrickers turn to, making our old girl as polished as her sixty-odd years of hard use will allow. Readying our salty craft for show is a greater motivating force for some than readying her for sea. Looking ever so fine and dapper, the Sofia says farewell to the Tuamotus and sets sail for the fairy-tale islands of Tahiti, Mooréa, and Bora Bora.

The passage is expected to take twenty-four hours, but we hit an unusually brisk following breeze and are making an uncommon, steady eight knots during the trip. This threatens to bring us up on the Societies around sundown of the day we leave Rangiroa. We reduce sail to almost bare poles and rein our galloping steed in tight to make a dawn landfall instead. It's a matter of seamanship. The charts and pilot books provide enough information that we can manage a night landing with the aid of a well-lit entrance to the harbor. But entering these islands after dark is almost criminal. They are notably among the easiest anchorages in the world to make by eyesight alone, and it would be a damn shame to waste the opportunity.

Charts for various cruising grounds anywhere on the globe are readily available, but they can be pricey as hell. The money spent on these necessities alone can drain a circumnavigator's kitty. The Societies, however, are an area famous for giving a financially strapped sailor a break, at least in this one respect. The entrances to these islands are so clearly delineated by the alleyways through the surrounding reef that many a mariner has traversed them by using nothing more than postcards bearing aerial photographs of the area. The change of color from sea to inlet to lagoon is so precise that from the air it resembles Day-Glo base lines cut on a psychedelic ball field.

We slow our old girl down to a gentle trot, which allows us to come up on Mooréa around noon of our second day out. In the first bay we enter, we again meet up with the rumor that has haunted us since Panama. "The *Sofia* shouldn't be here. She sank off Costa Rica, dontcha know?" Are we destined to be a ghost ship of sailors reincarnate? I keep hoping the rumor hasn't somehow reached the States. My family would not appreciate it. Anyway, we also encounter forty- to sixty-knot gusts in the harbor, so it is just as well that we mosey on down to a more hospitable anchorage.

Cook's Bay, named for the famous British explorer Capt. James Cook, proves to be a better bet all around. We anchor next to the *Club Mediterranean,* a four-masted transatlantic single-handed racing schooner. She is up for sale, a sad, dilapidated relic of her former self. Still, she is a marvel to behold, a ship comparable to the *Sofia* in length, yet rigged and outfitted to be operated by a single, solitary sailor. Hard to imagine.

Mooréa turns out to be a lovely island, offering many pleasant rustic hotels and good restaurants to supplement its inherent beauty and natural recreational facilities. Like the neighboring sophisticated metropolis of Papeete, Mooréa is more accessible than the atolls, which makes both islands popular destinations for the jet-set. We discover that a Club Med is tucked away on a secluded corner of the island. Resorts of its type aren't unfamiliar to most of us. Although the bulk of the *Sofia*'s crew is not tempted to risk crashing *that* party, a few of us are not inclined to miss such an opportunity. Lars and I, a bit of an item by now as a result of our joint ventures off and away from our shipmates, fairly jump at the chance to enjoy a little depravity.

At first light we pack our fanciest duds in waterproof duffels and swim around to an outlying sandbar frequented by the hotel guests for "Beginners Snorkeling." We hang out there until low tide, when we wade ashore and confidently join the throng of tourists mingling about the grounds. Sussing out the situation, we conclude that we'll have to find somewhere to stash our belongings. A row of bungalows way off on the perimeter of the property looks promising, so we try each door until we find one that is unlocked. We enter, determine that it is unoccupied, and move in.

Lars and I set out hand in hand, like a wealthy, handsome young couple on exotic holiday in the islands. I find it intoxicating. The risk we are taking makes our sojourn here far more thrilling than it would be if we were here legitimately. This awareness disturbs me ever so slightly, but my discomfort soon dissolves into a delightful arrogance. I am a Sofian, which somehow makes me feel superior, even here. Would I be at the Club Med on Mooréa in any other circumstances? Not bloody likely. Would I want to be? Probably not. But I am a Sofian—a world traveler, an accomplished tall ship sailor, a sea bum, a risk taker extraordinaire, and I hold my head high.

Like mischievous, truant schoolchildren, Lars and I dash off to play among the rich and famous. He can't wait to get back up on water skis. I wander down to the nude beach where I make myself comfortable on a plushy padded terrycloth lounge chair, noticing abstractly that I'm the only one here already sporting an all-over tan. Lars soon reappears. He has expertly slalomed up and down the lagoon and boasts, "I've still got it!" It is midday, so we join the caravan of privileged frolickers who are strolling toward the luncheon buffet. Lars is flagged down by his new fan club of adoring, water-ski enthusiasts, who urge us to join them. Two large carafes of French wine—one white and one red—are set at each table. An imposing spread, easily fifty yards long, is laid out down the center of the spacious open-air hall. Oooh-la-la, I can hardly contain myself. I keep giggling and nudging my coconspirator in the ribs. He, in turn, does his darnedest to ignore me as he engages our dining companions in lyrical conversation in a variety of languages.

When our companions ask why my fingernails—difficult to hide during lunch—are black, Lars pipes up to say that I'm an artist who, yes, strange as it sounds, dabbles in the eccentric medium of painting with pine tar. The odor is unmistakable and overwhelming. A few eyebrows are raised, but no one takes issue with the explanation. They are, after all, on vacation and ever so congenial. No worries! When someone inquires about the tropical ulcer scars that crust our ankles, courtesy of the evil Varmit, I get right into the rhythm of the charade, explaining that we stumbled into a nest of nasty sea lice while wading in the shallows. "Sea lice?" Our alarmed luncheon chums make a mental note to be especially careful of *them*.

Ultimately, though, the relaxed atmosphere, further oiled by several more carafes of cabernet, begins to have its effect on us. Soon Lars and I are spilling our guts. Our new confreres are intrigued. They make us promise to sneak them out to the *Sofia* for a full tour. And when we humbly suggest that perhaps we should be getting back to the ship, they simply won't hear of it. We've been the best entertainment of their trip, our tales of adventure on the high seas eliciting astonished ooohs, aaahs, and ardent pleas for more. Honored that we graced their table and chose them as accomplices in our victimless crime, they aren't about to lose us.

A few other yachts from the Marquesas have, like the *Sofia*, taken refuge in Moaréa before slamming headlong into the manic fanfare of the annual Bastille Day salute. Among the other boats on Cook's Bay is a yacht out of California, which we met up with on Nuku Hiva. Her captain is a real piece of work, an uptight, neurotic accountant whose cruising experience thus far totally belies his vessel's name—*Motivation*. He simply doesn't have one for being out here. Quite the contrary, he is a lovesick sad sack who blusters incessantly that he needs to go home to his girlfriend. That's all good and well, as nobody—with the exception of his two exasperated deckhands—really gives a damn where he goes. The deckhands had sold all their worldly possessions in order to board the *Motivation* for passage across the South Pacific to New Zealand. Although resigned to eternal misery in the company of their homesick skipper, by the time we reunite with them in the Societies they are facing an even more dismal future. The *Motivation* is turning back, and the accountant has threatened to dump or desert the deckhands in the middle of the South Pacific, unless they agree to return home to the States with their insufferably whiny captain.

The French authorities have prepared well for such eventualities. Orphaned sailors left on their doorstep is an all-too-common occurrence. So the islands' customs and immigration authorities require that each and every cruiser passing through their territory post a $900 bond. This is the

approximate cost of a one-way ticket out, to anywhere. The local government has no intention of playing nursemaid to a regular procession of
abandoned and destitute seafaring vagrants.

Darla, the female member of the *Motivation's* crew, is expecting her
boyfriend to fly in and rescue her. Joey, her fellow deckhand, has no such
option. He has hardly any money left and even less desire to pack it all
in and return home. Joe is now a bird of passage, midway in the tropics,
with an all-consuming New Zealand-or-bust fervor and an equally overwhelming quandary. Rick, a member of the *Sofia's* crew struck up a fast
friendship with Joey in the Marquesas and has a brainstorm. He
encourages Joe to join the *Sofia* as her official cook, in exchange for passage to New Zealand. Such an assigned position has thus far been unheard
of aboard our self-righteous cooperative, but the *Sofia* has amassed a sin-
gularly spoiled and demanding crew complement here in the Pacific. A
very vocal quorum of this bunch is passionate about not having to spend
one more day sweating over our behemoth diesel oven. Nor are these folks
polite when faced with questionable meals prepared by our ever-growing
company of pretty crappy chefs. The lobbying grows loud, fast, and furious, so Rick convinces Joe to join him for a little holiday while Joe decides
what his next move will be. Joe and Rick reckon that they too can pull
off a quick, illicit visit to a Club Med.

Rick is a card-carrying stonemason, as ruggedly handsome as he is
rough around the edges. Joey, on the other hand, is a young licensed phar-
macist from New York City, who perhaps under more favorable circumstances would have had the street smarts to pull off a Club Med scam.
Both have been cruising for some time, however, and in the laid-back, freewheeling style of the hobo sailor, they've let their hair down—waaay
down. They are unwashed, unshaven, uncouth and unadorned, muddy tan,
covered in oozing sores, overly enthusiastic, and inappropriately familiar.
This is the French playground of the Pacific and hoity-toity as hell. At
the Club Med on Mooréa, our two cheesy lads stick out like maggots on
a month-old brie.

After scoring themselves a bungalow where they stash their rucksacks,
Rick and Joe scamper off to join in the fun. Spotting a beach volleyball
class, they take up positions as though it's a regular old pick-up game in an
inner-city school yard. Dressed only in cutoff overalls with dirty kerchiefs
tied around their shaggy manes, they play like true urban cowboys—as
though their lives depend on it. They dive, they spike, they shove, they
curse, they bump chests and slap butts. They win. The other players are

frankly terrified of them. Returning victorious to their secret hideaway to clean up for cocktails and dinner, they charge through their bungalow door and are stopped short. The resort concierge and two big, burly security guards are convened on the bed. Their arms are crossed over their chests, and they wear smug smirks on their French faces.

Rick suggests to his accomplice that they make a run for it. Instead, Joe, in true "Queens" fashion, whips out his wallet and asks what the nightly rate is. Nightly rate? Oh, please! After confiscating their visas and seeing— thank gawd—that they aren't both from the *Sofia*, the authorities charge them exactly ninety-two hundred francs, the equivalent of U.S. $100, coincidentally the exact amount of Joe's remaining traveler's checks. Then they advise our sports, in no uncertain terms, to hit the road running. When Lars and I get wind of the bust, we quietly make our own exit, with our new Club Med buddies promising to visit us aboard ship. They do many times during the remainder of our stay on the island. It seems that no matter where the *Sofia* happens to be, she is where it is happening.

Joey, now in even more dire straits, consents to join the *Sofia* as her cook. But he still needs to officially clear off his yacht and sign on to the *Sofia* in Tahiti. Papeete is the capital, chief port, and business center of the Societies. Its yacht harbor is a quay running the length of the seawall that fronts the city proper. When we arrive, every flavor of floating craft imaginable is stacked up beam to beam like a colorful display of multinational bric-a-brac. Approaching the wharf requires carrying out a complicated series of maneuvers in heavy traffic. Vessels have to motor in stern-to and perpendicular to the quay, toss out and set a bow anchor, and then scoot backward into an open lane until aft mooring lines can be secured to the dock bollards lining the main street of town. The *Sofia*, hefty as she is, slips into her slot as slickly as a knife blade slips into its sheath. The best happy hour entertainment at the quay during the days surrounding the Fete, however, consists of watching one fancy yacht after another botch its docking. One of the more memorable of these fiascoes is played out by the *Motivation* and our pal Joey himself.

We can hear *Motivation* approaching long before we see her. Her skipper is shrieking at the top of his lungs at his mortified crew. We dash off to top up our cocktails and then settle in on deck for the show. As the yacht approaches, I recognize Darla back aft, holding the stern line in preparation for leaping ashore. Joey is on the bow, feeding out anchor cable. "Captain Maniac" is at the helm, red-faced and sweating profusely, demanding, "Faster, Joe! Faster, goddammit!" Joey responds by tossing out chain in handfuls as the boat speeds astern at an alarming rate. We are on the edge of our seats, I can tell you. Darla hunches on the quarterdeck, bracing herself and suddenly looking very pale. The skipper squeals one last time for Joey to "hurry the fuck up!" We all watch in elated horror as the bitter end of the chain sails through Joe's fingertips and disappears beneath the surface with a sickening plunk. Joey plops back on his butt with a thud. Someone has neglected to shackle the anchor chain to the yacht. Big oops.

Darla manages to grab hold just as *Motivation* plows stern first into the wharf and then bucks hard forward, tossing her irate and startled skipper ass over tin cups into the cockpit. He frantically sticks his head up like a flushed quail and continues to berate his deckhands but at a higher and wholly incoherent octave. The quay is in blubbering hysterics. Cackling laughter rises from dozens of boats in all directions. The *Motivation* bounces about stupidly in her slip. The crew of the *Sofia* is fortunate enough to have ringside seats. We cheer appreciatively as Darla throws down the mooring lines, marches on top of her ex-boss, storms below, snatches her already-packed duffel, and leaps ashore. She never looks back, save for theatrically spinning and double-flipping her nemesis the big bird. We give her a standing ovation.

Joey, ever the gentleman and thorough seaman, ignores the stammering, frothing recriminations of his soon-to-be former captain and adeptly secures the yacht to the dock. Then he gathers his belongings, cocks his head to one side, purses his lips in his compliant Joey grin, and gives the *Motivation* a farewell nod before disembarking and sauntering on over to the *Sofia*. We haul him aboard, hand him a drink, give him a slap on the back, and quietly move into the next chapter of the *Sofia's* saga.

On Joey's first official morning as ship's cook, he sets to preparing the special inaugural breakfast he's shopped for in town. Our kitty allots him 50 cents per person per day to supplement the on-board dry goods. Joe shoots the wad on eggs, lots of them, for a commemorative French toast feast. He neglects to notice in his shopping fervor, however, that the *oeufs* are hard boiled. So as the hungry crew waits eagerly, forks and knives clutched in meaty little fists, he whips up a mean cornmeal porridge instead. Then he concocts a truly sumptuous egg salad for lunch. Joey proves to be masterful with herbs and spices, turning even humdrum fare into gourmet delicacies. And he demonstrates that he can think on his feet. We are sufficiently impressed. The *Sofia* has herself a cook.

After five grueling days of cooking, cleaning, and shopping, though, the

Sofia stands to lose her new acquisition. Ship's cook is at best an unglamorous and thankless job. Joey longs to turn a splice, climb a ratline, or set a square sail. He will cook, he decides, as long as it isn't all he is permitted to do. Besides, he's a hell of a sailor whose culinary expertise, although impressive, isn't all he has to offer. He decides that he needs someone with whom he can share the galley chores. We commission him to go hunt up such a person.

Enter Tami, an eighteen-year-old blond bombshell of a surfer from San Diego who hopped aboard a yacht in Mexico skippered by an incompetent yahoo. She subsequently also finds herself adrift in Tahiti and is not inclined to be sent home. Our Joey first met Tami back in the Tuamotus when she bounded ashore after a looooong crossing, burbling, "God, it's great to finally be on Apitaki!"

"Yeah, but you're on Rangiroa," Joey offered.

"*Shit*," she guffawed, "I gotta get the hell off of that jackass's boat!"

She did just that and is now also conveniently in need of working passage to New Zealand. Joey and Tami form an alliance and present their proposal to the *Sofia's* crew. Our male constituency takes about a half-second to welcome young Tami aboard. They don't even bother to ask whether she knows how to cook. The rest of us—the female persons, that is—are almost as pleased to have her. Tami is full of infectious energy and youthful exuberance. She is also, by far, the youngest on board, so she is christened our resident "Kid." It fits and it sticks. So does Tami. The *Sofia* has herself two—count 'em—*two* chefs for the crossing. Ah, the decadence . . .

Joey and the Kid host a huge homemade pizza party to celebrate their new positions. Yachties and locals alike clamber aboard. Among the visitors for dinner is a big, comely native named Totu, who was once a bodyguard for Muhammad Ali. Totu is so taken with our ship, her crew, and the to-die-for pizzas that he insists on reciprocating. Totu informs us that should we need to get away from the hoopla for a bit, he owns his own *motu*, a tiny undeveloped atoll. It lies just off the island of Bora Bora, right next door to Marlon Brando's private *motu*, he confides. We are to consider ourselves welcome there any time. Totu's impressive entourage assures us that his offer is sincere. If we need to retreat to relative peace and quiet in the meantime, however, Totu suggests a mellow getaway just around the lagoon on the island's back side called Maeva Beach. Here, he says, we will find a nearly deserted anchorage fronting a surprisingly swank hotel. It sounds ideal. Much as we enjoy a good bash and the company of our fellow cruisers, the quay is becoming a mite close for comfort. The *Sofia's* immodest style of living is decidedly cramped by crowds. Swinging bliss-fully alone at anchor, where we can take care of business without skulk-ing about in the dark for fear of offending the tourists or violating some civic code, suits us better than squatting in the center of megalopolis. We motor on down, socking away in our memory bank a couple of the other snuggeries suggested by Totu: the outlying islands of Raiatea and Huahine.

The Fete is big, as big as any celebration I've ever participated in. Thou-sands of people from all over the world converge upon the tiny Societies for a gala that is a cross between Mardi Gras and an all-fraternity kegger on homecoming weekend. It is wild, upbeat, sultry, musically infused, alcohol-hazed, dawn-to-dawn, days-on-end communal debauchery. I'll say this much for the French—they do know how to throw a party.

Half the time the *Sofia* has piles of unidentified bodies crashing on board. Come dawn, most drift off to wherever they came from. Always, a few stay, and some even sign on. Sofians come in all shapes, sizes, and circumstances. Somewhere along the line, we acquire a Hungarian fellow named Julius, and what a story he has.

One night Julius divulges the truth about his mysterious past. He de-scribes to us how, as a boy, he dived from a freighter steaming off the coast of Italy. He swam the dozen or so miles to shore and exited the ocean wearing only his underwear. Then he strolled over to a portside bistro, swiped a Cinzano tablecloth off a counter, draped himself in it as though he were nobility, and haughtily demanded sanctuary. It was granted. Young Julius continued his quest for freedom, eventually making his way to New York City. He didn't know a soul there, nor did he speak a word of English, but he somehow managed to land himself a job as an apprentice in a company that manufactured false teeth, of all things. Continuing his pilgrimage in the promised land, Julius reached California and became a resident of his long-dreamed-of utopia, Hollywood. Ensconced, employed, and in possession of a green card, he was able to bring his family over from Budapest for a visit. But he was so concerned that his poor, peasant parents would suffer serious culture shock that he devised an elaborate plan for introducing them gently to the United States. At this point the story becomes just a tad suspect . . .

Julius said he met his parents at Los Angeles International Airport, wel-coming them with a huge batch of brownies secretly laced with a lid of marijuana. They munched these lustily as they drove straight to Disney-land. His eyes light up as he recalls how proud his parents were to find out that their son was such a successful young man in so sparkling a new land—which they have unwittingly experienced through a dreamy, chocolaty, hashish haze. When we press him about how he ended up aboard the *Sofia*, Julius lowers his mischievous ebony eyes, waggles his curly mop of hair, and pensively strokes his full, glossy beard. He confesses that, after all, he is a gypsy and born to wander. We are completely beguiled by him. He is, we determine, a Sofian of the first order.

I especially remember one discussion with Julius when he, Joey, and I are standing a night watch together. These are often special moments, quiet times when a sailor's thoughts run deep and conversation becomes meaningful . . . or not. This night we are on the subject of food, always a popular topic on board. Julius is marveling at Joe's ability to make magic meals in our spartan galley. He is curious to know how Joey learned to cook.

"Well," Joe explains, "when I was little and I said I was hungry, my mother would tell me to cook a meal."

"When I was young," I offer, "my mom always prepared everything for me."

We both glance over at Julius, who is mulling this over. Finally, he pipes up proudly, "When I was a boy, back in Budapest, long, long ago, and I was *so* hungry, I would say, 'Mama, I am *so* hungry.' And she would answer in her beautiful soft voice *so* full of love for her own small boy, 'Hey, you, Julius! Go steal sometink!'"

Among the multitude who come and go during the *Sofia's* South Pacific sojourn, Julius is a rare find, but others are also noteworthy. In the perpetual jumble of personalities, some become principals in memorable vignettes. For instance, one of our more highfalutin "passengers," as he prefers to think of himself, is a physician from San Francisco. This character—we call him Dr. Dutch—is instrumental in hiring Joey for the *Sofia*. He even tries to hire other crew members to do his routine shipboard duties. Dutch shamelessly advertises his single, driving desire to relax and score with as many French Polynesian beauties as his limited time and self-proclaimed prowess will allow.

As Dr. Dutch's luck has it, another crew member who finds her way to the *Sofia* at about the same time, an emerging feminist named Nan, very vocally deems our young doctor's attitude to be reprehensible. The squaring-off and sparring between these two provide the rest of us with steady entertainment. When he becomes especially exasperated by Nan's merciless condemnations, Dutch resorts to baiting her, making Nan the brunt of the abuse that she otherwise levels at him. He'll lie in wait. A large audience will assemble. Then he'll pounce with some quick-witted, evil-tongued attack. Actually, Dutch might be a pompous, sexist, obnoxious show-off. We Sofians, however, have long since given up engaging in the counterproductive act of judging the moral fiber of our compadres. What's the point? If you can sail—or you can pay—you can be here. We are a pretty forgiving lot. But Nan is new and as yet uneducated in the social mores, or lack thereof, of our unconventional society afloat. Live and let live is not part of her persona of "ethical woman of the '8os." She still cares, while Dutch, quite probably, never has.

Nan is determined to beat that dead horse, and Dutch delights in inciting her to publicly swing the bat. Nan takes offense at any reference to "making it." Whenever Dutch gets bored with the futility of the game, he resorts to more creative material just to keep it lively. He'll say things like, "Hey, Nan, a couple of us men are going ashore. You can tag along, but you'll have to *make it* back on your own, in case we *get way*laid."

The irony is that our randy lads are all pretty roundly rebuffed by the local womenfolk. I've witnessed their rejections in every pitiful way, shape, and form imaginable. On one occasion I am watching when the ever-hopeful Mikey jumps into a dance with a young Tahitian beauty. He is convinced that she has been making "hey there, big fella" eyes at him, and he just can't restrain himself. As the music gets louder, a large crowd encircles the pair. The island woman is moving to the drum beat in traditional Tahitian fashion, hips swinging, shoulders jittering, knees fluttering. Mikey is just kind of galloping around, trying to keep up. It soon becomes unavoidably clear that Mikey's excitement is rising as the dance progresses. But we can only watch helplessly, stupefied that he has set himself up for such an embarrassing public display. Finally, the music stops, and Mikey's dream of a young, lovely Polynesian conquest turns and walks away without so much as a backward glance. The crowd is not dispersing, however. Everyone is rooted, gaping at the forlorn Mikey, his pathetic little shorts looking ever so much like a pup tent.

Even Dr. Dutch eventually becomes resigned that the *Sofia's* young studs aren't in high demand among the island women. He settles, coupling instead with an itinerant tourist like himself. They become known aboard ship as Dr. Dutch and the Duchess.

It should be noted that the guys on the *Sofia* aren't the only amour obsessed island occupants. Lasciviousness seems to have reached near epidemic proportions in the Societies this summer, and Sofians are not the only aggressors. In fact, we female sailors receive our share of invitations.

Dozens of French military troops have been shipped in to participate in the Bastille Day celebration. I don't know how many soldiers and sailors have been dispatched to the Societies, but I'll wager that a fair number of them find their way over to our tall ship. Fresh young recruits in uniform seem to just love our boat, and the French are no exception. They swarm us whenever we're in spitting distance. We spend the proscribed period fending off their ardent advances. Soon they relax and we're able to become friends. These young Frenchmen are so docile and mild mannered that I question the appropriateness of their decision to join the military. "Aren't you lovers, not fighters?" I ask. "Oh, to be sure," they agree. They go on to explain that the French military is not in the business of building combatants. Rather, it is designed to educate young gentlemen and to provide them with the instruction required to pursue a profession. They further assure me that not only will they never be sent off to war but that they don't receive one lick of weapons training. "What then," I wonder, "do you expect will happen if your country is attacked?" "Oh, not to worry," the young cadets continue, "America will, of course, come to our rescue."

This final statement is delivered with the cock-eyed mix of complacent certainty and sarcastic disgust that I have come to expect whenever the subject of national security arises. The United States is often perceived as the evil, war-mongering big brother, a bully who brutally intrudes a gloved fist into another country's business when it is neither required nor appreciated. But what about, perchance, when it is needed and wanted? "Well, then, the Yanks had bloody well better high-tail it on over and be damn quick about it!" seems to be the universal consensus.

My new enlisted buddies escort me around the island. They are anxious to expose me to as many of the positive aspects of their people as possible, knowing that it will be difficult to dispel the American sailor's stereotypic notion of the French. By and large, we regard them as rude elitist snobs. But my pals are desperate for me to think well of them, both as individuals and as a nationality. They usher me all over, even into restricted areas where I am allowed only because I'm in the company of servicemen. All the while, the lads coach me in French, careful to instruct me in most of the subtle nuances of the language.

I find one French colloquialism particularly amusing. It flows off the tongue with such fluidity that I use it often, reciting it to waiters after a meal, visitors sharing a particularly magnificent bit of scenery, or just whenever I'm feeling fine. In French, the cliché is *Je prends mon pied*. It translates into "I take my foot." I understand this odd saying to be suitable as an expression of supreme pleasure following an exemplary experience. Each time I use the phrase, however, my cohorts drop their heads, make effusive apologies, and whisk me away. They finally clear up the misunderstanding. It turns out that this idiom is a double entendre used almost exclusively to express the bliss specific to a satisfying sexual encounter. They neglected to tell me that part.

When the time arrives for the *Sofia* to abandon the celebration, the young officers come down to the quay to see us off. We share tight embraces, kiss both cheeks European-style, and shed a few tears. These partings are hard. We all know that we'll probably never meet again. Yet we say farewell instead of goodbye, always leaving the door open, hoping that someday, somewhere, . . . perhaps. It's easier this way. For my part I find solace in being the one who is leaving. Staying means sameness, routine, and a sense of security that is for me somehow false, more disturbing than it is reassuring. Even so my heart aches with each separation. The soldiers are sorry to see us go. They have been touched deeply by our wandering tall ship. Were it possible, I believe these young men would come along. As a result, the *Sofia* again leaves behind her a trail of longing, a dockside of folks whose lives won't allow them to cut loose, jump aboard, and run away, no matter how much they yearn to.

As the *Sofia* pulls away from the wharf where she has long rested, I take my post on the quarterdeck and wave farewell to my friends. I watch as they snap to attention to salute our noble vessel. Then, turning away to immerse myself in the comforting exercise of shipboard duties, I hear a chorus of hoarse male voices carrying lightly over the water, barely audible as we drift off. "Je prends mon pied," it cries, "Je prends mon pied."

On the short passage to Bora Bora a few of us take ill. We might shrug it off as Bastille Day hangovers, except those afflicted aren't among the more notorious partiers of our group. Norman is ever the gentleman, in control and never, in my experience, a big drinker. And Andrea, who spent the better part of the last rough passage patiently holding her boyfriend's forehead as he wretched miserably over the side, possesses an iron stomach. But as we sail away from Tahiti, these two are green around the gills or, more accurately, yellow around the eyes. When the customs officials board the *Sofia* in Bora Bora, they are quick to offer a diagnosis. Hepatitis. Our ship is forthwith banished to an empty anchorage and put under strict quarantine.

Here we lie, off Bora Bora, often called the most beautiful island in the world, and we aren't allowed ashore—again! After shipping Andrea home to Canada and getting Norman on a strict treatment regimen, we sit and wait out the required incubation period that will ensure that the rest of us aren't also infected. When we're given the all-clear, we naively motor over to anchor with the rest of the yachties off the Bora Bora Yacht Club, only to find that we aren't welcome here, either. The club's mercenary pro-prietors seem to be congenial only to those who have a substantial amount of money to blow in their establishment. After the Fete, most of us on the *Sofia* are pretty well tapped out, so we definitely don't qualify. Besides, "Don't you Sofians have hepatitis?" We are beginning to feel like pariahs. Not a ship to be easily defeated, however, we traverse to anchor off the famous Bora Bora Hotel instead. Here, we are surrounded by magnificent snorkeling spots and have easy access to shore. I reassemble my trusty bicycle and set out to explore the island. A few inhospitable morons aren't going to ruin my trip. It's hard to keep a good sailor down for long.

I find that I am able to circumnavigate the island in a single day. On the far side I discover the Bloody Mary Hotel, a rustic bar, restaurant, and bungalow complex that sits right at the water's edge. George, the owner, is a big-as-a-brick-shithouse Polish flirt who boasts to me and to anyone else who drops by that he is featured in the movie *Hurricane,* which was filmed here a few years earlier. He doesn't have to try to impress me, how-ever. His mai tais are so yummy, his presence so companionable, and the scenery so lovely that he can tell me anything and I'll nod with effusive appreciation. I'm just thrilled to be welcome somewhere.

Nonetheless, a few random friendships, beautiful vistas, and carefree jaunts aren't enough to ward off the pall that hovers over us on this par-ticular island. We are being hounded by negativity, so incongruous at such a felicitous time in so impeccable a spot. The *Sofia* and her bohemian ways have become the object of malicious ridicule—and worse. On Bora Bora we are being scapegoated as the villainous blackguards responsible for all manner of petty (and not so petty) crime being perpetrated ashore. First, the yacht club lambastes us for swiping rolls of toilet paper from its stalls—OK, that could have been true. Then, the Bora Bora Hotel accuses us of absconding with tableware from the room service trays left outside in the halls. Well, I can't help but notice that a few new cafe-au-lait cups have found their way into our galley. But last, and most slanderous of all, are the vile accusations that a member of our crew has been behaving in-appropriately with the local youngsters.

The authorities have no proof, but they don't require any. They demand that we leave quickly and quietly. Demoralized by the charges, and knowing full well that we have no venue for contesting them, we are forced into compliance, thereby tacitly admitting guilt. It is abominable. Someone on the *Sofia* has gotten on someone's bad side on the island, and all of us are being punished for it. "One for all and all for one" swings both ways. There is no separating a single crew member's actions from the culpability of the vessel as a whole. The *Sofia* is being kicked off Bora Bora, expelled from the most beautiful island in the world, and told not to return. Oh . . . my . . . gawd! With as much dignity as we can muster, we weigh anchor and slink away, hoping to find some measure of sanctuary away from the French fast lane in the quieter outlying islands and *motus.*

On Raiatea we meet other sea bums like ourselves, bona fide cruisers traveling without the benefit of flash yachts or wads of dough. Kurt, a master shipbuilder out of Port Townsend, Washington, is here aboard his trusty *Ishmael* with his American girlfriend, Genna, and first mate, Jim, from New Zealand. Utes, an old German single-hander, is also in residence aboard his beamy double-ender, the *Frauken 10.* The *Longevity,* skippered by an intriguing fella named Dave, rounds out the anchorage. It feels like a fine old wooden boat regatta, and the *Sofia* fits the profile to a tee, both in body and spirit.

Genna and Jim are aspiring wooden boat builders, learning the craft from Kurt on the fly. The *Ishmael* is his prototype, and he has her out for a long shakedown cruise. Utes is just kind of sailing around, sampling local brews and chatting up the lasses. The only thing about him that seems even remotely old is the thick, weathered, leathery skin on his face, earned by decades of beating into his beloved sea while trotting about the globe aboard the succession of ships he's spent most of his satisfying seventy-odd years constructing. Dave is also skippering a fine old wooden craft, but he didn't build her. I later learn that he acquired her in a less than conventional manner, the circumstances of which make for a sea story that I'll not soon forget.

A fine web of channels stretches out in all directions to a sprinkling of tiny secluded islands and *motus* around Raiatea. The waters appear far too shallow for the *Sofia* to navigate, so when Dave invites me to come along for a tour aboard the *Longevity,* I accept. I need a stretch away from my crewmates. The developments of late rankle. Besides, I'm curious as hell to get the lowdown on old secretive Dave and eager to try my wings aboard *Longevity.* Sailing a tall ship is a unique experience, to be sure. However, handling a small boat is a wonderful sailing experience. It's a bit like the difference between racing a Porsche and driving an eighteen-wheeler. It is healthy to mix it up a little.

Dave is an artful sailor, as well he has to be because he carries no auxiliary power aboard his boat. He tells me that she was outfitted with an engine initially, but he followed in the hallowed footsteps of many a sailor before him by tossing his motor into the drink somewhere in the middle of an ocean. Strange as that sounds, it is a venerable and honored tradition among skippers since ships first took to the sea. A heap of coughing metal beneath a suit of clean canvas is something that a significant segment of old salts cannot stomach. Out in the wilds, I get around to asking Dave about the origin of his vessel's name.

Dave was a big city cop, on the force for about twenty years. When he was a rookie straight out of the academy, he and three other young cops had the pragmatic, albeit morbid, insight that they should set up a fund. The reserves were meant to be collected by whomever was fortunate enough to live the longest. They agreed that the survivor would use the money to retire from police work and would devote the remainder of his days to living out his one great dream. Each man had taken a solemn oath, making a pact to carry out this honor in memory of those who had not been granted that opportunity. Their chosen profession was admittedly a very dangerous one and they did not delude themselves. Dave confessed that the pact had created a bond among them that offered a glimmer of hope and served as a constant source of comfort during the tragedies that consumed the ensuing years. Each of the four officers contributed some portion of his salary for two decades.

By this point in the story I have deduced that Dave alone has survived. Following the death of his third and final partner, he keeps the promise. Dave leaves the force, withdraws the money, buys a boat, and sets sail for a world that is as far from the horrors of his past existence as he can get. This has always been *his* dream. I sit quietly as the storyteller pauses in his tale. Taking a deep breath, he concludes that the fellas had christened their collectively amassed assets the "Longevity Fund."

While exploring aboard the *Longevity,* Dave and I bump into the *Ishmael* in an idyllic anchorage hideaway up a deep, secluded inlet that leads to the isolated jungle village of Faaroa. By marking the depths along the channel, I know that the *Sofia* can navigate it. I can't wait to inform my crew. It is the consummate *Sofia* spot—remote, wild, and accessible.

The *Sofia* beats a path to the anchorage just as fast as her little engine can carry her. Once here, the rest of the crew concurs with my initial assessment. Faaroa is magnificent. A deep smoky lagoon winds upstream into dense jungle, where the most isolated tribes, almost completely untouched by outside influences, still live. We no sooner set our hook than entire families emerge from the trees and set up residence on the *Sofia's* deck, as though she's an extension of the landscape. We don't object. Cohabiting with the locals feels quite natural. They move in, we move around them. Everything is copascetic. We share foodstuffs, combining their fruits and vegetables with our grains. Fresh fish caught daily by the joint efforts of our crew and the village youngsters is always the entrée. Each meal is a feast. The natives cook on deck, making us slightly nervous on our all-wooden home. Joe and Tami cook down in the galley. Only when we prepare popcorn do the local women dare to venture below, their curiosity getting the better of them. They are fascinated by the process and ecstatic with the result.

They gather in a bunch, clutching one another in gleeful anticipation as they hover over our huge corn pot and wait for the eruption. As the kernels begin to pop, producing a tittering rhythm against the iron kettle, the gallery leans in. Then, too excited to contain herself any longer, one of the ladies reaches over and flings the hot lid off the pot, inciting the gawkers to shriek and go off like champagne corks as the steaming kernels and boiling oil fly about the saloon. Each time it is as if they're discovering the phenomenon for the first time. Popcorn becomes a mandatory side dish for every meal in Faaroa.

The day before the *Sofia* is to return to Papeete, we throw a party for the villagers to thank them for sharing their Eden with us. The festivities begin at dawn. Morning drifts into afternoon, afternoon melts into evening. The rum flows, the kernels pop. By midday the party has hit a crescendo. The local children, who have been climbing and leaping from the rigging into the lagoon all morning, are ready to rev their game up to a higher gear. They begin to jeer at us old folk, taunting us into participation. Eventually, our rum-tinged derring-do overpowers our good judgment and we take up the challenge. Matches are staged. As if in a vertical limbo contest, participants ascend the ratlines, clenching in their teeth the rope swing that is attached to the lower yardarm. Higher and higher we climb, coaxed into leaping from one batten after another. The farther up we go, the more slack we allow in the line. When we jump, it stretches taut, flinging us fifty feet into the air like the bitter end of a crack-the-whip and flipping us topsy-turvy out of control until we hit the water. The fearless youngsters fly through the sky, performing athletic flips and spins before entering the sea, making nary a ripple. We more bulky, drunken, and far less agile Sofians careen through space like ungainly buffoons, our bodies contorted in wholly unnatural poses.

Barney and I outlast even the youngsters. We tie for the record—the fifteenth ratline batten—and call it a day. The game is not over for everyone, however. No sooner have we settled down to nurse our drinks and our bruises than the curtain rises on an encore performance. Glen, an architectural student from Boston, emerges from the companionway in full costume. With a pareu draped across his shoulders, gaudy warrior paint streaking his face, and stripped down to his itty-bitty tighty-whiteys, he is the image of John Belushi's samurai from *Saturday Night Live*. Glen is of Asian descent, which contributes to the authenticity of his impersonation. Our valiant samurai mounts the rail, ascends the rigging, and jumps. Flying headlong out over the water with his arms, legs, and cape outstretched, he looks more like a fat flying squirrel than a superhero—and he has forgotten the rope. His startled body, spread as flat as a Frisbee, hovers parallel to the water for a few breathless seconds before it drops, smacking the surface face first. Glen sort of drifts there motionless like an inflatable floaty before sinking. Just as it is beginning to look like we'll have to rescue him, he emerges, grinning and waiting for his applause. The locals cheer enthusiastically. They have no clue what he's attempting to do, so they deem him the undisputed champion of the competition and try for the remainder of the day to re-create his winning stunt. Glen doesn't dare repeat it, though. In fact, had he not been "feeling no pain," I'm sure he'd hurt like hell. It is a day full of innocent fun, and it is a fitting finale to our stay in Faaroa.

The *Sofia* returns to Papeete, only this time we're here to work, not to celebrate. Our windlass needs restoration before we can continue on. However, the money required to cover the cost of shore power (electricity), materials, and leasing a working slip is substantial. Our ship's kitty is almost dry because upon entering Tahiti the *Sofia* had to float the bond for most of our less-than-solvent crew. These monies will not be returned to us until we leave the French territories. We ever-scheming sailors have prepared for just such a predicament, however. While in Costa Rica we laid in a huge stash of what promised to be a highly marketable trade good down the road—coffee beans. Our cargo hold is stuffed with hundreds of sacks of coffee purchased at 50 cents a pound but worth an easy $5 a pound in the pricey port of Papeete. That's a profit margin to sing a sea chantey about. We make a bundle, cover our expenses, and even have some reserves with which to stock up on our next trade item—the local wine, bottled in plastic one-liter containers, and sold for less than one American dollar each. We call it "Chateau Plastique." It isn't half bad when left to breathe for a day or so.

Refurbishing the *Sofia*'s ancient windlass is an arduous task that requires skilled labor. Besides Barney and Evan, only a few other shipwrights and journeymen on board will be responsible for most of the work. After disposing of the coffee—a transaction accomplished under the table to avoid the fat local taxes—the rest of us don't have a whole heck of a lot to do. So we take turns taking off.

I jump aboard the *Ishmael*, and we set out in search of Totu's *motu*. As I've been issued an open invitation and am not likely to be back this way anytime soon, I don't want to miss it. It turns out that Totu is the real deal. We follow his directions and find his lovely little landmass precisely where he said it would be, right next door to Marlon Brando's. The *Ishmael* can't get in close enough to anchor, so Jim and I lower the sailing dinghy and make for the private getaway. It is perfection. The thin lagoon that runs through the *motu* is chock full of sea life, more than enough to sustain us, just as Totu promised. On the island is a single open hut, a stone fire pit, a grove of coconut palms, a stand of wild lime bushes, and a net for catching fish—everything we need.

I return to the *Sofia* several days later to find that the windlass is almost ready. I soon determine, however, that the crew is far beyond ready. Just as sweet desserts consumed immoderately will putrefy in the gullet, Tahiti, such a delicacy, has made many in the *Sofia*'s company sick. We have glided about these fantasy isles as though sealed in a bubble, insulated and immune, but in fact the *Sofia* is way out of her league in Tahiti. We simply can't afford to remain in French Polynesia any longer. New crew (and even some of the seasoned veterans) have been seduced into believing that our shipboard life can drift indefinitely at this level of self-indulgence. They are dead wrong. If we don't leave these islands soon, they will be the end of us. The *Sofia* is a working ship. Her funds are all but depleted. The bulk of her crew is chronically hungover, and she is seriously "landlogged." Our vessel is as desperate to reach open ocean as her crew is to remember what it means to be sailors. It is long past time for us to get our shit and our ship together.

As we finally prepare to depart, I take curious note of our newest acquisition. Below decks, positioned in a place of honor on the bulkhead above the saloon table, hangs a work of art, a touching bon voyage gift from a friend we made on Mooréa. Her name is Heftsy, and she crafts exceptional batiks in her studio home on the outskirts of town. The batik that she presented to the *Sofia* is a square yard of cloth dyed in soft colors, depicting a Tahitian nymph nestled amid a wild profusion of tropical flowers. It is a beautiful piece, yet when I stare at it, an eerie uneasiness creeps over me. Something in the nymph's eyes is curiously knowing yet mysteriously sad. Her expression suggests a loneliness that belies her beauty and a despair that her free spirit might otherwise contradict. Ah, but the sun here is brilliant. The breeze now is fresh. These are the things that I am sure of. So I shrug off any nagging, disquieting feelings. The *Sofia* sails on, as do I.

Crew and locals on board *Sofia*.

chapter 9

Too Many Have Come before Us

The Cook Islands, the Samoas, and the Kingdom of Tonga

Somewhere, and I can't find where, I read about an Eskimo hunter who
asked the local missionary priest, "If I did not know about God and
sin, would I go to hell?"

"No," said the priest, "not if you did not know."

"Then why," asked the Eskimo earnestly, "did you tell me?"

—ANNIE DILLARD

INTRODUCTION

Discussing in a neat critique the three remaining island groups that we
visited is a formidable task. The Cooks and the Samoas stubbornly resist
a single classification. The Kingdom of Tonga, on the other hand, was just
that, a kingdom in and of itself that exuded security and comfort. It
was a calm and lovely setting that allowed us to catch our breath following our whirlwind ocean transit. One had only to look at the *Sofia*'s course
on a chart to see how far we sailors had come, both in terms of miles
logged and sea legs flexed. Tonga was an appropriate port of departure
from the crossing, a soothing interval between an energetic dash across
the Pacific and a long layover in New Zealand. But before Tonga came the
Cooks and the Samoas, and unlike the self-possessed Tongan group, they
appeared to be struggling with their identity.

In the Cooks we spent most of our time on the island of Rarotonga.
Part of a voluntary association with New Zealand, on which it depends
for defense while retaining self-rule, Rarotonga offered us a sampling of
a culture we'd sailed an ocean to experience. The Maori—as the South Sea
islanders occupying New Zealand's mainland are known—were reconciled
to their affiliation with the United Kingdom, of which New Zealand is a
part. But those Polynesians remaining on the small protectorate islands of
the Pacific found the British cultural influence to be insufferably irritating.

Similar circumstances existed in the Samoas. The three main islands that comprise this group are the American Samoan island of Tutuila and Western Samoa's islands of Upolu and Savaii. During the twentieth century a veritable smorgasbord of governments influenced and commanded the peoples of these obscure island groups. The resulting cultural schizophrenia was evident everywhere. I would catalogue a goulash of adventures there, yet any attempt to place my finger on the erratic pulse of this confusing and complicated culture would ultimately fail. The most powerful impression that remains with me today is of that which had already been lost.

∾

JOURNAL ENTRY
Bay of Islands
New Zealand
December 1980

Many of our newly acquired crew members married their souls to the *Sofia* while vacationing in the romantic Society Islands. But on the passage to the Cook Islands the honeymoon is over. It's a hellacious crossing, a fast, blustery bolt before fresh trade winds atop an exuberant sea. The *Sofia* is hoofing it at a steady twelve and a half knots, well exceeding her proscribed hull speed. Those who can handle her do. Those who can't get out of the way. Many are horrendously seasick. They're condemned to retch alone and uncomforted. We sailors have our own hands full, and for us it is a glorious ride.

After six wet and wild days we are coming up fast on Rarotonga, the capital of the island group and the *Sofia*'s predetermined port of call. We who have worked the ship are both exhausted and exhilarated, master tall ship sailors doing what we know how to do best. Those who have barely survived the voyage, either because of their own bottomless pit of nausea or an abominable inability to perform a single constructive task aboard ship, are dazed and bewildered. They wear that unmistakable look of "What the hell happened to paradise?" on their pale and drawn faces. The *Sofia* has reclaimed dominance to command the journey, in all her glory.

We tally the casualties. A cheerful young Swedish couple who hopped aboard in the Societies puked in tandem the entire sail to the Cooks, hardly cognizant enough to tend to one another's sorry needs. They are a mess. Karen, as usual, was wretchedly ill the first couple days and then sprang out of it and assumed her responsibilities as a capable sailor. She is a trouper, sick as a dog—and knows she will be—the first few days of every passage yet sticks it out as one of the longer-standing veterans on board. Some lucky people never get seasick. Some never get over it. Most, however, acclimate and are then done with it for the duration. But Karen gets sick, really sick, every single time we put to sea. Still, she never packs it in and runs home. Many who witness the repetition of this grim process think that she is just plain nuts. I think she is a champion. I am damn proud of her and always feel reassured to have her along. A few random others were also pretty well done in by the malaise of moaning, gagging lethargy, that ever-loyal accomplice to nonstop violent vomiting. The good Dr. Dutch and his duchess weren't too visible on deck this passage, nor was Nan. But it didn't matter. We knew better than to factor them into the watch schedule. They were froth, extras without whom we could manage quite adequately. One of our number who was necessary, however, also took ill with a vengeance and battled valiantly to continue attending to his duties. Joey was seasick.

A mariner since boyhood and a seasoned ocean sailor, this odd twist caught Joe off guard. We deduced that the diesel oven was the culprit. Being trapped below, preparing heavy greasy meals while inhaling bitter sooty fumes, was more than many a hardened seadog could stomach. Joey did his darnedest, nonetheless. We'd see him fly up on deck several times a day, spew explosively over the side for a few long, repulsive minutes, and then stumble back down to resume his cooking chores. For the rest of us, it was a less-than-appetizing prelude to a meal. We, of course, never let on that we were revolted. He was trying so hard.

Tami pitched in and helped out when it was clear that he needed a breather. Joe is happiest and healthiest on deck anyway, and his sailing abilities are invaluable. Tami was eager to test herself as a tall ship sailor during this passage too, however. She's bustin'-a-gut to learn everything and try anything, in fact. Fortunately, besides owning a steady belly she possesses boundless energy. Tami manages to do it all. She's like a puppy, racing around all excited, everywhere at once, then on a moment's notice collapsing into a dead sleep, only to later awaken and do it over, again and again. Kowabunga!

Just outside Rarotonga, the customs agent approaches by pilot boat to escort our vessel in. We assume that this is standard procedure as we are entering a new territory. Because the Cooks are a protectorate of New Zealand, we need to officially clear out of French Polynesia and enter the

United Kingdom. The officer informs the helm that once inside the narrow channel, we are to tie up to the wharf, where he'll complete the necessary formalities. "Lead on," Evan concurs. "We'll just crank up old Juni and motor on over."

Well, actually, the *Sofia* does not and has never maneuvered real slickly under power. Her prop is undersized and its pitch is slow to respond. Typically, we take this into account and are able to accommodate for it. But we have not been made privy to this port's peculiarities, and we are not given time to respond responsibly. In fact, as it turns out, the *Sofia* has no business being in here to begin with. This becomes abundantly clear once we get a good gander at the harbor. It is tiny—teeny-weenie—and packed. Anchoring is clean out of the question. But where is it that we are instructed to tie up?

The agent on the pilot boat motions crisply over to the dock. We look that way, shake our heads, and look back at the officer. He is making even more commanding gestures so we look again. Slotted between a long string of ships tied stem to stern along the wharf is one lone empty stretch of about, oh, say, 150 feet, tops. The *Sofia* measures just under 125 overall. But she possesses a jutting bowsprit, menacing catted anchor flukes, piercing yardarms, and cumbersome, protruding backstays. She is one hundred tons of lumbering snarl just waiting to tangle. As if on cue, all heads on the *Sofia*'s deck spin 180 degrees, searching for an avenue of retreat. No such luck. The harbor is shaped like a lightbulb, the ball too crowded for us to turn around in and the neck too narrow for us to squeeze out in reverse—not without taking a good half-dozen yachts with us. The customs agent is now gesticulating frantically and quite unprofessionally, I might add. Clearly, we are going to have to parallel park our ponderous old girl, and we are going to have to be pretty damn quick about it.

Everyone in the half-pint harbor is now on full alert, standing on the decks of their boats preparing to fend us off—another cruel joke as the *Sofia*, besides not being very maneuverable, is also not very "fend-off-able." In fact, when she has some way up she's patently unstoppable, like a tank.

Evan takes another hard look at the tight squeeze and sags visibly. Then he sighs, recovers, stands erect, and takes control. He is at the helm. Norman is at the pitch lever. Evan shouts out, and bites off his commands.

"One ahead! One astern! Half ahead! Half astern!"

Back and forth, inch by inch, we "unch" our ship, each series of screeching, grinding shifts nudging us negligibly nearer to the wharf. It is going to have to be a magic trick, a real sleight-of-hand, to pull this one off. So of course we are committed to accomplishing it. All our experienced crew members are at the ready, bracing around the yards, hauling in the running backstays, poised in an armored stance, electrified, prepared to perform whatever insane act will be required next. The inexperienced and unenlightened crew members are doing what they always do in these situations. They are hiding . . . but not where they can't witness every bit of the drama. This promises to be a feat, or a fiasco, not to be missed.

Standing on the raised quarterdeck, I straddle a stacked coil of three-inch hawser, which is the *Sofia's* stern line. I hold a half-dozen smaller coils of this line neatly in my left arm. In my right hand I grip a tight spiral of a thinner length of line with a monkey's fist (a heavy knot of intersecting loops) tied and dangling at the bitter end. It is ready to be heaved into the outstretched hands of the lads on the dock, who will then be able to haul in the attached, much weightier mooring line.

I am waiting . . . waiting . . . waiting. Now, I've got a bloody good arm, and I've successfully thrown a heaving line on numerous other occasions. This, however, is dicey—deadly dicey—and I definitely need to get it right on the first try. Deciding to defer to the skipper for the go-ahead, I glance over my shoulder at Evan. He is glistening with sweat and emitting a faintly familiar sour stench, one that I have detected on him only a handful of times during the years I've known him. I recognize it straightaway as his "nerve toxin," as he calls it. Suddenly, I realize that he isn't at all sure that we can deliver the goods. The amount riding on his bet is unfathomable: our ship, the ships around us, our crew, the hands on the dock, a major tussle with the authorities, endless red tape, and on and on. The toll, if we fail, will be enormous.

Evan knows his ship well. He knows that she is not going to be able to motor into that spot, and she isn't going to hold steady where she is much longer, either. We have kicked up so much turbulence with our propeller and our hull wash that we are being buffeted about like a child's bathtub toy. The boats at anchor are rocking like buoys in a wild open sea. The ships tied to the wharf are alternately stretching their spring lines taut and snapping them back, causing their beam ends to crash with thunderous force against the dock. Everyone in the miniature harbor is alert and appalled. Disaster seems imminent, and it has the *Sofia* written all over it. Wide-eyed and gape-mouthed, I hold my palms, full of line, up to my captain.

"Evan?"

"Swim!" he orders.

"Uh-huh . . . What?" I waver.

"Swim, goddammit! Now!" he commands, really loudly.

Aarrrrrggghh!

The surface of the water is roiling, black and slimy, with a thin coating of bottom muck dredged up in all the commotion. I lock my grip on the heaving line, pounce up onto the rail, and dive well out, careful to clear the whirring prop blades. Surfacing, I slip the rope between my teeth and sprint for the dock. The route is treacherous, blocked by the hulls of a dozen vessels, which are careening tumultuously back and forth. It is like swimming a gauntlet. Waiting arms haul me up out of the tide, drag in the hawser, and begin to sweat it in on a bollard. I run down the dock, catch the bowline, and line up with the pile of bodies that is arching to draw the *Sofia* in—sideways. She does fit but just barely. All in all, it is a perfectly ludicrous exercise.

The *Sofia* stays in her parking spot for the duration of our visit in Rarotonga. We have wedged ourselves in and are content to leave well enough alone. Besides, Rarotonga poses no problems for us as far as privacy and propriety are concerned. The authorities provide us with ample shore facilities for maintaining personal hygiene.

Rarotonga turns out to be a delightful experience. It is a little nibble of New Zealand life. The spoken language is predominantly English, the currency much like that in the States, the customs familiar. And the amenities are bountiful and affordable. The village is more like a small city, with its main street lined with a succession of shops and restaurants. A double scoop of full-cream ice cream costs 60 cents. Steaming meat pies are a dollar. And Steinlager, a damn good New Zealand beer, is on tap cheap, everywhere. We find actual grocery stores where we purchase fresh New Zealand dairy products and produce and discover one of the United Kingdom's treasures—a thick, waxy, salty, vitamin-rich paste called Vegamite. I love it, buy it in half-gallon tins, and spread it on everything. We also visit the local movie theater. Ironically, it is showing the film *Hurricane*. My old pal George from Bora Bora hasn't lied—totally. He isn't in a leading role, as he implied, but you couldn't miss him, bald, bloated, and sporting lipstick, one of the extras in the famous courtroom scene.

A bunch of us rent mopeds and venture off to explore the island. We find it to be a tapestry of mud roads slithering up mountains through dripping jungle to burgeoning rivers, pools, and waterfalls. Rarotonga is wet, with a significantly cooler and rainier climate than that of the islands where we've spent the past many months. This is a pleasant deviation, at first.

After a bit, though, chronic mildew begins to consume the ship, making her dank, dark, and musty. The *Sofia* is now a tropical gal. She requires gentle warmth, a regular shot of sunshine, and a soft, dry breeze to keep her in good nick. Consequently, in just a matter of days in damp Rarotonga, our ship begins to take on the disconcerting stink of rotting driftwood. This gives the newer crew members yet something else to be nervous about.

The people of the Cooks are native South Pacific islanders, and they've learned to speak English with a refined European inflection. But they don't appear to have embraced as readily the bulk of the British trimmings. The merchants are polite and formal, as are all the government liaisons with whom we have official dealings. Their interactions with us, however, feel stilted and rehearsed. Once we get out of town and are able to roam the countryside, we experience a very different brand of islander.

We find that the vast majority of the people of the Cooks are still very much Polynesian in character and culture, although they can and will turn British if they need to. These are inherently imperturbable people with no grudges to hold or battles to wage. But when they get away, loose in their own natural element, they behave as unconstrainedly as a pack of fourth graders liberated from a stuffy parochial school. Out in the wilds, these locals still maintain their native traditions and customs. Clothes come off, exposing intricate and elaborate body tattoos. Stiff upper lips relax into broad, open-mouthed grins and waggling tongues. Their behavior is playful and ecstatic, feeding an atmosphere both joyous and deliciously irreverent. Traveling back into the city is a bit like stepping through a time warp, or culture schism, or both. The inequities created by the naturalness of the Polynesian cultures and the taboos imposed upon them by the missionaries has reached the level of absurdity. As we visited the more heavily touristed areas of the Society Islands, we encountered posted notices on the peripheries of the hotel and resort grounds, advising vacationers to wear ample and discreet clothing when entering the local towns and villages. The resorts' dress codes had become quite lax, with nude bathing and topless beaches being commonplace, much in the style of the French Riviera. The signs, however, warned that the locals in the villages would be embarrassed and offended by what they now considered less than "proper attire." What a hypocrisy! The islanders had never given a thought to hiding their beautiful bodies until the missionaries barged in and taught them to be ashamed. It seems that the wealthy Europeans have bought back their God-given right to nakedness while the poor, frightened, and less enlightened islanders, still reeling from the missionaries' religious sermons about skin and sin, remain intimidated and overdressed. A dichotomy does exist here, but it's not manifested in mutual exclusion. It's just kind of . . . sad. Rarotonga is, nonetheless, fascinating. It whets our appetite for New Zealand and introduces us to the Maori culture.

The run from the Cooks to the Samoas is like that from the Societies but with substantially more tacking involved. We need all available hands for the frequent sail changes, so it is fortunate that by now most of our crewmates have found their sea legs. Everyone manages, and manages the ship quite well, but it is a squally sail, both above and below decks. The *Sofia*'s hull is being worked hard. Her fastenings are tired, and her seams are sagging. The large stretch of copper sheeting that we've patched and repatched and that covers her bow where the planks butt the stem is coming away once and for all. The wood beneath it is mushy, the fastenings rusty and bleeding. The crinkled metal is doing more to hold the sea in at this point than to keep it out. It's apparent that we'll need to haul the *Sofia* before we reach New Zealand. American Samoa is a likely spot to do it. So we duck our heads and charge on. The rough beat to the Samoas finds our crew manning the bilge pumps 'round the clock.

We use our manual pumps almost exclusively. We activate the auxiliary electric pump only when our Deutz generator is running and only in emergencies. Because we haven't filled up with diesel since Venezuela, we are now careful to conserve fuel. Our reserves need to last us until we make New Zealand, and we are already down to near dregs. Pumping has become a daily exercise—literally. It is the type of tough, rhythmical, aerobic workout that I personally thrive on.

The *Sofia* has two manual pumps. For the one that is set on deck amidships, a mate inserts a pole into its collar, which is flush with the planks, and push-pulls while a large black rubber diaphragm sucks bilge water straight up and out across the deck. The other pump, which is set into the forward port corner of the afterdeck house, is more intricate, however, and requires greater finesse in handling. It is my favorite. First, I heft a six-foot length of ten-inch plastic tubing from its slot next to the engine exhaust. Then I lay it across the deck, fitting one end into a sleeve at the pump outflow and pushing the other end through the scuppers. I jam a long, heavy rod into the neck of the diaphragm, grasp the bar with both hands at about eye level, stand hunched with legs spread-eagled, and begin rocking back and forth with a steady thrusting movement. Often a second crew member will hop up atop the paint locker that's set over the pump, cock a leg, lay a foot on the rod, face the other pumper, and kick down hard with each pull. It's a bit like wielding a two-person saw. The synchronization has to be perfect for optimum effect. The pump slurps, forcing water by the gallons to gush through the tube. Both "leg" and "arm" toilers work up a righteous sweat. It's a prime opportunity for some intimate interaction between the two people engaged in this effort. Julius, for instance, will dash over from wherever he is to assist whenever a female crew member is stationed at the big pump. He insists that he finds it oddly erotic, in a purely platonic sort of way, of course. While either standing or sitting across from him, swaying in unison, all sorts of spongy sounds emanating between us, Julius's dark eyes twinkling with mischief, a lascivious grin playing at the corners of his mouth, I find it impossible to keep a straight face. We pump and giggle, giggle and pump, until the bilges are bone dry—at least for the time being.

We swing that old rod nonstop all the way to our first port of call in the Samoas, Pago Pago, on the island of Tutuila in American Samoa. For nearly a century the United States controlled the Samoan Islands east of the 171st degree of west longitude, but in the 1960s American Samoa adopted its first constitution and established an independent local legislature. The port of Pago Pago was considered the only viable harbor in Samoa, though, so the United States set up and has continued to maintain a naval base here. It is still considered an important link in the chain of American bases in the Pacific.

All across the Pacific, we've been treated to horror stories about the port of Pago Pago. It is wryly referred to as one of the world's most beautiful harbors, which has been reduced to one of the world's most hideous garbage dumps. On the approach to the anchorage the first half of that description seems to be a pathetic understatement. A graceful dogleg channel is bordered on both shores by lush towering cliffs of dense tropical flora. As a seasoned veteran of at least several dozen anchorages, I could be jaded, but Pago Pago's first leg truly is breathtaking.

The long narrow seaway appears to snake through a lost valley between soaring mountains of vegetation that explode in color and scent. As we tack around the bend, however, the harbor draws anticlimactically into view. The town itself is a slapdash jumble of tin roofs and fading multicolored buildings constructed from a variety of incongruous materials. Aluminum siding is no stranger to this South Seas paradise. The most prominent edifice, perched high on the cliffside overlooking the bay, is familiar to any classic film buff. It's the Rainmaker Hotel, the site of the World War II movie of the same name. Upon closer examination we notice that the top half of the structure is missing. Amused locals later inform us that years ago the U.S. Navy, in an attempt to impress them and to generate some semblance of acceptance of the military's imposed presence on the island, orchestrated an elaborate Fourth of July gala, complete with bomber fly-bys. One plane failed to clear the roof of the hotel, crashed into the world's most beautiful harbor, and put an abrupt halt to the festivities. This is such an entertaining tale that I admit that I have never checked into its authenticity. Suffice it to say, it is the widely accepted truth among folks hanging out in the Pacific these days. As of our arrival, the hotel had not been repaired, nor had much of the other damage residual to the U.S. military's occupation.

The harbor is a traffic jam of hulking, rust-striped merchant and commercial vessels flying the flags of a dozen nations. The tropical sun's golden rays reflect in a slimey rainbow splash across a greasy slick of oil that smears the surface of the bay. Visibility is extremely poor in the tainted, murky water, making anchoring a nightmare. Invariably, no sooner is a hook set than it catches and fouls on some rotting war relic that clutters the junkyard of Pago Pago's ocean floor. It is not uncommon for a group of divers, braving the foul water and laboring for hours to clear their anchor, to raise a discarded jeep in the bargain.

After entering the harbor, we're body-slammed into the reality of having traded a bona fide paradise for paradise lost. The harbor patrol officer curtly instructs us to tie up to an abandoned, half-sunk tug that is moored in the dead center of the cesspool. This hurts our feelings, but as always we are resilient and decide to make the best of a bad situation. (It will be a while before we learn what some of our more delinquent crew have in mind in this regard.) Evan goes ashore to make arrangements for hauling the *Sofia*. Others row over to the clot of Taiwanese fishing vessels stacked up like scrap metal and overflowing with masses of dirty toothless little men who demand our attention the instant we enter the harbor. The foreign swabbies beckon us with high-pitched unintelligible squeals and a frantic waving of arms. They aren't allowed off their ships, so they try to induce our freewheeling crew to come over and barter. They look like refugees from a POW camp.

Still others from the *Sofia* decide to check out the vessel that we are so discourteously assigned to tie up to. This turns out to be a bad idea, one of the many we'll suffer for in the months that follow. I choose to venture ashore and get a feel for the island myself. I want to try to find evidence of its former beauty.

On my quest I run into two adorable, engaging, blond, decidedly American children. They look like they've been magically sucked up from the manicured playground of a wealthy stateside prep school and accidentally deposited here on the dirt roads of Pago Pago amid a passel of big, dark, wild Samoan street urchins. I'm astounded. Their father emerges from a shop and protectively collects them while introducing himself to me. He says his name is Bob. His children are Joshua and Sunshine and, yes, they are from the States, he allows. Why are they here on this least glamorous of all the islands in the South Pacific? Why not, he says, dismissing my question with a shrug. Bob and the children ask if they may escort me around town. I offer to bring them all out to the ship in return. They are wonderful guides, intimately familiar with the history of the island and the character of its people, as though they've been here for some time.

Industry, commerce, and the accompanying amenities do abound in this busy port. One has to make a hefty trek overland, however, to find any remnant of the natural state of the island or its original inhabitants. The locals, inherently large in stature and gifted athletically, are often engaged in baseball, rugby, and soccer matches. A veritable patchwork of playing fields dots the landscape all around the town. (We eventually are made privy to the sport in which the ancient Samoans were known to truly excel.)

When I return to the *Sofia*, I learn that a few of our lads have discovered what they presume to be a genuine cash cow aboard the foul commercial fishing boats of Pago Pago. They have traded moldy stacks of old *Playboy* magazines for several massive sets of shark jaws. Although they are pleased as punch with their end of the bargain, I fail to see the enterprise in these gaping, toothy monstrosities, particularly when I get a good whiff of them, which isn't hard to do because they reek. Braving a more thorough inspection, I notice maggots squirming around, and I put my bare foot down.

"You get these gawd-awful, putrid carcasses off the ship!" I demand.

"We traded for them fair and square and they're ours!" the guys argue limply as more and more of our crewmates begin to gather round, holding their noses and looking mad as hell.

"Take them ashore and bury them. Let the red ants and sand crabs have a field day," I scream. "They're fucking infested!"

The guys take a closer look, and when they realize that there is yet life in them thar skulls, they know they're beaten. Absently trying to brush themselves off while scouring their chest hairs for vermin, they complain, "But, well, what if someone steals them?"

They get no sympathy from us. Those who've puked most of the way
since Tahiti are frankly sick of being sick. The rest of us are trying to
clean up our act—both literally and figuratively—as best we can since
leaving the Societies. Our already soiled image will not benefit by having
gamy, ghostly visages hanging like bizarre voodoo ornaments and adding
their odors to the perpetually fetid, steamy heat of the stagnant harbor of
Pago Pago. A flag of skull and crossbones sent aloft to the *Sofia*'s top mast
couldn't do us more harm.

Evan finally settles the details of the haul-out. We will be allowed to
use an old facility that is rough and funky but ideal for our needs. When
the *Sofia* is on the slipway, her work area is anything but neat. We do all
the labor ourselves, attacking every diseased facet of our ailing wooden
vessel. Consequently, the job, while by no means slapdash, is messy, manic,
and continues 'round the clock. Therefore, shooing us off to somewhere
out of sight, sound, and way out of the way is always advisable. In Pago
Pago the authorities don't need to be warned twice. We are banished to
a deserted area where the amenities are nil. None! So a few of our fellas
grab four oars, a sheet of canvas, a disembodied commode, and, voilá, they
construct a makeshift restroom right here on the dock, complete with a
couple of rolls of fluffy French toilet paper ("gifts" of the Bora Bora Yacht
Club, no doubt).

This haul-out is alarming. The *Sofia*'s hull is in much worse condition
than we expected. For some of the new crew members, coming face to
face with it is a real wake-up call. For others it is a shrieking siren to
abandon ship. For the rest of us it is a call to arms—arms, hands, feet,
fingernails. The projects list is, as always, daunting. And, as always, we
plow through it. Every material we use is toxic. Each process is hazardous.
Because of the tropical heat, however, even while working we wear a minimum of protective clothing. Consequently, we also end up wearing much
of the evidence of our efforts: paint, tar, epoxy, varnish, and the like. And
as a result of this, we have to bathe in raw diesel fuel, rinsing our bodies
and our brushes with the same harsh solvent. Imagine! And we hardly give
it a thought. Well, most of us hardly give it a thought.

Extreme circumstances will give rise to strange bedfellows. Here Dr.
Dutch and Nan have a rare meeting of the minds and enter into an unlikely partnership. They both flatly refuse to dabble in noxious carcino-
gens. "Why should we take such a foolish risk? We've got no allegiance to
the *Sofia*. We're on holiday, for crissakes!" they argue. Their conscientious
objections don't go over big with the rest of the us. We remind them, "If

you want to eat, and you want to sail, you have to work. If not, adios and no hard feelings." They offer to buy us off. "Uh-uh, no way!" When all else fails, they reluctantly take their places on the scaffolding with the rest of us, except that they are incognito beneath grimy coveralls, old sneakers, ragged socks, big orange rubber gloves, wide-brimmed sun hats, and ill-fitting snorkeling masks. Grudgingly and gingerly, they pitch in. Ah, but they are a vision to behold!

Our new friend Bob helps us out on the slipway while his kids, Josh and Sunshine, flit about, injecting the whole dismal arena with a healthy dose of fun and light. When the time comes for the *Sofia* to leave Pago Pago, we invite Bob and his children along for a tour of the islands of Western Samoa. They leave us in Apia, our next port of call, but not before winning the affection of the entire crew and entrusting us with a secret that each of us will have to learn to deal with. On one watch during the passage Bob finally confides that he was a successful attorney in the States and therefore understood the U.S. court system exceedingly well. He was all too familiar with the current trend in family law: The mother has to be practically certifiable to be denied custody of her children. Bob and his wife had been going through a nasty divorce. He believed that his wife was an unfit mother who was about to hook up with a real louse. Certain that the courts would not assign him primary custody of the children, he grabbed his son and daughter and bolted. For the time being, American Samoa is a relatively easy place to hide out: same passport, currency, language, customs, and so on. When we meet Dad and the kids, they are officially on the run.

Bob couldn't have chosen a safer place to acknowledge his history, and surely he knew this. We on the *Sofia* are not in the blame game. This must be glaringly evident to anyone who becomes more than a passive observer aboard our ship. I reckon Bob is confident that his secret will be kept with us. Nonetheless, I do struggle with this information. It sparks some inkling of ethical outrage not yet totally dead in me, just in a remission of sorts. My window into truth and righteousness has gotten a bit fogged up, and my moral muscles are atrophied, but I still know what is fair and what is just. Sadly, I also know that in the circumstances Bob described, the legal system in our country can sometimes be neither. I also believe, however, that no parents should ever be sentenced to a lifetime of never knowing of the whereabouts or the well being of their children. So where does that leave me? Engaged only in a philosophical exercise. This personal insight comes as a revelation. I discover that out here I am becoming something alien, someone whom I sometimes have difficulty recognizing. Bob is correct in his assessment of us. We will not intervene. The *Sofia* will sail on. Lives will intermingle. Apathy will bury condemnation. Opinion will lie dormant. The tribunal will not assemble here. Judgment Day hasn't come to the *Sofia*. Not yet.

Beyond learning Bob's big mystery, our voyage from Pago Pago to our first stop in Western Samoa is pretty uneventful. It is a pleasant enough passage, save for the rack of shark jaws that is mounted back aft on the davits over the *Salty Dog*. Our guys' paranoia got the best of them, and they exhumed their trophies prematurely. When the *Sofia* put to sea, the jaws were still rotten and rank as a week-old roadkill. Even the Varmit doesn't go near them. We demand that either the fellas find a way to hang their prizes as far downwind as possible or we'll chuck them over the side. They make an effort, and it does become marginally tolerable on board until the wind comes around, which it has an annoying tendency to do, and carries the stench forward. Whenever this occurs, the crew, gagging and cursing, makes a mad dash for the bow. A great flock of seagulls has accompanied us out of Pago Pago, and they stick with us most of the way to Western Samoa. The birds hover, en masse, above our wake like a billowing white parasail. One or two routinely break formation to drop down and snatch a maggot from the sharks' gory gums. Consequently, we also have a light dusting of bird shit adorning the taffrail. Really delightful.

Our first stop in Western Samoa is the large port city of Apia on the island of Upolu. It is intended to be our only port of call in Western Samoa and our final destination in the island group.

Before World War I, the United States shared control of the Samoan Islands with Germany, but in 1914 Britain seized the port of Apia from the Germans, and the Versailles Treaty of 1919 awarded the rest of German Samoa to New Zealand. In the early 1960s the territory became a free and independent country, but the German and British influences are still very much in evidence when we visit.

Apia is a fresh surprise. We anchor well out in the harbor, just off a beachfront dominated by an austere-looking structure. It is the famous Aggie Grey Hotel. Reportedly, its namesake was the model for Bloody Mary in the musical *South Pacific*. No semblance of the colorful, exotic person depicted in the story is evident anywhere at the hotel, though. In fact, the lodge exudes an ambiance that is quite the opposite: polished and very fine. I soon learn that the hotel serves a proper English tea every afternoon, precisely at four. I vow not to miss a single one.

Every day I return from my wanderings or stop my work projects by midafternoon. Then I bathe and dress carefully, clean under my nails, put on SHOES, and row ashore. The hotel lobby is cluttered with wealthy European tourists. They artfully balance a delicate china cup and saucer in one hand while resting a small plate of beautifully sculpted, little triangular sandwiches in the other. The spacious dark wooden lobby is filled with several small, ornately carved, antique glass-topped tables around which are poised two or three similarly styled high-back tapestry chairs. A large buffet table is set against the far wall before a series of French doors that open out onto a superbly manicured garden. First, I help myself to a cup of Darjeeling and a few dainty sandwiches. Then I concentrate on finding suitable dining companions, all the while attempting to appear aristocratically blasé.

The anchorage in Apia is well stocked with yachts full of cruisers, some of whom also manage to make their way in for tea, and they are conspicuous in this crowd. The soft melody of hushed whispers and tinkling china is intermittently perforated by rough, heavily accented voices, jarring amid the otherwise prim conversational overtones. I chart my way in their direction as though guided by radar. Even with their mouths closed, the cruisers are pretty easy for any educated eye to spot. Their plates are piled ridiculously high with the bitesize tea sandwiches in a sloppy mountain of disarray. At Aggie Grey's I also taste my first cucumber sandwich. I'm quickly smitten, can't get enough, and vow to consume at least several daily, each with a thick slathering of Vegamite, for as long as we stay in port.

Another fascinating aspect of the island is the mammoth open market. It carries a startlingly varied and cosmopolitan selection of items, from English herbs and spices to an eclectic assortment of European delicacies. The market epitomizes the general flavor of the island, which is a colorful mix of diverse cultures. The sense one gets of the locals in Apia is that they're a comfortably genteel people. It is small wonder that Robert Louis Stevenson developed so intense an affection for these natives that he made this island his final home.

Stevenson came to the South Pacific with his family in the late 1800s and settled on Upolu. He became so beloved and revered by the Samoan people that when he died, sixty Samoans carried his body to the top of Mount Vaea, where he was buried and where his grave site remains today. They called him Tusitala, or Teller of Tales. This is how the locals still refer to him. I visit his grave. It is captivating, adorned only with the tiny mountaintop flowers that grow wild here. The words inscribed on the author's tombstone are his own. His now-famous epitaph ends with these lines:

> Here he lies where he longed to be;
> Home is the sailor, home from the sea,
> And the hunter home from the hill.

On the return from our trip to Robert Louis Stevenson's grave, we run into a burly fellow with a bushy beard and a quick smile who introduces himself as a New Zealander, or a Kiwi, as he prefers to be called, after one of the more prolific cash crops of New Zealand, the kiwi fruit.

In any event, we meet this Kiwi, who tells us he lives on the neighboring island of Savaii with his wife and children. He's part of a small New Zealand community that manages a large mill for a mainland lumber company. I, in turn, tell him that we're off a circumnavigating tall ship, bound for New Zealand, and invite him to join us aboard for dinner.

Once Evan gets wind of our new Kiwi friend's situation, he gloms onto him. Evan rarely deigns to scam for pocket change or toilet paper, but acquiring survival necessities for his ship seems to be a priority as well as a proficiency of our skipper's. It is decided by evening's end that the *Sofia* will leave Apia and set a course for the wild outer Samoan island of Savaii. Evan has long dreamed of resoling the main cabin and building a proper chart table in the aft cabin. Our new pal assures him that on Savaii not only will the finest timber be at his disposal, milled to his precise specifications, but it will be dirt cheap. The Kiwi will see to it personally, and he and his family will be at our disposal for the length of our visit. As Savaii is far less touristed than the other large islands of the group, the locals, he warns us, are less amenable to intrusions. Well, Evan is practically salivating. Actually, it sounds pretty darn sweet to the lot of us— a worthwhile stop for the ship's welfare and an adventure for the crew, to boot.

Before our new buddy takes off for the night, he and a couple other fellas from our crew hatch yet another scheme. They discuss going in halves on a cow—a dead cow, that is. Our carnivores are starved for fresh meat and leap at the opportunity to sink their teeth into a side of beef. So encouraged is the Kiwi by our crew's unbridled enthusiasm that he runs another proposition by them. How about a little hunting expedition? Patrick takes him up on the offer, and the two of them plan their outing. In the meantime, we pay for the cow and iron out the details for our sail to Savaii.

The following evening, as our hapless Joey is struggling to deal with the raw, bloody slab of steer that has been so savagely deposited in his tiny galley, our mighty hunters return from the bush with their booty. Patrick produces an enormous dead bat from his pack and thrusts it in Joey's face, offering to help him cook it up for supper. I'm sure I have never seen anything so grotesque in my entire life. Apparently, neither has Joey.

"It's a big dead rat with wings!" screams our discerning chef.

"No, it isn't," argues our great white hunter. "It's a flying fox."

"That . . . is . . . not . . . a . . . fox!" Joey declares.

Our Kiwi pal intervenes at this point and explains that this large species of bat, known locally and on the New Zealand mainland as the flying fox, is indigenous to this area and often hunted as game.

"How am I supposed to cook that?" Joey whines, pointing an accusing finger at the foul whatever it is (it's a mammal, we later learn).

"Why, make up a soup," our Kiwi mate suggests, hungrily smacking his lips.

Between the hunk of beast and the broth of bat, below decks on the *Sofia* takes on the carrion-choked stench of a slaughterhouse. I tip my metaphorical hat to Joey and retreat back aft to the relatively fresh air and suddenly less eerie company of the fermenting shark mandibles. Joe earns his passage this day.

The group of islands now known as the Samoas was once called the Navigator Islands, because of the fine seaworthy canoes that the natives built. But I see negligible evidence of this celebrated craftsmanship on Pago Pago or in Apia. The Polynesians we encounter in urban settings appear to be fully citified, well groomed in Western clothes, speaking English with refined accents. This irks me, as I have read so much about the physical beauty, spiritual joy, and raw athleticism of the Samoans. Encountering instead the clipped, smooth, assimilated, and homogenized version of these people is a genuine disappointment. I long to experience the islanders in all their unadulterated glory. (Perhaps we should be careful what we wish for).

The *Sofia* puts to sea, bound for Savaii. Even at first glance it is clear that Savaii is by far the least tamed of the islands we've visited in the Samoan group. There is no looming city, no harbor to speak of, and no other yacht in sight. The land erupts in a mat of jungle. A single narrow mud path squirts out onto a sturdy dock where our our host and his family are waiting for us and motioning for the *Sofia* to tie up.

Our itinerary has been predetermined for us. We are to visit the lumber mill directly and select our timber for the sole of the main cabin, Evan's chart table and miscellaneous other projects. We find the entire operation settled in a clearing in the middle of nowhere. It is a fully equipped lumber yard, run by what appears to be an even mix of New Zealand and Maori laborers. We watch our planks slide through the planer and get loaded onto powerful flatbeds that deliver them down to our waiting vessel. Many loggers accompany us to the *Sofia* and lend a hand off-loading the wood. Afterward, we invite them to join us for dinner and, of course, a little partying.

Savaii is nowhere near the cruisers' highway, nor is it in any fashion a tourist hangout. These Kiwis, uprooted from their homes and families on the busy mainland and deposited in the middle of the ocean, are almost desperate for diversion and entertainment. The *Sofia* is just the ticket. Somewhere between the second and third case of Steinlager, our guests present an intriguing proposal to us. They've spent long enough on the island to uncover its abundant mystery. So we're invited on a scenic tour that they assure us will never appear in any travel brochures. We aren't about to pass it up. We plan to meet on the landing the next day at dawn.

At daybreak we drag ourselves from our cozy bunks despite our hangovers and pile into the backs of the two flatbeds that brought us our lumber. All the "littlies" (as the New Zealanders refer to their offspring) from the previous evening are aboard and rarin' to go. These awesome urchins have already won our affection and admiration. They are dynamos, never still for an instant and never quiet. All during the festivities on the *Sofia* the night before, this pack of prepubescent powerhouses was climbing to the top of the rigging and leaping out into the sea, over and over again. No one was monitoring them, and their parents seemed utterly unconcerned. Having been raised where the jungle is their jungle gym, and weaned on perilous adventure and double dares, these kids are as adept as they are feisty. They exemplify the bold vitality of the New Zealand people.

The trucks trundle along the unpaved roads at a good clip. We stop often so that our guides can offer some commentary on the beautiful landscape and so that the children can go pee and run off a little pent-up energy. We pass crystal-clear streams beside gushing waterfalls, take dips in pristine inland lakes, hold our breath at lofty cliff-top overlooks, and huddle under vaulted jungle canopies. Nowhere do we see evidence of another living soul.

Our friends assure us that Savaii is quite thick with natives who still live much as the Samoans have for generations. Their island remains undeveloped and undiscovered by most outsiders, and this is just as the locals

prefer. They neither want nor appreciate the intrusion or influence of foreigners, and in their own way they make this abundantly clear.

One of the most spectacular sites on our tour is a blowhole carved into
a rock shelf way around the back side of the island. Our guides brag that
we will be able to walk right out to the mouth and stand on the trembling
overhang as the tower of compressed seawater shoots several dozen feet
straight up in front of us and showers down to drench us in a soft tropical drizzle. There are no fences, no guards, no "unstable cliffs" signs, no
"enter at your own risk" warnings, and we can't wait. En route, the trucks
stop at a large expanse of grassy meadow. I stand up, look around, and
see little to warrant my relinquishing my cushy spot amid a jumbled nest
of napping children's appendages. So I settle back down to rest and wait
while most of the crew and the Kiwis off-load. Eventually, though, my
curiosity wins out. What is out there to detain the gang for so long? It is
just a nondescript pasture littered with cow patties. Hmmm.

As I watch, my mates rise one by one and stagger, grinning, back to the
trucks. Guess there is more than lilies and cow shit in the fields. Our band
of grazers has unearthed magic mushrooms growing in acrid fungal clumps
all around the poop piles, and they have been chomping contentedly. On
the remainder of the ride to the blowhole, my mushroom-munching mates
treat the kids and me to a running dissertation on a veritable fantasia of
scenery that we aren't seeing. They insist on leaping to their feet to ooh
and ahh at things irresistibly marvelous in their personal psychedelic trav-
elogue, and it is a small miracle that no one is flung from the vehicles.

The blowhole, when we do reach it, is phenomenal, even in my unaltered
state. I can only imagine what the others in our party think of it. Mount
Vesuvius, perhaps? Our guides corral us back to the trucks pretty quickly.
It is getting late, and they caution that we don't want to be traversing the
jungle after dark. We are rearranging ourselves in the vehicles when I feel
that vaguely prickly but unmistakable sensation that I am being watched.
I glance around but spot only our own exuberant, clumsy party trying to
reboard and resettle. "Heck, why should I be paranoid?" I scoff. I am clear
and coherent. I am also, however, convinced that someone is lurking in the
lengthening shadows. As the trucks rev their engines in preparation for
pulling out, I hear a loud ping, followed closely by a volley of pings that
mimic the twang of marbles falling on sheet metal.

"Bloody hell!" our driver hollers. "Kids, get your heads down!"

Kids? I personally drop spread-eagle, flat as a cow patty, onto the truck
bed. The dope squad also hits the dirt hard, diving for cover, tucking their

limbs beneath them, and rolling into tight fetal balls. They think we're being bombed. One keeps screaming, "Where are the foxholes? Where are those foxholes?"

"We're off, lads!" our leader yells as he puts the pedal to the metal and spins out in the mud with our partner truck in close pursuit.

He is orchestrating as hasty a retreat as he can manage under the circumstances, but it isn't fast enough to keep us out of harm's way. A hailstorm of stones descends upon us from all sides. We are being ambushed by a foe we haven't even laid eyes on. These warriors, whoever they are, are pelting us with rocks, and they are expert marksmen. It seems that every missile hits its target, and we are all well battered by the time we get out of range. As the assault wanes, I risk uncovering my head for one quick face-to-face with my assailants. There, several yards off in the distance and standing in a relaxed phalanx, dressed only in lavalavas, is the enemy—a gang of embarrassingly puny native Savaii children.

Once our guides are sure that we've gotten well away, miles away, they pull over to take a body count and to apologize for that glitch in our gay little tour. They explain that the Samoan people historically were skillful rock throwers. It was both their means of hunting wild game and of defending themselves in battle. Their aim was known to be uncanny and their power unequaled. (Tell me again!) Any practical application for this natural gift has all but been eliminated from the big islands, so the talent of the locals there has atrophied. Not so on Savaii. These youngsters here still exercise their art. Not many interlopers wander onto their island, but those who do are notified straightaway and in no uncertain terms of the boundaries. We crossed them. Our escorts were well aware of this, but they gambled, hoping to get away with the minor infraction so that we wouldn't miss the incredible blowhole. We didn't miss it, the natives didn't miss us, and all told it is well worth it. I actually feel reassured by the Savaii natives' refusal to be absorbed into the assimilation steamroller that foreign interests level at the Polynesian peoples. Sure, these natives are a bit hostile in their resistance, but after what I've seen of the disintegration of the indigenous cultures in the South Pacific, I reckon this is about what it takes.

We return to the ship at sundown, mostly unscathed. We do have to backtrack to a nearby vista point to retrieve one child who has been misplaced, however.

"I thought he was in your truck."

"I thought he was in yours!"

"Oh, bloody hell!"

We eventually find him playing contentedly in the dirt, waiting to be collected. Our lads who are coming down off their vegetables are looking a bit shell-shocked, however. I wonder how their perception of the incident will play out in the retelling. Puts a whole new slant on "getting stoned."

We spend the following day seeing to ship's duties. The load of lumber we've laid in needs to be evenly dispersed on the deck. Then we need to lash it securely into place. The work is executed with careful attention to detail. A slip-up could prove disastrous. Many more nautical miles lie ahead of us, and we are likely to see several more good blows before the *Sofia* comes to rest in New Zealand. The threat that such a bulky cargo load will shift under stress at sea is a serious one, dangerous, even deadly. We tie every timber down tight. We finish by dark with enough time to organize one final celebration to thank our hosts on the island. Although a few loggers, those scheduled to be shipped home within the year, vow to find the *Sofia* wherever in New Zealand she winds up, the chances of ever reuniting with most of our Savaii friends is unlikely at best. We are saying goodbye. The littlies cry. They hug us all, hard and long. The family of the fellow we first met in Apia, and who has been our host on Savaii, presents me with an incredible farewell gift. Years earlier a Samoan tribal chief had given the couple a matching set of magnificently carved ceremonial spears made of one of the island's most exotic hardwoods, pau. The better-known hardwood that grows in these parts is ironwood, a dark, oily-looking tree whose branches will sink like heavy metal when dropped into the sea. Pau is the blonder of the two dense timbers and is easier to work with. It is the most beautiful wood I've ever seen, and I comment often on the unique style and grace of the mounted, decorative weapons whenever I have occasion to be in our friend's home. When the couple presses me to accept the spears, I adamantly refuse. They insist, imploring me to have something to remember them by. The benevolent spirit of the Polynesian people that we have come to know and love during the past many months is evident in the Kiwis as well. It is of vital importance to them to know that they have made a meaningful connection. I accept the precious gift, hug each of the children one last time, and signal for the lines that have safely secured us to the dock of this unforgettable land to be cast off, setting our restless tall ship on her way once again.

The passage down to the Kingdom of Tonga is uneventful. Oliver, Axel, Anders, Glen, Julias and a few other mates have wandered off at various points during the crossing, to jobs, families, different vessels, other adventures. Our remaining crew is pretty well seasoned, even those hitch-hiking wanderers who hopped aboard somewhere in the Pacific. With seasickness behind them, they are eager to practice real tall-ship sailing. Our watch teams are well manned. The *Sofia* drifts off, smooth and capable, tended by a group of knowledgeable, experienced sailors and a rabble of expectant wannabes.

Those of us with specific expertise are left to our respective responsibilities. Evan plots the course. I overhaul the rigging. Patrick mends sails. Norman tinkers with Juni. Joey and Tami crank out a steady succession of curious and delectable dishes. Karen swings her varnish brush like a pro. Barney fine-tunes his fine carpentry. Rick dives grinning into whatever manual labor is required. Billy is always here, sort of doing a little bit of something that never amounts to much of anything. He doesn't like working much, except when it comes to baking sticky buns. This we now know and accept. Billy is a pleasant fella, a good sailor, and a core member of the crew. Enough said. So it is an easy scoot south.

Tonga is often called the Friendly Islands because the people here have historically been exceedingly hospitable. Unlike many of the other island groups in the South Pacific, Tonga is a kingdom, a constitutional monarchy with a native premier and parliament. The kingdom has more than one hundred islands, which are separated into three main groups: Tongatapu, Haapai, and Vavau. We spend most of our time in Vavau, the northernmost group in the chain. But first we have to check into the kingdom in Nukualofa, the seat of government, which is located in the southernmost island group of Tongatapu.

Our time in Tonga is swell—fun but not fabulous, relaxing but just shy of carefree. It is the last stop on the tour, and we are already thinking beyond the holiday, symbolically packing our bags, as it were. Most of us are eager to hustle up paying jobs as we anticipate our ships impending extensive stay in New Zealand. But we all rise to the occasion and rally for what we know will be the *Sofia*'s final "South Sea island paradise" experience in this segment of her journey. In Tongatapu we check in at the busy port of Nukualofa and are cleared to enter the kingdom. Then the *Sofia* makes a mad beat back up north to the more pristine and undeveloped Vavau group to finish out our tour.

The northern Tongan island group is unique in that it exists as an off-the-beaten-path retreat for the jet set. The *Sofia* anchors alone on a stretch of lagoon near the main village of Neiafu, between the cruise ship landing and an imposingly opulent "Barefoot Yacht Charter" operation. At its rental office any marginally capable sailor who flies in can hop aboard an outfitted boat, act as his own skipper, round up a crew, and sail around the wealth of lovely islands and beaches that the Vavau group is known for. The diving in these waters is superb, the winds mild, the anchorages protected, the natives friendly. It's the perfect playground in which to be a yachtie for a week. What a great concept.

Simon, an interesting young Canadian acquired by the *Sofia* in the Samoas, purchases a used top-of-the-line windsurfer from one of these charter yachts. He is already adept at the sport, but while in Tonga he vows to attain his personal best, the "Force 5 Challenge" (sailboarding in winds exceeding Force 5 on the Beaufort scale, or up to 21 knots of fresh breeze). Now, Simon is a fella who likes things done a certain way, and is one of those types who seem just a tad out of their element aboard the *Sofia*. He is well educated, well traveled, used to somewhat finer digs, and accustomed to having more of a firm hand in the management of things. But he is a good sport and a capable sailor. We are quite pleased to welcome him and his expensive little water toy on board. Why, Simon even offers to give a few of us women some basic training in windsurfing and then gallantly allows us to take his prized possession out for a spin on our own.

Ever the optimist, I leap up on the board, grab the boom, assume the stately athletic position that I've seen postured by so many of the "beautiful people," and am promptly swept several miles downstream. I still don't get it, I guess. By the time my stubbornness gives way to disgust, I am way the hell out in the cruise line shipping lane. I gaily flag down a water taxi, whose driver tows me the couple of miles back to the *Sofia*. But he makes a hasty retreat once he sees and hears my obstreperous instructor. Simon is just furious! Oh, man. His prized board and sail turn out to be no worse for wear. Anyway, he should know better.

We have many memorable experiences on Tonga. Barney and Billy, practiced spelunkers who've done a fair bit of caving together in the Samoas, have heard tales of a spectacular spot in the Vavau group and are hot to explore it. They soon learn that it is accessible only by sea, so Billy begs off. He still isn't confident when it comes to operating under water. Barney has no trouble rustling up a couple of other capable divers, though, and soon the expedition is outfitting the *Jonah* with an ancient 2.5 horsepower British Seagull outboard that Barney bought off some yachtie when the Evinrude packed it in. The team loads supplies and is off on an overnight adventure to the famous Swallows Cave. They return a few days later with the now-routine tale of breathtaking danger and awesome beauty. They also return with a news flash. At the mouth of the cave they bumped into a swanky yacht named the *Pandora*; her steward, it turns out, is Deirdre, an infamous old flame of our good skipper's. Will wonders never cease? I swear, these ex-sweeties are everywhere. This particular reunion is untimely, though, and creates serious tension in our cooperative family. Evan is presently involved in a relationship with the Kid, whom we all obviously prefer and still feel protective of.

Evan perceives these chance meetings with former honeys as providence, flirtations with fates that he isn't inclined or equipped to ignore. Tami, faithful and wholly smitten, begs to differ. If I had a gold doubloon for every time I've witnessed this drama play out between Evan and his female fan club, I'd be one wealthy pirate. In Evan's defense, though, I do not believe that his intent is to wound his paramours. But he succeeds in doing just that, time and again. And although we Sofians are careful not to judge, we cannot help but empathize with the jilted women. Many crew who have sailed with Evan before have been offended by this particular behavior of his. Should anyone wish to pick a bone with our captain, this is one that is ever available—fresh, bloody and agonizingly exposed.

Through the *Pandora* and Deirdre we hook up with Vavau's fast crowd. Extravagant vessels and a highfalutin bunch of yachties are hanging out in Tonga's northernmost island group this season. We again offer to entertain the mob aboard our ship. Joey single-handedly prepares the banquet. Tami makes herself scarce, going off on a solitary walkabout for a spell. The party is grand, well attended by sea bums and the country club set alike. But we do have a few incidental, inconsequential catastrophes, the sort that one simply has to expect.

At some point near the top of the evening, the frenzied squawking of an irate guest brings the affair to a complete standstill. He is one of those rich Europeans on holiday who rents himself one very plush yacht. Arrogantly ignoring specific instructions to the contrary, this pseudosailor drove up to the *Sofia* in his nifty little motorized tender and tied up . . . back aft. Several of us tried to warn him, but some people just think they know better. Sometime during the night someone, or perhaps several people, hoist themselves up on the taffrail for relief without first checking for stray items below. When our unsuspecting visitor prepares to leave, he pulls his tender alongside and hops in, landing squarely on a fairly impressive mound of human excrement. He must have slipped, fallen, and flailed around in there awhile, because when he charges, raging, back down below, he is covered, and I mean *covered*—Brylcreemed head to tasseled Topsidered toes—in doo-doo.

Here he quivers, entirely apoplectic with his dapper little sailor suit all nasty and his face as red as a pomegranate. We are so shocked by the ghastly image that all of us are, at first, struck dumb. Then, as if on cue, the entire assembly collapses in writhing, howling hysterics. The harder we laugh, the more ballistic he becomes. Finally, he detonates, spinning his arms like pinwheels and flinging pieces of poop all around the saloon. We dive for cover. We later get him hosed off, shovel out his tender, and shove him off for home. But he is the undisputed hit of the party, congratulated around town with tentative handshakes and amused slaps on the back for days afterward.

A family of locals who attend the party invite a few of us to a Tongan feast and kava ceremony. Kava is a shrub related to the pepper plant and has been cultivated in the Pacific islands for centuries. The juice extracted and then fermented from the roots of this plant becomes a smoky, bitter beverage that has a mildly sedative effect when ingested. Kava has been an integral part of Tongan culture for generations, and we are all looking forward to giving it a try.

The feast takes place on the outskirts of the village at the home of one of the tribal elders. The house, or *fale*, is a large rectangular structure with a raised floor, open sides, and thatched roof. In inclement weather woven sheets of palm fronds are rolled down from the upper perimeter like Venetian blinds. A pit that has been dug just outside the *fale* and covered with fresh palm fronds is already emitting an exotically sweet, pungent steam when we arrive. It whets our appetites and our curiosity.

My new friend and our generous hostess, Fuauli Uile, explains that the pit is six feet deep, stacked first with smoldering embers upon which a fat pig rests, then is covered in layers of whole fish and local fruits and vegetables. Each course is separated by sheets of large palm leaves that will later double as serving trays. The meal has been simmering all day and is now ready to be eaten. We settle around the pit as the food is unearthed and, boy, do we feast! The dinner is a culinary masterpiece, each flavor distinctive, each texture crisp, every seasoning a new discovery for the palate. When we can't eat another bite, we are ushered into the *fale* and instructed to join the family in forming a large circle on the floor around a bucket-size wooden bowl that is filled to the brim with a thin, putrid-smelling, umber liquid—kava, or kava kava, as it is known in the islands.

Our hosts begin the ceremony. An elder cradles the bowl in his lap while he relates a short tale of Tongan folklore. At its conclusion he raises the bowl to his lips and gulps a lusty swallow before passing the mixture along to the next person in the circle. Each in turn tells a story, drinks, and then passes the bowl along. Whoever holds the kava has the floor. As the brew disappears, the stories become more elaborate and interesting. The Sofians are coming up with some real doozies. Clearly, we can't hold our kava. We are being drunk under the table, as it were, and soon we are sprawled helpless on the floor.

I'm feeling pretty queasy by the third or fourth round. The potion is thoroughly distasteful, and it floats like pond scum on the greasy feast coagulating in my bloated belly. I glance around and notice that a few of my mates are snoring. It is definitely time to call it a night. Apparently, however, the circle can't be broken until the bowl is drunk dry. Although most in my crowd pride themselves on being hard-drinking sailors, the Tongans have put us to shame. They take pity on us and guzzle the remaining dregs so that we can wake up and go home to sleep. We slur out our goodbyes and thank-yous, gather up our slumbering mates, and head for the ship.

Now, where is that darn boat? The jungle is black dark. We are dopey woozy. Finding our way back is like trying to tackle a maze while under anesthesia. Our sorry bunch eventually stumbles onto the right path and soon is gazing upon our lovely *Sofia*, swaying hypnotically at anchor on a glass flat lagoon. Bathed in moon glow, the mountain's reflection in the still water looks like a landscape stuck upside down, or a row of those silly little tea sandwiches sandwiched in, point first. Or is it the kava kava?

It has been a memorable evening. On the winding ride back to the ship—we just cannot seem to row in a straight line—I do hear a few disgruntled rumblings about kava's being inferior to mushrooms. Jeez, you can't take these guys anywhere!

The next morning Fuauli Uile meets me at the beachfront to escort me to the weekly tapa-making gathering. I am eager to see how Tongan tapa is made. Although beautiful, it is a very different finished product than the tapa cloth I saw in the Marquesas. As in Fatu Hiva the process of making tapa is a community effort. The sienna bark used almost exclusively in the Tongan islands comes from the paper mulberry tree. It's stripped, soaked, and pounded much as in the Marquesas, but after that the process is different.

The Tongans use either arrowroot or tapioca paste to glue together small sections of cloth to form much larger finished pieces. These average seventy-five feet in length and are commonly used as wall coverings, sheets, blankets, room partitions, and dance costumes. In Tongan culture these lengths of cloth are attributed a worth or status based on the number of sections included in them. Every line signifies a family event or represents a generation, and sections are often given individually as gifts for a birth, death, or marriage.

The Tongan method of decorating the cloth is also different, slightly more involved and more sophisticated than the Marquesan method. In the Neiafu tapa houses the women lay their cloth atop special relief design tablets that are attached to long convex boards. Then they rub a natural brown dye onto the cloth, embossing the raised designs into the bark. Once the tapa is dry, the women outline the brownish designs by hand with a natural black dye. The resulting objet d'art is as unique as it is stunning. With the help of my friend I am able to purchase several fine finished pieces.

The *Sofia* is scheduled to set sail for Tongatapu the following morning. I find myself once again saying goodbye to a dear friend, turning my back on a paradise, and closing the chapter of yet another unforgettable experience. The next and final stop in our tour of the islands of the South Pacific will be a business trip: We need to provision for the passage to New Zealand and tie up all the remaining loose ends of the last leg of this most momentous of voyages.

For all practical purposes the *Sofia* is going home. Many folk in New Zealand have kept tabs on our ship's progress and are eagerly awaiting her return. The *Sofia* is about to undergo a fundamental change. She will soon cease to be a working tall ship for an indeterminate period, and her crew will have to adapt to a long dry spell—no sailing or traveling aboard her. It will no doubt be a fascinating exercise, one that her aging adventurers anticipate with a combination of excitement and dread, for we will once again have to redefine ourselves. But for the moment, we are still just cruising, laying in supplies, keeping the old girl going.

I accompany Joe on a shopping spree to the marketplace in Nukualofa. It is large and well stocked with all the fresh produce we will need for the voyage. Browsing around, he and I are struck by two curious things. First, the center of the square is awash in watermelons—big, ripe, red melons for pennies apiece. Also, several stalls are devoted exclusively to the sale of vanilla beans. When we inquire about the vanilla, we learn that a series of hurricanes that hit Madagascar in the last decade decimated its crops. Madagascar has been the chief source of vanilla for this part of the world.

The Kingdom of Tonga then stepped up to the plate, set aside great expanses of fertile soil, and planted an impressive vanilla bean crop. The Tongans succeed in harvesting and marketing a major windfall for their islands. This doesn't surprise me. I've gotten the distinct impression that the Tongan people are as resourceful and self-sufficient as they are amicable and generous. What gives me pause, though, is the irony of how we egocentric wanderers keep inadvertently finding ourselves in the thick of events with global ramifications.

Most of us long-term Sofians have effectively cut loose, disconnecting politically, economically, geographically, and emotionally from the mundane preoccupations of our respective nationalities. We no longer vote, fight for, or even necessarily engage in thought processes that are motivated by our countries of origin. The *Sofia* is a nation unto herself. We on board are consummate explorers, going with the flow at any given time or place. Then, just as benignly, we veer away and move off down the next path that presents itself. "When in Rome, do as the Romans do" might well be emblazoned across our salty brows. Invariably, though, geophysics and geopolitics invade and control our realm. We repeatedly are touched by world affairs and political climates far beyond our immediate concerns—the breeze, the sea, the ship, and our whim.

Joey and I are busy loading up on foodstuffs when a ruckus on the main drag diverts our attention. Curious, we wander over and join the hoards of excited Tongans lining the street and are just in time to witness the spectacle. The king is passing by. Here is this enormous specimen of a man—three hundred pounds, easy—plopped into a Lazy-Boy that is perched atop a platform stretched across the customized cutaway back of a Ford Bronco with a raised chassis. The king is dressed in shorts, a floral print shirt, and a lei of live tropical flowers; he is waving and nodding enthusiastically. The king of Tonga looks like a parade float. His head is titanic, as rotund as any of the watermelons we've just purchased, and he has no neck. His face wobbles on his massive shoulders like a Weeble. What impresses me the most, though, is how joyous he is and how happy his people are to greet him. We are told that this king is very visible and accessible, an elemental part of daily life in and around the villages. It is a refreshing and hopeful national statement.

As Joe and I turn to resume our shopping, we bump squarely into Jane, of the *Jane*. What a surprise and what a treat! Of all the people whom I've had occasion to know in my travels, Jane stands out as one of my favorites. Each time I meet up with her, in whatever corner of the world, I feel like

I've found family. We embrace and promise to join her and Paul aboard their boat for lunch as soon as we've squared away our bundles. When Joey and I arrive at their yacht, they are waiting for us, having already set the table with a sumptuous, fresh ratatouille that they've just whipped up and a celebratory bottle of sweet vermouth. Jane apologizes, saying it is all the liquor she has on board but that she wants to be sure to have something to toast with.

"What are we toasting?" Joe and I ask expectantly.

"Why, you!" Jane gushes.

"Us?" we ask in confusion.

"Oh," Jane says, "we all knew it would happen sooner or later."

The "all" can only be our extended clan of South Sea cruisers but the "it" still confounds us.

"What would happen?" Joey and I risk asking, almost in unison.

"Why, that the two of you would get together, of course," Jane and Paul exclaim. They hold their glasses high, we follow suit, and we drink and laugh and share sea stories well on into the evening. By exchanging a glance, Joe and I agree not to disagree. What is the point? They are so thrilled for us. Besides, he and I are extremely fond of one another—like brother and sister, really. So, heck, let's drink to us and you and the run from Costa Rica across the Pacific and to the sturdy *Jane* and the stately *Sofia* and to fair winds, following seas, safe passage, and, the sea gods willing, many, many more happy reunions down the road. And who knows? (Some times in the course of an event mysterious mechanisms softly slip into place. Everything shifts, just that fraction of an inch. Who really knows anything for certain?)

The Varmit.

chapter 10

Deep in the Doldrums

Crossing the Horse Latitudes to New Zealand

The worst is not always certain but it's very likely.
—FRENCH PROVERB

INTRODUCTION

The passage from Tonga to New Zealand marked a significant departure. We were leaving behind the dreamy magic of the South Pacific and its complementary complacency on board ship. The South Seas had lulled the crew of the *Sofia* into a euphoric sense of well-being. Amid those tranquil islands, the tall ship and her crew were kindred spirits, hull and hearts buoyed in unison, soul mates sailing along the great equatorial pathway. We were bound for New Zealand, a destination that was to be a homecoming for *Sofia* and the crew members who had been aboard for her first circumnavigation.

New Zealand offered all the luxuries of the civilization we'd left behind—hot showers, shared language, similar currency, recognizable fresh produce. The cost of living promised to be affordable, opportunities diverse and plentiful. Certainly, this port should have boded well for us. Yet, between the Kingdom of Tonga and landfall in New Zealand's Bay of Islands lay the doldrums. The dictionary loosely defines them as equatorial ocean regions noted for dead calms and light, fluctuating winds. Mariners, using less flowery terms, define them as purgatory at sea—great expanses of ocean where sailing ships will make neither headway nor sternway and will encounter nary a breeze or a detectable change of weather. And no sailor worth his salt is a stranger to them.

In the past the *Sofia's* crew had taken advantage of these phlegmatic zones to work on delicate projects aboard ship that could not be facilitated when underway. I remember once painting the ship's topsides stem to stern with our bare rumps astride surfboards, our legs dangling like a kelp bed in a bottomless sea that stretched for thousands of empty miles in all directions.

Becalmed can be precisely that—relaxing and refreshing, a chance to swim, play, and sunbathe without inhibition in 360 degrees of endless horizon. Still. Silent. Serene. Not bloody likely! Rather, should you find yourself on the approach to a large landfall—say, a continent—that stands in the way of the omnipotent sea's charge across vast cordons of latitude, you will be treated to yet another phenomenon of the ocean. As these waves attack the distant shore, they meet resistance. Ricocheting off beaches and jetties, they recoil, climbing back on top of themselves and retreating toward open ocean in massive, lumbering, rhythmical mounds of unbroken water known euphemistically as groundswells. They sound innocuous enough, but on a sailing vessel lying well off shore and becalmed, they can be devastating.

Sails not only produce forward motion on a ship but also act as steadying agents. Without the benefit of the sails' towering counterbalance, the narrow, shallow hull of a boat will bob drunkenly atop the surface like a spastic cork as the swells catch the ship on her beam end. Still doesn't sound too dreadful? Now add thousands of ponderous pounds of spar, rigging, and equipment—rattling, slashing, crashing, and thunking with each violent lurch and counterlurch. Blocks and tackle are whiplashed into deadly weapons. Still air amplifies the slapping of canvas to a deafening volume. Gear breaking free of its lashings slices through open space, slamming and shattering against bulkheads and bulwarks. The crew is able to take only desperate, evasive action. Even while seeking sanctuary in your own bunk, you have to install snug bumpers on all sides of your body to try to allow iron-taut exhausted muscles a brief moment of relaxation.

Sailors cynically refer to the doldrums that the *Sofia* encountered between Tonga and New Zealand as the "horse latitudes." Historically, trade ships trafficking these waters would be carrying cargoes of horses. During protracted episodes of floating aimlessly beneath a relentless sun (in years past, ships didn't have the benefit of auxiliary power), the crew's patience would dwindle in direct proportion to the diminishing stores of food, water, peace, and quiet. The survival needs of the horses quickly became secondary to those of the sailors. Any profits to be gleaned from the safe delivery of horses ultimately had to be sacrificed to save the crew's lives and sanity. Consequently, the horses would drop dead of thirst or hunger, and the captains would order the carcasses to be dumped overboard. These rotting, hulking corpses floated on the swells, often for many days, and served as ominous portent to ships following in their wake.

Although the *Sofia* did not have the benefit of so vivid a presage, the past prophecy of the horse latitudes was, in fact, acting upon her.

JOURNAL ENTRY
Nelson, New Zealand
January 1981

In retrospect, *exhausted* most aptly describes how I feel during much of the crossing from Tonga to New Zealand's Bay of Islands. It is admittedly a demanding physical exercise, but I am used to this aspect of sailing and able to take most of it in stride. Rather, I am emotionally burned out. The final leg in the long passage across the South Pacific has beaten the hell out of my will and my good sense. I can no longer convince myself that I still belong on the *Sofia*, but somehow I manage to remain in denial about this. However, I find that operating a functional denial can be a bit like running a marathon. I spend half my energy just trying to make the situation seem less grueling than it actually is. I glamorize the effort I am making, persevere through the misery, and then totally miss the glory at the finish line in the Bay of Islands because I feel like sobbing, not celebrating, when we arrive. I just can't see the point anymore, and my tears hopelessly obscure the joy on the faces of the Kiwis on the dock. Somewhere in those horse latitudes, I realized that I may have finally had enough. I'm just not ready yet to ask myself what comes next.

Lars left the *Sofia* in Tonga. We shared a pleasant farewell dinner and parted as friends, but it was a regretful culmination of unfortunate events and marked a personal failure. He and I had been careful to orchestrate our relationship for success. We were both intelligent, independent, and self-motivated. We were sure that we alone would be capable of making a tryst aboard the *Sofia* work, to the mutual benefit of us and the ship. And for a time, when we were at our best and brightest, we were winning. Smug and self-congratulatory, Lars and I pronounced ourselves the summa cum laude of shipboard romantics.

As far as many of our mates knew, we never progressed beyond "hand-holding on the taffrail," as Evan so patronizingly put it. But this ruse was part of our plan. Contrary to general practice on the *Sofia,* Lars and I rejected external acknowledgment of our intimate relationship. We cared not what our fellow crew members thought of our affair. We deemed public displays of affection too vulgar and too revealing for us. We drew upon our own strength of commitment, drafted personal guidelines and expectations, and sealed our private bond in mutual respect. We had few rules, but those that we did have were firm and clear. The most cardinal was that neither of us would ever philander, meaningfully or otherwise, with a shipmate. We had both borne witness as indiscreet behavior of this kind repeatedly produced gut-wrenching, cataclysmic results within our floating society. Such action was far beneath us. We were savvy enough to avoid it. But, alas, it was this very conduct that Lars fell victim to.

A wild American in her twenties, single and on the party-hearty trail with a satchel full of recreational drugs that she was anxious to share, also happened to be hanging around the islands. She found the atmosphere aboard the *Sofia* irresistible. Most of our lads had already found her, her stash, and her noncommittal devil-may-care approach to life equally irresistible. When Lars's number came up, she reasonably reckoned that he too played it fast and loose, so she saw no reason not to invite him out to play. And out he came, poor sap. Can't hardly blame him, really. In the main, so much else on the *Sofia* is vague, and this particular visiting female amusement was nothing if not explicit.

When she eventually left our ship to embark upon her next fun-filled escapade, Lars crawled back to me consumed with remorse. I was rigid. He implored. I stood fast. He beseeched me to at least consider reestablishing our unique friendship, an infinitely more precious commodity on the high seas than a roll in the hay. But I was resolute. Although there was never a deep love between us, we had a profound trust, and he violated it. In full truth, however, as much as I loathed the realization and abhorred the implication of weakness, I was hurt. That I could not forgive. Lars forced me to examine a vulnerability that I was convinced would prove disastrous if I did not remain on guard.

From that point on, I treated Lars with the cool indifference of a casual acquaintance. He and I no longer gossiped, giving rein to our superiority complexes, about the pitiful pairings of our fellow sailors. We shared no more heart-to-heart dialogues on the relative merit of one political, religious, or philosophical viewpoint over another. The cerebral cortex of our connection was lobotomized and our association reduced to superficiality. The void left when I excised companionship from our interactions was immeasurably deep and ultimately unbearable. Strange, how critical this element is within our society afloat, how necessary to share some semblance of deeper humanity. Lars, left with no recourse, left the ship in Tonga. It will be a while before I allow myself to miss him.

Emotions in general are raw on the sail from Tonga to New Zealand, and they run the full gamut: excitement, frustration, pride, jealousy, compulsion, fury. Everyone is hypersensitive in some way or another. We are like overcharged ions, colliding in an atmosphere that is clicking and popping with energy. The slightest friction threatens to spark an explosion.

Patrick, a self-proclaimed martial artist, among other things, had been trying for months to scare up a training partner. He finally lands one in Tonga, an alley-tough Scot who was crewing on a yacht. While we're there, the two amicably agree to some full-contact sparring on the *Sofia's* main deck. We all gather to observe the spectacle and to cheer our boy on. At their level of the sport, no one purposely pulls punches or misses a kick, so they expect some pain and punishment, but both men are ruthless during their match and the retaliation is savage. In the end our lad is beaten to a bloody pulp. However, Patrick's pride suffers far more traumatic injury than his flesh. Long after the cuts and bruises heal, the wounds to his ego remain flinchingly tender.

At one point, while hopelessly becalmed in the horse latitudes, a fed-up bunch of us say to hell with whatever it is that we're doing and instead leap over the side into the ocean to swim and let off a little steam. Those who are not inclined to join in are soon tossed in the tide against their will. Most then get swept along in the game without much resistance but not everyone. Patrick politely declines. When a gang of fellows surrounds him, jocularly threatening to ambush him and force him overboard, he does an odd thing. He reaches into his belt and draws his knife. Caught up in the excitement, some in the group still don't get it. They naively continue their playful taunting and mock assault. Patrick then begins to sway like a street fighter, his eyes narrowed and his arms in fighting position. One hand flips the knife handle, rotating it 180 degrees in his palm as he swipes the blade in darting strokes and jabs in front of his face. His other hand is flexing that oh-so-subtle but unmistakable "come on" gesture. Everyone freezes. There isn't a sound. Then with nervous shuffles and forced laughs, the guys back away from Patrick, turn, and dive over the rail into the sea, sneering and jeering a trifle too loudly to suggest authenticity. Patrick slowly resheaths his knife and quietly returns to his chores. I keep my eyes on him for a while afterward, though, amazed at what he has attempted, impressed that he has pulled it off. Who is this man?

Rick, our happy-go-lucky stonemason, also discloses an intriguing personality quirk during this passage. He's put on some extra, unwanted blubber since joining the *Sofia* and vows to lose the fat before landfall in New Zealand. In the horse latitudes he embarks upon a patently insane diet and exercise regime. He slaps together a corral-like structure on the main deck and fills it to the brim with watermelons from the Nukualofa marketplace. These, Rick swears, are what he will subsist on for the duration of the crossing. The diet alone, he reckons, will not do the trick. So he augments his fast with an aerobic workout schedule that crosses clear over the border of reason and moves into the realm of the fanatic. Now, the *Sofia* has no weight room, no treadmill, no running track. So Rick jumps rope. He jumps rope fast. He jumps with dizzying spins and twists. He jumps forward, backward, and on one foot. Rick jumps rope all day every day until he pours sweat like it's watermelon juice—which it probably is. Exasperated, we insist that he move from station to station around the deck so the monotonous pound-and-slap, pound-and-slap isn't concentrated for too long over any one bunk ceiling. It's like Chinese water torture.

Tami, back on board but not yet back to her old self since her relationship with Evan went sour, impetuously tries to fire up the oven without properly priming it. She knows better. She just isn't paying attention. It blows up in her face, singeing off her eyelashes, eyebrows, and the first two inches of hairline on her forehead. Fortunately, her face is scorched only superficially, like a really bad sunburn. It could have been much, much worse.

Not surprisingly, a substantial amount of drinking is going on in these doldrums, and the empties begin to pile up. Some wise guy on board devises a brilliant scheme for ridding the ship of its garbage while engaging in a little harmless sport at the same time. This genius gathers up all the bottles and jugs, corks 'em, and tosses 'em over the side to bob like glass buoys on the waves. Then he runs to fetch his gun. The others on board who are also carrying contraband weapons follow suit, reckoning that there is no crime in a little target practice. I am stunned to see how many pistols and shotguns appear. We could have been put away for several lifetimes in any one of a dozen foreign prisons for smuggling all this artillery. I shoot an accusing glare at Barney, remembering the gun he stashed in the floorboards of the car that carried us through Central America. He backs away, hands in front of his face, warding off my attack, and defending himself by saying, "Hey, I'm unarmed. I traded that Saturday night special to a Kiwi in Savaii!"

The "infantry" commences taking potshots at the floats. The noise is deafening, and the growing fervor is horrifying. But this is only the beginning. Someone shouts that he sees a shark, and immediately all loaded barrels are trained on an obscure point on the ocean. Bullets rip the surface. Then one truly misguided lout spins and takes a bead on a seagull bobbing in our slack wake—an innocent "by-floater." That does it.

"Holy shit!" I shriek, "What the hell are you thinking?" I jump up on the transom and put my body between the barrel and the bird. What the hell am I thinking? Barney slinks over and kind of sidles up next to me, but we need an army. Finally, Evan intervenes and suggests that once the bottles are blown to smithereens, the guns go back to their respective hideaways. The shooters grudgingly comply. It is nuts. Who are these guys and who are we? Where are we, and where are we heading, for cryin' out loud?

Back in Tonga, while Tami was away, Karen helped Joey with the shopping. He prepared a list for her, but when Evan spotted canned mushrooms on it, he flatly vetoed the item. "Canned mushrooms have no nutritional value whatsoever, and they taste like crap," he asserted.

"But I can accent so many of my recipes with them," Joe pleaded. Joe lost the battle but not the war. Karen, never a big fan of Evan's anyway, stubbornly took it upon herself to buy Joey a veritable gross of canned mushrooms. In her spending frenzy, clearly designed to show up Evan, she forgot to buy cooking oil, a basic necessity that the ship was very nearly out of. What remains on board might last until New Zealand if we can make it in the anticipated week to ten days, but the trip takes longer, and the supplies dribble out.

Joey, desperate to cover for Karen, has an epiphany. In Panama we'd laid in two fifty-five-gallon drums of pigs' tails in brine—"*high* in nutritional value"—which had sat largely untouched until now. Joe begins scooping out squirmy buckets full of these obscene corkscrew appendages and renders them for oil. When Evan gets wind of this, which isn't hard because the odor is rank and the air below is still and steamy, he is furious. Karen could care less. He hasn't been able to intimidate her for years. The two had early on established their mutual dislike and consequently always seem to be at loggerheads over something. I've often wondered whether pure vindictiveness doesn't account for some portion of Karen's perseverance aboard the *Sofia*. It can be an awesomely powerful force. Karen stands up to Evan's scolding once again, firmly turning the tables and placing the whole blame for the situation squarely on his shoulders.

"If you'd have agreed to run the bloody engine just long enough to drive us the hell out of the doldrums, as most of us have been demanding that you do for days now, we'd have reached landfall long before our oil ran out!"—or, I'm thinking, our patience, and what minuscule scrap remains of our cooperative inclinations.

Out here, caught fast in these eerie horse latitudes, angry factions form. They are well fueled by the relentless sun, oppressive heat, questionable foodstuffs, unendurable rolling motion, and the sudden overwhelming urge to be anywhere else doing anything else with anyone other than our shipmates. Evan refuses to start Juni. Norman wants to. Patrick wants to. Karen, Simon, and a bunch of fresh, new upstarts who've felt snubbed at one time or another by our captain want to. Billy and Rick are riding the fence, as is their nature. A few others rally behind the skipper, for no other reason than that he is the skipper and it feels more comfortable to be in his corner. I'm conflicted. It is risky to waste diesel, knowing we'll have a fair bit of motoring to do to safely navigate New Zealand's lee shore. But at this point it is also risky not to. Tensions continue to mount, rising up in the sultry heat, being fanned by the brutal, thrashing elements. Our ship is threatening to rage completely out of control, and her crew is on the verge of a full-blown tantrum.

One night the lid nearly blasts clean off the *Sofia*'s emotional pressure cooker. I'm roused from a fitful sleep by the violent clanging of the ship's bell. Everyone scrambles into the saloon, stepping gingerly around the frenzied Varmit, who is crazed by the pealing metal, even though he hasn't been feeling too plucky himself lately. At center stage, waiting for us to assemble and practically spewing venom, stands Karen. We early arrivals begin to congregate warily as the latecomers straggle in, muttering, "What the fuuu . . . ?"

Karen paces, heaves, and glares for full dramatic effect. Her squinting eyes appear comically maniacal behind her Coke-bottle glasses as she pans accusingly around the room. We are waiting. We don't have to wait long.

"I . . . JUST . . . WIPED . . . MY . . . ASS . . . WITH . . . A . . . PAGE . . . FROM . . . LEVITICUS!!!" she bursts out.

In one hand Karen clenches the familiar thick black text. So we hazard a peek, and, yes, there it is. Dangling from her other hand hangs the evidence, crumpled and grody but still identifiable.

"Who put this Bible on the taffrail?" Karen booms. "Who? I'll kill 'em, I swear. I'll get one of your damn rifles and blow 'em to bits!"

The culprit, whoever he is, isn't any too eager to 'fess up. The gallery is drop-dead silent. Then someone, clearly overcome with a twisted case of nerves or else struck by the farcical nature of the entire episode, begins to titter uncontrollably. And it is contagious. Soon we are all snorting and drooling, trying desperately to choke back a flood of laughter. Karen becomes, if possible, even more unhinged. I truly believe she could kill us all right here and now.

"Where's a gun? Get me a gun, goddammit!" she squeaks.

Then, sucker punching us once again, she spins around and charges into the galley. Is she settling for a knife, I wonder? She skids back in, bounces into the middle of the ring, and begins rotating slowly, poking a gallon jug of Heinz ketchup in our faces. Karen is going to squirt us to death? No, something else . . .

"Where did this come from, huh?" she baits. No one is clear on where she is going with this, but we are definitely interested. We're a captive audience. "I saw this on the tug in Pago Pago, didn't I? Who stole it? STEALING IS EVIL! I'll kill ya, I swear I will!" she roars. We are caught red-handed. We are going to be slaughtered for pilfering condiments.

When the guffaws die down, we talk. In truth, we all feel a smidge better. The spectacle has been cathartic. Karen clearly has had it. She has reached the bitter end of her own idiosyncratic rope. We all have one and we are all approaching its end out on this long passage going nowhere. Slowly, more items that walked off the tug begin to materialize. The crew accepts collective blame for the theft. Those who hadn't actively participated in the act had eventually gotten wind of it and had done nothing to rectify it, so we are all guilty. The mate responsible for "misplacing" the Bible never comes forward, however. For days afterward, when whatever little breeze we get comes around from astern, it snatches up toilet paper as it is deposited off the taffrail and carries it forward across the ship. Karen abandons her varnish brush and races up to the foredeck to examine the refuse, making certain no further sins are being committed. It is gross, but she is compelled, on a mission, a missionary on poop patrol.

During this crossing any little thing seems to disturb the tenuous balance that we are struggling to maintain, and the boat is rockin'. Mutiny is on the wind. People want out, and they perceive the engine to be the easy solution, Evan the obvious obstacle. I don't want to hear it, don't want to think about it. The physical elements out here in the doldrums refuse to release us. Instead, a storm of passions and opinion is brewing. Will the inferior sailors on board actually resort to piracy simply to attain a semblance of control and equality, no matter how temporary or false? I'm afraid to imagine it, to imagine us. Our minisociety has as many layers as an onion. We generally function a stratum or two below the surface. But on the sail across the horse latitudes, as we approach the end of our enchanting South Pacific islands tour, the *Sofia*'s skin is peeled back nearly to her core. And what we have exposed isn't pretty. We are desperate to reach New Zealand before we're stripped completely bare.

The crew knows that we've reached a point of no return with respect to the condition of the *Sofia*'s hull. Her massive keel—a ship's backbone—has aged like an ancient spinal column crippled by osteoporosis. It measures a full eighteen inches higher at her middle than it does at her stem and stern. The effect of this grotesque bowing, or hog, is a relentless weakening of the vessel's structure.

The *Sofia* was built in the tradition of Baltic traders of her day. She was outfitted with a powerful engine amidships, a cavernous hold below decks, and a simple rig designed to be managed by two men and a boy. Her hull was fashioned from readily available and malleable pine, a soft wood of limited life expectancy. Someone had factored obsolescence into these old workhorses. By the time that group of college kids from Oregon found her, beached and forgotten on a European shore, the *Sofia* was already geriatric. Her refurbishing began straight away and has proceeded, as funds allow and seaworthiness dictates, to this day.

The earliest rehabilitation involved shifting her engine aft and installing a large forward gear locker for storing the sails and rigging required to run a three-masted gaff-topsail schooner. She also gained a secondary anchor with fathoms of heavy cable. Amidships was gutted to make room for a saloon, galley, and additional bunk space. Consequently, the *Sofia* rides heavy in her bow and her stern, with little counterweight in her midsection. This reapportionment has taken a serious toll on her posture. A friend and avid proponent of fiberglass yachts once smugly defined wooden boats as jumbles of separate and independent parts, all engaged in a constant struggle to get away from one another: keel, planks, frames, and fastenings—all pulling, grinding, twisting, and arching in different directions at once. Pretty accurate. In the horse latitudes this description could apply to the crew as well.

We reach New Zealand's Bay of Islands after an absurd twenty-eight-day drift, slog, and boil. The area proffers more islands—pretty enough islands, more people—nice enough people, more sailing, more sunsets, more, more, more of the same—too much more! Man, is it ever time for me to get the hell away for a spell. The port town of Russell welcomes the *Sofia* with elaborate fanfare. The villagers have been waiting for us, and I long to be a fraction as gracious or as enthusiastic as they are. Instead, I am disenchanted and drained. Before I can even begin to give this fine country its due, I know that I need some space. So I jump ship. Cramming all my trade goods—*molas*, tapas, wood carvings, wall hangings— into a woven basket from Tonga that is six feet high, I hitch a ride on an oyster truck to the city of Auckland. Here I board a plane for the United States, where I dive into family, am coddled with love, sell my pieces, hug my dog. When I return to the *Sofia*, I find her cozily re-ensconced down in Nelson, the absolutely delightful municipality on the sunny northern tip of the country's magnificent South Island, where she spent much of her first visit to New Zealand. This will be the site of our ship's long refit and the crew's primary base of operations for approximately the next twelve months.

Crew of *Sofia* in bilges drilling the keel bolts for the new keel. Nelson, New Zealand.

chapter 11

Roll On, Deep and Dark Blue Ocean

The Mutiny and the Sofia's *Final Passage*

> The worst form of inequality is to try to make unequal things equal.
>
> —ARISTOTLE

INTRODUCTION

When we hit New Zealand, most of the crew scattered like shrapnel—escaping, distancing themselves from the residual frustration and crumbling solidarity that menaced the *Sofia* and her sailors on the long, slow passage from Tonga. Some stayed with the ship, either by choice or by necessity. As time wore on, this distinction became hazy. The *Sofia* and her crew validated one another. At any given time, the tall ship was whatever her resident mariners made of her: a cargo hauler or a sail-training vessel, a renegade "hippy ship" or a youthful United Nations afloat, an ambassador of goodwill, a pleasure craft, our home, a trading vessel, a counterculture existence, or, finally, a ship that continued to sail the grand oceans of the world simply because that was what she was destined to do.

Truth be told, however, some of us had tied our identities so closely to the *Sofia* that we now defined ourselves by what this proud old schooner had made of us. An interdependency was implicit in the relationship between sailor and ship. Striking a balance between what we were willing to give and what we expected to get back from the *Sofia* would prove to be a cornerstone of the venture—elemental to success, mandatory for survival.

Because we were cognizant that the ship was stuck for the long haul, minute fragments of our former land-bound selves began to reappear in our fragile egos. And the delicate fabric of the cooperative began to unravel.

Throughout my years of traveling with the tall ship, I often found myself playing the observer, evaluating the behaviors within our self-contained ecosystem. So perhaps I should have been able to foresee what was about to happen. Instead, as the splintered remnants of our sailors' alliance disintegrated and mutiny threatened in earnest, I was way down South Island, taking my shot at earning some money.

∾

JOURNAL ENTRY
Nelson
New Zealand

My plane lands first in Honolulu, then on Fiji en route to New Zealand. Once in Auckland I find my way down to the wharf and chance upon an old friend, Jim, on the *Rebel Yell.* The *Sofia* helped him to repair his ship in Tonga after he was dismasted in a storm. We nicknamed his yacht the *Rebel Whimper* and set to getting him squared away. In Auckland he is happy to repay the favor by putting me up for the night.

From here I set out at first light, hitchhiking my way to Wellington, the nation's capital, which is located on the southern tip of the North Island. I make it in a day after a dozen different lifts. But what lifts they are! Each is a scenic tour. The locals are proud of their country's beauty and bounty and eager to be helpful. We stop for a spot of tea here, a quick look at the Maori Queen's Palace there, every vista and historical site worthy of a brief stop or a few miles' detour. No one drops me off without leaving me with her or his address and a promise to be available should I need them. They all give me a warm hug, a saucy wink, and a "Good on ya, lass!" before trundling off. I feel cared for and protected by these magnanimous folk who are yet strangers to me.

In Wellington I sprint to make the ferry across the infamous Cook Strait to the South Island. Everyone scrambles to help me toss my gear on board—more winks, more "Good on ya's." The ferry is imposing, complete with bars, restaurants, and lounges, but I spend the entire three and a half hours on deck, wet, cold, and beside myself with happiness. I'm back at sea. The salt air is manna for my soul. The strait and Queen Charlotte Sound are magnificent. The pass is rough, the weather drizzly, and I'm filled with pure joy clean through.

We land in Pincton, where I shoulder my bags and strike out on the final stretch to Nelson. A young couple picks me up, stops at a pub for a pint of grog to warm me, a roadside stand to buy me some apples and honey, and then on into the town of Nelson.

I finally chase down the *Sofia*. She's wharfed up alongside a retired cargo hauler, the *John Wilson*. Only Evan and the Varmit are on board when I arrive. This is fitting. I am home and these two are the longest-standing members of my shipboard family. Everyone else, Evan tells me, is off tramping or working. He has taken full advantage of their absence to dive into a major overhaul of the main cabin—grinding, sanding, varnishing top to bottom, from ceiling and bulwarks down to sole. The now tacit confirmation of commitment implied in my reunion with Evan is understood and unspoken; I stow my worldly belongings and pitch in. We work together like mad all week long, hoping to finish by the weekend when much of the crew will return.

Many local folk come by to visit, and we make some fortuitous contacts. Sport salmon fishers from North Island, Bill and Maureen Butler, want to be involved. Maureen insists on sharing her prize-winning thirty-pound catch with us. Bill offers to turn us some new belay pins—all gratis, all their pleasure, grateful offerings to a proud ship and to those who keep her sailing. We are humbled.

The young couple who drove me into town returns to invite us out to the local pub, where bluegrass music is playing. An old-timer climbs on stage while we're there and dedicates a sea chantey to us, banging it out on a broom and shovel. At ten o'clock, when the whole town literally shuts down, we're whisked off to the home of more new friends for more beer, more music, and homemade waffles. I'm patted on the back so often it's embarrassing. Crinkled eyes wink, leathery working hands deliver thankful praise. The *Sofia* is warmly welcomed home, and we are fairly canonized for getting her here.

At sunrise an old milk truck rattles down the dock and deposits bottles of fresh milk, cream, and yogurt at our gangplank. I go up to collect them and wave "ta," the Kiwi thank-you, to the milkman, who's dressed like he was lifted straight off the pages of my early primer, *Dick and Jane*. In the dusky dawn I notice that the Japanese mother ships have come into the fish-packing plant across the channel and reckon I'll wander over later to see about wrangling work. This afternoon I also have an appointment to meet with Dr. Kay Bradford, head of psychiatric care for children in Nelson, to sort out what's required for me to obtain a work permit to do counseling here. Meantime, some new mates will be carrying me out to Blenheim, in the countryside, to buy apple wine and fresh blackberry juice for one Kiwi dollar a flagon. As I stand on the dock, cradling my dairy bottles and feeling the first breeze of the morning, a scow full of divers motors over to offer me half its crayfish catch.

So far, New Zealand is everything I'd hoped for and more. The trepidation following the last crossing is quietly dispersing, rinsed away by this warmest of welcomes, this wholesome atmosphere. It's so sweet that the lingering bitter aftertaste of the horse latitudes is almost forgotten.

∿

JOURNAL ENTRY
Chez Elco—A little coffeehouse
Nelson, New Zealand

The local newspaper publishes an article I wrote about the *Sofia*. It creates quite an emotional stir in the hearts of Nelson's substantial sailing population, particularly among the old-timers. The *Nelson Mail* doesn't usually run such sentimental features, but this town has only one *Sofia*, and she truly is Nelson's. The piece is very well received but has nowhere near the impact of a subsequent article, about our Varmit.

The laws regulating agriculture and wildlife in this country are strict. When we first enter New Zealand territory and welcome customs and immigration officials on board, they ask if we have a cockroach problem. "But of course not!" we lie, confident that our seasoned roaches will know to lie low. We assure the agents that we are an exceedingly sanitary vessel. They request permission to do a cursory spraying anyway. "Sure," we chuckle, amused by the ridiculous little canisters they each then produce from their pockets. Like they have a prayer of fazing the indestructible demons that have plagued our ship across three oceans. Armed with their pathetic spritzers, they proceed to squirt at random around the below decks. Then we all settle, blasé as all get-out, at the long pristine saloon table (which of course holds its standard assortment of girly magazines, music tapes, and liters of grog) to go over our paperwork. We forget about the sorry extermination attempt, that is, until dead or writhing bugs begin raining down on us in a flurry of revolting fallout. The saloon is being dive-bombed by cockroaches with enormous wingspans, cockroaches the size of small animals, creepy opaque albino cockroaches, cockroaches with ghastly mutations, Panamanian cockroaches, Caribbean cockroaches, veteran cockroach–passage makers from Boston's Italian North End, too many and varied to catalogue. We are furtively picking them out of our hair, brushing them off the tabletop, kicking them out of the frenzied Varmit's reach, hoping the officers won't notice. Suddenly, squirming insects pour down, plopping into the cups of tea and becoming embedded in the neat little cakes we've prepared for the occasion. Corpses are dropping on the officers' shoulders and bouncing off their hat brims. The crew is mortified. The authorities just giggle. They're quite used to this scenario, although I have to say that even they appear a mite impressed by the diversity and magnitude of the *Sofia*'s infestation. This doesn't overly concern them, however. What does is our critter.

National law dictates that because of the threat of rabies, the Varmit either has to be confined to a small cage on board or be taken into custody and held in quarantine for the duration of our stay in the country. The Varmit, caged? Unthinkable, but clearly the lesser of the available evils. He isn't expected to take well to it, but he simply will not survive an indefinite quarantine away from us and the only home he's ever known. We have no choice. We promise to construct a pen and keep him locked up on the ship. The officers promise to visit the ship routinely to ensure that we are doing just that.

Needless to say, our elderly coati doesn't suffer his confinement well. He is already showing his age with a slightly less aggressive nature and more careful gait, particularly when making his regular tour of the ship atop the cap rails. However, his physical decline from the imposed incarceration is devastating. When I come back from the States, I notice it straightaway, and I fear for the welfare of this wild tropical creature once the cold weather sets in. I express this concern when the editor at the paper asks about Varmit's condition while going over my piece. Lordy, does that start a ball rolling! The New Zealanders are passionate about very few things, among which are their countryside, their littlies, their sports, and their animals. No one in Nelson warms to the idea of Varmit's being imprisoned. But the thought of his actually dying, here in their homeland, is intolerable. Many locals still remember Varmit as a pup when he was here several years ago.

The newspaper comes down, takes pictures, and writes an article. Then the television people get wind of it. Varmit and I are featured on a local children's program called *Video Dispatch*, and an exposé runs on the evening news. Soon all of South Island is on the alert and on the warpath. The poor Agriculture and Wildlife Department is deluged with angry letters and attacked in newspaper editorials. The *Sofia*, contrarily, is deluged with support, all manner of offers to help, and suggestions about how to fight the authorities. Then the visitors come—in force.

They come bearing gifts: eggs—a Varmit delicacy, kerosene heaters, lamb skins, little wool doggie sweaters, insects, reptiles, dead mice, homemade fruit salad—another Varmit favorite—and even chocolate Easter eggs. And I, Varmit's "surrogate mother," am drawn into a bizarre social scene. All the first graders from a local elementary school write the Varmit letters— "Dear Varmit, I'm so sorry you're a sick sailor," and the like. Then they come to visit, after which they write me letters—"Dear Varmit's Mother, we love you for keeping the Varmit well," and invite me to visit their class-room, which of course I do.

One entire wall is decorated with articles about and photographs of me and the Varm from the newspapers, plus the letters and cards I wrote to each of them, thanking them for their concern. The children sing special songs and recite poems written for me. They take me on a tour of the school grounds, all the while jockeying for position to hold my hand or hang on my shirttail. When we return to their classroom, they take their workbooks out to show them to me. As they are just learning how to write and spell, their pages are lined with the deliberate scrawl of six-year-olds: "A is for apple, B is for ball," on through the alphabet. The high point comes when we reach the latter pages in their books. They beam while showing me that "P is for Pam" and "V is for Varmit." I am sincerely touched. On the heels of the examples of disturbing human behavior to which I'd been subjected during the last passage, these small innocent faces, smiling up so proudly, so genuine and benevolent, are like tender fingers softly smoothing over the recent jagged edges of my soul. Years of rough mileage feel as if they're being melted away by the warmhearted goodness of these gentle Kiwi people, and I am thankful.

Varmit nearly does die. He contracts bronchial pneumonia and needs emergency medical attention. I spend weeks injecting him twice daily with penicillin and cradling him by the pot-bellied, wood-burning stove we've recently installed in the saloon. He makes it, this time—a true survivor.

In anticipation of the *Sofia*'s long-awaited return, dozens of Kiwis, plus a bevy of far-flung, aspiring tall ship sailors, had flocked to New Zealand's South Island and are now beating their way to the decks of our welcom-ing schooner. The general mood on board is elevated. The newcomers are openly thrilled to be here. And in the absence of many of our more iras-cible veterans, these initiates are free to bubble away, unfettered by the ancient smoldering negativities. Some damn intriguing fresh personalities are in our midst; temporarily liberated from the recent pernicious develop-ments of the horse latitudes, I find that I am free to delight in them. The atmosphere reminds me of summer camp when we're each first meeting our new cabin buddies. I am a returning camper, however, so I'm afforded the respect and admiration that my station suggests, plus something else—awe. I have paid my dues, so this should be a dividend well deserved and enjoyed, yet I can't help feeling protective of these fledgling sailors. "Wait," I say. "Test the water," I warn. "Be sure. Be very, very sure," I caution. The old guard will return soon for the refit, and I'm wary.

Karen is off living on a farm as part of an apple-picking crew. Tami snared a sweet job as deckhand on the salmon boat of a veteran of the *Sofia*'s first circumnavigation who has since settled in New Zealand and runs a lucrative fishing business. Patrick went off to work in forestry. Joey wisely reasoned that a few months in the States, working pharmacy for $15 an hour, beats the hell outta performing unskilled, manual labor for chump change here. Smart boy. He's back in New York City, expecting to return by the New Zealand winter. Barney went home to California for a spell. He's quite smitten with Barbara, who has graced the *Sofia* intermittently since Costa Rica and who is in the process of ending a relationship back in the States. If I had to lay odds, I'd bet that ol' Barn has something to do with that. And if I'm still trusted to know what it looks like, I'd swear these two are head-over-heels in love. I hope so. Barney deserves to be happy. Rick has gone tramping, the Kiwi term for hiking. So have Simon and Norman. Billy, I believe, is also apple-picking somewhere up on North Island.

In their spots are these bright new faces. Chris, a Yank, is just about jumping out of his skin to learn the ropes. I'm teaching him to be a boatswain. Byrds is a Kiwi from the North Island, an experienced traditional sailor, and he looks the part—full, bushy-red beard, wild tuft of orange hair, big and strong as an ox. He has gleaming, ruddy cheeks and a hearty belly laugh. He's doing a touch of everything, handy as you please. Mary, another Kiwi who's a nursing student but also has a fair amount of sea time under her belt—guess it's in the New Zealanders' blood—has also signed on, as has Bart, a middle-aged welder from Holland. His highly specialized skills will be well used around here, I'll guarantee that. Casey and Jenny are a young American couple. Rick is a local electrician. Michael, a fella who arrived from northern California after hearing me speak about the *Sofia* on a local radio talk show while I was visiting in Mendocino, has assumed some shipboard responsibilities. And there's a smattering of others. None of these fine folk is looking at sailing this old ship anytime soon but no matter. They're here and they're diggin' it.

I soon find a job working the loading docks across the way. Each dawn a pram (dinghy squared-off at both ends) full of boisterous young Maori men rows across to pick me up and ferry me over to the Japanese boats. The holds of the mother ships are deep, expansive, and piled twenty feet high with packed, crushed ice, chock full of dead fish. First, we slip on our "foulies"—rubber gloves, rubber overalls, and rubber gum boots—and hop onto the pallets, which are lowered away into the cavernous bellies of the fishing vessels. Then we pick a spot and begin clawing out fish by the arm-loads and tossing them in the bins stacked twelve high all around us. Finally, we load the filled cases on the pallets and whistle, signaling for the crane operator to haul them up and out.

Every three hours a siren blows and the hold empties—fast. We're lifted out and converge in the cafeteria, where we down gallons of strong, steaming hot tea mixed with whole milk and gooey honey, until the next siren blows. These breaks are called "smok-o's" and I soon begin to live for them. Often, I'll work back-to-back shifts, twelve hours straight at $1.65 an hour, a bloody fortune. Plus, the perks are noteworthy. We stuff as many fish as we can fit down into our pants and boots, to be smuggled home at work-day's end. I personally stock up on John Dory, a delectable, rare, and expensive local fish. The *Sofia's* crew is always thankful for my contributions to the evening meal, which is as often as not attended by a fair number of my fish-sorting mates. A good bit of bantering and harmless flirting goes on down in the holds. Consequently, these guys and I—I'm the only woman in the gang—have become grand pals.

While I am wading through dead fish and foul ice, my application for legal work status is approved. These permits are issued on an "as needed" basis, and at the moment the country is apparently short of qualified applicants to handle its growing troubled youth population. But in the interim I have also been volunteering as a caseworker with these kids. I find that the so-called serious juvenile delinquent problem is really more on the order of misdemeanor shoplifting and occasional truancy. "Bad kid" here is more like the "feisty kid" that I was used to in the States. New Zealand really need not be concerned about a crime wave. I'm told the entire country saw only one homicide last year and that one occurred in the midst of a domestic squabble. So I don't think I'll actively pursue my profession here. Besides, it's time to attend seriously to the refit.

Evan has rounded up a sterling jury of experts to discuss how to treat the problem with our keel. Most of the *Sofia's* wandering old salts have also returned for the occasion. Thankfully, we've all managed to keep our shipboard responsibilities in sight, despite the recent dissension and simmering hostilities.

Karen and Billy are back from the farm. Tami is done fishing until the next salmon run, and Patrick has returned from the forestry gig. Patrick tells us that his was a pretty cushy job. If conditions are such that the foresters' uniforms become wet, they are excused from work for the day. The area where he was stationed is famous for a weather phenomenon known as tully fog, a thick, low-lying layer of mist that settles on the bush (the Kiwi term for forest) each dawn and is quickly burned off by the rising sun. The forestry crew teaches Patrick to get out there good and early, roll in the grass until his khakis are soaked, report back to headquarters, and consequently be given the day off—with pay. His team does this routinely, scampering off to spend the remainder of the workday bending their elbows in the local pub. He says no one seems to mind much, not the laborers or their bosses.

New Zealand boasts a socialist government, with a significant number of its citizens contentedly living on the dole and not even bothering with the pretense of trying to scratch out a living doing something that isn't good fun. These are an exceedingly healthy, joyous people who celebrate life and simple pleasures. The country is an outdoorsman's paradise, and the locals take full advantage of every inch of it. New Zealand's compact South Island is crammed with geographic diversity. From its severe snow-capped peaks to its full-circle coastline, the landscape is dotted with alpine slopes and awash in vast stretches of open rolling countryside. It has many secluded coves, ice-carved sounds and fantastic fjords, ancient living glaciers, fertile river valleys, limestone gorges, natural sulfur pools, temperate rain forests, and an uncommonly varied blend of quaint townships and cosmopolitan cities. New Zealanders would much rather be with family, enjoy the outdoors, explore their natural wonderland, play rugby, drink beer, make new friends, and preserve old values.

Our wandering mates have also now found their way home to the *Sofia's* old worn decks, and they appear refreshed and revitalized. Evan has assembled a congregation of sailors, wooden boat aficionados, shipwrights, and marine architects. Each evening we gather in the saloon to hash out how to fix our failing hull. It is fascinating and I'm learning volumes. As we cannot consider completely rebuilding *Sofia* from the waterline down— one naively proposed treatment—we need to find a way to strengthen her existing framework without also further compromising it. This conundrum stimulates some sessions that run through numerous flagons, over many a dark night, and on into many a brightening dawn.

Ah, but with the dawn finally comes the light. After a week of brain-storming, we agree on what to do: fill the arc of space along the keel between the bow and stern with layers of soft pine, cut and fitted to form a wedgelike false keel. Then we will build a mammoth metal truss—I just knew Bart's expertise would come in handy—to connect the old and new keels externally while supporting the new planking. All this will be joined, squeezed together, and connected by a series of six-foot screws that will be bored clean through from the bilges of the original underbody and through-bolted to the worm shoe (sacrificial plank) on the foot of the false keel. The concept puts me in mind of the wooden block sets that I played with as a child: the crescent had a complementary half-moon that, inverted, slipped neatly into it, creating a solid rectangle.

We haul the *Sofia* at the slipway in Nelson, which is run by a pair of crusty seadogs named Ross and Solly, as scabrous on the outside as they are squishy on the inside. These dear old cusses become like our dads—or granddads. It's difficult to guess their age. Capable, responsible, cautious, solicitous, professional to the last, they beam with pride when we achieve and are disappointed and scolding when we misbehave. These mentors evoke from me a solid trust and a deep, abiding affection. But they seem much more comfortable being demonstrative about the *Sofia* and openly express an emotional attachment to us only by virtue of our association with the ship. They honor us simply by holding our fervent devotion to this old vessel in their very highest esteem.

For a brief time we become a solidified crew again, joined in our common bond, racing to rescue our tall ship. New crew and old alike work tirelessly, side by side. We are all betting on a long shot, albeit a well thought-out one. We are sprinting toward what we have convinced ourselves will be a victory. Of course, such is always the nature of life aboard the schooner *Sofia*. This is our arrogant and daring stance, our best profile. This is our face to the outside world. And we wear it with quiet dignity.

The slipway is chock-a-block daily, and for weeks, with curious, doubting, and cheering onlookers. They stretch out a meaty thumb in front of a squinted eye and survey the steady progress in our attempt at so novel and ambitious an undertaking. We wave confidently. Filthy and ebullient, we dismiss any reservations in the language best understood here, "Good day, mate! No worries! She'll be right!" The crowd is much more apt to be soothed than to scoff. Everyone *so* wants to believe.

Shortly after the refit is completed, Joey returns from New York. He is sorry to have missed this history-making event. He is also disappointed to learn that the old social stink, conspicuously absent on the hard, has begun to resurface on board. The glue that holds us all together is a common interest and a joint venture where the *Sofia* is concerned. Without this critical component we collapse like a house of cards. Many of us already are rediscovering our own selfish interests, as a result of the excessive downtime when the ship isn't sailing and we are no longer her sailors. The land has fostered individual exploration, and we have become something other than Sofians, moving in intellectual and emotional directions off and away, often colliding violently when we do confront one another. Those who can avoid getting caught up in the conflicts are able to maintain a decent quality of life on board. Those who can't are wise to distance themselves geographically and wait elsewhere while the dust settles. I am happy to run away again. I am not looking for a fight. Things will come right in time, I reckon. They always have before, more or less.

Joey has had all his rock climbing and backpacking equipment shipped out with him. He's heard wondrous tales of the beauty that abounds on this continent and is hungry to explore it. He and I decide to go off on walkabout together for awhile, while things calm down on board. I can tell that the opposing viewpoints within the crew are going to clash for a good while before they even have a prayer of coalescing into meaningful debate for reasonable consideration.

Our old Rick earned a decent wage working construction in Nelson and bought himself an automobile, an ancient Hillman Huskey; it's cream and chocolate brown, boxy and marginal, with two Brillo pads stuffed in the exhaust pipe to simulate a muffler. Perfect! Joe buys the car from Rick for a fat $200. He and I load it to the hilt and off we go. We begin our tour at a batch (the Kiwi term for a cottage or cabin) owned by friends and located on the shores of Nelson Lakes. Here, the aspen glow, a bright blue sheen that illuminates the surrounding snowy mountaintops at sundown, is acclaimed as the most magnificent of the South Island. From the batch we tramp the historic Abel Tasman trail, visit Marlboro Sounds, hike the famous Franz Joseph Glacier, and climb partway up Mount Cook in the great Southern Alps. All along the way we find ourselves overwhelmed with the country's raw, natural vibrancy and the people's gracious nature. We are also often overwhelmed by herds of sheep. New Zealand boasts that it has ten sheep for every one of its citizens, and I believe it. The grazing fields, or paddocks, as they're called, dominate the landscape. We frequently find ourselves chin deep in a run of sheep that takes a full hour or more to cross a road. The herder waves us a friendly "good day" with nary a thought to apologizing or hurrying along. This is Kiwi life, the pace and the priorities clearly in order.

We drive across the sprawling Canterbury countryside and then on through Christchurch. Our tired old Huskey can't quite muster the energy to climb the hill out of Queenstown on the way to the Fjordlands, so we bid it a sentimental farewell and abandon it there. We stow our excess baggage with friends and set out on foot to tramp the renowned Ruteburn and Milford tracks. Each trek entails several days of rugged beautiful wilderness hiking with a steady chain of batches, one every few miles, all along the trails. These batches, part of the national parks system, are incredible—fully equipped with firewood, axes, lanterns, cook stoves, kerosene, beds, bedding, and books. They are here to be used, a gift of the nation, and to be left tidy for the next tramper. Now that's something you won't find anywhere in the United States.

Somewhere between Nelson Lakes and Milford Sound Joey and I move a mite beyond a platonic relationship. In any event, by the time we reach the small hamlet of Hanmer Springs, we are enmeshed. Because I'm still uncomfortable with the dependency that I could develop as part and parcel of a relationship, I announce to Joe that he should head on back to the ship. I have landed myself a temporary job in town. The proprietors of the English Tea House, a fine gourmet restaurant, have not only hired me but they've offered me the free use of a little cottage while I'm in their employ. Joey is characteristically undaunted and exclaims, "Oh. OK, I'll get a job here too!" So we set up housekeeping. I set off to work and Joey sets out to find work.

Now, Joey is just about as engaging a person as I've ever known, so it shouldn't surprise me that he finds himself a job—three jobs, actually—quick as a wink, or "Bob's your uncle," as the Kiwis say when a deal is done. The manager of an establishment called the Lodge Hotel becomes immediately taken with him. Even though Joe has no actual experience, the manager hires him as weekday bartender, under his given name. Then he goes on to hire him as "Joey Vallachi," the weekend bartender. Finally, he hires him under the name of Joey Galliano, as wood chopper, fire layer, and all-around handyman. The manager resorts to all this pseudonym nonsense to avoid paying overtime, which seems a trifling concern because he's already hired Joe illegally and is paying him under the table.

So here's our Joe, an outgoing, magnetic personality with New York street smarts, entertaining rural rednecks and country bumpkins. And he's an absolute overnight sensation. The bar is always jam-packed. The manager, who looks like a Mafioso, loves Joey, introducing him proudly as "my nephew, the doctor from New York!" and me as "his lovely little missus."

Every day after work I stop in for a drink. I find Joey fully in his element, flipping glasses, pouring generous drinks, and rattling off a monologue of really dirty jokes to an enraptured audience. The jukebox will be screaming Grateful Dead or Jimmy Hendrix tunes, the crowd lined up three and four deep at the bar, and the manager strutting back and forth, all puffed up like a proud peacock.

Joe's boss makes sure that I'm given a stool at the bar whenever I come in. Then he'll motion Joey over, whisper in his ear, and soon Joe sets a drink before me, on the house. But not just any drink—Hennessy Cordon Bleu VSOP, no less!

Each morning Joey runs by the teahouse to bring me a bouquet of daffodils that grow wild all along the roadside. The owners coo that this is so sweet and that he is so adorable—that is, until it occurs to them that perhaps he's the reason that their business has dropped off so drastically of late. One night they decide to drop by the Lodge to see for themselves what all the commotion is about.

Joe and I have a pretty sweet setup in a gorgeous spot. And we are a comparatively happy couple. So it isn't totally unexpected when more and more of the *Sofia's* crew begins making regular pilgrimages to visit us in our little paradise. But the growing social unrest on board is the primary contributor to the increasing number of Sofians who seek sanctuary with us. On one weekend in particular our shipmates learn that the Lodge Hotel is showing *The Rocky Horror Picture Show*—the source of the *Sofia's* salacious unofficial theme song. An especially large contingency arrives for the occasion. Our compatriots also come in costume, as is traditional behavior for fans of this film. My employers choose this same evening to make their unannounced appearance at the Lodge.

The bar, as usual, is crammed. The raunchy soundtrack made infamous by the film is this night's music of choice. "The Time Warp" is blasting from the jukebox at full volume. Well-oiled locals are engaging in a bastardized version of "The Velvet Thrust" (a lewd dance number from the movie), with a chorus line of Sofians, who are in impressively authentic full drag. Joey is dancing on the bar. He isn't in drag however, but in a much more incriminating get-up, if possible. He wears a comically ill-fitting three-piece pinstriped suit with dress shirt and tie that clash loudly, patent leather shoes several sizes too large, and a jaunty little brown derby. Every stitch is borrowed from a back storeroom of the little batch on loan to us by my very proper English bosses. As our waning sailors' luck would have it, at this very moment my employers are standing in the bar's doorway, dumbstruck, not knowing where to look, or not to look, first. Finding it infinitely less embarrassing to focus on Joey, it takes them all of about one hot New York second to recognize their wardrobe.

Joey has been rummaging through the storage area for weeks, putting together ever-so-tasteful outfits for work, which he meticulously returns afterward, no worse for wear. Really, what's the harm? My formerly solicitous hosts are about to enlighten us.

This teeny infraction, plus Joey's employment by the competition, gets me sacked and us evicted. The townies, ever so ill at ease following their flamboyant exhibition of uninhibited dancing with the *Sofia*'s cross-dressing mates, are now a tad standoffish ("Hey, you guys realize it was just for the movie preview!" our macho sailors announce in self-defense). It is also evident that the situation developing back in Nelson requires our personal intervention. Joe and I have been inundated for weeks with frantic letters, ominous phone calls, and urgent visits from panicky crew members, who blather premonitions of all manner of revolution's erupting aboard the *Sofia*. All things considered, it is a good time to leave Hanmer Springs.

But we find no easy way to disentangle ourselves from Joey's "uncle" at the Lodge. Clearly the heir apparent of the establishment, Joey would be guaranteed a secure future if he chose to stay on. His boss is utterly distraught when Joe gives his notice. As the manager grudgingly bids us farewell, he slips us a couple of cases of the hotel's finest wines. "Cracker!" as the Kiwis say when something is particularly swell. So Joey and I, with our backpacks, sleeping bags, pillows, bags of souvenirs, and now two cases of wine, once again find ourselves on the side of the road with our thumbs out. A flatbed filled with goats picks us up and carries us all the way home to the *Sofia*.

Once back on board, we find ourselves in the company of eerily familiar strangers, mates with whom we've crossed an ocean, traversed a swaying foot rope in a storm, shared a revelation, celebration, and adventure. They are friends with whom I've survived a hurricane at sea, sailors who have bonded with me in a sober promise to be responsible for the vessel that is responsible for our lives. These same men and women have been mysteriously transfigured into politicians, victims, vigilantes, judges, and juries. Joe and I realize that we haven't come home a moment too soon. We only hope it isn't already too late.

∾

JOURNAL ENTRY
Nelson, New Zealand
January 1982

The *Sofia* has just come down off a whiz-bang haul-out after a three-day sea bashing—working her really hard under sail. We shook down the vessel, the swabbies, and the command right and proper. The ship's fancy new truss and green crew all performed damned smartly. I'm relieved to report that the keel is strong and the rookies are eager and capable. The new links in the chain of command, however, are only as sound as can be expected, considering recent developments.

The drama that ensued after Joey and I returned to the *Sofia* was captivating, with all the elements of a sordid soap opera. Misquotes from law books are boldly proclaimed. Bad performances of vignettes that could have been taken straight out of sociology texts are played out. Angry tears are shed. In the end, all the players, exposing themselves alternately as both great and small, emerge at the final curtain as fundamentally human, imperfect, impassioned, often misguided yet deserving of recognition and respect. Afterward, we trudge tentatively forward or at least onward. All indications are that our side has won. So why, in the hollow of my gut, do I struggle with persistent nagging doubt, dark and rasping like a gnarled pebble?

We stand victorious. We are the champions of futile debate, of controversy consumed by emotion, accusation void or reason, ultimatum decapitated from its rational consequence. Basically, we're what is left standing when everything around us disintegrates. Each one of us loses our way at some indeterminate point in the skirmish, loses sight of what it is that we are fighting for. In the final stages, I am just struggling to raise my head above water, to latch onto a lifeline that will keep me afloat. I only do what I can. There never really is much of a choice for me.

In retrospect, the conflict was a classic one. A small but vocal group united in an effort to force their personal agenda, which was to leave New Zealand straightaway. We'd been there a long time, and they were eager to get moving. Evan advised against it. The opposition demanded that the *Sofia* sail immediately for Australia. Evan warned that the newly refitted ship needed a tough trial under sail, followed by one more thorough once-over on the slipway before embarking on a long voyage. They want. He wants. They order. He refuses. They threaten. He shrugs. It is simply a contest of wills. The issues are never the issue. Or even if they once were in theory, they are soon sucked up into a tornado of obstinance. Eventually we each take a side. Our mere presence, no matter how benign, fortifies a particular position. The battle lines are drawn.

The insurgent Gang of Five, as they come to be known, is comprised of Norman, Karen, Patrick, Simon, and young Chris, the apprentice boatswain. They target the new recruits for conversion to their point of view, for obvious reasons. The Gang's plan promises immediate gratification and escape, sailing and adventure. It is, after all, why the uninitiated have come to the *Sofia*. Others on board, more seasoned sailors whose wary allegiance leans toward those with credentials, support Evan. A few are undecided but rally behind whomever has been nicest to them. Evan winds up with the wee short straw here. It isn't that Evan is unkind—not overtly, anyway. It is more that that he virtually never makes an effort to cultivate a following simply for its own sake. I have never seen Evan cater, kowtow to, or try to ingratiate himself with another human being. For whatever reason, he just doesn't behave in this fashion. Over the years I have seen many take this behavior personally, as a snub. It is no different in Nelson. Most of us old-timers are not in residence when the mutinous shit really hits the fan. And the insubordinates take full advantage of our absence. They assemble the jury, present their case, and reach a verdict. The majority believe that the *Sofia* should just go ahead and get on with the business of sailing across the Tasman Sea. Evan says no.

They cry, "But we voted, and you lost."

Evan says no.

They wail, "This is a cooperative. We followed due democratic process. You can't just say no!"

Evan just says no.

Norman, a member of the Gang of Five, was involved with the cooperative when its constitution was first drawn up. He is a veteran sailor who loves the sea and an idealist who has managed to find some measure of serenity in the life that he and the *Sofia* have shared for nearly a decade. In all his years with the cooperative, however, Norman has never managed to move beyond the marginally tolerable disaffection that has always existed between him and Evan. Their crippled relationship has been glaringly evident to anyone who has spent any time on board, but an acknowledged incompatibility was basically it's only manifestation, until now. Suddenly, as if out of nowhere, Norman pulls a fast one. He discloses a gavel with which he can finally hammer his long brooding animosity into action.

Norman places a call to the Farm, a commune in northern California (unrelated to the famous one by the same name in Tennessee). It's also the land-based version of the *Sofia* organization, home to many a past member of the sailing cooperative, as well as a few of the original architects of its sociopolitical framework. A man named Kansas is among those who still hang out there. The *Sofia*'s official documents are kept there, and Kansas's name is on them. It turns out that this man, whom I have never met and whose name I've rarely ever heard mentioned over the years, possesses a power over us that I didn't even know existed. Kansas has the legal authority to have Evan stripped of his command. This is Norman's ace in the hole. When I realize that he has had it all along, I am amazed that he has managed to resist playing it sooner.

Kansas, I later learn, is a true child of the '60s and ever the pacifist. He is the embodiment of the cooperative spirit. I find myself wishing that I could have known him under different circumstances. Upon being notified of the conflict, he announces that he intends to do one of two things. Either he will exercise his power of attorney to have Evan removed, or Kansas will defer to the rule of the majority on board. He apologizes, saying that he'll require some time to mull this over. He'll let us know.

And so, in an attempt to tip the scales, the games begin. The politics on board are brutal, the lobbying fast and furious. Accusations fly. Muckraking takes on a life of its own—despite efforts at prudence, we've revealed *way* too much to each other over the years. Evan, sensing the climate, surreptitiously contacts Joey and me down south, lassos Tami, who has been fishing out on the banks, and sends up a big red flare—he is in trouble. After stating his position—straightforwardly, honestly, without emotion— or even diplomacy—he instructs us to follow our best instincts and to keep him informed. He cautions us that no matter what we decide, we will need to act quickly. Then he uses the only strategy left to him. He goes AWOL, cunningly absconding with the ship's papers, which are necessary to check out of the country. Evan is not willing to concede, not without a fight. But reckoning that we are on the eve of a decisive battle, he wisely claims the high ground.

The Gang of Five assumes provisional command of the ship. Its members assert that because Evan is in clear violation of the basic tenets of this cooperative venture, as drafted by its original authors, he can be removed. They are confident that Kansas will concur.

When Joe, Tami, and I return to the *Sofia*, we collide head-on with a tightly compressed sphere of fury, a whirlwind of revolution that is already firmly entrenched. I am impressed. I hadn't realized that these guys had it in them. My regard soon gives way to disgust, however, as I survey the dilapidated condition of the vessel. These impassioned individuals, these righteously indignant resisters, these self-appointed bluebloods of the cause, have let the object of their inflamed devotion fall into such an obscene state of disrepair that it defies common sense.

The galley is a chaotic dirty slum. The engine room has become a fire hazard, a warehouse chockablock with abandoned projects, dumped in a junkyard clutter of open paint cans, spilled diesel, soaking brushes, discarded tools, and scattered miscellaneous spare parts. Above decks is no better. Gritty shrunken planks reveal gaping seams and cracked sealants. Tarps and covers have come away, exposing sails to the brutal elements, which are senselessly baking away days of their already limited life expectancy. Mooring lines are chafing through. Running rigging lies in unkempt heaps in the scuppers. Paint has chipped off the spars. Worn varnish lies dull and patchy on the rails. The old tar on the stays is clumped and caked. The ship is anything but shipshape. She is outwardly manifesting the rot that is infecting her soul. The *Sofia* has effectively been abandoned by those same folk who are trying to convince me that they should be at the helm of my ship and my life. NOT BLOODY LIKELY!

I try to reason with them, but they can't hear me. Their rage is all encompassing, their vision tunneled, blind to the consequences. Their vehemence is a maelstrom. Shouting into this darkness, I realize with horror the immense power contained in what we manage to convince ourselves is true. The small army that has formed from hurt feelings, bruised egos, and purely subjective notions is determined to proceed—with absolute certainty toward probable and calculable catastrophe. No one on board in the midst of this chaos is going to be able to stay this mutiny. So I take a chance and try reasoning with Kansas. He is peacefully planted in a sunny summer meadow, a million miles from the cold steel decks of the *John Wilson*, the old cement hauler where I spend countless hours speaking with him on a pay phone. We brainstorm. We philosophize. We are trying to find the answer. He and I discuss past hopes, the realities of the present, and a vision for the future. Kansas and I talk. Joey, Tami, and I talk. Others venture shaky opinion and plead for guidance. "What should we do?" "Who do we choose?" "Why is this happening?" I don't attempt to respond, don't know what to say, don't want that responsibility.

New Zealand's sailing community at large firmly supports Evan. They find the whole thing patently absurd.

"Oh course, Evan is skipper. Done!"

"Certainly, he's qualified. Hasn't he proven that?"

"A vote to determine command? Ridiculous! Unheard of!"

Informed that Sofians are debating the time-honored measures of sea-manship versus Evan's social graces, the Kiwis have only one response: "OH, BLOODY HELL!"

Of course, it isn't quite that simple. The Gang has accused Evan of tyranny at sea, of endangering the lives of the crew and risking the structural integrity of the vessel to further his own selfish interests—shades of life in the horse latitudes. I honestly don't know, and probably never will know, whether this claim has a shred of validity. But let's say for the sake of argument that a case can be made. Certainly, Evan has been known to stand alone, obdurate in the face of irate and often panicky objection. But isn't that what a leader must be willing to do? And doesn't Evan always remain fully accountable? I have never—not once—seen him shirk responsibility. Why, he has not ever even waffled, been crippled by fear, frozen into indecision, or stalled into submission. And I can honestly say that for all our nautical miles together, through storm and calm, he has seldom if ever been proved to be clearly or absolutely in error. In truth, the Gang has taken a stand based on shaky principles. Finally, I decide that I will not put to sea on principle. So I write a letter to the crew, tack it to the saloon bulkhead, and wait. Here's the gist of my statement:

by Pami Sisman

To whomever is interested—

I cannot condone the action taken by The Gang, in any way. I will not forget or ignore the fact that it is in violation of everything *Sofia* supposedly represents as well as violating the basic human rights of myself, the crew in general, and Evan in particular.

I won't compromise myself or *Sofia* by working or sailing on her with less than a whole heart or an easy mind. I don't have a handy rationale that allows me to feel other than sick, sad, and angry about what's been perpetrated here. And God, I'm tired of those feelings. So . . .

I'll wait until Kansas either exercises his power of attorney or decides to let the majority rule on board. If he defers to the crew, I'll participate in the crew's discussions and decision making. If not, then I'll not sail out of here on *Sofia*. My gut won't let me support you on principle. And my better sense, born of 3½ years on this ship, won't let me risk my life unnecessarily. The 2 arguments—1) that *Sofia* has sufficient lifesaving equipment in the event of a disaster, or 2) that she's sailed in a similarly unsafe and unstable state before and survived—just don't allow me to sigh with relief and resignation, somehow. I won't sail across a notoriously volatile body of water, in tenuous weather conditions, on a vessel of questionable seaworthiness, with a predominantly green crew, skippered by Norman. Bloody Hell! Although I believe Norman to be a qualified seaman, I don't feel he is capable of instructing, organizing, or commanding an inexperienced crew in the best of conditions, let alone the aforementioned. Nor is anyone else on board.

At the recent meeting, I attempted to explain any reservations and found you unreceptive. I can't take responsibility for you, nor can I single-handedly protect *Sofia* from you. Sadly, I reckon you'll have to learn for yourselves. With all my heart, I wish you an untragic lesson. And I'll see you at its end. Because I love this ship and I'll be God-damned if I'll throw her away to this crap presently befouling her and all of our lives.

If things don't come right here, I'll meet you in Australia and rejoin *Sofia* there. I'll help square her away when she isn't laboring under the destructive handicaps of petty politics, inexperience, hurtful emotions, and time limitations that you're naively allowing to dictate priorities where your own and the ship's safety take an unconscionable second place.

I can't deny what I know. With knowledge and understanding we have to learn to assume and exercise responsibility in and for our lives and others in our midst. This is the only responsible position I can take. For those of you who don't know *Sofia* and the people in question, I guess the decision is easier. Or perhaps no decision is easiest yet. My position is clear, and I'm relieved finally to be able to explain it to you. It's a consideration I would have appreciated from others of you. I do care, very much.

Pami

In California, Kansas decides not to exercise his power of attorney, and Evan is voted in as skipper. Anticipating what might happen if we wait to go to Australia is an easier scenario to accept than imagining what could happen if we don't. Quite simple, when taken down to its bare bones. But, sadly, these aren't the only bones that now lie exposed. A graveyard of skeletons has emerged from the closets of too many of the key players during the revolt, making it impossible for them to stay on after they are defeated. Simon, who's largely driven the attempted mutiny, packs up and heads for Australia. Patrick, Norman, and Karen soon follow. Chris hasn't had time to accumulate anywhere near the pile of dirty laundry that the others leave behind, and he has barely gotten his feet wet on the old girl, so he decides to stick around. Evan comes home. Life on the *Sofia* shifts back into gear, and we soldier on, albeit a trace more cautiously and soberly than before.

Marge, an old friend of Evan's, owns a house in Nelson that has in the past many months become a refuge for us. A mother of three grown boys, Margie is smart and sassy, an independent woman with a heart as big as the great New Zealand outdoors that she so cherishes. We are invited to enjoy many festive occasions with her family and are introduced to a colorful assortment of characters as well. Among them is a well-known local artist named Roger Morris, who specializes in maritime paintings. Morris is in the process of compiling a collection of watercolors for a book to be called *Sail Change—Tall Ships in New Zealand Waters*. He asks if he might be allowed to paint the *Sofia*. We are moved. To return the compliment, we ask the artist whether he would be interested in piloting the *Sofia* during the country's upcoming annual Anniversary Day Regatta. Morris says that he would be honored. Later, when *Sail Change* is published in 1981, he makes certain that we receive a copy. In it, as an introduction to the painting of *Sofia*, he wrote:

> I was impressed by the philosophy of the crew; this was, basically, the ship comes first. While unorthodox in appearance and the manner in which she is organised—the ship is run by a co-operative—there was nothing unseamanlike in her gear which was well maintained and cared for. A running battle with poverty was apparent but strength and safety had not been sacrificed.

With respect to piloting the *Sofia*, he went on to say:

> Steering down-harbour with Varmit, the coatimundi, making passes at my toes, I was further impressed by the sail handling and ability of the five crew that managed the ship and the seventeen or eighteen raw recruits. A few quiet words, a whistle and some hand signals and within minutes of bearing away down-harbor all fore and aft sails were set, followed by flying jib, topsails and squares—twelve sails in all.

Morris's painting of the *Sofia* is stunning: bow-on under full sail, charging through a tossed sea, with crew aloft, straddling foot ropes, releasing the square sails. The artist concludes his series with this painting and uses it on the cover as well. So far, my association with this fine tall ship is the proudest accomplishment of my life, despite the recent troubles.

We meet another artist in Nelson, a sculptor who offers to carve a traditional figurehead for the bow. We agree, and he begins work straightaway.

Life settles more or less into routine once again. We have to apply for another visa extension—these are granted in increments of six months—as the ship is deemed not yet seaworthy. (This wise sailing nation is of the same mind as our captain.) As long as the *Sofia* can stay, we can stay. Without the ship we'd each be booted out of here on short order. So we find ourselves riding her wake once again.

In the lull that followed the failed coup I had occasion to leave the *Sofia* for another three-week work stint. I had been feeling strangely restless, as though on the verge of some momentous personal leap of faith. Fairly raging into my thirties (if in fact I turned thirty at all, as *Sofia* crossed the International Dateline on my thirtieth birthday, October 7, 1980, relegating that day to drift forever in some chronometric limbo), I was experiencing an expectant tingling, a sense of pause as though holding my breath, stuck in the rests between the notes of a musical score, waiting on the next beat in the movement. High on the tablelands of the North Island overlooking the Tasman Sea, alone save for my company of cows, goats, and sheep, I found my next step.

I'd landed a job running a monitoring station for a geophysical survey for offshore oil drillers. My duties were to watch over my beacon tower, Yagi antennae, SSB (single sideband) radio, and generators. I'd check my guy wires and lashings and climb the tower to readjust the Yagi when it blew off its compass bearings. I'd maintain regular audio contact with base camp and keep a detailed log. That's it. The total and complete solitude was like a spiritual retreat; it afforded me endless hours to ruminate over current events and ponder my future. Some recent developments warranted particularly careful scrutiny.

A film company had approached the *Sofia* and proposed a movie deal. The project would consume the better part of the next year. It was too lucrative a prospect to turn down, so the *Sofia's* immediate future had been determined. Also, Joey and I had entered into a phase of our relationship that hinted at commitment and consolidation, a surrendering of freedom, a threat to my direction, my independence. This situation rattled me to my core. I wasn't looking for it, didn't welcome it, was not prepared, was not being won over easily. Actually, Joe had been working on me from the outside in, a tactic that was succeeding. My internal resolve had been a hard compressed knot, impregnable and unyielding. But recently I had been experiencing life light and bright through Joey's innately optimistic, confident, adoring eyes. And despite myself, my gut was giving me permission. Also, this damned annoying nesting and nurturing urge kept sneaking up on me.

Up on the mountain I realized what I needed to do. For several days I'd watched a very pregnant cow graze with her herd. Each morning I'd race out to the paddock in anticipation of a calf. On the morning of the day that I was to dismantle my station and be flown off the headlands, she gave birth. The wobbly new life, still wet and sticky with a ragged tassel where its mother has chewed through the umbilical cord, was already mingling with the big gals, mewing and butting, demanding to be noticed. Birthing time: Everyone out of the womb! And in an instant, I knew. I would soon resume my autonomy, free of both the *Sofia* and Joey. I would leave them to their film careers and strike out on my own once again, maybe for Indonesia to climb some mountains, chat with some gurus, perhaps for quite a while. I'd find the *Sofia* again, wherever she was, when the time was right, and I'd know then if I still belonged. I'd find Joey too, and the future would be whatever Providence so deemed.

Sofia's Keel Project haul-out and crew. The ways in Nelson, New Zealand.

chapter 12

Off the North Cape

The Storm

Watchman, what of the night?

—ISAIAH 21:11

INTRODUCTION

Although the *Sofia* survived the mutiny attempt intact, the attendant under-mining of her fragile social structure was irreparable. Wounds inflicted by long resentments and brooding angers left scars. A huge well of sadness filled the void created by the defeated and consequently disembarking crew. Those of us who stayed claimed a hollow victory. We'd won the battle but at what cost? We'd lost once-trusted friends, companions with whom we'd shared the adventure of a lifetime.

With quiet and efficient dignity Evan resumed command of the tall ship. The skipper was by then a close comrade of adversity, the state, I've heard it said, in which we become best acquainted with ourselves because we are notably free of admirers. Confrontation simply reduced Evan to his fighting weight. He was prepared for it, resigned to it. True to his style, the captain had remained resolutely unyielding. The crew was swayed.

Throughout my days aboard the *Sofia*, amid countless debates concerning the ship's care and course, despite often furious posturing and vociferous diatribes delivered by a revolving cast of characters, the outcome was always the same. The captain remained resolutely unyielding. The crew was swayed.

Evan based his decisions on research, meticulous calculations, and the time-worn tradition of consulting books, charts, and the esteemed opinions of other sailors. His position held up well to objective scrutiny and rational debate. Rather than being his salvation, however, such validation often further alienated him from his crew. We Sofians gathered in a saloon instead of a boardroom. The captain was a young sailor, not a CEO. And our democratic process commonly fell victim to the temptations of anarchy. Evan found that being right too often, particularly when compromise was not part of one's working vocabulary, was lethal. By definition, a cooperative rejects a hierarchy. But a circumnavigating tall ship and no viable chain of command are mutually exclusive concepts. Herein rested the ever-present *Sofia* quandary.

The venture, always a cost-plus operation at best, could not survive without continually tapping its most renewable resource—new paying members. Whatever a person's reasons for coming on board, whatever her or his expectations, the ship's requirements of each individual remained static. We were shamelessly uncivilized in our lack of a class system. One could not simply purchase, say, a nicer bunk, fewer night watches, a stand-in for galley duty, vacation time during haul-outs, an excuse from foul-weather sail handling, or guaranteed camaraderie with the captain.

However, the world seems to have a marked shortage of functional adults who will pay for the privilege of working hard, feeling lousy, and being ordered about. So, unfortunately, most novitiates approached the *Sofia* with the daft notion that accomplishments in some other phase of their life would carry over and provide them with status aboard ship. On a vessel such as ours, however, newcomers were promptly pigeon-holed as one of three basic types: someone who knows what to do and does it; someone who has no idea what to do but will follow a command and is willing to learn; or someone who doesn't know what he's doing, pretends that he does, and habitually endangers the lives of everyone on board. This third brand of sailor was always represented among the transients in the crew of the *Sofia*. Those used to wielding power and authority in a former existence are fiercely resistant to being regarded as greenhands (tallship terminology for someone straight off the farm).

Finally, everyone who lasted either came on board as a member of a cooperative and learned how to be a sailor or came on board as a sailor and learned to cooperate. Evan never equivocated. His allegiance was always to the ship. He was a sailor first, a cooperator merely out of necessity, and he failed miserably at disguising this, if in fact he tried at all. Actually, I believe that the great majority of those who sailed on the *Sofia* with us derived comfort, security, and a sense of freedom from the certainty that

Evan would assume capable command and ultimate responsibility. The bottom line was that Evan understood the ship and the elements of seamanship far better than most on board at any given time. But his stumbling inability to pass along this knowledge diplomatically proved to be an often debilitating handicap for the vessel. Because I understood both the ship and her captain, the crew was willing to cooperate with me. Thus, I took on a significant role in the *Sofia's* final days: the intermediary trusted by both sides.

JOURNAL ENTRY
New Plymouth
New Zealand

In preparation for scheduling sea trials for our newly refitted hull and the final haul-out in Nelson, we constructed a tentative pecking order in the ship's reinstituted and now openly acknowledged chain of command. Evan approached me the evening before the organizational meeting and asked me to accept the position of first mate—second in command. The job previously had been held by one of the mutineers. I balked, suspicious of the motives of this marked man in bestowing upon me so dubious an honor. Without a hint of defensiveness or any pretense of winning my affection, he stated quite academically that immediately restoring order, routine, and discipline aboard the *Sofia* was imperative. He believed that together we could work methodically and constructively toward this end. I offered that if the crew approved of my appointment, I would accept it conditionally: I would consent to function as acting first mate, a temporary stand-in, until a qualified successor could commit to seeing the *Sofia* through the next chapter in her saga. I had already decided to take off on my own for a bit and was reluctant to give up my autonomy. Although a couple of people on board have more sailing experience than I, no one has more sea time aboard the *Sofia*. Also, and perhaps more important, I can and will work with the captain. Although Evan and I have no deep friendship, what we do share is infinitely more practical. In our years of sailing together we have achieved mutual respect and acknowledge a shared sense of commitment and obligation. The captain will command the ship, the mate will organize the crew. So I agree, the resident sailors overwhelmingly approve my commission, and I begin bearing my heady responsibilities. It seems to be working. The ship is coming around, the atmosphere is positive, and we're once again progressing toward a common goal.

Of the veterans who sailed into New Zealand with the *Sofia* more than a year ago, only Evan, Billy, Joey, and I remain on board. Tami has hired on for the next season's salmon run, and Rick high-tailed it outta here when the politics got dirty. I expect they'll both continue to pop up on board in the future.

In their place is some fresh new blood. Margie's youngest son, Mark, has come aboard with his mom's mixed blessings. His cousin Betty has also signed up for a short holiday. Two young local fellows, Trevor and Rodney, are here. Trevor is an apprentice shipwright who worked with us on the refit. Rodney has just been sort of hanging around us for months. We also have a Big Scott and a Little Scott in our company. Little Scott is a mate of Billy's, a youngster, really—can't be much out of his teens. Big Scott is a Canadian, a traveler, and large and loud—that's about the gist of him so far. A fine young Englishman named Nigel is also new to our crew. He is obviously bright, self-possessed, and an experienced sailor. Imogene is from the country, a clean swatch of homegrown New Zealand farmland. And then there's Julie, who is very new, very young, and very quiet. Mark and Joey met her while she was waitressing in a Nelson health food restaurant. That makes seventeen Sofians in all.

The demands of my new position have caused me to reorder my immediate priorities. I'm now responsible for organizing, instructing, assigning, implementing, and supervising. I run the crew, Evan oversees. As a result, I'm polishing my skills for walking on egg shells. I've had to rediscover a functional diplomacy and a savoir-faire that have been buried by the grittiness that accumulated while I was just getting myself through many a long year and across endless ocean. However, I'm just putting one foot in front of the other along the path that stretches directly in front of me—my direction. Nothing fundamental has changed on board. But I am somehow moving apart. My own course still dominates my focus. For the time being my present bearings are setting me on the same tack as this new bunch, that's all. I did affect the outcome of the mutiny attempt, and I've accepted the consequences of my actions. So I will remain on the *Sofia* until I am done with her, and she with me. I owe the ship that much. I owe it to myself. When the time for an honorable finish does arrive, it will feel right, even though it often feels less than that now. This is what I tell myself.

We will be saying goodbye to so many good people here. I am closer now to some of them than I have been to anyone in a very long while.

Many are elderly, and although I promise to return some day, in my heart I know it won't be soon enough. It seems so sad, so strangely final. I don't recall having this ache before. Something is changing.

A whole slew of travelers came and went while the *Sofia* was in Nelson. They lived, worked, and played on board without ever sailing a lick. In Norman's absence one of these fellas, Kiwi Rick, rewired the engine room. His time ran out before he got much of a chance to sail with us. But before he left, he completed his pet project: He rerouted the electric bilge pump, running her straight down from the generator. He promised that this would make it function much more efficiently, and our initial sea trial proved him right enough. It worked like a charm.

The Varmit just ambled back aft to say "gudday." He's become so civil, cuddly almost. He barely survived the winter and appears to now need constant reassurance that his significant others are still around as well. The official agents assigned to monitor his incarceration eventually took pity on him, or else they got plumb worn down by the vigilant protesters. They took to calling old Jimmy, the watchman on the *John Wilson*, to alert him that they were on their way over. Jimmy would signal us, and we'd round up Varmit and stick him in his pen. The officers would come below, look at the critter, nod, wink, and be on their way. They'd done their duty. We'd kept our promise. As soon as they were gone, we'd release the Varm to roam free until the next bed check.

Our coati has definitely slowed down a mite, but we're not fooled for a minute. Should he make overtures and warm to affection, we'll supply it in bundles, but it has to be on his terms. A hard case, to be sure. If he's not in the mood, we know not to push our luck—woe is the sailor who tries to steal a hug uninvited.

Jimmy and I have become close friends. He actually got me inducted into the Wooden Hullers Association, a local group of old sailors who cut their eyeteeth on ships like the *Sofia* more than a half-century ago. I've spent countless dreamy hours sitting with Jim in his spartan little quarters, listening as he recalls sea stories from his boyhood, while he patiently teaches me how to spin rope in every imaginable shape and purpose outlined in *Ashley's Book of Knots*, the bible of traditional sailors. I know that I will miss him and Margie the most. Front and center on the wharf when the *Sofia* drifts away from Nelson for the last time are Marge and Jimmy, along with Ross, Solly, and my Maori fish-sorting mates. Pretty much the whole town turns out to send us off, as we head to Auckland where we are to meet up with the film company. Tears are shed, promises made, prayers whispered. It is like leaving home again. God, it is so hard, and I'm not sure why.

Our generous sculptor finished the figurehead in the nick of time, but we haven't managed to mount it yet. Actually, we aren't quite sure what we're supposed to do with it. The artist obviously put in a great deal of time and effort, and he completed an impressive, albeit odd, piece—a larger-than-life bust of a woman coifed in a prim brunette pageboy and outfitted in a high-cut, olive green housedress. Her pale blue eyes are trained to the heavens, her severe black eyebrows arch expectantly, her thin, deep scarlet lips are pursed into a smirk . . . not exactly what we were expecting. I have to admit that I've heard more than one Sofian mutter under his breath, "What the bloody hell are we to do with her now?" Until we come up with a solution, she's lashed to the main mast like an errant swabbie on a pirate ship, right snug up next to Joey's deep purple classic Bantam Major motorcycle. Joe had been spoiled by the Huskey. No sooner had we returned to Nelson than he set out to find another set of wheels. Since purchasing the Bantam, he's been pleased as punch, tooling through the countryside with me astride his hot new machine—Joey wearing a Green Bay Packer football helmet, me with one of Billy's caving caps, complete with carbide lamp jiggling atop my bouncy curls.

We've alerted the movie company that we're on for the film. The British-Kiwi team wants our ship to star in a project about the infamous local pirate Bully Hayes. Among other inducements, the production crew promises us an occasion to visit Fiji, where much of the filming will take place, a new engine to ensure our arrival on schedule, and—plum of plums—spots as extras for all the male crew members. Our fellas are already grooming swashbuckling beards, sporting shiny gold earrings, and practicing their saltiest "Aaarrrggghh, mateys!" The historically accurate project has no parts for women.

The film company's attorneys are waiting for us in Auckland, where we'll have our new engine installed. They're busy ironing out the details for yet another visa extension for the *Sofia*. With our sea trials completed, all that remains is for us to get the ship up the North Island to meet them. No rush, no pressure, just a place to go, a reason to leave, and an opportunity to put unfortunate circumstance behind us.

The first leg out of Nelson, en route to Auckland, is illuminating, to put it mildly. Beating for almost three days through near gale-force winds and heading seas smacks the rookies with the realities of open ocean sailing, and Evan and I get barely any sleep. At least one of us is on deck the entire time. The ship holds up, the crew hangs in, and we're now readying for the last leg, a hefty stretch that'll loop us up around the North Cape of New Zealand and back down along the Bay of Islands and on in to the east coast's Hauraki Gulf.

Departing Nelson from the Tasman Bay of New Zealand's South Island, we needed only to make a short hop across the Cook Strait to reach the North Island and a proverbial fork in the road. There are two routes to Auckland. We can follow the example of generations of local fishermen by sailing up the west coast of the North Island. This passage, colloquially known as "North About," is the rougher of the options. It promises fluky winds, heading seas, and many miles before landfall. The other route, up the east coast and around the Bay of Plenty, will, on the other hand, put us on an almost constant reach (winds blowing sideways to the ship), with the prevailing breeze shoving us into a lee shore. Few things at sea are more unsettling than sailing for an extended period while the immense effort of the malevolent "Roaring 40s" (as the latitudes there are known, for their extreme winds), forces you into mile after protracted mile of jutting, jagged, reef-rimmed coastline.

We have to keep in mind our current liabilities: We are comprised largely of a green crew, and we are setting out for the first ocean voyage with our new keel and truss. Byrds, a member of the crew who hails from New Plymouth, a city on the west coast of the North Island, intercedes. Eager to introduce his family to the *Sofia* and vice versa, he proposes a short layover in his hometown that will give us a chance to reassess and rejuvenate partway along in the passage. Weighing the pros and cons, we decide to head North About.

All in all, we have a fine rest here in New Plymouth. Byrds's family, friends, and the entire community have been grand to us. We very much want to repay their kindness with a day sail, but the weather has been uncooperative—cold, gray, damp, and blowing like stink—and we're waiting for a break in the wind so that we can take them out. We've had to run additional mooring lines from the wharf, four feet high across the *Sofia* to the cleats mounted on her outboard rails, just to keep her on an even keel at the dock. As we can anticipate that these adverse conditions will hold until we've rounded the cape, everyone seems eager to get it over with.

Each morning we wake to face a crowd of expectant and beaming daytrippers, dressed in foulies, toting potluck contributions and cameras, and gripping the hands of rowdy littlies. And each morning we must shake our heads regretfully and turn them away. "No worries, mates," they console us. "Perhaps tomorrow," they offer. "Perhaps," we answer guardedly.

Evan alone calls this shot and turns a firm thumb down on each successive blustery day. He will not take such a risk. For what? Frustrated crew members spit out angry words and demands, but these are the wailings of cranky students. Evan stands firm, quiet, unemotional. He is the teacher, instructing them in a sailor's patience.

∾

JOURNAL ENTRY
New Plymouth
New Zealand
February 14, 1982
Valentine's Day!
8:15 in the evening

It's still light out! There's a clean, fresh breeze and some partial clearing. We finally have our day sail—seventy guests, Force 5 winds, lousy seas but manageable. I hate it, hate the day sails in general—too much bloody work and worry for a few hours' sea time, and then you end up right back where you started. We owe these folks, though, so we do it. The weather is markedly better than it's been, and the locals seem to have a fine time. I'm just relieved that it's over and there are no casualties. Soon we'll weigh anchor for Auckland via the Bay of Islands, a sentimental full-circle journey for the few of us who entered New Zealand there, well over a year ago. It is definitely time to get going. The people here are wonderful, though, like those in Nelson. They make me feel proud. Proud to be a sea bum. Proud to be a Sofian. I'm aware that I'm part of something priceless and majestic, a cherished tradition that these people still hold in reverence and that we are honored to be allowed to carry on. Thank god for old sailors.

AUTHOR'S NOTE: My final letter home was dated February 21:

> Just a quick note to say hi and tell you we're on our way again. New Plymouth has held us longer than planned but we were made so welcome here. We expect twenty-five to forty-knot southerlies up the coast, so it should be a quick trip north. I'll call you from Auckland in a week or so.

It rained like crazy the last two days. Very depressing and uncomfortable. I miss you guys. I love you. Keep warm.

P.S. The ship 'The Bounty,' built for the third remake of the film, may be heading across the Pacific, San Diego-bound, in May. Hmmmm . . .

Talk to you soon.

Please be well.

Love, Pami

AUTHOR'S NOTE: I posted my final journal entries, pictures, and that letter from New Plymouth to my hometown in Michigan the morning we set sail. The events that follow are as I remember them.

I set up a watch rotation of four teams, four to a watch. Each team has one experienced watch captain and three relatively green crew members. We stand three hours on, nine hours off, around the clock. The wind is fresh, the weather cool and drizzly, the current strong. In other words, the conditions are normal for this area. We are working the ship hard. The rookies are at times overwhelmed. It is admittedly an unpleasant passage.

We are hauling up the coast, averaging a good five knots, expecting to round the cape on the second night and make Auckland by the fourth day. Our schedule is ambitious, but the weather is foul. None of us wants to be out bashing around in it any longer than necessary. The voyage has not lent itself to instruction in basic sailing techniques. Rather, it's more suitable for a sailor's master's thesis, and some recruits are frankly alarmed. The weather has not yet presented a major concern for us veterans. We've each experienced similar conditions on numerous occasions without incident. We are, however, all thinking about the truss, picturing the keel, visualizing the *Sofia*'s underbelly as it labors underwater—willing it to stay strong.

The pilot charts for this area warn that fall brings with it a considerable increase in the number of gales, particularly in the higher latitudes, where the more frequent and violent storms increase the force of the prevailing westerlies. But this is February, still late summer in New Zealand, and we are sailing above the westerlies of the 40th parallel and below the bottom of the trades at 25 degrees. This interim area that we need to traverse, specifically, the waters off Cape Reinga, is in a 15-degree stretch where the winds are reported to be simply "of a variable nature."

We make Cape Maria Van Diemien, the island's northeasternmost point, in the late afternoon of the second day. As dusk approaches, conditions appear to worsen. I'm not sure whether this is fact supported by our actual readings or just the vague foreboding that accompanies the prospect of weathering a rough night at sea without the reassurance that daylight can afford a weary sailor. The crew is showing fatigue. The ship is taking on water. Both are consequences that we anticipated and prepared for. We spell the watch. We pump the bilges steadily. We are keeping up, holding our own—sailing.

Moments before dark we sight a beacon from the cliffs above a small secluded inlet off our starboard bow. In the tiny cove we make out what looks like a single masthead light. Someone suggests that perhaps we should follow the lead of that vessel and tuck in for the night. No severe weather has yet been predicted for the area, no storms are reported looming off on the horizon. Still, the prudent thing to do is to get an update.

Almost everyone on board gathers back aft, coming on or going off watch, or just finding comfort in company, anxious to know the plans before they can rest assured down below. Evan flicks on the single sideband and waits to pick up a current weather report. Nothing. He flips the toggle off and then on again and listens, hard. Still nothing. Dead quiet, not even a buzzing. No static. No life. Reaching a hand behind the instrument panel, he dredges out a fistful of dismembered bits, a clump of torn wires. Earlier in the day someone had noticed the Varmit behaving strangely. He was tearing around the chart room in a frenzy and had at one point wedged himself into the radio well, where he was heard to be routing and thrashing wildly about. For some reason Varmit apparently ripped the wires from their sockets, stripped the connections, and left the works in a tangled nest of useless garbage. He had unplugged us.

Aware that it will take hours to repair the damage, Evan takes a chance and tries the VHF radio instead. If we can raise the boat in the anchorage, we can at least solicit from its occupants a current account of the weather for the immediate vicinity. Evan gets some juice from the VHF, but the signal is weak and intermittent. Varmit left this one radio only marginally operational. Under the circumstances the anchored vessel will very soon be outside our limited range. So will any chance for safe harbor for the night, as we are nearly beyond the cove and will not be able to battle the strong current and backtrack into it once it is off our stern. We hail the yacht. They respond jovially. No, they haven't heard of a storm bearing down, know of no appreciable change since the last report we've received. "This is the weather off the North Cape, dontcha know?" They've just snugged up to rest for the night.

There remain a panicky few who still lobby to head in, just in case. The anxious faces on a number of the others in the gallery reflect this same sentiment. But none is seasoned. All are inexperienced. They are miserable. And they are scared. Those of us who have been there and done that on many a rocky ride in the past defer to the clinical, unemotional laws of the sea in making our decision. We calmly discuss the options back aft, out in the open in the encroaching darkness and howling wind, surrounded by a dread-filled group that is hanging apprehensively on our every word.

The small harbor, if we chance it, will be a gamble. The anchoring exercise will be lengthy, complicated, and physically demanding. It is certain to be followed by a wakeful, watchful, worrisome long night, at the very least. The winds, on the other hand, are fresh, yes, but nothing the *Sofia* can't handle. The channel is tossed, the seas confused but just for another couple hours. The pumps are keeping up. The dawn will see us in to the golden, serene, tropical Bay of Islands, which lies just around the bend. The wind will then be on our beam, the tremendous effort will be off the rigging, the stress on the hull will ease. The deciding factor, finally, though, is the current. It is wicked strong, impossible to confront under sail. We are flying along *with* it now and will continue to do so for only another three or four hours, tops. Then it will turn and run against us. If we wait until morning, it will be heading us then too. OK, we all decide together, we can grind it out through this night. It is just one night.

I take the watch from six to nine. My team looks back as the light at Cape Maria Van Diemien fades away and dissolves into darkness. The course alters slightly during my watch, putting us on more of a beat, sailing close-hauled, sails sheeted tightly in. Consequently, we've begun to heel over, which is natural in these conditions. Then the auxiliary pump chokes and abruptly stops. It creates a kind of implosive sensation, as if all the oxygen has been drained from the atmosphere in an instant. It sounds like the end of the world. I dive into the engine room, crawl under the generator, and stare into the swilling bilges. The pump's hose lies at the deepest point, precisely where Kiwi Rick had led it, just where it ought to be. But it hangs naked and exposed, pathetically dry and marooned. The gallons of seawater gushing in have shifted into the outer underbody as we heel well over. The pump, sucking air, has lost its prime and died out. Clearly, it will do it again and again, each time we suffer such a severe roll, each time we're forced to abandon our dominion over an even keel. Sure, it's more efficient—when the *Sofia* sails upright. How had we missed this? Bloody, bloody, bloody hell!

We'll have to depend solely on the manual pumps. They move volumes, but we'll have to pump nonstop. We'll just have to, that's all. And we will. We've done it before. I set my team to manning the pumps. The watches will overlap shifts if necessary. We should be able to maintain until a few short hours later when we'll alter course again, tack over to a beam run south and a more tractable point of sail.

Confirming the latest developments with the skipper, I then share the information with Joe, the oncoming watch captain. I turn the helm over to his team but stay on deck well into his watch—pumping, verifying, overseeing, pacifying. Everything appears to be stable. The *Sofia* has been through worse, much worse. She can handle it. I go below at around eleven.

At one point during his watch Joey goes down into the galley to put up a pot of tea. The young woman from Nelson, Julie, who doesn't have a bunk and so is sleeping in the saloon, is wide awake when he gets there. She whispers that she is frightened. He urges her to try not to worry.

His watch pumps steadily. Whenever the crew slows down, the bilges fill rapidly. The team pumps them until they suck air, rests a few seconds, and then resumes pumping with a will. When Joe turns the watch over to Byrds's team at midnight, he communicates the severity of the situation. I hear Byrds express concern that the manual pump diaphragms must be faulty. Joe says no, the ship is laboring, the hull is working especially hard, and he needs to just keep pumping. Byrds slaps him on the back reassuringly and says something like "Right, then, mate."

The next thing I'm aware of is an instinct. Everything is wrong, out of sync, shifted ever so slightly. Something has crossed mysteriously over the line by just that fraction of an inch. I struggle to gain the deck, feeling my way along, scrambling, falling, moving in slow motion. As I reach the top of the aft companionway ladder, I spot Big Scott at the helm. He is gripping the wheel with white knuckles, forcing it this way, that way, hunching way over, burning his eyes into the compass. He's hopelessly lost his heading. Only terror is holding him erect. Is it happening?

"EVAN!" I yell first down the hatch to alert the captain. Then I scream at Big Scott: "Where's Byrds?" The other two members of the watch team are clinging to the helm where they sense that there is some obscure semblance of control. And no wonder. The aft quarterdeck is still partially illuminated by the flickering chart room lamp, whereas the entire forward half of the ship looks as if it has been swallowed up into the dark belly of the moonless night.

"Why aren't you pumping?" I demand. They answer weakly that Byrds is in the engine room cutting new diaphragms for the manual pumps. "They aren't working properly," they assert. My voice is shrieking inside my head, "Oh, no! Oh, God, no! No one is pumping!"

Evan is on deck, hollering for Byrds to try to get the portable gas pump running, commanding me to call all hands to reduce sail, "NOW!" Pulling my way forward to the main deck hatchway, I lean my upper body in and whistle loudly three times. "All hands on deck!" I shout, "Report back aft and prepare to furl the mizzen." It is so dark—a heavy, suffocating blackness. The running lights are dim. Below decks looks fuzzy, like a dream. Crew members pop out of every orifice, pulling on a shirt, a boot, a pair of glasses. Their eyes are like saucers, their mouths agape, mute, not asking the question.

It takes the entire lot of us to drag down the mizzen, except for Big Scott, who is still wrestling with the wheel. "I can't see the compass!" he cries. Evan commands the crew to "prepare to furl the main!" No one moves. They are paralyzed with fear. Evan orders me to "get a torch for the helm!"

I drop below and my stomach shoots straight up into my throat. Seawater swirls around my ankles. The main batteries are half under water, drowning. The auxiliary diesel generator's starting battery is completely immersed. I know that we will not be able to engage the engine or the pump. I reach for a torch and return to the helm, where everyone is packed in like desperate, cornered animals. I press the flashlight into someone's hand. "Train it on the compass!" I demand.

Byrds and Evan are now at the starboard rail near the forward corner of the after-deckhouse, furiously trying to start the gas pump. Mary is attacking the big manual pump heroically, futilely. She screams, "Why don't we sheet out? Can't you see we're heeling too far over?"

As Joe and I move forward to furl the main alone, I catch a glimpse of Julie, who is crouched on the main deck, clinging to the fore boom crutch next to the companionway. She asks me what she should do. She looks so scared. I think I tell her to hang on. I think I say that it will be all right.

As I pass the companionway, where minutes earlier I'd called the "all hands," I glance down. The saloon looks odd. Once the site of celebrations, angry confrontations, new faces and old—so many faces, so many years, so many echoes of voices, so much hope, so much life—it is now deserted, misty, silent—and the bilge boards are floating. The sturdy ladder is gone. The cabin sole, newly varnished and shiny still, lies buried beneath a foot of water. We aren't heeling over. My God, we are listing, filling up! I think about the life jackets—plenty of 'em, more than enough. I think about them then for the first and only time in all my days on board, except for the recent drills. We've had drills. I've run them myself—safety drills, man-overboard drills, abandon-ship drills. The Coast Guard–approved bright ocher bundles are suspended in nets beneath the cargo hatch. Without the ladder they are now inaccessible—maybe still even unnecessary? No one has said the bad thing yet. No one has given it a name.

Joe and I inch our way to the main throat and peak halyards. Mine is on the port side, the leeward side. As I reach it, I notice that I can dip my hand into the sea from the deck. "Oh, lord, are we riding that low?" Just then the ocean bursts over the bow, and in an instant I am wading in waist-deep water, wedged against the bulwarks, straining to keep my footing. As the sea trails back aft, I numbly return to my mission, my mind throbbing, "Furl the main. Just furl the main. What else can you do? This might not be happening. Probably isn't happening. Do something! Furl the main!"

Now Evan confirms that it is happening. "Release the forward life raft," his voice wails and then sails off. Go up there? Where? Only the sea is there, that sea, Joey and me. I see Joe take a step, stop, and lurch again, one last time, toward the void. Then it hits.

The *Sofia* under sail.

chapter 13

Sinking

The Life Rafts

The moment one definitely commits oneself, then Providence moves too.
All sorts of things occur to help one, that never otherwise would have
occurred.

—GOETHE

Spinning, Evan gestures furiously toward the bow. I see panic on his face,
but his words become absorbed by an inorganic groan so deep and all
encompassing that it presses me to my knees. Craning my neck, I pivot
toward the sound and confront a gargantuan wave hurdling the foredeck.
In an instant the monster has nimbly snatched the heavily secured life raft
from its pedestal—the one that Joe had lunged for just a fraction of a
second earlier—and is thundering toward me, expanding as it advances.

My throat clamps down on a small piece of cry before the charging
ocean buries me with the malevolent force of a steamroller. Consumed
whole, I am tumbled over and over inside the cylinder of sea. Then, as
abruptly as I have been propelled, I am yanked around to a full stop with
my arms stretched at the sockets. The line that I still clutch in my fists is
snapped iron taut. I was attempting to reduce sail when the wall of water
struck, and mindlessly I retained my grip on the main halyard.

Struggling against strange, uncertain gravity, I thrust up my head, gasp
for air, and find myself not in the sea but still on the ship. I realize then,
with the absolute certainty of one who knows that we are sinking, that the
sea is now also in the ship. Lifting my eyes, I consider the disorienting
perspective of the *Sofia*'s main deck, which is rising vertically in front of
me. The vessel seems to be teetering oafishly, suspended on her port
beam. Black foam gathers around my thighs as I become aware of forward
motion. Still undefeated, the *Sofia* is making stubborn headway, sailing on

her buried rail, slicing through the hollow trough between the looming
peaks of the waves that are relentlessly enveloping her.

Like the achingly deliberate tunnel-vision camera pan of a suspense
film's opening scene, my head rotates toward a vague incessant slapping
sound. In the murky gloom a whip of brilliant orange snakes across my
fingers, now splayed and clawing for a grip on the *Sofia's* slick deck planks.
I grapple dully for the flailing Day-Glo line, recognizing it as the main
topsail brail, the one that I had marked conspicuously when I was boatswain to avoid confusing it with a halyard. Rarely used, the luminous coils
of the topsail brail rest neat and secure, patient and ready, on the mid-
ship's starboard pin rail. On this night, though, this darkest of nights, it
reaches down to me in a long, lonely, beckoning strand.

Twisting the cord around my forearms, I begin to scale the *Sofia's* main
deck. The now upward-reaching cap rail is as far as I can climb. Thick
bulwarks extend out over my head, a four-foot shelf of familiar, tired,
and worn timber, an old friend that I can't muster the will to maneuver
around. I hang there, dangling somewhere between a black sea and a black
sky. Then I notice that Billy is sitting on the outer hull. His legs are swaying and he is absently twisting his mustache with the deliberate fingers of
one hand. Somehow sensing that I need to be careful not to startle him,
I murmur his name. He drops his free hand toward me, all the while continuing to stare serenely out to sea. I release the brail and clasp his arm
in one single, desperate motion. Kicking hard and swinging out from the
deck, I arch a leg up over the rail and am able to mount the hull. Suddenly, I find myself standing on the *Sofia's* starboard beam end, looking
down as my ship slips sideways beneath my feet, deeper and deeper into
the ocean. "Billy, we have to go now," I say gently, still holding his arm.
He stands, we turn together, and without a word we step lightly off into
the sea.

Tensing for biting cold, I instead find the roiling, dark demon that is
sucking me down to be welcomingly warm beneath the surface—and so
bright! The *Sofia's* running lights, weak and dim against the slate black
night sky, still illuminate the ocean's depths with a cartoonlike surreality.
Today, if I close my eyes, I can see the *Sofia* as I saw her in that paralyzed
instant, underwater in suspended animation in front of me, close enough
for me to reach out my hand and touch.

Ripping me from my mellow reverie, a hazy yellow object the size of a
station wagon is rising in billowing undulations below me. To avoid being
run over, I veer aside and begin kicking and straining toward the retreating

surface in full panic. As I break from the softly lit quiet of the sea into the obscure, shrieking violence of the storm, I collide head on with the hulking yellow blob.

It turns out to be the life raft that went down with the ship and then, just as it was designed to, self-inflated at a predetermined depth and exploded into the open air, thanks to the pressure-sensitive device that we installed in each raft in New Zealand, almost as an afterthought. Sofians scattered about in the water begin clambering into it. A few meters away, the other life raft, the one that was wrenched from the bow, is inflated and already filled with crew. Everyone aboard it is shouting in an effort to gather the struggling sailors from the sea, while Evan kneels and waves his torch in broad, arcing circles. I start toward the nearest raft. Then I freeze. From somewhere behind me, I hear fragments of a muted call for help. Whirling about, I confront what seems like immeasurable emptiness. Then I hear it again. "Help me," the feeble voice cries.

"I'm coming," I scream. "Keep calling," I plead into the aloof, angry face of the gale. Taking a few quick strokes and then straining, waiting, I hear no human sound. "Where are you?" I beg. Nothing. Twisting back around to alert the crew, I am stunned to find the rafts nearly out of sight and drifting fast, their bulky windage tossed helplessly on the storm-swept seas. I turn back one last time. "Where are you?!" I wail. But there is no further cry to lead me.

Far off in the distance, a twinkling glimmer of light catches my eye just barely above the surface. The *Sofia* has finally made her peace with the sea. She has raised herself upright. The very tips of her topmasts stretch proudly straight toward the stars as she sails down and away and disappears forever. In front of me now lies only the omniscient ocean and its storm. I know that I am alone. Behind me, Evan's torch, bleak and only intermittently visible above the swells, offers me my only direction. I swim toward it.

I am the last one to reach the rafts. "Someone is still in the water!" I shout. "They called for help. Over there!" I gesture wildly. Turning to point the way, I am lost. Where? Over where? There is nothing anywhere. Visibility is arm's length. Direction is nonexistent. The sea swirls indiscriminately. The storm spins in chaos.

"Take a head count!" someone orders. There's a pause before we hear, "Sixteen!" "Count again!" the voice screams. "Sixteen! Sixteen!" Someone is missing. Who? Julie. It is Julie. Oh, god.

"Julie! Julie! Juuuuulieeeeee!"

All that exists now is sheer pandemonium. Frantic, we try to seize some control. It has all happened so fast that it isn't real to us yet. It simply isn't possible.

Evan takes command. "Lash the rafts together!" he orders. "It's imperative that we're not separated." Minutes have passed. Some call Julie's name. Some sob. Almost everyone is vomiting. It isn't seasickness. It is raw, unadulterated horror and disbelief. Evan cautions us all to hold it back, retain fluids, try to avoid dehydration. It is a futile admonition.

The smaller raft, the ten-person that the fatal wave liberated from the *Sofia*'s bow and flung well clear of the sinking, is remarkably intact. Both flotation pontoons are holding air and the canopy is secure. It bobbles like a tiny, spinning dreidel atop the lathered ocean. The second raft, the larger one that holds thirteen, went down with the ship. It is the one that automatically inflated underwater and floated to the surface, but it was damaged during ejection, perhaps punctured by gear or tangled in rigging during its escape. It is logy and soft, its canopy nowhere to be found. Only one pontoon is inflated. The other one hangs in weighty tatters beneath the raft's floor. This is the raft that someone hauls me into.

All night we battle the brutal elements. We in the broken raft are totally exposed to the storm—wet, cold, bailing nonstop, pushing water over the sides in armfuls. And we are ridiculously unstable. Each wave that doesn't engulf us threatens to flip us. The sea picks up our raft, buckles it in half, and tries to fold it in on itself. We fly, bodies hurled, crashing from side to side, clinging to the slippery rubber, balancing, forcing ourselves against the onslaught. We assume that this is the best that we can hope for. We fight on through the night.

Evan sets up a watch, one person per raft, to collect whatever flotsam we find—there should be so much—check and recheck the lashings, bail, look for ships, call out. Call for Julie. Never stop calling for Julie. It is about 1:30 A.M. It will be an insanely long night.

The rafts seem so minuscule, so flimsy. It feels as if the sea and the storm conspire to bully and taunt us without mercy. With numb bloody fingers we reknot lashings. Aching arms grasp each other from raft to raft across the water. The sea slams the rubber boats violently together. They bounce off each other with tremendous force, parting the thrashed lashings, ripping the handholds from the pontoons, slipping our grips. Screaming, we paddle, reach in desperation, find one another in the blackness, hold on, all night, a forever long night.

First dawn comes quietly in a damp gloom of soggy gray sea and bloated sky. We see little evidence of so catastrophic a storm. We alone remain out here, the only evidence that the *Sofia* has ever existed. We take stock and decide to be proactive survivors. We will shake it off, suck it up, do whatever has to be done. We are, however, secretly careful not to think too much, not to ask, not to feel. Not yet.

Our poor, sorry raft turns out to be less disabled than we originally feared. It has only one inflated pontoon, yes, but it also has its canopy, which we now realize has been dragging in the water all night. Our raft is upside down. Jumping off into the sea, we right it, clamber back aboard, and prepare to erect the canopy. The raft is still goosey and wobbly but better, so much better. The pole to support the canopy, however, has gone missing in the night, as have the life raft's stores, of course. But the raft's small wooden paddle is still lashed on, so we use it to prop up our tent.

The other raft has its paddle, food and water stores, a manual foot pump, medical packet, skimpy patch kit, and fishing gear. Everything is pint-sized and minimal but functional. We also have a signal mirror and a small compass, plus three hand-held signal flares. All this comes with pages of detailed instructions, which are completely worthless to us: They are all in Japanese. They prove good for toilet paper, though.

In yet another strange tilting of fortune, these two life rafts were purchased, inspected, and installed on the *Sofia* only recently, during her long stint in Nelson. The tall ship had sailed for decades virtually free of incident, serious injury, or casualty, without ever having these safety devices on board. In fact, even after acquiring them, we smug seasoned veterans asserted that, in light of the countless survival tales reported in many of the books in the *Sofia's* library, we would still rather use one of our hard-bottomed dinghies, on the outside chance that the need ever did arise for us to abandon ship.

A single, sealed white plastic bucket banged into the smaller raft during the storm. Mary snagged and tossed it onto the floor, assuming that it would be just one of many items that we'd retrieve. When we open it the next morning, we discover that it contains survival stores—canned water, foodstuffs, and flares that can be shot off and will be visible from a good distance. The bucket is one of the dozen we'd prepared and secured in the *Salty Dog*. It somehow broke free and found its way to us. It is all that we will ever see of the *Sofia* again.

As those of us from the large disabled raft tread water during the righting operation, it becomes quietly, tacitly understood among us that we will remain in this raft, come what may. We do not need to discuss it. Later we learn that the floor will need repeated patching and the pontoon require constant pumping. We exchange solemn looks. The nods that follow acknowledge our realization and acceptance of what we all know. We are in the death raft. If we are not rescued fairly soon—hours? days? weeks?—we will be the first to die. Just like that, it is done.

Still, we do a good deal of temporary shifting from one raft to the other for a variety of reasons—for attending to medical issues, giving comfort, sharing information. By and large, however, my raft's company is made up of me, Joey, Byrds, Billy, Little Scott, Imogene, Mark, Chris, and Rodney. We nine form a tight, close unit throughout the ordeal. Evan, Nigel, Bart, Mary, Betty, Trevor, and Big Scott remain crammed into the ten-person raft. We drift on.

The night of the sinking, most of the crew came on deck and went into the sea in various states of undress. In the rafts we try to apportion what little clothing we do have among us. Byrds was on watch when we sank and therefore was sensibly attired. He both went in and came out with his rubber boots on. We allocate one boot to each life raft. These funky, old size thirteens quickly prove invaluable, used alternately for bailing, puking, and eliminating. A very few, only one or two really, remain too cold, too angry, or too frightened to share, and that is all right. We don't pressure them, don't judge. Some of the *Sofia's* basic tenets yet carry on. We share only what is volunteered—an oilskin, a t-shirt, a poncho.

Evan remains clearly in command. This is never an issue. He maintains order and dictates function, thus giving us blessed purpose. The watch holds the signal mirror. Joey takes on the role of medic. The survival stores are very strictly rationed and doled out. We trail a fishing line. We watch for signs of land, look out for other ships, listen for passing planes. We take obsessive care of what little we have—our clothes, our rafts, our supplies, each other—and still we make potentially fatal mistakes. Someone panics and shoots off a flare at a 747 that is easily several thousand feet overhead. Evan commandeers the remaining cache of flares—now down to five. We lay wet items of clothing on the canopy to dry and find that they have blown away when we go to retrieve them. We try to shift our positions, take the weight off chafing rubber and the pressure off broken skin, but an attempt at relief in one area only increases the damaging effects somewhere else. We monitor each other's physical and mental status. Nonetheless, some bodies are deteriorating and some minds are insidiously losing their grip. But we are alive. We have made it this far, and we are determined to survive.

Finally, we talk. During the next few days we reconstruct the sinking, piecing together from our individual accounts a somewhat plausible explanation of what happened.

The sea was not more than we had expected, but somehow it was different from what most of us had ever encountered. The current that ran across the North Cape was ungodly strong—a steady five knots. When it ran with the prevailing winds, it produced a rocket of a ride. But when it turned and ran against the winds, the confusion created unnaturally steep peaks with deep, empty troughs between them. When the tide began to turn, the *Sofia's* 123 feet from bowsprit to transom were wedged between those peaks. Her nose would plunge over the face of one wave into the hollow trough. The next wave would be upon her before she could recover. As the ship's hull worked harder, enabling more water to seep in through her seams, she began to ride lower and lower, thus furthering the deadly process. Wave after wave would thunder over her bow, leaving her main deck increasingly awash and distended. Her bilges, filling from beneath the surface, eventually overflowed, invading her belly. The *Sofia* was being buried alive.

Chris recalls lying in his bunk on the port side of the forward cabin just before I called the all hands. He heard a cracking and then detected a low "fump, fump, fump" sound coming from somewhere outside his bunk wall. Evan deduces that this was probably the *Sofia's* death rattle. The storm had exposed a structurally vulnerable point in the hull—the garboard strake, the planking next to the keel that runs the length of the keel from stem to sternpost, tracing a vital connection where the old and the new planking met. The *Sofia,* already too heavy from the water she had taken on, began to lumber. On a severe heel this planking would then feel immense pressure from both the external forces and the internal weight. The garboard would be the likely strake to give, and this would be fatal.

As it turned out, Byrds's decision to go below to cut new diaphragms did not affect the sinking any more than Kiwi Rick's rerouting of the electric bilge pump. Members of the crew had not failed to report to their assigned emergency stations to release the lifeboats, activate the new EPIRB (electronic position indicator radar beacon), send a radio message, distribute the life jackets, and grab the survival stores. They had not failed because I, the mate, had never ordered them to do so. We never officially abandoned ship. She had abandoned us, sailing down and away while depositing us in the water, stunned and disbelieving. It had all happened in less than fifteen minutes.

Why was Julie the only casualty? In fact, we are not so much perplexed that she hasn't survived as we are bewildered that we have. The survivors have no magic lessons to impart. We possessed no special attributes that came into play and kept us alive. Julie did nothing wrong. We did nothing right. It just happened. In a single instant the ship was over and going down. Almost everyone on board was back aft when it happened, on the coach roof or the quarterdeck, and they simply floated off. Joey and I, amidships and low, were just plain lucky. We should have been tangled in the miles of rigging, trapped beneath the walls of set canvas, sucked into the pit a mile off the shelf, swallowed up in the vacuum created by a downward-spiraling, hundred-ton vessel.

I think I may have been the last to see Julie, there at the boom crutch. Mary thinks that she saw her later, also near the companionway. Joe remembers seeing her there too. The next time he looked, the companionway was empty and the stairs were gone. Someone mentioned that Julie had said a couple days into the trip that she didn't know how to swim. I never knew that. We didn't ask. I'd sailed for more than two years with Patrick without knowing that about him. Ensuring that crew members could swim, or assessing *any* single fact of a personal nature, for that matter, simply wasn't something we did on the *Sofia*. I suspect that had I known, and if Julie had worn a life jacket as a consequence, she might have survived. I live with that. I do know that I was the last one to hear her, in the water, and I couldn't find her. That I will have to learn to live with.

Another casualty of the sinking, which we all quickly realize but no one can quite manage to mention, is the Varmit. Joe thinks that he saw him hiding in the aft cabin after his watch. No one remembers seeing him anywhere in those final minutes. We'll never know what happened to him, but we all soon become resigned that our critter has met an appropriate end. He would have torn the rubber rafts to shreds, further endangering us all. We would have had to leave him in the water, even if we had rescued him from the ship, and that would have been unspeakably heartbreaking. He could not live anywhere else anyway. The *Sofia* was his only home on the planet. I like to imagine that the Varmit was nestled deep in someone's bunk, euphorically lathered in a private stash of toothpaste or deodorant. Or maybe he was feasting, up to his eyeballs in raw eggs in the storeroom and having one hell of a last supper while we were all otherwise engaged. I hope that wherever he was, he went calmly down with the ship and that he is peacefully and forever home.

We sank just off the North Cape, almost within sight of land. The storm blew us well off shore, but the current is pushing us back, and maybe we'll get one more shot—a long shot—at reaching the coast. We are still in busy shipping lanes, but we hadn't gotten to set off our EPIRB. No one will be looking for us, expecting us, or waiting to hear from any of us for days. We are on our own but still have good reason to be hopeful. We refrain from eating or drinking for the first two days. Then we calculate that with a thimbleful of water, one glucose tab (like a potent Sweetart), and one two-inch square of biscuit a day, we can survive eight, maybe ten, days out here. We need to keep the rafts together. We need to keep ourselves well—and catch water if it rains, dry clothes if the sun breaks through, move around to avoid getting sores, stay warm, rest, be positive, and perhaps, most important, trust. Nonetheless, in the too-quiet moments, I begin to wonder, almost against my will, when it is that we begin to doubt someone. When do we finally risk asking ourselves whether that person has failed us, is dragging us down, and whether we are willing to go down with them? We never confront this in the life rafts, not openly. In fact, by all outward appearances we have managed to somehow keep a tenuous faith, both individually and as a crew. None of us, I'm sure, can predict how long this faith will last, however, and I truly believe that the prospect of losing it frightens us far more than any other single thing.

On the second day in the life rafts, we spot the tip of Cape Reinga well off in the distance. Land! We can see land! We are saved, right? Not bloody likely. Nothing so simple. The current that Evan warned us about now holds our tiny rafts full in its clutches and is barreling along on its mad dash to the Tasman Sea, with us helplessly locked in its charge. Evan commands us to stroke constantly, taking turns, each raft with an oarsman, each raft with one silly little paddle. We try. As we come closer and closer, we try harder. We hang over the sides and kick. We dig with our hands. We pull. We try. We watch as the land gets nearer. The cape is rugged, as rugged as any shoreline I've ever seen. Sinister boulders jut up everywhere, as do towering cliffs and jagged walls. One after another, in no rhythm, formless raging breakers are pounding the beachless shore with the force of tidal waves, crashing, exploding, thundering with a deafening, sickening finality. Still, we are trying. In our tiny foolish rafts we paddle toward that looming nightmare for twenty-four hours straight. It is, after all, land: dry, warm, and somewhere inhabited—although not as far as we can see.

Joey quietly voices the concern that the lighthouse appears to be unmanned, the bluffs sheer and at least a hundred feet high. Evan assures him that a cottage lies up behind and a ways down from the lighthouse. We'll climb to it, but we'll have to wait until morning, he says. Instead, we'll find shelter for the night on the shore and then attack the ascent at daylight. Shelter for the night? Joe presses him. Yes, according to Evan's relative bearings, we'll be off the nearest approach to the beachhead sometime during the night. We'll have to make our approach in the dark, that surreal moonless darkness. Joe is convinced that we won't make it, that the rocks will shred the rafts and we'll be thrown into the raving mad sea, ripped apart and drowned right here, oh so close to land. God, it is dark. God, the crashing off the cape is horrendous. God, we are tired, thirsty, hungry, cold, sick, and alone. God, we are scared. Joey suggests that we wait and hail a passing ship in the daylight. Aren't we in busy shipping lanes? You never know, Evan cautions. Besides, he tells Joe, it would be better if we don't have to, better to rescue ourselves than to need to be saved. This is what Evan personally hopes for, but to the rest of us this doesn't matter. We have sunk, survived, and now are fighting for our lives. And there is land. We all know we have to go for it. It quite possibly is our last best chance, and it just doesn't matter that it doesn't look remotely like we can make it.

It doesn't matter. We paddle futilely all that second night until the threatening, welcoming detonation of the sea upon the shore is nothing more than a distant echo. We are stuck in the groove of that current, swept on by. Nothing we do or could have done would alter the course that the sea has set for us. When the sun comes up on the third day, we are once again lost, no ship, no shore in sight.

At dusk the night before, a great family of dolphins appeared all around the rafts. They were leaping and spinning, darting in and out, bumping and caressing the pontoons, playful, manic, insistent. None of us interpreted this as a random act. We all had heard sea stories—dozens of them—of dolphins' coming to the aid of imperiled sailors. But are they warning us away, we wonder, or offering to escort us in? Someone suggests that perhaps one of us should get into the water, swim ashore with the dolphins, go for help, alert someone that the rest of us are out here. More than a few of us think about it, although the plan is viable only if we aren't going to attempt to land the rafts. Even so, it is an incalculable risk. But it doesn't matter. By the time it is clear that the current is rocketing us past the cape with no chance in hell of reaching it in the rafts, it is much too far to swim, and the dolphins have abandoned us.

During the next day, day three, our slightly deflated hopes are bolstered once more when we spot a large tanker close enough for us to read the

word *EXXON* painted on its bow and to hear the engines droning. We signal with the mirrors, we holler until we are hoarse. We set off a flare that
could be seen, *should* be seen, if just one sailor—anybody—is on deck, on
the bridge. That Exxon ship is so close that we can smell its exhaust. It is
by far the closest we've been to any of the dozens of ships that we've spotted and likely the last we'll see because we're almost out of the shipping
lanes, and they have not noticed us. They may never know that we were
ever here.

The days in the rafts slip away. With each successive sundown, a sliver
of hope is dashed, a dire eventuality made increasingly inevitable. One day
put us within reach of the shore. The next reduce our chances of reaching it to minus zero. Now the current is propelling us past the Three Kings
Islands, the very last bits of land until the tip of Australia, about forty
days away at the rate we are moving. With his characteristic impassivity,
Evan suggests that we'll all be well dead by then.

On the third day Rodney phlegmatically announces that he hasn't uri-
nated yet—not once. Before the *Sofia* set sail, he was recovering from a
serious kidney infection that had landed him in the hospital in Nelson.
He apparently has relapsed. When he refuses to drink his daily allotment
of the scant remaining freshwater stores, we assure him that if he is the
first to die, which looks likely, we won't hesitate to eat him. He drinks.

This same day Evan and Joey discuss diluting the freshwater stores
with seawater to extend the number of days that they'll last. We also make
a curious discovery. We have assumed that in our all-consuming haste to
release the *Sofia* from the force of the storm by frantically reducing sail, no
one had time to even think of trying to salvage anything of personal worth
from the vessel. Right? Wrong. When Billy came up on deck in response
to my all-hands call, he had with him his passport, his cash, and, as ship's
treasurer, a fistful of the *Sofia's* cash as well. How odd. He guesses that
he'd had a premonition. How positively unfathomable.

In our raft we practice a tough-love form of "whiner squelching." We
treat sniveling as an annoying self-indulgence that we will not tolerate. But
I should also note that we lavish praise when it is warranted. For example, we'll compliment each other on our new svelte physiques. For those
who'd been practically mainlining the notorious dough bomb, feeling for
now rapidly diminishing love handles results in proud exclamations of
"Hey, I'm looking good!" and we all enthusiastically concur.

No, we aren't in denial, nor are we delirious—yet. As I see it, we survivors have made an unspoken and crucially important choice. We have

chosen hope over despair. We practice generosity rather than selfishness. We opt for humor in place of solemnity. We battle valiantly to maintain life-affirming—albeit unrealistic—optimism rather than surrender to pessimism's death knell. It seemed then like no real choice then. It still seems that way to me now.

On the fourth day Trevor is still crazy as a loon. He has been basically non compos mentis almost since the *Sofia* sank. But on this day his psychotic yammerings have revved up to racing gear. Trevor lost his glasses when the ship went down, and without his eyesight his version of reality is reduced to fanciful fairy tales and terrifying delusions. When Trevor insists yet again on taking his turn at watch, we patronize him. When he reports hearing Maori singers and seeing whales breeching, we quietly post a secondary watch. When Imogene sings beautiful ballads through tears she can no longer contain, we hum along. When someone shivers uncontrollably, we huddle around, cuddling them in our body heat. When Nigel gathers me under his poncho and blows his breath into it to envelop me in warmth, I know that although I'll never be able to properly thank him, I will not need to.

Big Scott has lost his will to be obnoxious. Unlike Nigel, who has been consistently strong but quiet, or Bart, who is somber and passive throughout, Big Scott has been a reliably vociferous pain in the ass. When Big Scott has whined, we have quacked gaily in unison, drowning him out. Now he is silent. In the absence of this distraction, we become alarmed.

By the end of the day the winds have calmed and may even be a touch warmer. We shiver less convulsively, but maybe we're just spent, our bodies depleted of the energy required to generate their own heat.

As we awaken on the morning of the fifth day to our now strangely familiar routines, we each appraise the situation. Matted, nappy heads stick anxiously out of canopy ports in renewed anticipation of a good omen. This is always the first order of business. Sky and sea—an indistinguishable silver blend, like being immersed in a mercury bubble. Air—so heavily infused with chill dampness that we feel it in our bones. Swells—obese, unbroken, rolling monotonously from some far distant shore toward a safe landfall that by all appearances so longer beckons the surviving crew of the lost schooner *Sofia*. We are alone.

With one deep gulp of fresh oxygen—which is exhilarating after a long night of sucking the stale, fetid air of the enclosed raft—we again cast aside our initial crushing disappointment. We get busy, checking and resecuring the battered lashings that unite our two rafts, greeting the neighbors—

"Any new developments over there?" "How is the sky? Might it be sunny enough today to dry these sodden, rotting clothes? Is there weather on the horizon—a storm [which would mean blessed drinking water]?" Reluctantly, we slip back inside and see to household chores. We always have bailing to do. Where's the boot? Ah, being used for the morning ablutions. We wait our turn . . .

Although we all pretty much remain in whichever raft we first sought refuge, we often need to rotate between them. Our raft is disabled, wet, and wobbly, but it is also larger. It is almost possible to stretch out in it, whether for pure comfort or to receive medical attention. Joey has the most training in this area, so his capable hands swab our seeping lacerations. By this time we collectively suffer from a free clinic's worth of ailments, but the most troublesome to all of us are the skin ulcers, gaping, bleeding sores from the incessant chafing of raw, soggy skin against the tight, rubber, salt-encrusted sheath of the raft. Joe cleans the wound and applies a minute dollop of the mystery ointment that he found in a first aid kit tucked away in a sealed compartment of one raft.

The only other real advantage to being in the larger disabled raft is that we maintain the more jovial atmosphere. For instance, the other raft has made food a taboo topic, whereas we enforce a must-discuss-foods policy. Whoever clambers aboard our marginal craft is encouraged to supply us with graphic descriptions of favorite meals in every mouth-watering, stomach-cramping, almost aroma-inducing detail.

On this fifth day we realize that we no longer are seeing distant ships off on the horizon or the occasional plane soaring high overhead. And we hear far fewer heralding cries or have welcome visits from curious shore birds venturing out to examine our unnatural presence. Already well outside the shipping lanes, we have been carried steadily out to sea, on our way to nowhere. When incurably wide-eyed and ever-hopeful Chris asks Evan if we still have a good chance of being saved, Evan fixes on his imploring stare and answers with accuracy and uncharacteristic gentleness. "No, Chris, not much," he replies. Evan then lays his head on my shoulder and sleeps. In nearly four years of countless highs and lows across half the planet, this simple gesture is the most sincere and spontaneous intimacy that my captain and I have ever exchanged.

We need to patch the raft yet again, a prospect now both futile and horrific. We are being barraged by a family of sharks. They rub their sandpapery bodies along the thin, grainy raft floor, bumping us about like we are on a carnival ride. By the second day in the rafts, I was forced to announce to my captive audience that, whether we liked it or not, I was menstruating. Amid a chorus of alarmed male sighs, the other women raise their hands in a reluctant but resigned "me too" acknowledgment of undeniable feminine unity. As is so often the case when women live together, our cycles had synchronized. Nature delivered us yet one more cruel jab: There would be blood in the water. The sharks are now our nearly constant companions, a patient and persistent entourage. Patching the leaks is no longer an option. Besides, our raft is almost beyond repair. Our having to go into the ocean for good is imminent, and we all know it.

During my watch that evening the clouds part, inviting one final splash of magic sunset to streak the heavens. But it is unlike anything I've ever seen, and I have certainly experienced my share of magnificent, unbearably brilliant sunsets, the kind that might make a holier person drop to her knees in reverent awe. This one sunset, however, truly might be divine. The sky is emblazoned with a flushed splatter of such intense iridescence that it does take my breath away. Suddenly, I discover that I'm feeling fiercely bold and crystal clear, so I whisper, "God. Is this you? Are you here to help me? If the answer is yes, then do. Please do! But if this isn't you, or if you aren't going to help, well, it doesn't really matter. Because I'm going to get out of this. Understand me. I will not die here! Help me if you want, but either way I will survive. If this really is you, though, and you choose not to help, then you had better know that I will never, ever, forgive you for doing this now to my family." One of my hands is clenching the port flap tightly around my chest. The other hand is stretched out into the night, reaching toward the incomparable sky—the once in a lifetime sky—and this hand is raised in a fist. Right or wrong, I am not begging to be saved. I am giving notice.

Later, as I try to get comfortable resting against Joey, he whispers that he doesn't think Evan is going to last much longer. Then he takes a chance, asking me, "Would you let the skipper marry us at sea?" And I understand. "Oh . . . yes," I murmur, adding, "now let's try to get some sleep." But we of course have no privacy, and the raft erupts into spasms of applause and volleys of congratulations.

On that fifth night adrift I overhear Joe suggest to Evan the long-shot, last-ditch most drastic, possibly fatal tactic of implementing saltwater enemas—a more efficient and benign way of absorbing seawater than ingesting it. We glance warily at the only tool available for infusion, our pathetic little foot pump. Its offending gray plastic nozzle, grotesque, creased, and exposed, attaches to the end of the clear flexible hose that protrudes from the ribbed plastic paddle and greasy bellows. The instrument lies inert and discarded—for the moment—on the putridly soiled floor of the rubber raft. Evan winces visibly. It is on this night that we each succumb to personal reflection, perhaps for the first time since we've gone into the sea. Tonight the atmosphere in the rafts is melancholy, filled with the whispers and murmurs of individuals reconciled to making their peace.

When exactly does living make this turn, come around the bend, and begin its inevitable descent into dying? Is it different for each of us, dictated by something specific and personal? If we are called upon to express our druthers when facing the end, do we choose to submit, go gently, and accept defeat, or do we insist that we will triumph simply because we intend to fight to the death? On this night my thoughts run along these lines, curious, philosophical, raw. I notice, however, that I am not frightened. And within this bizarre realization I find my greatest comfort.

It is late, probably around 1 A.M., when young Chris, on watch in our raft, chirps up cheerily that he has spotted a ship. Yeah, yeah, we all groan, another ship, one of the dozens we've sighted so far. OK. A few minutes later Chris alerts us that the vessel appears to be—yes, definitely is—coming closer. No one is inclined to rally. It is late, maybe too late. We are spent and fearful that our fragile optimism might not survive another throttling. Reality has insidiously begun to grab our blind faith by the throat. Better not to look just yet. Besides, if we've managed to settle into a painfully tolerable position, we are reticent to relinquish it for one more false alarm.

"Guys, I really do think that this ship is coming nearer," Chris continues animatedly. He can be reassuringly or irritatingly indefatigable, depending on the circumstances. On what now marks our sixth day adrift, we sigh and condescend to encourage him to keep us appraised. His spirit is still astoundingly resilient, a priceless life force that no one wants to risk injuring.

Finally, after his fourth or fifth insistent pronouncement, Chris manages to raise our skipper. Evan is not doing well. His metabolism has always been jet fast, leaving him with little or no physical reserves to feed off. I reckon he's already lost nearly half his muscle mass. Also, he'd gone into the water wearing only a t-shirt and trunks. The t-shirt is one of his favorites, one I'd recently seen him tie-dye himself down in the *Sofia's* galley. Apparently, the dyes are not colorfast, nor are they nontoxic. They are acting as a catalyst for the corrosive effect that the saltwater and abrading latex are having on Evan's bony torso. He is rubbed raw and bleeding at every knobby point of his skeletal structure. It is a dreadful sight. I've observed him getting weaker and fading physically, frighteningly fast, but he never acknowledges this. He remains steadfast, in command, in control and invincible, or so he leads us to believe.

With Chris's most ardent plea, "Hey, Evan, you really might wanna have a look at this," the captain crawls to the lookout port of his raft and sticks his head out. He remains there, silent for several seconds, as Chris prattles on incessantly. "So what do you think? Am I right? Closer, right? What should we do? Should we holler? Should we fire off a flare? Hey, Evan!"

When Evan finally does speak, everyone is listening. "Lower the canopies," he orders slowly and calmly. "Commence shouting for help. When the ship is in range, I'll ignite a flare. It's our last flare, gang. If the vessel doesn't spot it, and no one aboard her hears us, then you must all prepare to immediately abandon the rafts. This ship is powering full steam ahead on a direct, unfaltering course, and unless we can raise her crew, she's aiming to run right clean over the top of us."

In an instant everyone in the rafts is up, on full alert, and screaming for our lives. We yank the canopies down as a jubilant chorus of shrieking voices—weak, hoarse, joyous, and frantic—rises up into the night. "Help!" "Save us!" "Please!" "Over here!" "We're here!" "We're right here!"

The mammoth ship's engines are thundering. Great gray clouds of diesel exhaust billow across the ocean's surface. The propellers are kicking up so much turbulence that the sea is boiling. The vessel is monstrous. It is steaming down on us. It is all that we can see, hear, or smell. And it isn't slowing down. It isn't altering course. I again think, be careful what you wish for.

Evan raises the flare high in his right hand, supports his shaky forearm with his left hand, and over his shoulder he speaks his final directive. "If this doesn't work, mates, dive into the water and swim for all you're worth!"

Then he squeezes the trigger. The crimson fireball sails over the bow, trailing a fuzzy streak of rouge across the ship's foredeck before becoming eclipsed from our view by the vessel's towering pilothouse. It is a spot-on perfect shot. We wait, cocked, every fiber of our beings poised to go, praying to stay. The gears of the ship whine and grind and then, like the Christmas tree in Times Square, the entire vessel is suddenly bright with hundreds of lights flashing on, off, and on again. It's a signal. They are answering. They have seen us.

On the first approach the wash off the hull of the *Vasili Perov* nearly capsizes the rafts. She comes back around a second time and on this pass shuts down her engines and just drifts downwind, within arm's reach of us. The ship's aft quarter looms above us, about forty feet straight up. As we stare, trying to imagine how in hell we are going to get up there, her crew tosses a series of flimsy rope ladders over the rail, and they tumble down the hull like some poor sot's red carpet.

"No way," I think to myself. "No bloody way will any of us be able to manage that." But as I am shaking my head in total rejection of this prospect and desperately wracking my soggy brain for a plan B, the first Sofian, a gal from the good raft, slowly begins to climb. One by one we follow her, reaching, grabbing, careening, smashing, swinging, climbing, climbing, climbing. The ship rocks. The ladders flop around violently. We hang on, deadened muscles somehow finding a way.

After what seems like an eternity, only Evan and I are left in the raft, kneeling, dragging on the bottom rungs, keeping tension on the ropes. He motions for me to go. He'll be the last, he insists. I'm not sure that I can climb. I feel certain that he can't, but I know there is nothing more to say. I nod my acknowledgment to my captain, and I start up.

I press my face into the coarse heavy rope. I can smell the rust on the ship's hull, taste it, even. I don't know whether I'm near the top when, all of a sudden, strong arms like forklifts are reaching down and hauling me over the edge. I land on my feet on the deck and immediately collapse. My legs don't work. A scrum of bodies huddles over me. One of the strange men stoops down and scoops me up like I am a small child. He rubs a bearded cheek against mine, smiles into my face, cradles me against his soft black jacket, and carries me away. I never get a chance to look back. Within seconds I'm propped up against a sickly greenish wall in an open hall that resonates with a hollow din. My Sofians are here. We hug and we cry. Then we look around us.

"Where is Evan?" I risk. I allow myself only a brief moment to consider the possibility that he hasn't made it out of the raft before I see him walk in, staggering slightly but fully under his own steam. He is escorted by a squat, stocky, older gentleman in a dress uniform—the captain of the *Vasili Perov*. The two skippers stand side by side, and a great cheer rises up in the hall, a rolling cheer like a wave. But this one is a warm caressing wave. We are alive. We are saved.

One by one we have been carried into the stark mess hall of the *Vasili Perov*, where the Russian captain, beaming like an expectant child, presents each of us with a glass of vodka. This he proudly pours from the last of his private stock. We have had no food or water to speak of for days and find it impossible to imagine taking a straight shot of liquor as our first nourishment. It would, however, be unconscionable to risk insulting the benevolent skipper. And, in fact, as the captain intends, the drink proves medicinal, desensitizing the otherwise convulsing gastrointestinal muscles of our recently atrophied digestive systems.

The wobbly crew of the *Sofia* raises an assortment of mugs, tins, and cups in a tearful salute to our saviors. Scanning the montage of bright faces illuminating the perimeter of the harshly lit room, my gaze meets Evan's. Turning deliberately, he lifts his glass toward me. With a knowing grin he speaks his toast softly, "Here's to you, Number One." This commendation, with the cascade of emotions that it evokes, signals the beginning of what will evolve into a long, grueling process of my coming to terms with my *Sofia* experience.

Composite of *Sofia* survivors in Wellington, New Zealand, and aboard the *Vasili Perov* with her crew.

chapter 14

Coming Home

Great occasions do not make heroes or cowards; they simply unveil them to the eyes of men. Silently and imperceptibly, as we wake or sleep, we grow strong or weak; and at last some crisis shows what we have become.

—BROOKE FOSS WESTCOTT

INTRODUCTION

We spend two disoriented days powering back to Wellington Harbor aboard the Russian vessel. Though we share not a shred of language with our hosts, the communication is clear. They give us everything. We are humbly grateful. A poor ship compared to so many we've seen, the sailors of the *Vasili Perov,* a cargo vessel hauling frozen fish, nonetheless provide us with all that they have: the last of their fresh food stores, their mattresses, medical attention, live folk music, gentle company, their warm woolen uniforms, space, quiet, and privacy. Although we try to look away, we are drawn repeatedly, as if by an irresistible magnetic force, to the portholes of the great deckhouse. Here, we, the surviving and bedraggled crew of the tall ship, find ourselves congregating and exchanging conciliatory nods and shrugs as we sit hunched and mesmerized, staring silently at the now too-familiar horizon. For us, squinting at the silhouettes of the miragelike specks of ships in the distance is gut-wrenching, too powerful a reminder of the endless hours we spent in the rafts, looking, hoping, praying, calling, signaling, and finally accepting that each glimmer of fading light extinguished a tiny spark of faith, another day of our lives. Here, in the sure, safe confines of the *Vasili Perov* and on our way home, we somehow still feel compelled to stand watch.

We are in a groggy stupor, locked into an almost constant state of hallucination. Sleep ambushes us with utter immediacy, only to be pierced without warning by a terrifying urgency. We shudder drunkenly awake, find our legs, and stumble about in a punchy trance, never knowing where to go, what to feel, which expression to paste on our faces. We know we may not have been capable of maintaining our lofty humanity in the face of the drastically worsening conditions that were imminent in the life rafts. We'll never know what we might have become had we not been rescued. Consequently we have been allowed to hold each other forever in memory as heroes, brave and unselfish. And this perhaps is how we can remember ourselves.

Fifteen of us are sleeping in an open corridor that has been converted into a makeshift dormitory. Mattresses carpet the floor. The lights are always on. Evan has been allocated a cabin, as befits his rank, I presume. We see him at meals. He rarely joins us otherwise. The night before we are to land in Wellington, I feel the need to speak with him. I naturally expect that New Zealand officials will hold an inquiry, and I want to discuss what we will say.

Searching out his cabin, I find him lying on the lower berth of a double bunk in a cramped room outfitted only with a shallow locker and a built-in metal desk. The locker is empty, the table top bare. He motions for me to sit next to him on the bed. Instead I move to the stool beside the desk. I have tough issues to confront, hard questions to ask, and I may receive answers that I might not be ready to hear, things I wish I never had to know. The room is so tiny. The cold steel stool is as far from Evan as I can get, putting three, perhaps four, feet of dead air between us.

Evan asks how I am. Better, I answer, and ask him the same. He smiles and says he is fine, as if we've just bumped into each other on the street and are exchanging a polite greeting. Then he asks after the welfare of the rest of the crew. I am able to give him a positive report, and he seems sincerely pleased. We agree that the ship's doctor—a gnarled, compact middle-aged woman, who looks much like the stereotype of a Russian peasant—has worked wonders with our wounds. She has also presented me with a dress, one of two that she owned. The garment is hideous and infinitely less comfortable than the cozy Russian sailor's uniform that I had been wearing. Nonetheless, I accept it appreciatively and wear it with pride each time I enter the dining hall. I do look ridiculous in it, but no one dares to snicker. The gift is a pure expression of her heart, and none of us would risk hurting the good doctor's feelings for the world.

Evan and I, after having learned of the circumstances, take a few minutes to muse about the prodigious moment when the *Vasili Perov*, heading to Wellington and running two days ahead of schedule, mysteriously diverts miles outside of the proscribed shipping lanes and sets a course across empty ocean in a black-hole–void kind of darkness, toward us. We can agree that there is no rational explanation for this miraculous stroke of fate that saved our lives. Then we regretfully move on to the more difficult topics. I wonder aloud what I am expected to say when someone asks me why the *Sofia* sank. He assures me that I won't be asked. The authorities will question only him. So I ask what he proposes to tell them. "The truth," he answers.

I lean forward, stare earnestly, and try to discern some evidence of greater depth or substance than he has revealed to me during almost four years of sailing side by side with him. Then, well aware of the gravity of the risk that I am taking, I ask Evan how he feels about losing Julie. As he begins to respond, Evan impresses me as being utterly undisguised. My captain ponders abstractly that he never got to know Julie personally, and my body goes rigid, bracing for what I fear his next remark will be. He goes on quite impassively to state that he expects he will mourn the loss of his ship more than he will the loss of a transient crew member. Now, whether this is true or not doesn't matter. Clearly, at this time, Evan believes it. And whether it is right doesn't matter, either. I am absolutely certain that Evan would express these sentiments regardless. He has always struck me as a basically guileless man, incompetent at pretense even when it is in his best interest to engage in some. His answer is merely his truth, and he seems neither proud nor ashamed of it. It is, for him, simply accurate.

I had long suspected that some broad chasm stretched between Evan and me, a philosophical breach that we probably would never cross. Suddenly, there it was—deep and expansive. Yes, I too would miss the *Sofia* for as long as I lived. I would dream of her, romanticize about her, grieve for her, and ponder my part in her life and in her loss. And although this process would be grueling, it would ultimately fall fathoms short of the emotional anguish I felt at the loss of the young woman from New Plymouth, New Zealand—a virtual stranger to me. This was my truth. I recognized it even then, and, just like Evan, I accepted it.

Early on in my sailing sojourn, I had deduced that if we were not strong self-possessed people when we arrived on the *Sofia*, we would need to become so or we would not survive her well. And in fact, during my years on board, I had witnessed this process play out time and again. Some submitted grudgingly to the ship's demands and stayed on. Others were crushed by their own shortcomings and left in pieces. Still others struggled to maintain their cocksure identities and stubbornly dug in, often hanging on only by the ragged fingernails of their hammered self-esteem. Finally, a few individuals, like Evan, just seemed born to the *Sofia* and were in their element from day one.

While aboard I had always been aware of the inherent dangers of sailing on a tall ship. I knew we could die. I realized only much later that, short of dying, everything might fall catastrophically apart and be lost forever, leaving us to figure out for ourselves how to proceed with the difficult business of living. For me this would be the greatest challenge. For Evan I suspect it was never an issue. His future held no deep soul searching. He might, however, be idly distracted with the scientific question of what actually occurred structurally that caused the ship to sink. But even that would merely be a passing preoccupation. She now rests more than five thousand feet down, and all the theories set forth will never amount to anything more than conjecture, anyway. In the end I reckoned that Evan would move on with significantly more internal ease than I would.

So our relationship is what it is. Evan offered me an opportunity for an incomparable sailing adventure and steadfastly provided me with capable leadership. It's everything I'd ever asked of him and honestly all that I had a right to expect. The rest has always been up to me and to me alone. As I sit in this tiny cabin, eye to eye with my captain—this strange man with whom I've traveled a world that I've come to know intimately; sailed a proud ship that I'd grown to love well; and worked, played, lived, and almost died—this is precisely how I feel: utterly alone.

We continue to gather in the *Vasili Perov's* great, barren dining room to consume copious pails of water sweetened with jelly, devour fried eggs by the dozen, and swallow down wads of steamy, doughy bread. We assemble in the pilothouse and gaze hypnotically at the horizon. We spend hours brushing each others' clumped, knotted hair, tenderly swabbing damp cheeks, clinging together and reminding ourselves that we were nearly gone. Evan is not part of this therapeutic group process. I can only assume that he has chosen not to be. In two days we are back in New Zealand's capital city.

When the ship does make landfall, we Sofians are aghast at what awaits us. The New Zealanders, still paranoid about communists, send agents aboard the *Vasili Perov* for the purpose of deprogramming us, in case we have been brainwashed since our rescue. Although we soon allay the officials' fears in a series of revealing interviews, they make us stay on board until they can present us with boxes of clothing donated, with an awkward air of probity, by the Salvation Army. According to the local authorities, it is imperative that we not disembark in front of the local media while wearing the uniforms of the Russian seamen. So we reluctantly shed the warm, thick, comforting coats and trousers of our fellow sailors and don instead a collage of ill-fitting, garish costumes.

Evan is correct. He alone is sequestered and questioned at length about the circumstances surrounding the sinking. None of us is present. We will not learn his account of the sinking until much later.

When we finally set foot on shore, things begin to happen rapidly. We contact our families, informing them that we have sunk, survived, and been saved. They, of course, knew nothing.

We all want to attend the memorial service for Julie at her family's home up North Island, but we are destitute. Most of our possessions went down with the ship. As in the past, however, the benevolent people of New Zealand take us under their wing. The newspaper sees to arranging our train fare to Auckland. One crewmate's brother puts us up in his home in the interim. A local shop provides us with free haircuts. After dividing up the ship's cash, which Billy had snatched, we each have about $40 to buy suitable funeral attire. Then immigration officials abruptly inform us that without our ship, they can no longer allow us to remain in New Zealand. We now qualify for only very temporary visas. In two short weeks we all have to be out of the country. In a frenzy we begin to make plans, sorting out our brand new lives.

During one of my earlier visits back to the States, I had traveled to San Pedro, California, where I had sat for the test and been granted my hundred-ton merchant seaman's ticket. Although I never intended to actually serve on a merchant vessel, I regarded gaining my certificate as a practical necessity: holding that license guaranteed me free medical attention and/or free working passage home from any U.S. base or aboard any U.S. vessel anywhere in the world. Pretty nifty, I thought at the time, never imagining the circumstances under which I'd have to use it. Desperate to complete this final leg of my journey under my own steam, I manage to wrangle a position aboard a merchant ship leaving Auckland, bound for New Orleans. I will work as "wiper," while Joey, my new "fiancé," will be allowed to accompany me at half fare as a spouse. Ultimately, though, our plans change. My father learns that he requires emergency surgery, and, in view of my recent near miss, he wants me there, so he arranges for my air fare. Although I had to pass on the monthlong ocean passage back, that I had secured my return ticket and would have completed my journey on my own terms remains a source of personal pride and satisfaction.

During those last two weeks in New Zealand, it feels like we're stuck in the fast-forward setting. We attend Julie's funeral, and it is dreadful. We are literally total strangers to her mourning family and friends. Many didn't even know that she had come on board. For Julie the *Sofia* may well have been a lark, an impulsive detour from her otherwise snug existence, a spontaneous adventure that she would have excitedly revealed to family and friends a few short days later. The memorial service also confronted us with the excruciating irony that we had all been there with her, and we survived. In retrospect I think it would have been easier for the family had we not come. I approached Julie's mother, a tall, stately, and handsome woman who instantly reminded me of my own mom, but her face was ashen and stony. Her eyes were filled with disbelief. I sobbed that I was so sorry, but she couldn't respond and didn't acknowledge me at all. Why should she? Who am I anyway? Part of the reason that her daughter died? Why am I still here?

Afterward, we sailors stay together at Mary's brother's house. The newspaper and magazine reporters who kept a respectful distance until after the funeral now hound us mercilessly. I stand apart, listening to the various accounts of the disaster that my mates are reporting, and I am stunned. The drama that they recount is deformed, full of embellished detail and warped in scope. Suddenly, I am desperate to distance myself from my fellow survivors. I am not yet prepared to know them, or have them know me, as less than we were in the rafts. Yet I see us falling from grace, hear us prattling inanities, feel us once again donning the trappings of mere mortals, and I'm not ready. So I run.

When an official who helped me and Joe secure passage on the merchant ship offers us her family's vacation batch on a beach down on the Coromandel Peninsula, we leap at the chance to escape. It is the ideal hideaway: a rustic, quiet, solitary spot of sand and ocean, with not another living soul in sight. While here, I grieve privately, barely even speaking to Joey. Each day I run barefoot on the beach for miles until I can't catch my breath. I develop crippling shin splints and still I don't stop running. I retreat deep inside myself and search frantically for something noble. All that I know for certain is that I will never be the same again. I swear that I won't. Because to go back to the person I was before, I'll have to take this difficult journey again some day. Maybe the only good thing about going through hell is getting through hell. I am just praying that in the end I wind up above and beyond it.

Joey watches patiently. It's my nature to seal myself off whenever I'm hurting, and a lesser man would not be able to wait until I resurface. When we determine that I have to fly home instead of boarding the merchant ship, Joe chooses to be with me. Together, we return to Mary's brother's house, only to find that our mates have already dispersed. Suddenly, we are out of time. But this cannot be the end, not goodbye. That is inconceivable.

Joe and I go home to our respective, anxious families and vow to reunite soon. Then we learn that in response to complaints, an official investigation is underway. The U.S. Coast Guard expects to bring formal charges against Evan.

On August 15, 1983, almost a full year and a half after the sinking, Evan receives an official copy of the case against him; it alleges that he has violated federal regulations. The maximum fine associated with the charges is $500. Although the sum seems nominal enough, what is at stake is significantly greater than money. When he receives the notice, Evan is working as skipper of a vessel engaged in studying a humpback whale migration, taking its crew and a group of students to the banks off New England and up into the North Atlantic, off Greenland. The case threatens his current employment, and if he is convicted, his career and life's work as a sea captain will be effectively over.

When I receive a copy of the weighty legal document—it includes Evan's own statement as well as statements submitted by some ex-Sofians, more than thirty pages in all—it is accompanied by a handwritten cover letter from Evan:

> Sorry to boggle you down with all this stuff, but I am in a bit of a jam.
> Am assuming that only Norman, Chris and Kansas made statements
> re: the sinking. So would very much appreciate your reviewing this
> material and giving some thought to it all and responding to my lawyer.
> Call me in California if you have any questions. P.S. We only have until
> October 1st to get this in!

This is all he has written, except for a short list of addresses and phone numbers that I might need. The message is straightforward, professional, unemotional—Evan.

The case presents Evan with three options for responding to the charges: He can admit wrongdoing, pay the fine, and the charge will stand; he can

request a formal hearing; or he can waive the hearing and submit written statements presenting evidence or information to refute the charges.
On the advice of counsel—and perfectly in character—Evan has chosen
the last.

The legalistic and wordy document boils down to accusing Evan of
negligent use of a vessel, endangering the life of a person; carrying passengers for hire without a licensed operator on board; and operating a
passenger-carrying vessel without a certificate of inspection.

An addendum attached to the report by the commanding officer of the
Marine Safety Office in San Francisco reads as follows:

> July: Topsail Schooner Sofia, VI 1034, capsizing and sinking, Cape Reinga
> 20 nm. N. of North Island New Zealand in the Pacific ocean on
> February 23, 1982 involving disappearance and presumed death of one
> passenger.
>
> 1.) Forwarded approved
> 2.) This report submitted beyond the six month time specified in
> section 75–5-10D because of the unusual nature of the case, which caused
> time delays as well as unusual coordination efforts. The fact that the boat
> was registered in the Virgin Islands, that the accident occurred in the
> area off New Zealand, and that the parties in interest were spread across
> the United States made for no simple fact gathering exercise. Also, we
> had several dealings with New Zealand authorities; though they were
> responsive in providing information, each evolution did consume
> additional time. Because of these problems, the case incurred further
> delays because it got transferred between a departing and a new
> Investigating Officer, further losing momentum.

I barely have the momentum to wade through it all. Clearly, someone
has been doggedly persistent in ensuring that this case does not fall
between the cracks. I hope that Julie's family has moved on, choosing to
deal with their loss privately. I must assume that someone else is looking
to hang Evan out to dry, and I am once again struck by the awesome ambi-
tion of vindictiveness and the power of what we think we know.

The findings of fact include a brief summary of what happened, a detailed description of the vessel, an impersonal profile of Julie, the number
of survivors, the weather and sea conditions at the time of the sinking,
and a forty-item detailed account that Evan had given to the agents in
Wellington right after our rescue. I also learn that the Coroner's Court in

Wellington held an inquest into Julie's death, ruling that she was presumed to have drowned in the sinking, and that the Marine Division of the New Zealand Ministry of Transport wrote a letter saying that although the inquest and its proceedings were open to the public, the coroner did not have the authority to include in the public record the information contained in the depositions. I also read a list of conclusions and recommendations offered by the Coast Guard's investigating officer that takes into account Evan's statement as well as those of Norman, Chris, and Kansas. In rebutting their allegations, Evan has proceeded in the fashion of a professional master seaman, going point by point through their statements, exactingly, clinically, obsessively attentive to detail, precisely, and without personal bias:

[Simplified from:]
Department of Transportation
U. S. Coast Guard
Case: 12–071–83
Date: 15 August 1983

In response to the charges of negligence, Evan moves item by item through the allegations. With respect to the question of whether or not a sufficient and reliable bilge pumping system was in place on board, Evan describes the function, capacity and condition of each pump on *Sofia*. He takes care to detail the upgrades and overhauls specifically made on these apparatus in Nelson, just prior to the ship's final passage. Evan concludes that although *Sofia* had a total of eight pumps using four separate power sources, the engine room deck pump normally covered 99% of the ship's pumping needs.

In response to the question concerning the vessel's watertight integrity, Evan is confident that it had been maintained commensurately with the building weather, and that it was normal for *Sofia* in a gale. All her hatches were closed and dogged down, with the exception of the main and aft cabin companionways so as to allow access below deck. He further explains that *Sofia* had weathered dozens of gales in this fashion, as her stiff rolling moment due to 27 tons of concrete ballast allowed her to sit light on the sea, rarely taking water on deck, which the scuppers always handled more than sufficiently. Evan goes on to explain that he had, nonetheless, conscientiously installed freeing ports aboard the ship himself, soon after he joined her several years earlier, but that they had always been superfluous. He concludes his rebuttal to this particular allegation by stating that the single only time *Sofia* had ever buried her lee rail was moments before she sank.

In answering the question of whether or not sufficient sail changes were made soon enough to come head to wind and seas, to ride out the storm, Evan states that the *Sofia* had been *head-to* all through the gale. She was carrying the precise sail combination which had been taught to him by the former captain and which had been successfully employed in all the gales they'd encountered during their three and a half years of sailing together. Evan adds that as an extra precaution he had further reduced sail on the night of the sinking by *reefing* (reducing by rolling or folding in the sail area exposed to the wind) the fore and the mizzen, due to the unusually steep head seas. He had reckoned that regardless of *Sofia's* attitude to the seaway (running or beating) she would take a bashing, and the bow would be the strongest point with which to meet this adversity. He concludes that she was indeed riding the gale comfortably until the sudden leak occurred. Evan asserts that *Sofia's* rolling, as she was designed to carry cargo under sail, was much more affected by the sea than by the wind. He goes on to state that in fact, she had historically been unresponsive to winds whose strength did *not* exceed 20 knots.

In reply to the insinuation that *Sofia's* stability was compromised by the deck load of lumber [we never did have time to resole the main cabin in New Zealand], Evan counters that the cargo of timber—measuring three feet by three feet by sixteen feet, and situated abaft the main mast on the main deck—weighed one ton or less and in no way adversely affected the vessel's stability. He further explains that five years earlier, *Sofia* had carried ten tons of Lignam Vitae—a particularly dense tropical hardwood—for six months and two thousand miles. This load had, quite to the contrary, succeeded only in slowing her already stiff rolling moment and in so doing, had kept her from spilling wind out of her sails in light airs, thus actually improving her sailing characteristics. The one-ton load of lumber, Evan is certain, had had little effect on the ship's stability at the time of the sinking.

In answering the charge that *Sofia* lacked "structural" watertight integrity, Evan states simply that the fact that something had failed in the hull was evidenced by great volumes of water entering the ship below the waterline. Reiterating that although the keel project's design and implementation was a result of exhaustive research and discussion by the entire crew in conjunction with two marine engineering firms, three professional shipwrights, and two professional steel workers, it still may have been at the crux of the sudden leak that occurred just moments before the ship went down. Although the eventual solution and implementation of the project was the culmination of an in-depth group process, Evan adds that he had contributed largely to what became the final decision for the keel, and that yes, ultimately it may well have been the source of the *Sofia's* undoing.

Lastly, in response to the accusation that the crew was not sufficiently trained to handle the weather which he knew or should have known would be encountered, Evan replies as follows:

The crew of seventeen was comprised of five veteran sailors and twelve relatively inexperienced crew. Of the five veterans there was: myself with 8 years at sea; Pam, first mate with 3½ years on *Sofia*, a thorough and efficient mate; Billy, 3 years on deck on *Sofia*; Joe 1½ years on *Sofia* plus small boat experience, and Wayne ["Byrds"], a veteran ocean sailor with 2 months sea time on *Sofia*. All these five were knowledgeable and experienced at handling *Sofia* and were put in the position of watch captains. Of the other twelve, nearly all attended the three weeks' worth of day sails and three- to five-day shakedown cruises prior to the sinking. Every practical effort was made to prepare the crew for sailing in the waters around New Zealand. However, as often happened during long stays in port, a large crew turnover (⅔rds) had occurred. In choosing a route for the passage from Nelson to Auckland, two options were open to me; either "North About," as the fishermen there call the route we took, or via the Cook Straight and East Cape. Each of those routes are equally well-known to have possibly adverse weather conditions. In fact, I have spent five days in the waters off North Cape in which two were light to moderate, two were fresh breezes, and one was a gale. Likewise, Cook Straight is a funnel for both wind and currents and has been the site of horrendous storms and maritime casualties. The waters around New Zealand are notoriously littered with 1,800 recorded shipwrecks. That the ship was in a potentially hazardous sailing area with the relatively inexperienced crew was a situation I did not create, but was forced to deal with as well as was practically possible. In preparation for this passage, 14 days of practice sailing was done, everyone was given regular sail stations to man during practice maneuvers. Maneuvers were explained in detail beforehand, and questions answered afterward. . . . Were *Sofia* still a cargo vessel, she would have been crewed by 5 people, the same approximate number as our experienced crew. The extra 12 provided so much extra manpower and rest intervals.

With respect to the allegations concerning the *Sofia's* "carrying passengers for hire" without a licensed operator on board, and operating a "passenger carrying vessel" without a certification of inspection, Evan deals with these issues patiently and almost by rote. As always, the operative word is *passenger*. This is no new question for anyone who has ever sailed aboard the *Sofia*. It refers to a strict maritime regulation, one that our ship's owners had danced handily around ever since she became a cooperative venture. The *Sofia* did not and had not ever carried passengers, nor would she ever. Every single sailor or sot who ever stepped foot aboard knew from the get-go that he or she was crew—albeit *paying* crew. But we were crew nonetheless and were expected to be worthy of the title, which carries with it responsibilities and liabilities. Although we were told simply and clearly what was expected of us as the *Sofia's* crew, what that meant often became evident only in the doing.

After reviewing the entire document, I am once again seriously impressed. Evan has remained calm and calculated in formulating his response. I would have been a portion more corked-off frankly. In drafting my own account of the sinking, I nevertheless follow his lead by remaining painstakingly stoic. I include as objective an overview as I can dredge up of the *Sofia*, both as a sailing vessel and as a way of life. In conclusion, I offer my impression of Evan as a sailor and as a captain. I am careful not to offer any personal opinions or to make any excuses. I do not wish the outcome of this investigation to rest upon my shoulders in any way. I was just a Sofian. The finding of fault and resolution of punishment will have to be decided in a higher court by those wiser than myself. Of this I am certain. I am equally convinced, however, that an attempt to fix blame will fix nothing. No repairs can any longer be made here. To the best of my ability, I revisit my experience on paper. I assume that I am not alone in doing so.

The charges against Evan are dropped. He returns to his command, I to my life, and everyone else to their own preoccupations. Nearly two full years after the tragic sinking of the tall ship *Sofia* and the disastrous loss of one of her crew, the episode is finally put to rest, at least officially.

The passing of time and marking of distance do inevitably soften a brutal blow. And despite an almost deranged compulsion to stay true to the agony of the experience, our pain does become dulled by life's perverse encroachment. The obvious finalities notwithstanding, the issue of closure remains one that the principles involved will each have to determine for themselves. If someone were to ask me whether the tragedy could have been avoided, my response would be the same today as it would have been more than twenty years ago on that dark February night in the cold, apathetic waters off the North Cape of New Zealand: maybe.

Double miracle saves 16 shipwrecked in (

Force 8 gale

A Soviet trawler rescued 16 survivors of the capsized schooner Sofia after they had drifted in life raf

Schooner crew cheer rescuers

16 safe after sea ordeal

Tragic end to Sofia dream

Crew rescued
16 safe, after 5 days
one is of agony and
missing nightmares

Russian rescuers cheered

Sixteen

SIXTEEN survivors of a shipwreck have told how a double miracle saved them from certain death on seas lashed by Force 8 gales.

Short notice of sinking

survive
five days
on rafts

Local woman saved at sea

Pam Sisman, 31, daughter of Dr. and Mrs. Bernard Sisman of 3575 N. Custer Rd., has been rescued after five days on a life raft after the ship she was on sank in a storm off New Zealand.

All personal effects were lost fo 17 persons on the ship. One p was killed.

Dr. Sism
takic Sism

E PALE beam of a small torch yesterday ended a five-day
htmare at sea for 12 men and four women in two life rafts

Collage of newspaper accounts of the rescue.

Epilogue

I am part of all that I have met.

—ALFRED LORD TENNYSON

INTRODUCTION

Where do I begin and where do I end in committing to print the designs left forever on my soul by those with whom I sailed the *Sofia?* The people I knew during my travels all were part of a grand tale, and I will never completely forsake any one of them. But what actually happens afterward? Where do the players go? Are we hopelessly lost to one another when we shed the roles once so crucial to our collective identity? I am often asked about my fellow Sofians, particularly those with whom I shared the life rafts. When I answer that we are no longer in close contact, people stare at me incredulously. How could I have allowed this estrangement to occur? How could so momentous an experience fail to bind us forever? I have given this a great deal of thought.

Perhaps one of the most difficult tasks that we are expected to accomplish in this life arrives in the aftermath of such a dreadful ordeal. Be it a war, act of violence, illness, accident, profound personal loss, or disaster at sea, we must then shoulder the awesome burden of how to incorporate this reality-altering experience in our lives. If we convince ourselves that we must be better human beings for having endured, do we search for new meaning? If we dare ask, "Why me?" do we commit ourselves to finding an answer? If, during the course of our traumatic experience, we attain a heightened level of consciousness, must we forever after engage in an earnest struggle to regain that elevated state of being? And should we attempt to share the details of the ordeal?

Because far too often, language is so piteously inadequate to convey the true depth of emotion that we feel that we end up trivializing it. We are then left with the sick empty sensation of having betrayed something vitally personal.

In the final analysis, many of us who survive such a test feel bilked. We realize that we may not have survived because we were chosen, and we therefore should not expect to experience some cosmic rebirth. We are only mortal. We are flawed. And for a time we are hopelessly lost and desperately alone. When (or if) we return from our journey, after sifting through all the multifaceted dimensions of the event and processing their intense impact on our lives, we often emerge to find that we have traveled vast distances, not only in terms of years and miles but conceptually and spiritually as well. I have been on such a journey. As a result, I have chosen through the years to avoid rehashing what happened with the other members of the crew. I have moved on, and life has filled up the spaces left in the wake of the *Sofia*. I expect it has been so for us all.

We are today as we existed then—separate beings who once combined on a magical stage to form one fantastic, albeit temporary, ensemble. And, yes, we are inextricably bound to one another by this fact. Together we did occupy an enchanted place and share an inimitable time. Although our respective paths may never cross again, I will always feel an imperishable connection to those with whom I journeyed. Where they venture, what they accomplish, and who they become will always matter.

The lives of my fellow voyagers have unfolded in a tapestry of ironic, mundane, and disastrous patterns since we parted. I have been made privy to some of the details. Here are just a few of their stories.

The film company that had originally contracted to use the *Sofia* proceeded, almost without missing a beat, to make the movie. It used *Eye of the Wind*, a traditional tall ship skippered by a sailor named Tiger, who was a longtime friend of Evan's. The project was completed. The film was released under the name *The Pirate Bully Hayes*.

The replica of the *Bounty* sailed back across the Pacific to star in a third remake of the film by the same name. When she landed in Los Angeles, her boatswain was none other than the *Sofia*'s young Chris. And the skipper for the last leg of the *Bounty*'s journey was Roger Morris, the New Zealand artist whose painting of the *Sofia* now decorates thousands of his books around the world.

The ancient schooner that the *Sofia* met in Barbados, the *Anne Khristine*, sailed on for many more years before finally being claimed in "the perfect storm" that blew up off the East Coast in the autumn of 1991. She was well more than one hundred years old when she went down. Barney, who had earned his captain's license by then, had been enlisted to deliver her on that fateful journey. At the last minute, however, something prevented him from taking the command.

Mother Boats has obsessively kept in touch, calling or simply showing up every couple of years. He's been like the hub of a great wheel, collecting and disseminating "the dirt" to any and all old Sofians who will listen or pretend to listen. I always listen. He attempted to establish a nude commune on the island of St. Lucia, but the local authorities wouldn't have it. Finally, he settled in Australia, where he built his own boat, a ridiculously large multihull that serves as his home, base of operations (in all their questionable detail), and as a nude commune.

Evan has worked at a variety of positions—always on ships, always at sea, and always with a mind toward building another traditionally rigged tall ship that would continue to sail around the world. Indeed, he has succeeded. Today the *Alvei*—a 126-foot, three-masted, main topsail schooner—graces the open ocean somewhere on the planet. She is eerily reminiscent of the *Sofia*, both in appearance and character, but with a few very distinct differences. Her hull is riveted steel, the organization of her crew is something other than a cooperative, and her skipper is Evan—period. If you aspire to sail a mighty tall ship, learn the venerable art of marlinspike seamanship, or ghost into elusive and exotic ports covering the globe, the opportunity does yet exist. All you have to do is find the *Alvei* in whichever distant ocean she now sails and boldly step aboard.

Tami returned to southern California, where she continued to sail and to work on boats. In the process, she met and fell in love with a South African named Richard, who was cruising on his boat, the *Mayaluga*. Together they departed San Diego, bound for South Africa and all that lay between. In Tahiti a disgruntled cruiser beseeched the couple to deliver his yacht to the States for him. They accepted, thankful for the opportunity to announce their recent engagement to Tami's family before continuing on halfway across the planet. En route, Tami and Richard were pursued by a hurricane that, try as they might, they were not able to outrun. Tami regained consciousness three days later, still down below, where, on Richard's orders, she had lashed herself beneath the salon table. Upon making the deck, she discovered that the boat had rolled several times. Its masts and stanchions had been ripped away. The vessel was completely disabled and only semi-afloat.

Richard was gone. Tami was adrift and alone. With only a jury-rigged storm sail, a lapwatch, a sextant, some salvaged food and water stores, a case of beer, and a box of cigars, Tami rode the current the several hundred miles back to the waters off the Hawaiian Islands where she was finally spotted. She was rescued more than a month after encountering the hurricane, lost at sea for forty days. Today she has her hundred-ton captain's license. She and her husband live in the Pacific Northwest with their two young daughters. Tami has written her and Richard's story and in so doing has, I hope, put her own private ordeal to rest after many difficult years. The book is titled *Red Sky in Mourning*.

Joe and I consecrated our life-raft promise. This year marks our twenty-second wedding anniversary. We have two remarkable children whom we raised aboard our own fifty-foot brigantine, which we have recently had to let go. She is being refurbished yet again, so that she may sail proudly for many years to come.

Today our bright and breezy home by the sea echoes our travels. It is richly appointed with molas, tapas, and wood carvings from people and places long gone and very far away but not forgotten. On one wall, in a particular place of honor, hangs a very special piece. It is a square meter of cloth, a batik in soft hues depicting a Tahitian nymph nestled amid a wild profusion of tropical flowers. At the lower left-hand corner, the author has signed her piece. It reads: Heftsy, Mooréa. But this one is dated 1983.

When Tami summoned the courage to return to Tahiti to collect her and Richard's personal effects from the *Mayaluga*, she found the batik carefully stowed away. They had commissioned this gift for Joe and me, an exact duplicate to replace the one that went down with the *Sofia*. It was to commemorate the arrival of our firstborn.

On a day long ago, before Tami and Richard first set out across the Pacific together, Joey and I joined them for one last sentimental day sail together aboard the *Mayaluga*. I was pregnant at the time. While lazily tacking about San Diego Bay, reminiscing about our extraordinary pasts and imagining our glorious futures, we four mused over names for our baby. Richard rolled out a star chart, rested a finger on the heavenly body marking the left foot of the constellation Orion, and looked up at us, beaming. The navigational star was familiar to us all. In fact, it was the brightest star in the universe—Rigel. And so, Rigel it was. Had they remembered to pack the batik on the cruiser's yacht to present it to us when they reached California, it would have been lost in the hurricane. But they left it behind in their eagerness to get home and share the news of their wedding plans, so the gift arrived much later than it should have. By then our son, Rigel, was a year old and Tami had to present it to him, with love forever from her and a Richard he would never know.

A few years later, our second child was born, a strong, bright, and beautiful daughter. We named her Hallie. Hallie means "lover of the sea." We named her Hallie Sofia.

And so we sail on.

The author and a fellow crewmember leaving port aboard *Sofia*.